Mindhacker

60 Tips, Tricks, and Games to Take Your Mind to the Next Level

Ron Hale-Evans
Marty Hale-Evans

WILEY

Wiley Publishing, Inc.

Mindhacker: 60 Tips, Tricks, and Games to Take Your Mind to the Next Level

Published by
Wiley Publishing, Inc.
10475 Crosspoint Boulevard
Indianapolis, IN 46256
www.wiley.com

Published by Wiley Publishing, Inc., Indianapolis, Indiana

Published simultaneously in Canada

ISBN: 978-1-118-00752-5
ISBN: 978-1-118-16641-3 (ebk)
ISBN: 978-1-118-16643-7 (ebk)
ISBN: 978-1-118-16642-0 (ebk)

Manufactured in the United States of America

10 9 8 7 6 5 4 3 2 1

For general information on our other products and services please contact our Customer Care Department within the United States at (877) 762-2974, outside the United States at (317) 572-3993 or fax (317) 572-4002.

Wiley also publishes its books in a variety of electronic formats and by print-on-demand. Not all content that is available in standard print versions of this book may appear or be packaged in all book formats. If you have purchased a version of this book that did not include media that is referenced by or accompanies a standard print version, you may request this media by visiting http://booksupport.wiley.com. For more information about Wiley products, visit us at www.wiley.com.

Library of Congress Control Number: 2011932270

To all the magical things patiently waiting for our wits to grow sharper — we're getting there as fast as we can.

Credits

Executive Editor
Carol Long

Senior Project Editor
Adaobi Obi Tulton

Technical Editor
Timothy Buck

Production Editors
Nick Moran
Kathleen Wisor

Copy Editor
Luann Rouff

Editorial Manager
Mary Beth Wakefield

Freelancer Editorial Manager
Rosemarie Graham

Associate Director of Marketing
David Mayhew

Marketing Manager
Ashley Zurcher

Business Manager
Amy Knies

Production Manager
Tim Tate

**Vice President and Executive
Group Publisher**
Richard Swadley

**Vice President and Executive
Publisher**
Neil Edde

Associate Publisher
Jim Minatel

Project Coordinator, Cover
Katie Crocker

Proofreader
Nancy Carrasco

Indexer
Robert Swanson

Cover Designer
Ryan Sneed

About the Authors

Ron Hale-Evans is a writer, thinker, and game designer who dwells in those parts of the multiverse commonly called the Pacific Northwest, with his wife and co-author, Marty, and their Pomeranians, Humphrey and Bridget. He has a bachelor's degree in psychology from Yale, with a minor in philosophy. Thinking about thinking led him to create the Mentat Wiki (www.ludism.org/mentat), which led to his first book, *Mind Performance Hacks* (2006), which has been translated into Polish, Japanese, Korean, and Dutch, and in turn led to *Mindhacker*.

Ron can speak Esperanto, draw ambigrams, compile a kernel, ken a kenning, and locate a letterbox. He owns a copy of the *Codex Seraphinianus*, craves the acquaintance of a Curta calculator, believes deeply in the principles of jury nullification and calliagnosia, and passionately desires to go to Mars.

You can find Ron's projects and social networks at his home page (http://ron.ludism.org). To date, he has won four small game design competitions, both with and without Marty. He has also written a series of articles on game systems for *The Games Journal* that have received attention from gamers and academics.

Ron earns the upkeep on his personal Amazon bookstream as a technical writer, and is the only copyfighter and free and open-source software advocate he knows who has worked for the Free Software Foundation, the Linux Foundation, and Microsoft. He would enjoy hearing from you at mindhacker@ludism.org.

Marty Hale-Evans lives just south of Tacoma, Washington, in the octagonal Groovagon with Ron and the Troublesome Yet Adorable Quadrupeds. Marty was a developmental editor for Ron's previous book, *Mind Performance Hacks*, to which she contributed several hacks herself. She has chosen the first-class upgrade to co-author for *Mindhacker*. Her professional title is usually technical editor, under which she has worked for companies such as Microsoft, Boeing, WGBH Educational Foundation, and the University of Chicago Press.

Between professional gigs, Marty works on several nonprofessional projects. She is currently serving as chair of Foolscap, a local literary science fiction convention, which she has helped to produce for three years. She has worked with Peninsula Hands On Art, for whom she has served on the board of directors and researched, written, or taught several art lessons. She has designed and co-designed several award-winning board and card games, and plays weekly with Seattle Cosmic Game Night, which she co-founded with Ron in January 2000. This autumn, Marty plans to begin graduate school at the University of Washington School of Information, with the goal of earning her MLIS.

Marty spends other time designing and making jewelry, dreaming up experimental confections, compiling themed music mixes, and writing nanofiction. She likes to study art and history, analyze pop culture, and talk to people about it. She aspires to learn Japanese, to add to her passable French, fragmented Esperanto, and pitiful Italian. She adores good coffee and good ice cream, finds all dogs irresistible, and is fascinated by cooking shows, despite not actually cooking all that much. She is a big comedy geek, soaks up song lyrics and random trivia like a manic ShamWow, and is passionate about fat lib, feminism, and politics in general. You can usually find her with her nose in a book; this has been true since she was a child, and she isn't about to stop now.

About the Technical Editor

Tim Buck worked for 15 years as IT Manager for a small software development company. Being the sole source of IT support there, he was responsible for server management, desktop support, web development, software testing, and wore many other hats as well. As a result, he learned a little about everything.

Now Tim works as a web application developer in state government; in this role, he continues to learn a little about everything, supporting legacy applications as well as developing new ones.

Tim lives in Santa Fe, NM with his partner, two cats, two dogs, and five chickens. He is a voracious reader, as well as an avid music fan, skier, hiker/backpacker, and traveler. He can be reached at timbck2@gmail.com.

About the Contributors

John Braley took Branko Grünbaum's University of Washington course — Special Topics in Advanced Geometry — about eight times and loved every minute.

Matthew Cornell is a terminally curious ex-NASA engineer, an avid self-experimenter, and an accidental philosopher, with degrees in electrical engineering and computer science. His current focus is on creating the Think, Try, Learn philosophy that treats life as an experiment, and on teaching it to everyone. He is developing Edison, the Think, Try, Learn experimenter's journal (http://edison.thinktrylearn.com), is a contributing editor at *The Quantified Self* (http://quantifiedself.com), and consults for companies in the burgeoning self-tracking field. He blogs at *The Experiment-Driven Life* (www.matthewcornell.org/blog).

Jonathan Davis is an Irish-South African autodidact, critical thinker, omnologist, and doting father. He lives in Belgrade, Serbia, with his wife and daughter, where he is the CTO for a global cloud computing services company. Jonathan blogs at Limbic Nutrition (www.limbicnutrition.com/blog) and can be found on Twitter as @limbic.

M. W. Fogleman attends St. John's College in Annapolis, Maryland, where he is reading the Great Books in preparation for a bachelor's degree in the liberal arts. He keeps a blog at mwfogleman.tumblr.com.

Meredith Hale is a teen services librarian by day and cake decorator by night. She lives in Tacoma with her two dogs. She considers herself to be pretty talented at figuring out how to communicate with people — have you ever tried to communicate with teens? Not an easy task.

Dave Howell, pioneering e-publisher, game designer, and artist, first remembers putting multimodal principles to work when designing the original Magic: The Gathering cards.

Lion Kimbro uses notebooks as both art and thinking tool, a practice that he has developed over 10 years. He lives in Seattle, Washington, and loves to talk with readers. He is an avid Python programmer, and is passionate about creating societies of dream.

Mark Schnitzius has a degree in computer science and mathematics and has been writing software ever since his father brought home a KIM-1 in 1977. He is a six-time winner of the International Obfuscated C Code Competition (www. ioccc.org), and currently resides with his wife in Melbourne, Australia.

Paul Snyder first became interested in inner worlds and alternate dimensions as a means of escaping the social stigma of his childhood sesquipedalianism. Today, he is a computer scientist researching self-organization, and designing biologically inspired distributed systems. Continuing evidence of his deep-seated, pathological eclecticism can be found in his blogs at www.zenoli.net and www.pataprogramming.com.

Professor Solomon, aka Michael Solomon (who describes himself as an "amateur professor"), has written six books: *How to Find Lost Objects, Japan in a Nutshell, How to Make the Most of a Flying Saucer Experience, Coney Island, The Book of King Solomon,* and *Visitors to the Inner Earth.* These books may be downloaded free at www.professorsolomon.com.

Chad Urso McDaniel has been a software engineer for 16 years since his graduation from Carnegie Mellon University. He is a foodie, a board gamer, a video gamer, and a resident (and fan) of Seattle.

Brett Douglas Williams, also known on the Internet as "mungojelly," and to the Lojbanic community as "stela selckiku," is still human. His education has included singing lessons, Buddhist meditation, BBSes, the *Principia Discordia,* Rowe Senior High Camp, Sudbury Valley School, Rainbow Gatherings, speaking with plants, and libraries. He loves his husband, I X Key!

Acknowledgments

First, thanks to our unflappable and ever-cheerful agent, David Fugate, of LaunchBooks Literary Agency, who saw the potential in this book and helped us revive it when it had flatlined for more than a year. Second, thanks to Carol Long at Wiley, who bought the book and trusted in us despite a missed deadline or two.

Thanks also to the Wiley editorial team, especially Adaobi Obi Tulton, who led the project capably and was a great pleasure to work with, never suggesting we drop a hack, no matter how bizarre it might seem on its surface.

Thanks to the even dozen *Mindhacker* contributors named in the last section. You rock! Thanks also to various people who contributed in important ways that are less visible, some of whom are also hack authors, including John Braley, Pamela Evans-Schink, M. W. Fogleman, Clark Rodeffer, Paul Snyder, and Tim "AlphaTim" Schutz.

Thanks to our friends for putting up with our neglect and absences, including those in Seattle Cosmic Game Night, Experimental Game Genesis of Seattle (EGGS), the Island of Misfit Games, and Seattle IF. We hope to be back among you by the time you read this.

Thanks to our families for their love and support, including Darlene, Ken, Meredith, Melinda, Keith, Pamela, Eric, Bryson, Ciaràn, Humphrey, and Bridget.

A special hello and thanks to readers who are meticulous or nosy enough to read all these acknowledgments.

Ron would especially like to thank his co-author, Marty, for once again pulling his irons out of the fire. Marty, you are the Brock Samson to my Rusty Venture, and (please don't take this the wrong way) the Claire Simmons to my Philip Cavanaugh and Gilbert Selwyn. You are also my favorite person, as you well know.

Marty would likewise thank Ron for pulling her onto this roller coaster again, even though she often makes herself tiresome company by complaining about standing in line and shouting curses on the drops instead of throwing her hands in the air with delight. She appreciates how many times Ron pulled his act together and Got It Done, because she knows just how hard that is for him sometimes. Thank you for keeping the vision when I get bogged down in practicalities. And, even after all these years, my dear — and, more important, my friend — thank you for continuing to be so damn interesting.

Contents at a Glance

Contents

Introduction

When we bundled up *Mind Performance Hacks* and sent it out to make its way in the world, we suspected it wasn't the last we had to say about techniques for boosting your brain power. Like keeping a sourdough starter, we had a little bit of lively material still fermenting and bubbling away. Over time, by ourselves and talking to readers — some of whom became contributors — we found and mixed in more tasty ingredients, let them sit and expand, punched them around a little, shaped them and baked them up just so, and now we have a new treat to offer you, *Mindhacker*.

This book is informed by two fascinating ideals for human behavior from science fiction. They come from different sources (and we discuss them in more detail in Hack 31, "Mine the Future"), but briefly they are the *mentat* and the *asarya*. The mentat aspires to mimic and even replace computers by training to perform prodigious feats of cognitive and analytical skill. Obviously the inspiration for the Mentat Wiki, the mentat was also, to some extent, the spirit of *Mind Performance Hacks*, wherein many of the hacks have to do with acquiring and honing those kinds of skills. The mentat is still present in *Mindhacker*, but we've added a colleague, the asarya. If the mentat is a strongman, the asarya is an acrobat, focused on flexibility of mind. The asarya aims to hold all possibilities in mind at once, to "look upon the universe just as it is and affirm every aspect," to say "yes" to all things. With the hacks in *Mindhacker*, we hope to help you amp up your mental skills, but also learn to bend and flex your viewpoint, to see things in new ways and focus your growing mental skills effectively. In the end, it's adding the right pipes and valves that turns a fountain into a fire hose.

Perhaps we should also explain up front that, to us, "hacker" doesn't have the negative connotations it has for many people. It has nothing to do with unauthorized breaches by either software viruses or hatchets. Rather, we subscribe to the belief that hacking something means opening it up and tinkering around, with the intention to make it better than it was, and possibly better than it was designed to be in the first place. It requires intelligence, skill, creativity, and work focused on improvement, not destruction. Nothing you can try in this book will harm you; the worst that will happen is that nothing will happen. With your brain, you don't even have to worry about violating a user agreement or warranty; you own it and you can make it as fast, tough, and agile as you want. We hope to lead the way and show you how — let's go!

Overview of the Book and Technology

The hacks in *Mindhacker* tend to be longer and less basic than those in similar books. However, they are firmly grounded. Some are grounded in contemporary neuroscience, as with Hack 53, "Train Your Fluid Intelligence," which explains how to perform the "n-back" exercises that have recently been shown in laboratory trials to increase your intelligence. Others are grounded in time-tested mental techniques, as with Hack 2, "Build a Memory Dungeon," which gives the classical mnemonic technique of the memory palace a twist that ought to appeal to video and role-playing gamers. All in all, we aim to include a variety of techniques based on a broad selection of sources that you'll also find interesting for their own sake.

A few hacks, but not all, require the use of a computer and some free software; see "Tools You Will Need."

How This Book Is Organized

Chapter 1, "Memory," covers mnemonics and other memory-enhancement techniques, including remembering to remember and recalling long-ago events. Bring your past along into the future!

Chapter 2, "Learning," covers techniques for education and self-education, synthesizing memory and information into knowledge. Learn to learn by pretending you're a dog or a grad student.

Chapter 3, "Information Processing," helps you manage both information and attention, so that you can choose among attractive options, catch the choicest informational fish with the Internet, and know what to do with them when you catch them.

Chapter 4, "Time Management," will aid you in your efforts to marshal a resource as precious as air or water: time. Get control of your time with a mental datebook, new types of clocks and calendars, a step-by-step algorithm for finding lost objects, and more.

Chapter 5, "Creativity and Productivity," will show you that making new stuff and getting work done go hand-in-hand. Work more productively by playing games, mine ideas from the past and future, and dare to be creative while not worrying whether the results are a little odd.

Chapter 6, "Math and Logic," will enable you to develop critical skill sets for clear thinking and solving real-world problems while having fun. Learn new mathematical notations, roll dice in your head, then visualize the third dimension — and the fourth!

Chapter 7, "Communication," will improve the quality of your interaction with other people. Communicate and clarify (or conceal) delicate shades of emotion, compress your chat messages, and learn to read lips more quickly.

Chapter 8, "Mental Fitness," will help you improve your "brain tone" so that you won't mentally pant and wheeze when you try to solve a hard problem. It includes a method for actually increasing your intelligence, and teaches you to try new things and acquire new tastes that will keep your limbic system limber and your neocortex nimble.

Chapter 9, "Clarity," works with the first eight chapters to wipe the smudges off the lens of your mind and focus your concentration into a narrow, powerful beam. You'll also learn to rid yourself of long-standing misconceptions, and when to throw everything you think you know away and start over.

Who Should Read This Book

We assume you're smart and you want to be smarter. It takes a fairly smart person to understand the need to be smarter; telling someone else that they need to be could lead to a shouting match or worse.

You don't need to be able to get into Mensa before you read *Mindhacker*; this book is not meant to exclude anyone. As we argue in the final hack of the book, most people are functionally about as smart as one another, even if some people think faster than others or have more information bottled away in their liter or so of gray matter. If some of the hacks in this book look intimidating, you can still spend some time with them and learn to implement them in your own life, slower than some people, faster than others.

No matter how smart you are, or think you are, not every hack in this book will fit your personal needs. We hope, however, that almost anyone will find something useful and interesting within these pages.

Tools You Will Need

For all hacks you will need

- Your brain, running an open mind
- Ordinary office supplies, such as pen, paper, and index cards

A few hacks have some extra requirements:

- A computer running Linux, Mac OS, or Windows
- A web browser, preferably Mozilla Firefox
- A version of the computer language Perl, either as preinstalled for Linux or Mac, or free from www.activestate.com/activeperl for Windows
- The scripts from the *Mindhacker* website (see "What's on the Website")

Many of the hacks that use Perl scripts contain instructions for running their scripts. The book's website also contains documentation. In general, to run a Perl script, you must open a command line in the directory that contains the script, and then type `perl` and the name of the script. For example, to run a Perl script called `mindhacker.pl`, you would type this at the command line:

```
perl mindhacker.pl
```

There are also ways to run Perl scripts by double-clicking them or using various other shortcuts, but they vary according to your operating system and are outside the scope of this introduction. However, don't be afraid to experiment; Perl rewards trying new things.

What's on the Website

At Wiley's website for *Mindhacker* (www.wiley.com/go/mindhacker) you can find the following items:

- Free, multiplatform software in Perl and JavaScript for the hacks that require it, as well as the accompanying data files
- Documentation explaining how to run the scripts
- Color versions of the monochrome images in some of the hacks, such as the Kilodeck cards in Hack 41, "Engineer Your Results"
- Errata, as they become available
- A few surprises

What's Next?

The book is not designed to be read in order, although you can do that. Rather, we expect people to dip in wherever it looks interesting and follow the cross-references in most hacks as it suits them. Read what looks fun and useful now; tomorrow, you may have new needs that call for a different hack.

We hope you learn at least as much from reading this book as we did from writing it. If you want to share your ideas and experiences with our hacks, we'd love to hear about it at mindhacker@ludism.org.

Memory

In classical Greece, Mnemosyne — usually translated as "Memory" — was considered to be the mother of History, Music, Astronomy, and all the other Muses. Memory is fundamental to learning and knowledge, so we've placed our chapter of memory-enhancement techniques first. They include how to build memory on previously memorized environments (Hack 2, "Build a Memory Dungeon"), how to use technology to remember most efficiently (Hack 4, "Space Your Repetitions"), and how to draw old memories that you thought you had lost back to the surface (Hack 5, "Recall Long-Ago Events").

Boosting your memory will help you both gather new information and track where you've been in your life, bringing your past with you into the future. Our goal is to help you hold onto all the intangible treasures your academic pursuits and life experience bring you.

Hack 1: Remember to Remember

Ever use a fancy mnemonic only to forget that you memorized anything at all? Prospective memory is remembering to do something in the future. Learn to cue your prospective memory in ways that go far beyond a string around your finger.

The traditional method to remind yourself that you need to remember something (and a staple of clip art collections) is a string tied around your finger, but there are many ways you can improve your *prospective memory* – or remembering to remember. We'll explore two very different ways to cut that string while retaining its effectiveness, as well as how to harness the humble checklist and improve prospective memory in general.

In Action

The character Uncle Billy in the Frank Capra film *It's a Wonderful Life* is an example of someone using mnemonics (badly) for prospective memory. Not only does he have the stereotypical string tied around his finger, he seems to have dozens, and he can't tell them apart. It's no wonder that he forgets important things and gets flustered, and this drives the plot of the movie.

To avoid having dozens of identical strings tied to your fingers — metaphorically or literally — we've found there are two main paths to using physical memory cues to remember to remember: either *differentiate your cues* or *overload a single cue*.

Differentiating Cues

A memory cue, such as a string around your finger, is only one bit of information: It tells you either "Remember something!" (string on finger = 1) or "Nothing to remember here!" (no string = 0). Uncle Billy's problem is that he has a lot of strings on his fingers all shouting "Remember something!" — but none of them are telling him what it is he should remember.

The key is to associate each "string" with what it's supposed to make you remember, and to strengthen that association through repetition. For example, when Marty notices that the car is nearly out of gas, she puts a blank sticky note on the windshield over the dashboard. When she sees it in the morning, it reminds her to look at the dashboard, which indicates she is out of gas and needs to go to the gas station.

NOTE The sticky note on the dashboard is like a prospective memory hack you're probably familiar with: putting your briefcase or purse in front of your front door so you won't forget it in the morning. (This is the number one trick people are eager to share with Ron at parties when he tells them he writes books on memory.) What's interesting here is that Marty doesn't write a message on the sticky note, just as you probably don't write on your bag — the required information is conveyed by the proximity of the memory cue to what you're trying to remember.

Marty has formed this habit over years, so now it's almost automatic. In this way, she is able to eke more than one meager bit of information out of the memory cue. Over time she has developed several such standard cues for herself, and now she has access to a whole armory of differentiated memory cues that not only remind her to remember something, but remind her *what to remember*.

Overloading a Cue

Ron takes the opposite approach. Rather than have multiple memory cues, each of which provides a small amount of information, he makes one cue represent many items of information. He calls this *overloading*, not in the sense that the cue is carrying more than it can bear, but as in some computer languages like Java, where the "+" sign might mean addition in an arithmetic context, but something different — concatenation — in a string context.

For example, Ron wears a wristwatch, and like most people, he usually wears it with its face on the outside of his wrist. However, because it's uncomfortable to wear a watch with the face on the inside of his wrist, doing so can be an irritant that serves as a memory cue. Thus, when Ron wants to remember something, he rotates his watch so that it is on the inside of his wrist.

But that's still only one bit of information. To overload the cue, Ron uses an old mnemonic device called a *link system* (www.ludism.org/mentat/LinkSystem). Because it can be indefinitely extended, it's usually sufficient to capture any information he needs to save while he's momentarily without his notebook or voice recorder.

Here's how the link system works. Let's say Ron has a list of three items to remember while he's driving: He has to buy gas on the way home (like Marty), he heard a review on NPR about a book he wants to check out, and he just remembered he has a meeting at work when he arrives. To remember these three items, he tells himself a connected story about what he has to remember, starting with his watch as an "anchor":

- First, he imagines that a gasoline pump nozzle explodes through the glass on the front of his watch, spraying gas everywhere.

- Second, for the book, which let's say is *The Hidden Reality: Parallel Universes and the Deep Laws of the Cosmos* by Brian Greene and is about cosmology — the Big Bang, multiverses, string theory, and the like — he imagines that the gasoline all over his car is ignited by a spark within the cabin and causes a new Big Bang. But he wants to remember the title is *The Hidden Reality*, so he imagines that the Big Bang is sucked into his back pocket, where it forms a hidden "pocket universe."

- Finally, he wants to remember the meeting, so he imagines that the people who will be at the meeting decide to hold it in the pocket universe in his pants.

Absurd? Yes. But you'll remember a story like this because it's absurd, and the next time Ron checks his watch (such as when he gets to work) and he's somewhere he can write or type, he too will remember he has a list of items "attached to" his watch. He will then transcribe them promptly to his catch (Hack 3, "Mix Up Your Facts"), performing any to-do items immediately if he can, such as getting to that meeting.

Checklists

In his 2009 book *The Checklist Manifesto*[1], physician Atul Gawande describes how adopting the simple technique of creating and filling out checklists is revolutionizing medical treatment. Like flying aircraft or spacecraft (aerospace has used checklists for years), medical procedures have become too complex to rely on human memory alone.

Thus, in 2001, Peter Pronovost at Johns Hopkins Hospital made a list of steps for doctors to take before an operation that can help prevent infections (known as *central line infections*) from use of a catheter pushed through a vein into the heart. Many of the steps were as simple and obvious as the doctors' washing their hands with soap. Pronovost asked nurses in his unit to observe the doctors and check the steps on the list; in more than a third of the cases, the doctors skipped at least one of these simple steps.

Pronovost then persuaded the hospital to allow nurses to stop doctors if they skipped one of the steps. He and his team followed the number of ten-day central line infections for a year. The rate went from 11 percent to zero, with similar results for the next 15 months. Gawande recounts how Pronovost's team estimated that in slightly more than two years at Johns Hopkins, the checklist prevented 43 infections, saved 8 lives, and saved the hospital $2 million dollars. Thus began the use of medical checklists at Johns Hopkins — and, as Pronovost taught others the technique, throughout the United States.

You can use checklists yourself to good effect. For example, as we've written elsewhere, Ron constantly used to leave the house without some item he needed and had to waste time doubling back to get it, or do without until he returned. But then he made a checklist of the 10 or so items he uses every day (medication, cell phone, and so on), and now he never leaves wherever he is without making sure he has these items. He also has a "PM checklist" for getting ready for bed, including such tasks as taking the dogs out one last time, turning off lights, and packing his 10 things to bring for the morning — nested checklists!

Don't forget, checklists can be surprisingly effective when you use them for procedures and routines that you think you know well but want to ensure you do correctly, or things that you want to do more effectively. Just like the Johns Hopkins doctors, you can easily forget the things that seem obvious, simply because you're comfortable with them. It may seem silly to write them down, but you may be surprised at the benefits in the long run.

NOTE If you find the checklist technique useful, try combining it with Hack 20, "Meet MET."

Planning

Here's something else we know about prospective memory that you can use to improve your chances of remembering to remember: *planning helps.* Try actually planning to do your to-dos, mentally walking through the steps before it's time to do them. If you *expect* to do something, and make a *commitment* to do it, you will remember it better than if you just expect to have to memorize it. It's especially useful to keep an eye on your clock or calendar as well.[2,3,4]

Other than planning, external mnemonics (such as those described above) are generally considered more effective than internal ones for prospective memory.

How It Works

There is still some question about whether prospective memory is qualitatively different from the usual, retrospective kind. For example, why is remembering a list of things you must do in the future significantly different from remembering a list of things you've already done?[5] However, given the flurry of research on prospective memory since the mid-1980s, as well as all the advances in neuroscience, brain imaging, and so on since then, we will probably have some answers soon.

Meanwhile, it shouldn't be too problematic for the *Mindhacker* reader. If it turns out that prospective memory is just like any other kind, we already have a library of proven mnemonic techniques developed over thousands of years. These should help.

If, conversely, prospective memory is different from any other kind, we soon ought to have a list of techniques that will improve it uniquely, such as the *implementation intentions* or planning described earlier.

See Also

- Atul Gawande, "The Checklist," *New Yorker*, December 10, 2007. The article that led to the book mentioned above, *The Checklist Manifesto*. Available online (www.newyorker.com/reporting/2007/12/10/071210fa_fact_gawande).

Notes

1. Atul Gawande, *The Checklist Manifesto: How to Get Things Right* (New York: Metropolitan Books, 2010).

2. Daniel Siu, *Planning for Success: Mnemonics for Prospective Memory* (master's thesis, The University of British Columbia, 2004).

3. Robert Tobias, "Changing behavior by memory aids: a social psychological model of prospective memory and habit development tested with dynamic field data," *Psychological Review*, Vol. 116 No. 2 (2009): 408–438.

4. Peter M. Gollwitzer and Veronika Brandstatter, "Implementation Intentions and Effective Goal Pursuit," *Journal of Personality and Social Psychology*, 73 (1997): 186–199.

5. Henry L. Roedinger III, "Prospective Memory and Episodic Memory," *Prospective Memory: Theory and Applications* (Mahwah, NJ, US: Lawrence Erlbaum Associates Publishers, 1996).

Hack 2: Build a Memory Dungeon

Paul L. Snyder

Memory palaces are one of the most ancient and reliable memory hacks, but it's not always easy to find a suitable real-life building for one. Today, role-playing games and video games offer rich, elaborate, and ready-made imaginary buildings and landscapes for use as "memory dungeons."

The classical art of memory lays out a system for using your established knowledge of physical locations as a *memory palace*, a framework to store and order memory images. Many authors have described this technique, in which you create concrete mental images of things you want to remember, then place these images in a mental landscape you know well in memory, such as your home. The idea is to harness your kinesthetic memory of moving through the familiar space and your predilection to notice changes in familiar surroundings, so that as you imagine moving through the space, you see the images you created in your mind's eye, which triggers you to remember the related information.

Most sources discuss using this technique with real places (such as your neighborhood or the inside of your house), but the places that you use need not exist in the real world at all. One of the earliest texts discussing mnemotechnics, the *Rhetorica ad Herennium* (http://penelope.uchicago.edu/Thayer/E/Roman/Texts/Rhetorica_ad_Herennium/home.html) suggests creating imaginary locations, but they do not need to be invented on your own. If you've spent a sizable amount of time playing video or role-playing games, you may have a ready source of prefabricated spaces available to you.

In Action

While you've been using video games, either to reduce your reaction time or just for fun, you've also been building up a supply of locales for your memory dungeon. Any number of games may provide suitable fodder, but some are better than others. Some games (such as *Doom*, *Quake*, or other first-person shooters) have multiple levels, not all of which will be ideal. A good choice of game will have a clear flow through its space; you should be able to choose a logical path that you can reproduce repeatedly without confusion. It's also better if the game space is visually varied, without many similar repeated areas or complicated mazes.

Unless you know the level very well, you may wish to refresh your memory of the level by playing through it several times. Disabling enemies so you can wander freely (if the game engine allows) will reduce distractions during this process.

When you have the layout of the level established clearly in your mind, pick a path through it. As you walk through this path in your mind, identify locations (called *loci* in the classical art) where you will place images. Pick out obvious locations (like corners) or distinctive features (like pillars or torches).

> **NOTE** As an alternative, you could also use a strategy like the Nook and Cranny Method (www.ludism.org/mentat/NookAndCrannyMethod) to select a consistent pattern of locations in each room.

As you move through the route in your mind, create memory images for each item you are trying to remember and place them in successive locations. The images should incorporate multiple *hooks* to make the image as memorable as possible: exaggeration, sexual suggestiveness, humor (even bad jokes), and strong emotional associations all serve to add "stickiness." Memory images need not relate to the game or its content; often, objects and people who are out of place are easier to remember.

Eventually, you may wish to clear out an area of your memory dungeon to store new images. It's a good idea to do this intentionally, rather than hoping images will fade on their own. You could blow up your images with imagined dynamite, but many games offer a more exotic selection of implements of destruction.

In Real Life

For testing this hack, I chose a level that I've played many hundreds of times over the years, and remember better than some houses that I've lived in: the first mission of the original *Doom*. Figure 2-1 shows the layout of this level.

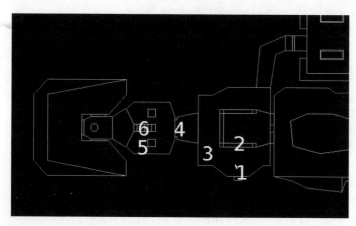

Figure 2-1: Doom level layout

While *Doom* was originally shareware, id Software released it as open source in 1997. You can install one of the many free versions of *Doom*. The version called *PrBoom* (http://prboom.sourceforge.net), for example, is licensed under the GNU General Public License and runs on Linux, Mac OS X, and Windows.

INSTALLING AND RUNNING PRBOOM

On Ubuntu Linux, *PrBoom* can be easily installed by running the following:

```
% sudo aptitude install prboom
```

You will also need the level data files for the first episode of *Doom*:

```
% sudo aptitude install doom-wad-shareware
```

For most versions of *Doom*, you can remove the distractions of being ambushed by demons using the `-nomonsters` command-line option, and you can jump to a specific level: `-warp <episode> <mission>`

On Ubuntu, with *PrBoom* and the data files installed, you can freely explore the first level with this command:

```
% prboom -iwad /usr/share/games/doom/doom1.wad -warp e1m1 -nomonsters
```

In this example, I chose to use the first two rooms of this level to remember the Julio-Claudian emperors of Rome. Here's how I did it:

Figure 2-2: Position 1

1. **Julius Caesar:** A man is leaning on the entry door to the level, wearing a laurel crown and the uniform of a Central American generalissimo. He is drinking an Orange Julius. (I want to remember that Caesar was

a dictator, not the first emperor.) See Figure 2-2 for an image of this location.

2. **Augustus:** A giant calendar is hung between the two pillars in front of the entrance, with a pin-up picture of a gentleman of Roman physique known as "Mr. August." See Figure 2-3 for an image of this location.

3. **Tiberius:** In the corner to the left, where a health vial usually sits, is a giant beer bottle with a garish necktie tied around it ("Tie-beer").

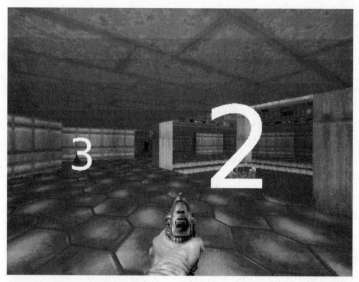

Figure 2-3: Positions 2 and 3

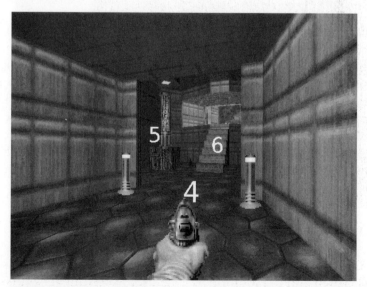

Figure 2-4: Positions 4, 5, and 6

4. **Caligula:** A giant combat boot sits between the two lights in the archway, blocking the passage. ("Caligula" means "little boot" in Latin.) See Figure 2-4 for an image of this location.

5. **Claudius:** A man is hiding behind the pillar to the left as you enter the side chamber, holding a pumpkin. (The Praetorian Guard supposedly found Claudius hiding behind a curtain after the assassination of Caligula. A satire was written about him called *The Pumpkinification of Claudius*.)

6. **Nero:** A man in a toga is sitting on the stairs, playing a burning lyre (fiddling while Rome burns, except fiddles hadn't been invented yet).

Additional mnemonics can be layered onto each image to store more information, such as the years of each emperor's reign. We might decide on a convention to record dates, such as an additional feature at the top for the first year of the reign, and another at the bottom for the last. Tiberius, for example, became emperor in 14 C.E. and died in 37 C.E. We could add this to our image by imagining the beer bottle being capped with a tire ("tire" being the pegword for 14 in the Major System), rather than a bottlecap and sitting on top of a Macintosh laptop ("mac" being the Major System mnemonic pegword for 37).

NOTE For more information on the Major System, see `www.ludism` `.org/mentat/MajorSystem.`

Hack 3: Mix Up Your Facts

Expand your vocabulary and knowledge of general facts with Google, a voice recorder, and an MP3 player set on shuffle.

This hack will teach you how to use the shuffle mode of your MP3 player to learn many different kinds of fact, from vocabulary words to entire encyclopedia entries. This technique can not only help you study for a class, but also help you consolidate what you glean from your independent reading as well. You are in control of what to learn, when to review it, and when to stop reviewing individual items.

Logophile Donald Sauter developed the original version of this hack back in the 1980s with cassette tapes. Adapting to modern technology has brought some refinements that cassettes couldn't offer, such as using shuffle mode and the capability to edit the mix of facts quickly and easily. As audio technology continues to improve, this hack may too.

How It Works

Learning facts by listening to a recording of your own voice can work very well. Ron tends to learn more by reading and writing, but has, at times, studied subjects like American history by obtaining an outline of a class's curriculum and recording a tape of it. All he had to do was listen to the tape twice while lying down in a dark, quiet room, and he routinely aced the tests.

Of course, he actually made *three* trips through the material, twice by listening to the outline and once by reading it. If you prepare the outline of the material you're learning yourself, that adds another iteration, and enables you to learn by teaching since you're essentially preparing to teach yourself (Hack 9, "Learn by Teaching"). Finally, using shuffle mode mimics flash cards, enabling you to learn each piece of information independently, instead of as part of a long rote series of facts.

This hack works partly because the web is the biggest unabridged dictionary and encyclopedia in the known universe (among many other wonderful things) but that merely speeds the process. It worked well enough for Donald Sauter when he developed this system with a highlighter, a paper American Heritage Dictionary, a one-volume 1950 encyclopedia, and a cassette tape recorder, starting in 1987 (www.reocities.com/donaldsauter/word-power.htm). Sauter's own explanation for the hack's effectiveness is as follows:

> What's nice about this "highlight and tape-record" self-education system is that what you study is precisely what you need to know, when you need it. There's no uncertainty as to whether it will be of value or not; it's immediately useful in understanding what you are currently reading. You can extract just the necessary essence of the new subject, or you might find yourself pulled into it and exploring it far beyond what you needed to make sense of the writer's passage.
>
> In a way, this approach knocks down the wall between fiction and nonfiction. I often find myself putting a story on hold to read complete articles on a topic that the author brought up or briefly alluded to. Like my dictionary, my encyclopedia has highlighted passages sprinkled throughout. If there were a contest to see who reads a story the fastest, I'd lose by a country mile — but so what? It takes me longer, but I cover more territory. I certainly don't claim this method is for everyone, but I know that for me it's far more enjoyable, exciting and satisfying. Consider trying something like it yourself, and if not for yourself, with your child.

In Action

This section explains in detail the following six steps you must take to make a vocabulary audio file:

1. **Consult:** Suppose you're looking up a vocabulary word like *apocopes*. Type **define:apocopes** into Google. Be sure to use a colon after the word "define" so that Google returns a special definition page for the word, aggregated from various online dictionaries and other sources. If you omit the colon, Google will just return a regular list of web pages that contain the words *define* and *apocopes*. Try it and see. You may not need to use a

general dictionary if you have a specialized glossary to use, such as the Infinite Jest wiki (`http://infinitejest.wallacewiki.com/`) — but we didn't know about it until we started writing up this hack.

Choose the definition that makes the most sense. Make sure you also learn how the word is pronounced when you look it up.

If you're looking up a historical figure, a country, a date, or the like, you may want to try typing it into Wikipedia instead. You may also want to use your mouse cursor to highlight the parts of the encyclopedia entry you're going to record.

2. **Record:** Start the sound recording software on your computer or smartphone. Ron uses the Sound Recorder application on his Ubuntu netbook. It's best to record the sound file as an MP3 or another format your audio player of choice can recognize, so you don't have to convert it later. However, it doesn't need to have particularly good sound quality, because you're only recording your own voice. Thus, you can probably use a low bit rate and keep the files small.

3. **Speak and spell:** When your sound recorder has started recording, speak the word or name aloud, then spell it carefully, being sure to note any accents or diacritical marks, or any other special features. In our example, we'll just say the word "apocopes."

4. **Contextualize:** Provide your word with some context. First, read the name or title of the source of your word — for example, "*Infinite Jest*, page 57." You don't need to be overly detailed here (e.g., you don't need the ISBN number), just a way to find your word again in its original habitat.

   Next, read the sentence in which your word appears, or the relevant part, if it's a long sentence. For example, from *Infinite Jest*, "the way menacing criminals speak in popular entertainment — d's for th's, various apocopes, and so on."

5. **Define:** Read the definition of the word into your voice recorder. If you are reading the secondary or tertiary meaning of the word, be sure to also note whether it's archaic, foreign, or anything else notable. Because Google aggregates several sources of definitions, it's a good idea to note the source of your definition too, such as WordNet.

   In this case, Ron read, "Definition, *apocope*: abbreviation of a word by omitting the final sound or sounds; 'the British get pud from pudding by apocope.' *WordNet*."

6. **Save:** Stop recording. Our audio file now says,

Apocopes. a-p-o-c-o-p-e-s. Infinite Jest, *page 57. "... the way menacing crimi-nals speak in popular entertainment — d's for th's, various apocopes, and so on." Definition,* apocope: *abbreviation of a word by omitting the final sound or sounds; "the British get pud from pudding by apocope." From* WordNet.

Save the audio file you just made, using the word you're defining as the filename, such as `apocope.mp3`, which uses the singular of the word for the filename, or `apocopes.mp3`, which uses the plural because that's how the word appeared in the book.

After you run through these six steps a few times with some vocabulary words, they'll become habit; after recording a few dozen words, you'll have enough to start reviewing them.

Reviewing your vocabulary files is simple. Load them into an MP3 player and put them on shuffle. Shuffle mode is one advantage that MP3s have over Sauter's original method of recording vocabulary words on cassette tape. Having words or other pieces of information come up randomly keeps you alert and makes you learn each piece separately, as you would with flash cards. Conversely, having them as one long piece, as they would be on a cassette, makes it easier to tune out and miss sections, or only learn each word in its new context on the tape.

Another advantage of MP3 files is that you can easily tweak and edit your vocabulary mix. If you find that you've learned certain words thoroughly, take them out of the mix. However, don't delete them. Each file represents a valu-able minute or two of your time, and that can add up. In a couple of months, you can look at the names of the files you saved; if there are any you no longer remember, you can drop them back into your mix. You can also trade them with a friend who's reading or studying the same material.

It wouldn't be hard to improve on this hack with spaced repetition (Hack 4, "Space Your Repetitions"). Of course, ordinary audio playback, shuffled or not, is preferable to interactive presentation when driving or doing anything else that requires sustained attention.

In Real Life

You may find that there are certain environments in which you can't use this hack immediately. Maybe you're reading in a quiet place, like a library or office, or maybe you're somewhere without Internet access. In such a situation, you can note the word you need to define and where you read it in your *catch*, which is basically a notebook you always carry in which to record spontaneous ideas. You may even come to prefer this method, because you can "batch process" 10 or 20 words at a time later, when it's convenient.

Alternatively, you can note your words on an index card that can double as a bookmark. When Ron was reading *Infinite Jest* by David Foster Wallace along with the Infinite Summer project (http://infinitesummer.org), the book had so many unfamiliar words that he noted them with their page numbers on an index card that he was using as one of his bookmarks. (As everyone who has read *Infinite Jest* knows, you need at least two bookmarks for it, one for the body and one for the endnotes.) Eventually, he got tired of writing words down and just underlined them in the text, which is always an option if you own the book you're reading (Hack 7, "Write in Your Books").

When you're back in a private environment with Internet access, harvest the words you've collected by recording a vocabulary file for each of them.

Ron has even found himself using this hack while driving — not just listening to his vocab mix, but noting words for later recording. Last night, for example, while driving home from work, he was listening to an audio version of Kim Stanley Robinson's science fiction novel *Red Mars* when he heard the word "massif" used in connection with a Martian hill. He had heard the word before and knew how it was spelled, so he committed it to his mental "mnemonic catch," which is basically a number-shape system (www.ludism.org/mentat/NumberShapeSystem). When he got home, he jotted it down in his paper catch. He looked it up by Googling **define:massif,** and the second definition Google returned was the one he wanted. He found the original sentence in his e-book version of *Red Mars*. Finally, he recorded the word, context, and definition. Here's what his MP3 file for *massif*, which is exactly 45 seconds long, says:

> *Massif. m-a-s-s-i-f.* Red Mars/Green Mars *e-book, page 148. "We drive around to one of the tongues of ice that drop to the sand. They're like ramps up to the central massif, and once there, we drive right to the pole!" Definition:* massif, *noun. A large mountain mass or compact group of connected mountains forming an independent portion of a range. From* Answers.com.

Hack 4: Space Your Repetitions

M. W. Fogleman

Discover open-source flashcard software that makes memorization easy and astonishingly powerful by means of algorithms that optimize your review sessions for maximum efficiency.

Our memory is simultaneously magnificent and pathetic. It is capable of incredible feats, and yet it never works quite like we wish it would. Ideally, we would be able to remember everything instantly, but we are not computers. We can hack our memory with tools like memory palaces, but such techniques require effort and dedication. Most of us give up, and outsource our memory to smartphones, cloud-enabled computers, or plain old pen and paper.

There is a compromise between easy-but-impotent digital outsourcing and extraordinary-but-laborious mental techniques. Psychologists have long known that a learning technique called *spaced repetition*, which efficiently organizes information for memorization and retention, can be used to achieve near-perfect recall. Nonetheless, the technique only began to catch on with the rise of personal computers, which can organize and track the mechanics of the technique easily. One of the first software programs to combine an efficient algorithm for spaced repetition with a user interface was SuperMemo, a proprietary Windows-only program that is still available. In the last few years, however, several free, open-source alternatives have recently appeared. If you use a flashcard deck made in one of these programs every day, you can guarantee near-perfect long-term retention.

How It Works

SuperMemo and its descendants are highly efficient for two reasons. First, you are actively reviewing the material with virtual flashcards instead of passively reading a textbook. Second, these programs use an algorithm based on spaced repetition that intelligently decides which information should be reviewed at a given time, based on your responses about each card's difficulty and how long it takes to respond to each card.

Spaced repetition was first discovered by the German psychologist Hermann Ebbinghaus in 1885. You may remember diluted versions of his findings from your teachers: instead of cramming, start studying early, because you're more likely to remember the material in the long run. Scientists and psychologists have gradually expanded this principle into a more exact science of predicting when you are going to forget a piece of knowledge. Using this information, the algorithms of the flashcard programs judge when you're likely to forget each word or fact, and test you just before you do. Being tested on the material you want to memorize just before you are likely to forget it strengthens your memory, and you'll spend less time doing so. If you mark a card as easy when you first see it, the program will give it to you again in a week or so; at that point, if you still mark it as easy, it might give it to you in two weeks, and then a month, and so on. Why waste your time reviewing simple concepts that you don't need to review frequently when you could be memorizing harder concepts?

In Action

While there are several spaced-repetition programs available, I prefer Anki, as it is free, open source, and actively developed. Its proprietary grandfather, SuperMemo, costs $50; the older, open-source Mnemosyne has not been updated since 2010. Additionally, Anki has many flashcard decks you can choose, and it's available on almost every desktop and mobile platform, complemented by an online synchronization and review service. To begin, download Anki from `http://ankisrs.net` and install it on your preferred platform. If you have a smartphone or tablet, I recommend maintaining your deck on your desktop and synchronizing it with your mobile device.

As an example for this hack, I will demonstrate how you can use Anki and a pre-made deck to learn advanced English vocabulary. Open Anki and click the Download button at the bottom of the screen. A new window will pop up with an enormous list of all the available decks and a search bar. We'll be using a deck called "5000 Collegiate Words (SAT Vocabulary)," which is currently the second most popular deck on Anki. Find it and click OK at the bottom of the screen. Anki will open this deck by default, and you can begin reviewing by pressing Review. The basic review screen for any deck is modeled after a flashcard: One side is the question, and one side is the answer, as shown in Figure 4-1. The first word in the deck is "abase," which I do not know, so I click Show Answer.

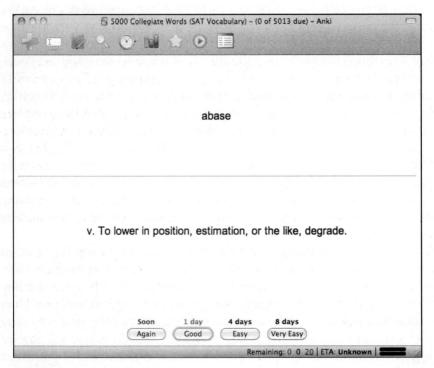

Figure 4-1: Anki in action

When it shows me the answer, I commit it to memory because I did not know it, and then I select one of the difficulty options. There are four options: Again, Good, Easy, and Very Easy. If, like me, you didn't know what the word "abase" meant, you click Again, and Anki will show it to you soon, most likely toward the end of your review session. If you knew what the word meant, you decide how hard it was for you to remember its definition, and click the corresponding level of ease or difficulty. Anki uses this response to judge the optimal time to show you the card again.

After you've figured out how Anki works, you need to make a few decisions about the kind of information you want to memorize and how you want to organize it. In addition to supporting basic text input, Anki is also able to use multimedia, as well as the LaTeX markup language for mathematical and scientific symbols, so you can use it to memorize almost anything. Some common usages are memorizing vocabulary, learning foreign languages, or preparing for a test.

Another choice you need to consider is whether you will make your own flashcard deck or use a pre-made deck. If you're memorizing something personal (the faces and names of your business partners) or obscure (varieties of flora and fauna near the Congo River), you will have to make your own deck, but in many cases you will be able to find pre-made decks in Anki's vast online database. These pre-made decks are best used in combination with some form of learning outside of Anki, such as taking a course or reading a textbook. There is one notable advantage to making your own deck: Although it can be arduous, the process of making the flashcards will further help you to learn, understand, and retain the information. If you do decide to make your own deck, I recommend exploring Anki's repertoire of features, many of which can make your job less difficult, and memorization more powerful. One final point worth considering is whether you should use one deck with many kinds of information or multiple decks with separate purposes (such as different languages, but not individual lessons from a textbook, as Anki has a tagging system for that kind of information). I prefer to have multiple decks, but you may find that having one deck is easier and more powerful.

While spaced repetition programs like Anki make your studying efficient to an almost transhuman degree, you still have to study. I recommend setting aside a specific block of time to study each day. It's okay to miss a day once in a while, but it's best to keep as regular a schedule as you can. How much time you want to spend using Anki depends on why you are using it. If you just want to pass a test, you can spend 10 or 20 minutes a day for a month beforehand and you will almost certainly ace it, but if you want to become fluent in a foreign language, you can spend more time per day and you will be able to retain more information. Of course, you can always decide to spend more or less time studying with Anki. You'll soon realize how powerful spaced repetition is, and you might just want to tackle more than you thought you could.

In Real Life

I first used Anki to memorize Ancient Greek vocabulary, paradigms, and grammatical concepts for my language courses at St. John's College. While I could have studied my textbook rigorously, I realized that Anki would enable me to spend more time learning the material properly for the first time and less time reviewing that material. I did have to spend some time making my own Ancient Greek deck, which was tailored to the idiosyncratic textbook that the language courses at St. John's use, but in that process I reviewed the textbook very thoroughly in order to decide which parts were important and worth memorizing. Additionally, I made my deck freely available to others, so that it will continue to be a resource to the college community for some time. Most important, I accomplished my mission and became more than adequate at Ancient Greek. Since then, I have also used Anki for memorizing music intervals, poetry, and English vocabulary.

A friend of mine is learning Mandarin Chinese with Anki, using a plugin with several Chinese-specific features. Each character is color-coded for the tone that it is pronounced with. Clicking on a character opens a link to its entry in a Chinese dictionary in his browser, and pressing a button plays a recording of its pronunciation. Similar plugins are available for Japanese and German.

See Also

- Anki has excellent documentation, including a series of introductory videos, a user manual, and a FAQ: http://ankisrs.net/docs/.
- Wired published an article about Piotr Wozniak, author of SuperMemo, and spaced repetition: www.wired.com/medtech/health/magazine/16-05/ff_wozniak.

Hack 5: Recall Long-Ago Events

You can improve your recall of life events with journaling, footwork, and other exercises. Remember more about your life than you ever thought you could!

In recent years, neuroscientists have begun studying a group of people who have more-or-less perfect autobiographical memory: They seldom forget anything that has ever happened to them (www.cbsnews.com/stories/2010/12/16/60minutes/main7156877.shtml). These people usually have an enlarged temporal lobe, which is associated with storing new memories, and an enormously enlarged caudate nucleus, which is associated with forming skills and habits, and with obsessive-compulsive disorder. When asked how much bigger the caudate nucleus was in these subjects, one researcher explained that the equivalent in height would be to be ten feet tall.

Unless you meet this description — and there are only a few people who are presently known to — you will probably never have perfect recollection of your entire life. However, you can recall directly, and reconstruct, much more about your past life than you think you can, through a combination of rumination, note taking, and detective work. This hack will show you how.

In Action

The following sections look at six different techniques you can use to enhance your autobiographical memory and reconstruct distant events, even if you never remember every detail.

Priming

To recall an event, thinking about related facts can help, even if they're only very loosely related. This is called *priming*. Thus, if you're trying to remember what you gave your spouse as a birthday present five years ago, you might naturally think about what your spouse's interests were at the time, or who was at the party. However, try to remember also how your favorite sports team was doing that year, who was living next door to you, and what jobs the party guests had. Even facts that don't seem to relate to the event can help, because they reconstruct more of the context, and because you can never be sure what, exactly, your brain will connect to the original event. In effect, you're googling your brain, metaphorically typing in haphazard keywords to get at just the search results you want. The curious thing is, it works.

Googling

Don't just google your brain — google the world. Search the Internet and other reference sources for facts about the period in question, and use them to remind yourself about what happened. This technique is especially useful if you have a Gmail account or other service that permanently archives all of your e-mail and enables you to search it.

Journaling

Of course, an e-mail archive like Gmail's only records facts about your world inadvertently. This is useful in its own way, but a journal is a purpose-built record of your world that records what you're sure you want to remember. Keeping a journal will prepare a record of your daily activities for when you want to recall them in the future, and it hones your observational skills so that the events of the day remain sharp in your memory. Ron has kept a journal since 1982, and he has found it invaluable.

If you want to improve your autobiographical memory but don't have time to recount the entire day's events in a diary or blog, merely jotting a few keywords about the day has been shown to have a significant impact on recall. (See the "How It Works" section.)

Scott Hagwood is a four-time U.S. National Memory Champion. His book *Memory Power* is one of the few books by mnemonists to address recalling past events, rather than just trying to stuff your brain with more data. Hagwood suggests that to enhance your recall, you ask yourself questions such as the following when you journal:

- What did I do today?
- What phone conversations did I have?
- Was major time spent on minor things and activities?
- How much stress am I under, on a scale of 1 to 5?[1]

Friends and Family

Talking to friends and family about the events you're trying to remember can be a big help. They will almost certainly remember some things you forgot, and they can corroborate things you remembered. They can also interview you, even asking the same questions you would ask yourself; it's often easier to remember facts in answer to a question from someone else, especially if you start telling a story.

Ratcheting

As you recall more and more information with the preceding techniques, leverage the bits and pieces of information you've recalled to pull up more. Feed the techniques and sources into one another: if you got a critical date and time from your e-mail, go look up that date in your journal. If you turn up a valuable clue in your journal, use the clue to remember more information with the priming technique, and so on.

Timelines

When you have gathered as much information as you can, draw a timeline of the period you're trying to remember — whether it's a day, a year, or your whole life. Mark out the period in the appropriate units; if you're trying to remember a weekend, that would be days and hours; if your life, probably years and months.

Fill out the timeline and try to get the order of events correct: Did that happen Friday or Saturday night? Was this the summer before or after my junior year? Putting events in order can solidify memories that are vague, and even bring up further details sparked when you see events next to each other. It can be surprising to see how memories snap into place and focus this way.

A timeline of your life can be quite useful. In researching this hack, Ron came across a timeline he had created of a roughly ten-year period from volume 1 of his journal, when he was 16, to just after he married Marty, at 25. It was so valuable to him in helping him set that portion of his life in mental order, both when he wrote it and later when he recovered it from his files, that he intends to expand it to cover his entire life, with shorter, denser, more detailed timelines for more interesting events, such as the one described in the "In Real Life" section below.

How It Works

With the act of priming, you're trying to find an alternate pathway to the desired information in your brain. By thinking of random related facts or memories, you're setting out on multiple pathways at once. With luck, one of them will connect to your target memory. The more pathways you try, the greater your chance of reaching your goal, or something near it.[2,3]

The keyword technique in journaling has been explored experimentally. Psychologist Willem Wagenaar recorded 2,400 events from his daily life over a period of six years, with short notes describing four features of the event: *"what* the event was, *who* was involved, and *where* and *when* it happened." Years later, Wagenaar tried to recall the other three features of an event based on only one of them. For example, given where an event happened, he asked when it was, what happened, and who was there. He concluded that "what" was the best memory cue, followed by "who", "where", and "when", in that order. He also noted, "Although the number of irretrievable events can rise to about 20%, there is some evidence that in fact none of these events was completely forgotten."[4]

In Real Life

In search of an event from his own life that he could use as an example of reconstructing long-forgotten memories, Ron was reminded of being a "Nifty Guest" (a rung below Guest of Honor) at Penguicon in Michigan several years ago. (Penguicon is an annual convention that brilliantly focuses on the geek trifecta of science fiction, gaming, and free/open-source software.)

Ron still thinks he had the most fun at Penguicon of any con he's ever been to, so he had some very pleasant memories already. Nevertheless, some specific details had been eluding him.

- What was the name of the all-white, 3D board game he played with his friends Clark and Matt?
- What was the book on "serious games" and policymaking recommended to him by the fans of Ron's previous book, whom he met while waiting in line for the Brazilian barbecue?
- What was the name of the friendly open-source hacker group into whose room party he stumbled on his way out of the hotel?

Ron began by searching for "penguicon" in his Gmail account. This brought up about 200 message threads, but he didn't look any further back than 2006, when his first book came out, because this was one of the reasons he was a guest at the con. He found a mention of a live-action chess variant he had participated in at the con called ChessLARP, so he opened that thread and found a mention of the Penguicon wiki, where he was able to determine that the Penguicon he had attended was Penguicon 5.0, from 20 to 22 April 2007, in Troy, Michigan. Ron was able to obtain the event schedule for the con from the Penguicon archives, and the gaming schedule from the Internet Archive Wayback Machine (http://web.archive.org/).

Ron then searched Gmail for "april 22 ticket" and immediately found his itinerary for the trip to Michigan, reminding him that his friend (and convention committee member) Matt had taken the trouble to pick him up at the airport at 5:30 in the morning before the hotel opened, let him crash at Matt's own apartment, then drive Ron to the hotel around 11:00. He was grateful to Matt for his hospitality, so this remains one of his fondest memories of the trip. It's all too easy to forget favors others have done us, so remembering things we ought to be grateful for is another advantage of this technique.

Memories of the con began flooding back, and Ron began jotting notes. He had a detailed memory of meeting Howard Tayler, creator of one of Ron's favorite webcomics, *Schlock Mercenary* (www.schlockmercenary.com/), and asking Tayler a sincere but probably intrusive question about how Tayler reconciled his transhumanism with his Mormonism. (Tayler said, "I'll tell you later," and proceeded to sign books for other fans for about an hour, after which he gave Ron a somewhat nonsensical answer that probably amounted to a polite "Go away kid, you bother me.")

And so on. After reminiscing for a bit, Ron dug up his Moleskine notebook for April 2007 and found what amounted to a timeline of the con's events, as he recorded them over three days. He might have done this in the first place, but all that googling was necessary to obtain the correct notebook to look in, since he has dozens of them. It was also good for a couple of hours of constructive rumination that clothed his bare memories of the con experience. He was able to answer two of the three questions he had asked himself:

- The book was *Policy Games for Strategic Management: Pathways into the Unknown*, by Richard Duke and Jac L. A. Geurts. Ron found one Amazon review, which seemed to hold Professor Richard Duke in as high an esteem as Ron remembered his interlocutor did. Unfortunately, the book was scarce and expensive. Too bad.

- The peculiar, all-white 3D board game was Santorini (www.boardgamegeek .com/boardgame/9963/santorini), which Ron discovered was highly regarded by abstract gamers and due for a reprint in Spring 2011, as he was writing this hack. What luck!

As for the local hacker group that opened their room party to Ron, who knows? He can recall they were a LUG (Linux user's group), or something like one. There were two or three men and one woman; they wore T-shirts, and adorned the hotel room wall, with their group's logo. The real culprit here in Ron's memory block is probably the alcohol he shared with the party. Perhaps if Ron decided to have a couple of drinks right now, he could remember a bit more about the occasion, but "state-dependent memory"[5] is a hack for another day, and probably another sort of book.

Notes

1. Scott Hagwood, *Memory Power: You Can Develop a Great Memory — America's Grand Master Shows You How* (New York: Free Press, 2006).

2. Endel Tulving, *Elements of Episodic Memory* (Oxford [Oxfordshire]: Clarendon Press, 1983).

3. L. E. James and D. M. Burke, "Phonological priming effects on word retrieval and tip-of-the-tongue experiences in younger and older adults," *Journal of Experimental Psychology: Learning, Memory and Language,* 26 (6) (2000): 1378–1391.

4. Willem A. Wagenaar, "My Memory: A Study of Autobiographical Memory over Six Years," *Cognitive Psychology* 18 (1986): 225–252.

5. Memory Disorders Project, "Memory Loss and the Brain: Glossary: State-Dependent Memory," Rutgers University, accessed May 10, 2011, www.memorylossonline.com/glossary/statedependentmemory.html.

Learning

The "Learning" chapter bridges the "Memory" and "Information Processing" chapters, because it's related to both. Learning is the skill and activity that brings memory and information together, synthesizing them into knowledge and, if you're diligent and lucky, eventually wisdom. Our learning hacks range from understanding the learning process at its most basic (Hack 10, "Play the Learning Game"), to expanding how you use your written resources (Hack 7, "Write in Your Books"), to finding new resources you might not have thought were available (Hack 11, "Pretend You're a Grad Student").

Whether you're officially enrolled in school or a free-range academic, this collection of techniques aims to help you learn as much as you can. Learning is growth for the mind, growth is life, and like it or not, learning never really ends. Why not go for the A?

Hack 6: Establish Your Canon

"Great books" are the books that teach you more every time you read them. "Sacred books" are the books that made you who you are. What are your personal great books and sacred books, and what can you still learn from them?

Whether they know it or not, all literate people have a *canon* of books that they treasure, learn from, and return to over and over. You can choose your own canon in many ways, from picking books because they're fun, to picking them because they're difficult, to picking them because they always offer something new.

Besides examining how to establish a canon of great books and why you should, this hack cites a few examples of great and enduring books and authors. Bear in mind that they're from our canons, not yours, so you might find reading them to be like wearing someone else's shoes, but you never know — we all might wear the same size, or close enough.

In Action

This section discusses a few criteria you can use to select which books to establish in your canon.

Adler's Hierarchy

Mortimer Adler was perhaps the twentieth century's greatest advocate for the concept of *great books*. He was a professor of philosophy at the University of Chicago who also served on the board of editors of the Encyclopedia Britannica and founded their Great Books of the Western World program. Adler claims with Charles Van Doren in *How to Read a Book* that the number of truly great books, or at least the number for any given person, is less than 100. This might seem extremely low until you consider their definition of a great book. They say that great books

> *cannot be exhausted by even the very best reading you can manage . . . you discover on returning that the book seems to have grown with you. You see new things in it — whole new sets of things — that you did not see before. . . [The] book was so far above you to begin with that it has remained above you and probably always will remain so. . .*

> *Our point . . . is that you should seek out the few books that can have this value for you. They are the books that will teach you the most, both about reading and about life.*[1]

The principle of general intelligence, as described in Hack 60, "Trust Your Intelligence (and Everyone Else's)," can be summed up in the idea that most mature human brains are, functionally, about equally intelligent, although some take more time to process information than others. If this holds true, then there must be few books indeed that will remain beyond you, no matter how long and diligently you study them in your finite lifetime.

Adler and Van Doren also describe what they call *good books*, beneath the level of the great books. Good books stretch your mind the first time you read them, but seem to have shrunk when you return to them. Adler and Van Doren claim these make up less than 1 percent of all books published, and possibly as little as .01 percent. The other 99 percent or more are useful only for "amusement or information." This ranking of books into the categories of great, good, and possibly amusing or informative is what we call *Adler's pyramid* or *Adler's hierarchy* (Figure 6-1). Of course, amusement and information are fine, and amusing information even better.

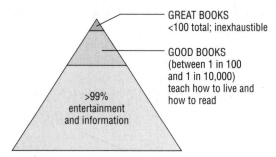

GREAT BOOKS
<100 total; inexhaustible

GOOD BOOKS
(between 1 in 100
and 1 in 10,000)
teach how to live and
how to read

>99%
entertainment
and information

Figure 6-1: Adler's pyramid

Enduring Influences

This criterion focuses on what books are the most meaningful for you personally and have changed your life the most. Based on our informal survey, a typical book that falls into this category for many people, but which few would claim is a great work of literary art, is *Illusions* by Richard Bach, author of *Jonathan Livingston Seagull*.

A canon based on enduring influences can help to fill your life with joy and meaning, but at a potential cost. The drawback of basing your canon only on books that appeal to you personally is the drawback of autodidacticism in general. At your current stage of intellectual maturity, you may not know what's best for you to study next. After all, as a child you might decide to read nothing but *If You Give a Moose a Muffin* for the rest of your life; if you stuck to that resolution, you'd be stuck indeed. In other words, it's best to accept some input on your canon. You'll learn more about how to sort out whose advice to take in the "Reading Guides" section below.

Ranking Authors

Ron and his friend Karl Erickson have similar tastes in literature and science fiction and have developed a language for ranking authors and books. They mainly use the system when recommending books to each other. It's a "fuzzy" or analog version of the crisper expressions "first-rate author," "second-rate author," and so on.

If they conclude upon reading an author that her best work could scarcely be better, that author is a "1.0" (first-rate) author. Authors they've agreed are 1.0 include Jorge Luis Borges, Stanislaw Lem, and Philip K. Dick. The 1.0 authors usually combine high literary quality with the capability of opening the reader's mind.

An author who writes books that one reads primarily for entertainment or basic information, similar to the bottom tier in Adler's pyramid, is a 2.0. An author whose books one can barely force oneself to read at all, even for entertainment or information, is at best a 3.0.

The analog nature of the scale enters when trying to rank certain authors who don't quite fit into the 1.0, 2.0, or 3.0 categories. For example, Karl and Ron read a Vernor Vinge novel for more than just entertainment or information (2.0), but his work doesn't usually fling open the mind's shutters to the degree that a 1.0 author's work does, either. Therefore, they call Vinge a 1.5-rate author. Authors closer to 1.0 but still slightly flawed might rate 1.1 or 1.2, or even 1.1227. The analog nature of this system suggests that Adler's system could also use an in-between category, for books that are less than great but better than good.

Ultimate Books

Ron also enjoys reading a class of books that he calls *ultimate books*. Ultimate books are often great books as defined by Adler, but may be merely good. The important thing about them, other than their being good or great, is that they are both long and difficult, almost ergodic.

> **NOTE** Ergodic literature is literature that requires a special effort to read beyond just turning pages, such as the *I Ching*, or interactive fiction such as Zork.[2]

In an age when the longest bit of prose many people read is a Facebook entry, ultimate books can teach sustained concentration. Phrases often applied to ultimate books include the following:

- *all-encompassing*
- *phone book*
- *sprawling*
- *epic*
- *mind game*
- *unreadable*

Far from being dismaying, these phrases merely pique the ultimate book adventurer's interest. Ultimate books Ron has completed and can heartily recommend include the following:

- *Gödel, Escher, Bach*, Douglas Hofstadter
- *Gravity's Rainbow*, Thomas Pynchon
- *Finnegans Wake*, James Joyce

- *Tristram Shandy*, Laurence Sterne
- *Infinite Jest*, David Foster Wallace

Books Ron is currently attempting or considering out of cussedness and intellectual vanity — for him, the two are boon companions in this quest — include the following:

- *Ulysses*, James Joyce
- *Don Quixote*, Miguel de Cervantes
- *House of Leaves*, by Mark Z. Danielewski
- *The Thousand and One Nights*, Anonymous
- *Manuscript Found in Saragossa*, Jan Potocki
- *In Search of Lost Time*, Marcel Proust
- *War and Peace*, Leonid Tolstoy

Marty also enjoys an ultimate book. She's working through *Finnegans Wake* and from Ron's list also aims to tackle *Ulysses*, *Don Quixote*, and *In Search of Lost Time* at some point. She also has her own separate list as well, which includes *The Making of Americans* by Gertrude Stein, Pynchon's *Mason and Dixon*, and Anthony Trollope's Palliser novels (taken as a whole, as they were meant).

Reading Guides

A final help to establishing at least part of your canon is reading guides, which range from simple reading lists, such as the Modern Library's "100 Best Non-Fiction Books" (www.modernlibrary.com/top-100/100-best-nonfiction/) and "100 Best Novels of the 20th Century" (www.modernlibrary.com/top-100/100-best-novels/), to more ambitious "reading plan" books with extensive commentary, such as *The New Lifetime Reading Plan* by Clifton Fadiman and John S. Major, to ready-made great books collections such as the *Great Books of the Western World* and the *Harvard Classics* (one volume of which is a reading plan for the rest of the collection).

The advantage of consulting a bibliography, book review, reading list, reading plan, or great books collection is that it prevents you from falling into a sterile autodidacticism, as if you really did decide to read nothing but *If You Give a Moose a Muffin* for the rest of your life. You are one of more than 6.7 billion people on the Earth; the chance of your being the single smartest and best-educated person among them is vanishingly small. This means that you may not always be the most qualified person to pick the next book you're going to read, especially if you're studying a field where expertise counts for a great deal and there are many cranks, such as physics. Therefore, we propose that you sometimes consider the advice of other people — or their proxies, reading guides — about what to read when establishing your canon.

You might object that when trying to determine a reliable source for reading advice by yourself, you're likely to fall into "second-order autodidacticism," or even third-order or higher if you've really managed to tie yourself into a strange loop. However, it's not as if you know *nothing* to start with. Candle flames are yellow, aren't they? To quote William Blake, "If the fool would persist in his folly he would become wise."

NOTE After you've established your canon, you might want to hold a gathering with several of your friends and compare your canon with theirs, whether theirs were chosen formally or informally. Lion Kimbro, one of the contributors to this book, once sponsored such a gathering to great effect at Seattle geek gathering place Saturday House. His criteria were centered on what he called "sacred books" and we've called "enduring influences" above, but any of the criteria in this section could apply at your gathering, and possibly all of them.

How It Works

The concept of great books grows naturally from the concept of a liberal education. A "liberal education" is not necessarily politically liberal or left-wing. Its emphasis is on teaching one to think for oneself, an aim that has no particular bias.

There are some colleges and universities, such as St. John's College in the United States, with a curriculum based entirely on great books, which encourage liberatory discussion and work with such books. People who want to educate themselves or their children with great books can buy the Encyclopedia Britannica's *Great Books of the Western World* set (www.britannicastore.com/Great-Books-of-the-Western-World/invt/greatbooks&bklist=), selected by Mortimer Adler, or the "Five-Foot Shelf" of the *Harvard Classics,* all of which are now free to download to your e-book reader and carry in your pocket (http://wiki.mobileread.com/wiki/Harvard_Classics_Available_at_MobileRead).

Why would anyone want an undergraduate education devoted entirely to the great books? In the United States, you can point to any career you wish and chances are excellent that it will be either automated or outsourced away soon enough. However, thinking — whether critical, creative, or some other kind — is a universally applicable skill, and it can be applied not only to existing jobs, but also to any new jobs that might appear, which you might not be able to fill or retrain for if you opted for a more narrow technical training (www.mckenzi-estudycenter.org/education/articles/practic.html).

The more you give to the process of educating yourself with great books, whether as part of a college education or independently, the more you receive from it, and the more you have to give.

In Real Life

In surveying possible books for his canon, Ron found that the three books that have probably influenced him the most are *Gödel, Escher, Bach*; *The Glass Bead Game*; and *Finnegans Wake*.

One of his earliest enduring influences was *Gödel, Escher, Bach*, which he read at 14. It was mentioned in Martin Gardner's column in *Scientific American*, and the review drew him irresistibly. *GEB* influenced his choice of college and career, and his sense of humor. Regrettably, 30 years later, he finds he's outgrown it because after years of school, work, and independent study, he understands the concepts in it much better than when the book introduced him to them. Thus, it's a good book, not a great book — for him.

Another book that had an enormous influence on him was *The Glass Bead Game* by Hermann Hesse. He heard about it in college, bought it, shelved it, picked it up a few months later, and hasn't put it down since. It's not only inspiring in its vision of an all-encompassing intellectual game, a "hundred-gated cathedral of Mind," but its playful, ironic spirit makes him suspect he keeps missing something, as if he glimpsed something with peripheral vision in a mirror.

We've already written at length about *Finnegans Wake* elsewhere, so we'll merely point out that one of Joyce's stated aims in writing the book was to keep scholars busy for hundreds of years. Ron's second time through the *Wake* is with a reading group, Allforabit Funferall. "Inexhaustible" is an inadequate word for the *Wake* and its many enigmas — "exhaustively inexhaustible" is more like it. We will be exhausted before it is.

See Also

- Umberto Eco's concept of the antilibrary: Unread books are more valuable than read ones, and the bigger your library, the better (http://ruchir75 .blogspot.com/2008/01/umberto-ecos-anti-library.html).

- Christopher Beha, *The Whole Five Feet: What the Great Books Taught Me About Life, Death, and Pretty Much Everything Else* (New York: Grove Press, 2009). A memoir that describes his experience with reading all of the Harvard Classics in one year.

- Pierre Bayard, *How to Talk About Books You Haven't Read* (New York: Bloomsbury USA, 2007). Funny and thought-provoking, this book discusses both the culture's canon (or as he calls it, the "collective library") and the interactions of individual canons (or "inner libraries"), as well as many other topics of interest to anyone who likes to read and discuss books.

Notes

1. Mortimer Jerome Adler and Charles L. Van Doren, *How to Read a Book* (New York: Touchstone, 1972).

2. Espen J. Aarseth, *Cybertext: Perspectives on Ergodic Literature* (Maryland: Johns Hopkins University Press, 1997).

Hack 7: Write in Your Books

Lion Kimbro

Do you find it repellent, or even shocking, to write in a book? Learn why some of the greatest minds in history were obsessive scribblers of marginalia. Remember, a book isn't really yours until you talk back to the author.

This hack is about extending what books can do for you. By the time you finish this hack, you'll know how to do all of the following:

- Quickly find specific parts of a book when you want to read them again.
- Understand an author's thoughts clearly, even when the writing is muddled or confusing.
- Develop your own thoughts clearly, and identify where your thoughts and the author's ideas align and diverge.
- Get a book ready for critical study, analysis, and quoting.
- Remind yourself of next-action steps, which will clearly indicate how reading the book made a difference in your life.

All of these techniques result from some variant of writing in your books. In this hack, you'll explore a few techniques you can use to get these great benefits. These techniques work for everything from *The C Programming Language* to *The Last Unicorn*, from the Bible to *The Forever War*. You can write on anything containing text, from the most technical to the most holy, to more deeply engage with it.

As an experiment, write in *this* book, and vow to write in the next book you read, to see what happens.

In Action

Traditional techniques for annotation — underlining, highlighting, putting checks next to text, and, most important, writing notes in the margins — are all worthwhile and beneficial. Because they are well known, they are not covered here. If you don't already do the traditional things, start with those, but far more is possible, including the following three techniques:

- Extending the index
- Agreeing and disagreeing with text, using blue and red (or any colors you prefer)
- Repurposing books for storing notes

Extending the Index

I'll start with the most powerful technique I have found: extending the index. This hack works for anything you read.

First, look in the back of a book that you're reading to see if it already has an index. If so, great! If there is no index — add one! To quickly make an index, see if the book contains some blank pages at the back or the front. If there are no blank pages, find pages that are almost blank — you can often build an index using extra space around the dedication in a book, for example. Figure 7-1 shows an index created on a book's inside cover. Figure 7-2 shows a similar index created on a title page because no other spaces were readily available.

Figure 7-1: A hand-constructed index, written on the back cover of a book

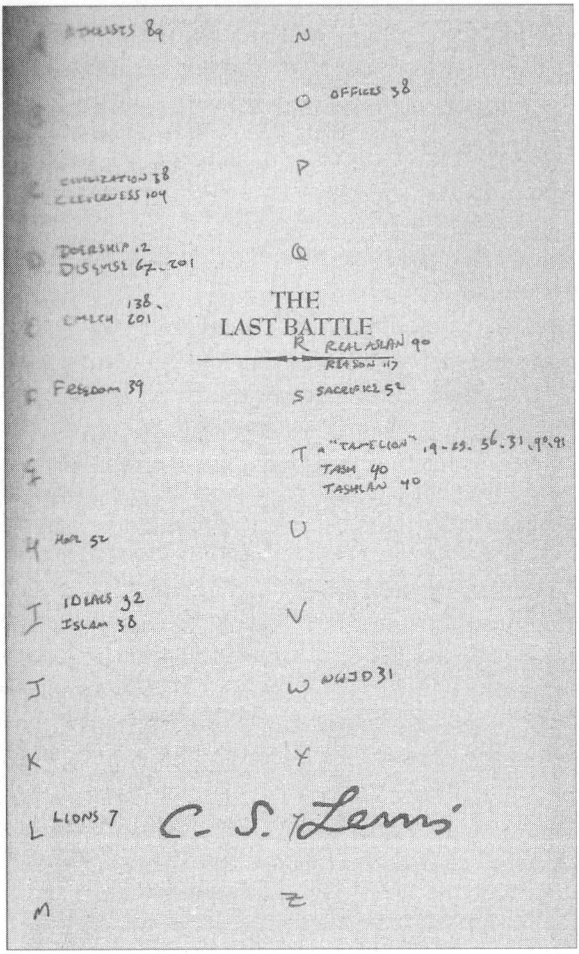

ATHEISTS 84   N

                                     O   OFFICES 38

CIVILIZATION 38   P
CLEVERNESS 104

DICTATORSHIP 12
DISGUST 67-201   Q

        138.   **THE**
EARTH 201   **LAST BATTLE**
                                     R   REAL ASLAN 90
                                         REASON 117

FREEDOM 39   S   SACRIFICE 52

                                     T   a "TAMELION" 19-29. 36.31, 90.91
                                         TASM 40
                                         TASHLAN 40

HOPE 52   U

IDEALS 32   V
ISLAM 38

                                     W   WAJOD 31

K   Y

L   LIONS 7   *C. S. Lewis*

                                     Z
M

                                         A N G s T

Figure 7-2: A hand-constructed index, written around a title page

To roughly organize the index, put the letter A in the top-left corner of the
left side, M at the bottom-left corner, N at the top center of the page, and then
Z at the bottom center. G goes at the center of the left side of the page, and T
squarely in the center. Then fill in the letters between, so that A through M
line the left side, and N through Z run down the center. They should be spaced
evenly, more or less, although some letters (such as Q, X, and Y) will have fewer
entries and others will have more.

This is the framework for your new index. Again, if the book came with
an index, there's nothing you need to do — you'll just add your entries within
the index that's already there. (If it's tightly spaced, you can draw a line between
two index items to indicate position, and then write the new entry beside the
line, where there is space.)

Now you can begin extending the index as you read the book.

For some reason, in June of 1948, Teilhard de Chardin neglected to use the word "blogs" — therefore, we must add that entry in the index for him (see Figure 7-3). However, on page 240, he *did* write "the surest affirmation we can make about the human future is that nothing will ever restrain Man from seeking to think and essay everything to the very end."

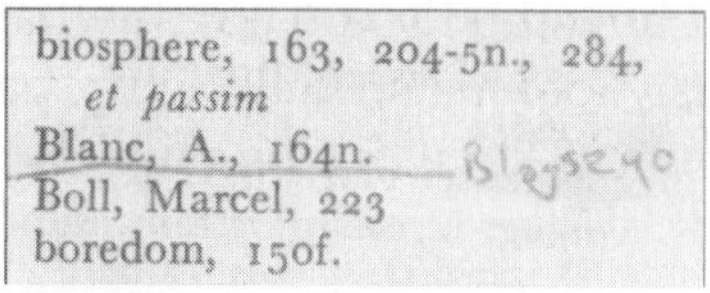

biosphere, 163, 204-5n., 284,
  et passim
Blanc, A., 164n.   *Blogs* 240
Boll, Marcel, 223
boredom, 150f.

Figure 7-3: An added index entry

Most indexes are indexes of keywords that are literally represented in the text, and many go a step further and organize the information in the book. I'm going to recommend that you go another step further, and personalize the index. Readers who are familiar with *tagging* will recognize the idea of organizing that is also personalized. A brief example to explain: Suppose you are reading a book (*The Future of Man*, in this instance), and the author makes use of a model that resembles an intellectual model your friend Peggy is currently working on. Note the page and open the index. Write your friend's name ("Peggy Holman") in it, and link it to the relevant page number (252). Now, whenever you want to remember where that model is located in the book — the one that reminded you of Peggy — you can just look up "Peggy" in the index. What could be simpler?

NOTE "Tagging" here refers to an online convention, such as the one at http://delicious.com. The idea behind tagging the Web is to link web pages with your mental associations, so that you can relocate pages that you've seen before — your own personal Google. Does it work? It works fantastically well.

If you find that the book is important to you, and it is suggesting a lot of *"to do"* items, just find a nice, easy-to-access spot in the book — say, the inside cover — and add a heading such as "Impact On My Life" or "To Do," and start your list under that heading. Include "Talk with Peggy" under it, and add the page number of the conversation (again) next to it.

Now, when someone asks you what you got out of that book, you can say something like, "Well, I found corroboration for an idea that Peggy is advancing," or "My ideas about man and the universe were challenged," and so on. Moreover, you can back everything up with specifics: exact texts and exactly what you were thinking about (you wrote in the margins, right?), and thereby gain mastery over the contents of the book.

As the names of people, places, key images, and ideas occur to you — anything of significance that comes to your mind — add them to the index. There's no law dictating that the words in an index have to appear in the book. Authors have no way of knowing how what they write about will match the specific situations or circumstances of your life. That is for you to discover.

If you do this regularly, you will be amazed at how fluidly you access what is in the book. If you ever find yourself laboriously looking something up, be sure to note where it is in the index after you find it: That way, you only ever have to look it up the hard way *once*.

There are other similar things you can do to gain mastery over the contents of a book. You can make your own maps of the book (complete with page numbers). If the book contains timelines or geographic maps (such as the geography of Middle-earth or Narnia), you can put page numbers directly onto the map, to show where in the book action took place at that spot. This makes it very easy to leap directly to the different parts. You can also create what I call a *reverse table of contents*. Instead of making a map that maps contents to page numbers, create a proportional map that starts from page numbers and maps contents onto them. This may sound like a silly exercise, but I've found that I've developed a much clearer understanding of Teilhard by visualizing his thoughts in a reverse table of contents of my own making, rather than relying on the given table of contents.

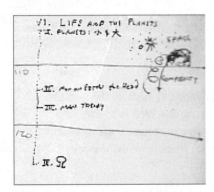

Figure 7-4: Part of a reverse table of contents

The numbers 100, 110, and 120 on the left in Figure 7-4 identify the page numbers. You can see in this diagram that the text dedicated to "Planets" is relatively long, "Man on Earth, the Head" is relatively short, and then "Man Today" is relatively long again. The drawing indicates that the author talks for several pages about the stars, space, and the development of complexity on Earth, leading into "Man on Earth, the Head." A spatial map of contents reveals not only the order of subject material, but also the author's emphasis, by showing graphically how much of the book is dedicated to each topic.

Annotating in Two Colors

The second major technique will help you anytime you're reading a persuasive piece. The idea is to use two colors as you read a book: *blue* to annotate what you agree with, and *red* to annotate what you disagree with.

When you read something that you agree with, or can endorse, or are sympathetic with, inspired by, or just generally feel positive about, underline that text in blue. When you read something that you disagree with, or have serious caveats about, or are otherwise alarmed or cautious toward, underline that text in red.

When you are writing notes that are inspired by or supportive of what the author is saying, use blue. If you can find some value in what the author is saying, but within limits, write that in blue, and list the situations where the author's point makes sense. When you are writing notes in contradiction, perhaps supported by counter-experiences from your own life, or pointing out arguments that the author hasn't addressed, use red, red, and more red. Explain why you disagree, and include a few words about any experiences from your life that support your position. (For information on pens that write in several colors, see Hack 17, "Write Magnificent Notes.")

By articulating agreements and disagreements with the author on the page, you can clarify the differences between your own thoughts and the author's thoughts, or the point at which the author has moved from what you understand to what you do not understand. It's clear because it's right there, visually, on the page, not just a thought in your head that *might* be evoked when you look at the page again. In other words, when you look at the page again, it is readily apparent where you disagree, because the text transitions from blue to red. Your attention is brought immediately to the core point of difference, and thus you don't have to spend a lot of time rereading and reconstructing arguments. You don't have to wonder what you disagreed with, because the book has been personalized to your brain already.

There have been many times when I have underlined something in red, only to later come back and underline it in blue. Our minds continuously process information; we're always thinking. You'll sometimes find that later you'll come back and say, "Wait, I see now what the author meant." You'll cross out the red and change it to blue, maybe adding a note that says "I had this life experience, and I saw these things, and now I understand what the author meant." And there will be other times when you say, ". . . and the author was just plain mad," because your opinion hasn't changed.

Using a Book as a Notebook

Finally, my third technique for transforming how I use books is to completely repurpose them.

We see books, conventionally, as vehicles for the transmission of knowledge, from an author to ourselves as recipient learners. We have worked in this hack already to change that thinking, to see ourselves in collaboration with the author towards understanding (writing in the margins, marking in red and blue), or weaving in the territory of the book with our own lives (creating a personal index). This technique is something very different: using the book as a storage device, ignoring the author and tailoring the object itself to our own goals, rather than just the content.

This is an unusual idea, and somewhat difficult to explain, so I'll try to clarify the concept by way of a story. Imagine that you wanted to learn about Colombia. To help with this task, you buy a blank notebook for taking notes. In this case, you are entirely responsible for bringing structure (or "partitions") to your journaled thoughts. For example, you could follow all the steps in Hack 17, "Write Magnificent Notes," and make a pretty good notebook on Colombia.

How will your notes be structured? You could allocate pages for studying geography, pages for studying the cities, pages for studying the political struggles, pages for studying the flower trade, and so on. Alternatively, there may be no overall structure, but only a series of investigations into information about the country as topics interest you over time, like a journal with no apparent order except a chronological listing. Could it be structured differently?

Here's a different story: Imagine you bought a book on Colombia, but it was misprinted. The index, the table of contents, the chapter and section headings, everything that reveals the structure of the book, was printed correctly in solid black, but the content of the text is a very pale gray, so pale that you can hardly differentiate it from the color of the paper. Imagine repurposing this misprinted book — all structure and no content — as your own notebook. Now, whenever you want to record a note on some aspect of Colombia, you have a functioning index, chapter headings, and sections, and when you look up "Barranquilla," you find exactly the pages that talk about Barranquilla, and you can write your notes there. The book has a place for your chosen subject, one that is easy to find again in the future and near related subject matter.

This is repurposing the book as a place for your own thoughts, and it's like having an "instant book kit" you can make yourself — just add content. It does not matter what the text says, just that it provides good terrain and structure for storing your ideas and notes. The structure makes it easy to find your notes again in the future, and places notes proximate to other related notes.

How It Works

When you read something, or when you hear something, you're only halfway to understanding it. To truly understand, you need to put it into your own words, into your own frame, into your own language, into your own metaphors.

Writing in books generates clear understanding in your own mind, because you yourself are kneading the material and reshaping it in a way you can digest. It's easy to become hypnotized by the sound of other people's words in your head; if you really want to understand what is being spoken, *you need to be able to bring it into form and feeling yourself.* Adding your own navigation and words works marvelously to that end.

For most people, the hardest thing about writing in books is making it past long-held philosophical hurdles or objections to it. The following FAQ addresses a few of these:

Q: "It's a book! You're not supposed to write in books!"

A: If you have an original Gutenberg Bible, please don't write in it. If you have an illuminated manuscript, please don't write in it. But if the book itself is not an artistic or historical artifact, then realize that it is there to communicate ideas, and that the clock of time is ticking. A book is an approximation toward telepathy, mind-to-mind communication, and it's the ideas that you want to focus on, the web of information — not the object that carries them. Develop thoughts and ideas, and remember priorities!

Q: "But I might want to lend the book to someone."

A: People on the Internet slave day and night to get annotation systems working, not just for personal annotation, but for sharing. Why would it be any different with our books? Why assume that your friend wouldn't want to read your thoughts? Isn't that an unexamined assumption? Which would you prefer returned from a friend: a "clean" book or a book that your friend has added his or her thoughts to, one containing your friend's thoughts as well as the thoughts of the author? Personally, I beg those to whom I lend my books to write in them. How often do we ask, upon a book being returned to us, "How did you like it? What did you think?" At worst, if the notes in your annotated copy are too distracting, you can buy a fresh copy for friends, they can buy their own, or they can take it out of a public library.

Q: "But I might want to sell the book."

A: Consider the difference between price and value. The *price* of a particular book with and without marginalia is often about the same; usually annotations bring the price down a little bit. Now consider the *value* — the meaning and connection with your life — that the book that you've written in acquires, compared to the book that is kept virginal. The value can double, triple, or increase vastly more. I once lost a copy of a book I owned. I bought a replacement, but of course it lacks all the index additions and maps I had made. The only way to reconstruct them is to read the book again, and remake the markings. How much value there is in those markings! It's often true that even seemingly inconsequential books turn out to be repositories of high value after you think about them and interact with them.

Q: "Aha! You say annotations are valuable, but you can lose the book!"

A: True, but keeping the notes in a computer has no functional comparison. There is no substitute for simply writing on the paper. The index, diagrams, and images are immediately accessible. Writing notes on the side can slow you down, but beyond that the cost of writing in the book is tiny: The vast majority of the labor is in the reading itself. Conversely, the cost of writing everything on a computer is high, including starting the computer, opening a program, locating a file, and manipulating the user interface. It is much simpler to just look at the page with writing on it. The value of writing in the moment and then quickly finding the relevant notes greatly outweighs the risk of losing the book; while using a computer is possibly safer (although subject to things like hardware malfunction), it lacks the value of writing in the book.

Own your books. Read the book for the ideas, and the development of your intellect. Forget mercantile bantering about prices and "value." After you're dead, it won't matter how clean the book is. What can be of infinite value are Granddad's and Grandma's notes in the margin, which transform an otherwise ordinary un-noteworthy baby of a book into a mature adult full of ideas, work, and wisdom.

The simple fact is, it's a book. You learn faster and connect more easily with the content if you write in it. Its value is increased by your participation, and it doesn't cost you anything.

This is not an all-or-nothing proposal: You can start small. Challenge yourself to find a book that you might like but don't have strong feelings about, and try writing in it, applying the techniques in this chapter. Anything will work. Perhaps you have a copy of a fantasy novel you thought you might read, or you bought a popular book in the airport because you were bored. If you buy something, choose something inexpensive and buy two copies, to alleviate your guilt about putting the pen of corruption to holy paper. Then apply these techniques, and see what happens.

In Real Life

This section offers some examples from several of my books, scanned in. The first example, shown in Figure 7-5, shows an annotated index.

Notice that in some cases existing index entries have been given additional page numbers, which for some reason were not noted by the original indexer, and that some entries are entirely unknown to the book's indexer (for example, "biological value of moral action") or even unknowable to the indexer (for example, "blogs").

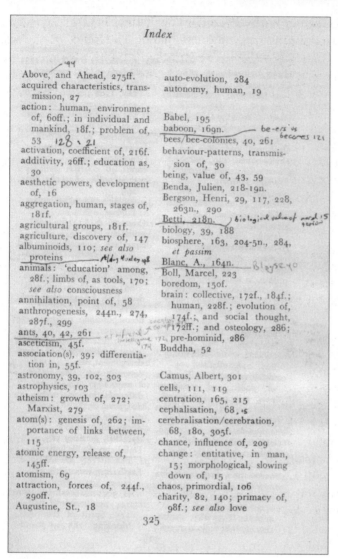

Index

Above, and Ahead, 275ff.
acquired characteristics, trans-
    mission, 27
action: human, environment
    of, 6off.; in individual and
    mankind, 18f.; problem of,
    53
activation, coefficient of, 216f.
additivity, 26ff.; education as,
    30
aesthetic powers, development
    of, 16
aggregation, human, stages of,
    181f.
agricultural groups, 181f.
agriculture, discovery of, 147
albuminoids, 110; *see also*
    proteins
animals: 'education' among,
    28f.; limbs of, as tools, 170;
    see also consciousness
annihilation, point of, 58
anthropogenesis, 244n., 274,
    287f., 299
ants, 40, 42, 261
asceticism, 45f.
association(s), 39; differentia-
    tion in, 55f.
astronomy, 39, 102, 303
astrophysics, 103
atheism: growth of, 272;
    Marxist, 279
atom(s): genesis of, 262; im-
    portance of links between,
    115
atomic energy, release of,
    145ff.
atomism, 69
attraction, forces of, 244f.,
    290ff.
Augustine, St., 18

auto-evolution, 284
autonomy, human, 19

Babel, 195
baboon, 169n.
bees/bee-colonies, 40, 261
behaviour-patterns, transmis-
    sion of, 30
being, value of, 43, 59
Benda, Julien, 218-19n.
Bergson, Henri, 29, 117, 228,
    263n., 290
Betti, 218n.
biology, 39, 188
biosphere, 163, 204-5n., 284,
    et passim
Blanc, A., 164n.
Boll, Marcel, 223
boredom, 150f.
brain: collective, 172f., 184f.;
    human, 228f.; evolution of,
    174f.; and social thought,
    172ff.; and osteology, 286;
    pre-hominid, 286
Buddha, 52

Camus, Albert, 301
cells, 111, 119
centration, 165, 215
cephalisation, 68,
cerebralisation/cerebration,
    68, 180, 305f.
chance, influence of, 209
change: entitative, in man,
    15; morphological, slowing
    down of, 15
chaos, primordial, 106
charity, 82, 140; primacy of,
    98f.; *see also* love

325

Figure 7-5: A scan of an index page from *The Future of Man*, by Teilhard de Chardin

I have a hard time, generally, following Teilhard — I find his sentences long, and his explanations even longer. Figure 7-6 shows an annotated page within the book. In this case, I read the words "universal law" (near the middle of the page), but by this point I'd forgotten what law he was talking about. Earlier on the page, he'd written "everything is the sum of the past." By drawing a square around "everything is the sum of the past" and linking it to the words "universal law," I brought Teilhard's point, and the page itself, into new focus.

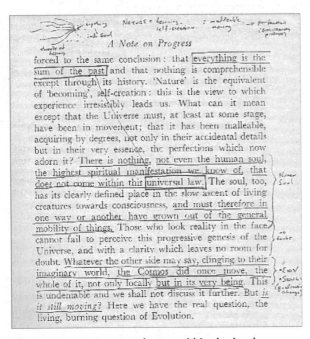

Figure 7-6: An annotated page within the book

Figure 7-7 shows a page from a reverse table of contents. Note that not all of the boxes are filled in; there are still parts of the book that I have not read. As I fill it in, it becomes clear to me what I've studied, and what I have not. To my way of thinking, it's more important to understand the ideas than to say I read every word in the book.

Figure 7-8 shows an index I constructed for *Reborn to Live: The Second Book of the Initiate*, published by ValRA at Damanhur. This is particularly useful, because the book has no index; it doesn't even have chapters or a table of contents.

This index has entries for A–H on the left, I–P on the right, and then from Q–Z on the following page. It's not important to perfectly space each letter. If you run out of space for a letter, bleed into the space for the next letter.

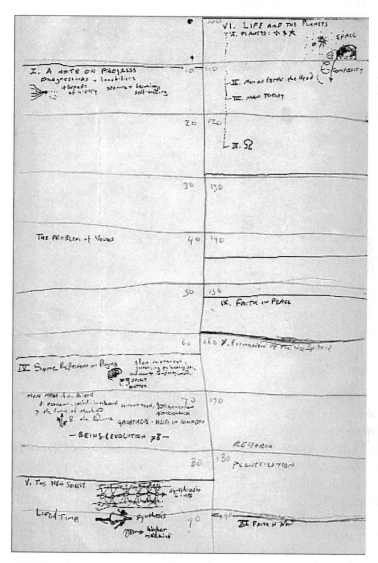

Figure 7-7: A page of a reverse table of contents

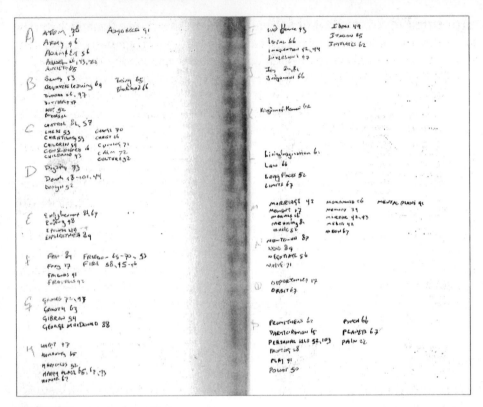

Figure 7-8: A constructed index

See Also

- *Marginalia: Readers Writing in Books*, by H. J. Jackson (Yale University Press, 2002). The value of annotation is well established historically, as this scholarly but fun examination of marginalia and the history of marginalia makes abundantly clear.

- Mortimer Adler, "How to Mark a Book," www.tnellen.com/cybereng/adler.html

- Bert Webb, "Twelve Ways To Mark Up A Book," http://hwebbjr.typepad.com/openloops/2006/02/twelve_ways_to_.html

Hack 8: Read at Speed

Significantly increase your reading speed with a few basic techniques. Rather than slog through several books on the subject, just read this hack.

"Speed reading" has a huge mystique, and many people have made fortunes out of other people's curiosity about it. There are always so many books and so little time — could we really change that ratio by devouring them faster?

First of all, it's important to understand the limitations of speed reading, or simply reading very quickly. The bad news is that, all else being equal, the faster you read, the more you will miss. Much so-called speed reading is little more than skimming, and you glean only the most cursory information from it; as the old Woody Allen joke goes, "I took a speed-reading course and read *War and Peace* in twenty minutes. It involves Russia."

The good news is that all else need not be equal. You can change your reading habits in certain ways that can make a significant difference in how much you understand and retain when you try to read faster.

No claims will be made in this hack about exactly how much faster its techniques will help you read, especially not the comical and probably fraudulent claims you occasionally hear in advertisements for speed-reading courses, such as learning to read and fully comprehend a page a second. Nonetheless, if you apply the techniques described in this hack consistently, you'll probably read both faster and better.

In Action

Here are five tips to help you improve your reading speed while reading well, and your reading comprehension while reading fast. These tips have been sifted from a bad lot of books about speed reading,[1,2,3] and I have found they help me read faster, although not so fast that pages ignite from friction when I turn them.

Get Comfy

Make yourself comfortable. Relax and make the following items part of your reading environment:

- Comfortable chair
- Comfortable desk or lap desk, if you use one
- Good lighting that illuminates your book fully without glare
- Eyeglasses or contacts, if you need them
- Dictionary and other reference materials
- Quiet surroundings, earplugs, or "mind music" (music you find conducive to concentration)
- Annotation materials (Hack 7, "Write in Your Books")
- A pacer (see "Pace Yourself," below)

Gather everything you need before you start, and take your reading seriously enough to provide yourself with the right tools. Removing the distractions of uncomfortable seating, glare or shadows from bad lighting, and having to get up and retrieve some forgotten item will improve your concentration, and therefore your speed.

Preview

Preview the book before you try to read it, including the following items, if the book has them:

- Front matter
  - cover text
  - table of contents
  - foreword
  - introduction

- Back matter
  - glossary
  - index
  - bibliography

After this preview of the book's structure, skim its content thoroughly, including any section headers and summaries. This technique works best for nonfiction. As a rule, novels won't have an index, and you probably don't want to spoil the plot for yourself by skimming ahead, unless you don't care about the experience of reading the book and are merely reading for information or a grade.

Knowing what you want from the book almost always helps. When you are reading with a purpose, you are less likely to miss important material.

Pace Yourself

Pace yourself through a page by moving your finger, a pen or pencil, or a chopstick down the text, line by line. If you let your eye follow your "pacer," it will serve almost as a metronome and help you to move ahead in a quick, even rhythm. Without it, your eye is likely to waste time wandering over the whole page, rereading phrases and lines, or skipping ahead and back.

Many speed-reading books tell you to drag your finger across each line. Ron seldom does this himself, but places his finger below the center of each line he's reading. Other people may run a pacer down the margin of the page, touching the beginning of each line. Experiment to find what works best for you.

Pacing with a finger or pencil can be useful even for ebooks. Of course, with many ebook readers, you also have the option of automatic pacing; many ebook reader software applications have an "autoscroll" feature that scrolls the text at a fixed rate, forcing you to pay attention to keep up. If you want to increase your reading speed, you should set the scroll rate to a little faster than you're already comfortable with.

Don't Reread

Rereading breaks your smooth forward motion. Chances are good that if you immediately reread text, you won't understand it any better, and you'll find yourself rereading it several times. *Wait until later to go back and review, when you'll have more context.*

Improve Your Vocabulary

A good vocabulary can aid both reading speed and comprehension. If nothing else, you'll pause less often to look up words as your vocabulary improves (Hack 3, "Mix Up Your Facts").

How It Works

This hack is really a bundle of related techniques that people (including myself) have found to improve their reading speed. Therefore, some parts of this hack have scientific support, and other parts are more anecdotal. For example, we don't know of a specific scientific study that shows your reading speed will improve if you sit in a well-lit, comfortable chair rather than lie on a bed of nails in near-total darkness, but do you really need one? People continue to try to get serious reading done in all kinds of crazy conditions. We're here to advocate for the comfy chair.

The claims found in many speed-reading books, such as that the perceptual span of the eye can be stretched to encompass whole sentences, paragraphs, or even pages rather than individual words, are controversial at best. Peripheral vision has much lower resolution than the part of the eye usually used for reading, the macula. The eye's physical structure doesn't enable it to easily parse small objects like text in peripheral vision, even with training.[4,5,6]

Similarly controversial is the common claim that reading speed can be increased by eliminating subvocalization, or silently "sounding out" words as you read. Marty finds that occasionally subvocalizing, or even vocalizing aloud, actually *helps* focus her attention when it wanders, and keeps her moving forward, much like a pacer. Research seems to bear out that subvocalization can improve reading comprehension.[7,8]

"read in an undertone"

In Real Life

Mortimer Adler, philosopher and proponent of the Great Books concept (see Hack 6, "Establish Your Canon"), formulated a golden rule of reading speed:

Every book should be read no more slowly than it deserves, and no more quickly than you can read it with satisfaction and comprehension.[9]

To this we'd like to add a corollary: You shouldn't read any slower than necessary, either.

If, for some reason, you must plow through a stack of books you don't expect to enjoy, you'll do yourself a favor if you read them at top speed. In general, the worse the book Ron has had to read, such as hard science fiction loaded with badly expressed but interesting ideas (Hack 31, "Mine the Future"), the more he enjoyed the experience if he read it as fast as he could — and because he was having a good experience, his mind was more receptive and he was more likely to retain the ideas. One of the "secrets" of speed reading is learning that some of what you read doesn't matter, and that you can get what you need from such material by skimming it.

On the other hand, don't cheat yourself. The right speed for reading can sometimes be very slow. We read and savor James Joyce's *Finnegans Wake* with a group of friends at the rate of about one page a month, and we are considered *fast* by the organizer of the Finnegans Wake Reading Groups Directory.

See Also

- "The 1,000-Word Dash," Timothy Noah, accessed June 2, 2011, `http://www.slate.com/id/74766/`. Nicely skewers claims that anyone can read with full comprehension at more than about 600 words per minute, or twice the human average.

Notes

1. Tony Buzan, *Speed Reading: Third Edition* (New York: Plume, 1991).

2. Stanley D. Frank, *Remember Everything You Read: The Evelyn Wood 7-Day Speed Reading & Learning Program* (New York: Avon, 1992).

3. Tina Konstant, *Teach Yourself Speed Reading* (New York: McGraw-Hill, 2003).

4. Keith Rayner, "The perceptual span and peripheral cues in reading," *Cognitive Psychology,* Vol 7 Issue 1 (1975): 65-81.

5. G. W. McConkie and T. W. Hogaboam, "Eye position and word identification during reading" (technical report no. 333, University of Illinois at Urbana-Champaign. Center for the Study of Reading, 1985).

6. Marcel Adam Just and Patricia A. Carpenter, *The Psychology of Reading and Language Comprehension* (New York: Prentice Hall, 1987).

7. Ronald P. Carver, *Reading Rate: A Review of Research and Theory* (New York: Academic Press, 1990).

8. Keith Rayner and Alexander Pollatsek. *The Psychology of Reading* (London: Routledge, 1994).

9. Mortimer J. Adler and Charles Van Doren, *How to Read a Book* (New York: Touchstone, 1972).

Hack 9: Learn by Teaching   yes!

Look for ways to learn by getting out from behind the student desk and into the front of the classroom.

If you're interested in learning something, do you immediately consider taking a class on it or perhaps finding a book that will teach it to you? Most of us do, and these can be effective methods. However, there are many opportunities to learn beyond the somewhat passive traditional ones, especially if sitting in a classroom taking notes doesn't work well for you. The advent of the Internet and widespread availability of production technology has enabled more people to produce and distribute a plethora of teaching and learning materials. Why not try being a teacher instead of a student for a while? You may find you learn more that way.

In Action

Before you can teach an idea, you must understand it. Therefore, teaching situations can be proving grounds for your own knowledge. Accelerate your learning of a subject by agreeing to teach it. Volunteer to tutor younger students, or try teaching a community education class. (Check with your local parks and recreation office about how to sign up.) You can learn together with your friends by starting a group around your area of interest, where you each take turns teaching the rest of the group. If no one wants to learn what you're teaching, *hire* some students!

Learning by Homeschooling

Alternatively, make some little students of your own. If you're a homeschooling parent, your kids are the perfect captive audience. Homeschooling provides a strong motivation to keep learning, because you have a responsibility to know more than your kids do so that you can teach them at the appropriate grade level and be prepared for tough questions. In the case of simple information, this won't be difficult — even if you don't know every country, capital, and flag in the world, for example, they shouldn't be too hard to pick up ahead of your kids, especially with some mnemonic hacks, such as Hack 2, "Build a Memory Dungeon," or Hack 4, "Space Your Repetitions." Then you can be prepared to move beyond the basics and put together that information to come up with the tough questions first: How did that city become the capital, anyway? If you're teaching your kids elementary Spanish, be sure you're learning (or brushing up on) your own Spanish at an intermediate or advanced level. Of course, all this means that when you homeschool, you're continually learning.

As mentioned in Hack 12, "Study Kid Stuff," homeschooling course materials — textbooks and so on — are a great way to learn things. In that hack, we are talking about kids' courseware; in this hack, we mean the manuals for adult teachers, which have all the answers to the exercises in the students' books, as well as much else that you'll need to stay at least a few steps ahead of your kids, including some deeper theory about what you're teaching, and even the educational theories behind the textbooks.

If you need even more motivation, consider joining a homeschool co-op, where you can teach other kids as well. If you don't have kids of your own, you can get a similar experience by tutoring. There are many tutoring opportunities, from paid jobs to volunteer work with kids who need help. You can even work online, tutoring kids at a distance or for a "homework help line." Ask around at your local schools and libraries for ideas about how to get connected.

Can homeschooling your kids help you follow your own interests? Indeed it can. Remember what we said about kids being the perfect captive audience? Get them interested in what you're doing. Younger kids especially tend to be interested in whatever their parents are doing; as a homeschool teacher, you have much more flexibility with the curriculum than a public school teacher. As long as your kids are learning all the regular subjects at or above grade level, why not challenge them with some things they wouldn't get in public school? If those things happen to be subjects you're particularly interested in, so much the better. Ron's sister Pamela, who is homeschooling her two sons, was delighted when the older one asked her to teach him sewing and knitting, things she herself loves to do. Teaching him will likely deepen her own understanding of these skills she already has.

Learning by Writing

A special case of learning by teaching is learning by creating written documentation. This can be easier than teaching if you have trouble speaking in front of a class, and it provides some of the same benefits. Get to grips with the basics of clear technical writing. For example, if you are having trouble learning some of the hacks in this book, why not try to explain them on the Mentat Wiki (`http://ludism.org/mentat`)? You could also try to create instructions for public use on Instructables.com or WikiHow.com.

If you would really like to be sure you understand a topic and are not obfuscating your ignorance with big words, try explaining it in Basic English (a constructed dialect of English with simplified grammar and a core vocabulary of only 850 words) at `http://simple.wikipedia.org`. There are software tools available to help you do so (`http://simple.wikipedia.org/wiki/Wikipedia:Aids_for_Writing_Simple_English`).

If you would like to teach someone directly before you document what you have learned, you can voice-record your explanation to a student and transcribe it later.

How It Works

To teach a subject, you have to understand it in detail, so that you can explain it fully and in a logical way. Trying to explain a subject can show you what you don't understand about it in very graphic ways; even if you think you already understand the information, actually having to articulate it can be tricky. This, plus the fear of looking like an idiot in front of someone else, can be a great motivator for learning! Additionally, students' questions in response to your teaching can act as a feedback loop to expose holes in your knowledge, and you can help your students further by working together to find the answers you don't know already.

In Real Life

Although Ron and Marty are technical writer and technical editor, respectively, the best examples in their lives of this technique are the two books of mind hacks they have written together. They have had to learn a great variety of things well enough to teach them, from polyhedral geometry to Morse code. Fairly often, one would know more than the other about a specific hack topic, and then Ron had to teach and learn from Marty, or Marty had to teach and learn from Ron.

Hack 10: Play the Learning Game

Are you smarter than your dog? Can you learn a complex action with extremely limited instructions? Trying to do so can help you understand the pitfalls of learning and teaching by stripping the process down to basics.

One of the most popular and effective animal training techniques of recent decades is *clicker training*, often used to train helper dogs. The trainer uses a *clicker*, a device that makes a short clicking noise. She creates a positive association of a click with a treat by making the noise and then giving the animal the treat. Then, when the trainer issues a command and the animal does the right thing, an immediate click gives the animal positive reinforcement at precisely the right moment. The animal knows it will get a treat, and the correct action is rewarded, without the delay (and attendant confusion) caused by the trainer getting a treat out.

Some trainers recommend that dog owners try receiving clicker training themselves to understand the process better, especially if they plan to take over the training. This helps owners understand what a dog experiences, which helps them become better trainers and express less frustration toward the dog. However, trying to receive and give clicker training can be enlightening for anyone interested in learning. It's quite challenging for people who are used to relying on complex language to communicate ideas, and multiple modes of delivering information (Hack 48, "Communicate Multimodally"). Stripping down the process to its minimum lays bare some basic facts about how it works, what can go wrong, and how to maximize success.

In Action

To play the learning game, you'll need a clicker and two people, one to teach and one to learn. (At the end of the first game, you might try changing roles and playing again so that both people can experience both sides of the game.)

The teacher takes the clicker and thinks of a "trick" that she wants the learner to learn. This should be a fairly simple, very specific action for the learner, such as "pick up the glass on the table." When the teacher indicates that she's ready to start, the learner can begin moving and trying to guess what the trick is. Neither person should speak — all communication should transpire via the clicks and physical movements.

Trainers don't teach dogs complex actions all at once. They "shape" behavior by rewarding intermediate actions. For example, if a trainer wants a dog to roll over, she first teaches it to lie down on its side, then possibly to roll from there. In the game, the teacher should reward intermediate behavior with clicks, to give the learner clues toward working out the target action. For example, if the teacher is teaching the action "pick up the glass on the table," she should click the learner for approaching the table, for touching the glass, and so on.

The learner should be using the click feedback to close in on correct steps toward the target action. Repeating actions to see if they garner clicks is helpful, of course. Timing is crucial, so the teacher must watch very carefully to click at just the right moment, and the learner should listen carefully to *exactly* which action is getting a click.

With luck, time, effort, and patience, the learner will collect a correct sequence of actions and eventually perform the trick. If you're not exhausted, switch roles and try again.

How It Works

Clicker training as an animal training technique was initially developed by Marian Bailey and Keller Breland. As students of the behavioral psychologist B. F. Skinner, their studies indicated that previous methods of operant conditioning using reward didn't give the animal enough precision and immediacy. Better information, they found, formed better cognitive connections, and faster training. Furthermore, it removes the imprecision that voice commands can carry through vocal tone, pronunciation speed, and other idiosyncrasies of human speech.

This game uses only *positive* reinforcement, so communication is usually simple and clear, but limited. When you try it, you may see just how much we normally rely on more complex information, as well as using both negative and positive reinforcement (roughly, being able to designate some actions as wrong as well as right). For comparison, try a learning game with two clickers or just the words "yes" and "no" to see how adding only one more piece of information speeds the process.

Effective clicker training takes a lot of attention, because the timing of the clicks must be exactly right. Deciding on-the-fly which actions would lead the learner toward the goal and clicking those actions can be very tricky. At any given moment, the learner is doing a lot of things that could possibly be correct; when he hears a click, the learner must decide which of those things is being rewarded. Is it the arm movement he just made? A step? The direction that he just turned? His facial expression? And so on. We don't usually realize all the ways that feedback can be interpreted.

If the teacher clicks the wrong action (possibly accidentally) or the learner misinterprets the click to be attached to a different action than the teacher intended, it can create *superstition*. Superstition is a belief that feedback attached to an action is meaningful in a certain way, when the connection could actually be random, or the feedback could be meant for another action. This can lead the learner down a long wrong path, and can be very difficult to correct. Sometimes the attempts to correct it even reinforce the superstition.

In both roles, the learning game should offer some insight about the intricacies of communication and the learning process, which should improve your ability to learn and communicate more clearly. In addition, it may generate some sympathy and patience for your friends, teachers, students, children, and pets when they aren't as successful as you'd like, even when they try hard.

In Real Life

When we first started clicker training our dog, we thought it would be only fair to try this process ourselves. Marty started as the teacher, with the goal of teaching Ron to go to the patio door and squat on the floor. With some effort, Ron learned that he was to go to the patio door, but once he got there, he tried many actions — some repeatedly — but couldn't guess the right thing to do. Marty found that it was difficult to convey an intermediate action to squatting: Was leaning toward the wall the right idea, since it got him to move lower to the ground? Clicking that, however, led Ron to believe he needed to place his hand on the wall, no matter what position he was in. Ron turned around, closed his eyes and opened them, and moved his hands and feet, but never thought to squat.

After nearly an hour, Ron was not much nearer to doing the target action, and both of us were confused and frustrated. We finally ended the game, and while Marty never managed to train Ron to do her bidding, we both agreed that we learned a lot from the experience . . . and we feel that we understand our dogs and their well-meaning attempts to do the right thing much better!

See Also

- Karen Pryor, *Don't Shoot the Dog*! : *The New Art of Teaching and Training* (New York: Bantam, 1999). An excellent book on clicker training, and the place we first learned the Learning Game.

- Karen Pryor has a large and extensive website full of clicker-training resources and supplies at www.clickertraining.com.

- TAGTeach International (www.tagteach.com) is an organization that teaches educators and coaches real-life techniques for clicker-training humans. It's particularly effective for working with athletes and autistic children.

Hack 11: Pretend You're a Grad Student

Assuming you're not, in fact, a grad student, learn to take advantage of both the privileges and the discipline of being one anyway.

There's a new freedom of thought these days about what education means and how it happens, which is broadening opportunities for taking your own path to knowledge at any age. There are more resources available than ever before, on every subject imaginable, and it's easier than ever to get hold of them.

Whether you're years out of university, or you haven't gone yet, you can avail yourself of creative and educational resources for your projects, resources that you would normally never have access to, by formally declaring yourself an "independent scholar."

In Action

If you're engaged in a creative or scholarly project, you can benefit from learning and employing methods of scholarship developed in formal academia. Claiming the title of independent scholar can help get you access to the selfsame resources to which the students and professors in your local university have access, even if you are not already affiliated with a university.

University Library Card

Chief among these resources is the university library card, which will grant you access to a world of knowledge that even an excellent urban public library cannot provide. If you can show your local university library that you are engaged in a scholarly project, and pay a fee (probably by semester), the library may give you a library card with access to all their resources, including databases of scientific and scholarly papers, and interlibrary loans from other universities.

> **NOTE** If you can't obtain a university library card for some reason, a New York Public Library card, available to nonresidents for an annual fee, might be a good investment. It grants remote access to many of the library's online databases.[1]

icpl.org

Loose Parts

Getting a university library card can be a foot in the door to other privileges *à la carte*, what the excellent *Independent Scholar's Handbook* calls a "loose parts package."[2] In other words, although no university is exactly likely to grant an independent scholar a full professorship, you might be able to piece together a valuable mix of educational resources from your local school, or even multiple public and private institutions. These might include a mentor, a courtesy title, the right to attend lectures, a quiet private workspace such as a desk or carrel, and so on. For example, if you're looking for a mentor or someone to champion your unorthodox affiliation with the school, you might start by finding out who teaches the subject you're most interested in and what she or he specializes in. If you think you're compatible, offer your services as a sort of informal intern and research assistant, in exchange for academic advice and criticism. In time, your new friend might introduce you to other professors, some of whom would permit you to audit their lectures, again informally. Now you're building a relationship, and have found a colleague as well as some useful "loose parts."

If you want to eventually pursue a more formal educational path, you may well be able to get university credit for your independent study, if you conduct it seriously. If you become familiar to the faculty at your local college and gain a champion who can advise you, this can be an excellent way to design a major in a really unusual or cutting-edge subject, if that interests you and you want the validation of a degree at some point.

Your Personal Library

There are other steps you can take as a scholar outside the university. For example, having better access to your own books and the information in them may be almost as useful as owning a bigger library or having access to a better one. Know what you have; organize and catalog your books. The following sites have excellent free or inexpensive resources for doing just that:

- **calibre** (http://calibre-ebook.com): Manage your e-book library. This open-source, multiplatform e-book multi-tool for desktop and laptop computers does everything from cataloging your e-books, to converting them to other formats, to displaying them for reading.
- **LibraryThing** (www.librarything.com): The best tool we know of for managing your paper book library; it's also a social networking site centering around your books.

Your library is a crucial tool for writing and study. Learn how to select and hone a high-quality collection of reference books about your subject matter at the beginning of a project. You'll never be sorry you did.

Scholar's Dates

It can be hard to work on an independent project when you also have the demands of a full-time job, family, or other obligations. Improve your chances of success by making a regular schedule of dates — a fund of time — for yourself and your project. Make yourself a "class schedule" and keep to it, just as if you had a class and teacher to report to. Give yourself gold stars for excellent attendance! Write yourself a plan and a curriculum describing what you want to study and in what order, with milestones and dates, and then keep yourself on track, class by class. You might think of these techniques as being like the Artist's Dates described in Julia Cameron's book *The Artist's Way*,[3] but dedicated to a scholarly, rather than an artistic, pursuit.

How It Works

Studying as an independent scholar works largely due to a shift in attitude: There's a distinct difference in what you can get done when you start taking yourself seriously. When being "interested in something" becomes considering yourself a scholar on the subject, it changes how you pursue your field and how you work on it. Taking yourself seriously gives you the confidence to seek out and gain tools and opportunities for your study, too, because it means others take you seriously as well.

There are many nontraditional students on most campuses these days; rising unemployment, changing work styles (like telecommuting and flexible hours), and simply living longer have provided many more people with extra time and energy to pursue scholarship. Most universities are responding to this by expanding the services and privileges they can extend to such students. In addition, there are a number of experimental and nontraditional colleges and universities throughout the country, such as Evergreen State College in Olympia, Washington, that are more flexible and more willing to admit those with an interest in independent scholarship.

In Real Life

Hack 6 Establish Your Canon, discusses how to choose and study the books that will enrich you the most. After writing that hack, Ron calculated in January 2011 that if he lived to be 80, at the rate of about a book a week, he could read approximately 1,800 more books. To make the most of this limited number, he started a reading plan — what might be thought of as a lifelong curriculum — of 1,000 books he plans to read (www.ludism.org/tinfoil/ ReadingPlan). As of this writing, he's filled only 167 of the slots, and read 13 of those. (Why 1,000 and not 1,800? Some of the books will probably take longer than a week, and what if Ron doesn't actually live to 80?)

Ron is keeping his reading list on a wiki page so that he can add and delete books over as time goes on. Because your own needs — not to mention your interests — will probably also change over the years, you might want to do something similar.

Of course, a curriculum is more than just a loose list of books. It's structured, for one thing. Ron has begun organizing the books he plans to read into courses. He arranges books on similar subjects into a logical (usually chronological) reading order. For example, as shown in the following list, the books in his Science and Culture course are not only in chronological order, but each title contains explicit comments on and references to the preceding books in the course.

1. C. P. Snow, *The Two Cultures*, 1969

2. E. O. Wilson, *Consilience: The Unity of Knowledge*, 1998

3. Stephen Jay Gould, *The Hedgehog, the Fox, and the Magister's Pox: Mending the Gap Between Science and the Humanities*, 2004

And here is Ron's fledgling Women's Studies course so far:

1. Mary Wollstonecraft, *A Vindication of the Rights of Woman*, 1792

2. Virginia Woolf, *A Room of One's Own*, 1929

3. Simone de Beauvoir, *The Second Sex* (new unabridged translation), 1949

4. Betty Friedan, *The Feminine Mystique*, 1963

If he really wanted to simulate a university course in these subjects, Ron could write papers about them, initiate seminars, and so on. Instead, he will probably blog about his reading and engage in discussions about them online. Since he knows how fast he reads (as mentioned earlier, roughly a book a week, not counting more substantial books such as *Ulysses*, the King James Bible, and philosophical and scientific texts with a lot of math), he will also block out a reading schedule for his courses, when he has more of them and more books in each.

Once this book is published, in pursuit of his next project, Ron may seek to fill out his loose parts package with a more formal academic affiliation. It may help that Marty will be attending graduate school at the University of Washington by then.

Notes

1. Kevin Kelly, "Digital Library Cards," *Cool Tools*, June 27, 2006, www.kk.org/cooltools/archives/001285.php, accessed April 27, 2011.

2. Ronald Gross, *The Independent Scholar's Handbook* (Berkeley: Ten Speed Press, 1993). Available as a free e-book from www.sfu.ca/independentscholars/isbook.htm.

3. Julia Cameron, *The Artist's Way: A Spiritual Path to Higher Creativity* (New York: J. P. Tarcher/Putnam, 2002).

Hack 12: Study Kid Stuff

Why read The Complete Idiot's Guide to Yak-Shaving **when** Yak-Shaving for Kids **is less condescending and will often get you up to speed faster?**

Not everyone learns the same way. The target audiences of conventional learning methods always reflect some kind of average; the methods work for the large percentage of learners who fit the profile, but others may benefit from a different approach. That may mean a different medium, a different way of talking about the subject, or a different educational model altogether.

One of those models you might find quite effective is to study material originally developed for young people. If your focus strays easily when you try to digest dry text and your learning goes down better with a little bit of fun sauce, consider using kids' resources to ground yourself in the basics of many subjects.

In Action

If you're just starting to learn a subject and looking for the fundamentals, there's a whole publishing sector that breaks subjects down to the basics. Some of these books range from the implausible (*The Complete Idiot's Guide to Calculus*) to the inadvisable (*The Complete Idiot's Guide to Amazing Sex*); but in all fairness, despite their risible titles, many such books are quite good. As we write this, Ron is working his way through our own publisher's *Existentialism for Dummies*, which he is finding very enlightening. Of course, there is probably no corresponding *Existentialism for Kids* explaining to children why Albert Camus considered killing a stranger to be an exemplary instance of the absurdity of all human life.

Nevertheless, if you want something even *more* basic than a book for dummies or idiots — and maybe more colorful and engaging — you might find it fruitful to check out books written for kids — and not just kids' books, but kids' videos, websites, comics, games, and toys. Here is just a partial list of our favorites:

■ *Greedy Apostrophe*, by Jan Carr:[1] Ever wonder what the difference is between *its* and *it's*, and why so many people yell at you about it? If so, this book will set your mind to rest forever about apostrophes in a fun and friendly way. It should be read by every English-speaking person.

▪ As far as learning from kids' videos goes, there are perhaps more educational videos available for toddlers and preschoolers than for older kids, which is where you should probably be looking. However, there are indeed some standout learning videos for older kids, such as the video DVD and audio album *Here Comes Science* by They Might Be Giants (a Hale-Evans household favorite). For example, do you understand the difference between speed and velocity? Let TMBG school you:

When I'm on my Big Wheel
Skateboard
Roller coaster
Race car
Motorcycle
Rocket ship
Into outer space

Motion (keep movin', keep movin', keep movin')
Direction (which way, anyway, uptown, all around)
Acceleration (let's go faster)
Acceleration (let's go faster)

I've got speed (that's how fast I am moving)
I've got velocity (that's my speed and direction)

▪ **Schoolhouse Rock**: If you're younger than 40 or so, you may not have encountered the Schoolhouse Rock series (www.schoolhouserock.tv), another great example of useful educational music aimed at kids. These songs, accompanied by animation, were shown on network TV Saturday mornings in the 70s, and a generation learned multiplication, grammar, science, and American history from them, as well as how a bill becomes a law. Marty learned them as a kid and still uses them to remember her multiplication tables. If she ever forgets, the videos are available on DVD and YouTube.

▪ **Howtoons** (www.howtoons.com): This website uses comic strips to teach kids basic science and engineering skills. You will learn the same sorts of physics-with-real-stuff you might see on *Mythbusters*, with the exception that the author, Saul Griffith, will never warn you "Don't try this at home!" Check out *Howtoons* to build goggles out of soda bottles, understand the physics of making ice cream in a zip-up plastic bag, and get a grasp on the Beaufort scale of wind speed. Books are also available from the online store.

- **Educational games**: These can teach you a variety of subjects quickly and painlessly. Because you encounter the information in a fun, interactive setting, your brain is primed to take it in and retain it. There are many, many online sites that offer quiz games for both kids and adults to help practice languages, science, math skills, GRE and SAT prep questions, and so on. You can also find educational games for console systems, and apps for your phone or other mobile device to help you learn on the go. Next time you're in a doctor's waiting room, have fun learning about Japanese language and culture with the Flash games at Kids Web Japan (http://web-japan.org/kidsweb/games/), for example, rather than flipping through that old hunting and fishing magazine.

- **LEGO robotics**: LEGO, especially LEGO NXT, excels as a way of learning to build and program your own robots, among other endeavors. Of course, LEGO started out as a kids' toy, and most users are still children, but it's deep enough that it can keep an adult busy and learning for a long time. (If you want to learn more about 3D geometry, however, we stand by the sources in Hack 42, "Enter the Third Dimension", especially *Zome Geometry*[2] and *Steven Caney's Ultimate Building Book*,[3] which are both technically kids' books as well.)

- **Homeschooling materials**: If you're looking for less elementary materials, or you want a more comprehensive system of educational media, try homeschooling curricula. Widespread access to production tools and a motivation for nontraditional education have led to an embarrassment of riches in this area as more and more people create and release their own stuff. However, this also means you should be careful to evaluate the materials before you use them, to be aware of any mistakes, holes, or philosophical bias. You can find many resources online to check reviews and ratings for a homeschool curriculum, and it pays to use them. (For more information on homeschooling materials as a way to learn, see Hack 9, "Learn By Teaching".) Here are a few of the more respected homeschool curricula:

  - Oak Meadow Bookstore: www.oakmeadowbookstore.com/Curriculum-c135/

  - Calvert School: http://homeschool.calvertschool.org/why-calvert/homeschool-curriculum

  - Ambleside Online: www.amblesideonline.org/ (almost an open-source approach; many of the materials are freely available on the Web)

How It Works

Learning from materials designed for kids works well for fundamental information because children's content is carefully designed to be effective while also maintaining a level of fun and interest. It often focuses on practical applications, and it's also great for people with a short attention span. In addition, educational content for children is often expected, or even required by law, to meet certain standards of quality, so you can usually rely on its soundness.

In Real Life

When Ron became interested in number theory and wanted to learn about the Riemann Hypothesis for some reason he no longer remembers, he visited `http://simple.wikipedia.org`, an edition of Wikipedia that is written for children, as well as adults who are learning English. The math articles in the standard English Wikipedia are well-written and well-maintained, among the finest in all of the site, probably because there is so little contention about them. However, they are written by mathematicians for other mathematicians. The Basic English math articles are much easier to understand. The Riemann Hypothesis article in the Simple English version of Wikipedia does not assume too much knowledge on the part of the reader. For example, it assumes you know what complex numbers are, but not the zeroes of a function, and it explains them.

Ron is also learning to cook by using a couple of cookbooks written for kids. The authors of these books don't assume that you know a lot of cooking terms or techniques already, and they go into detail about even the most basic parts of preparation. The kids' cookbooks also contain fun food ideas, and have a lot of pictures that clarify what needs to be done.

See Also

- The Khan Academy (`www.khanacademy.org`). A fabulous collection of free video lectures for older kids, mostly on mathematics, but branching into other academic areas, such as history.

Notes

1. Jan Carr and Ethan Long, *Greedy Apostrophe: A Cautionary Tale* (New York: Holiday House, 2007).
2. George W. Hart, and Henri Picciotto. *Zome Geometry: Hands-On Learning with Zome Models.* (Emeryville: Key Curriculum Press, 2001).
3. Steven Caney, *Steven Caney's Ultimate Building Book.* (Philadelphia: Running Press Kids, 2006).

## CHAPTER 3

Information Processing

In the so-called Information Age, information is abundant and cheap, but time and attention are scarce and valuable. This chapter demonstrates a number of strategies for managing both abundant information and scarce attention, including how to choose among a number of attractive options (Hack 15, "Sift Your Ideas"), how to fish out the choicest ideas from the Internet (Hack 16, "Ask the Hive Mind," and Hack 14, "Integrate Your Interests"), and how to record ideas and what you think about them once you've caught them (Hack 17, "Write Magnificent Notes").

Attention works best when it's under conscious control. Without control and discernment, you're left grasping at anything shiny that happens to catch your eye as a river of valuable information flows by. Learning to discern what information deserves your attention and what doesn't is surely a skill that deserves your attention.

Hack 13: Polyspecialize

Instead of knowing a lot about one thing or a little about many things, why not become adept at several mutually reinforcing skills that don't usually go together?

The ancient Greek poet Archilocus said, "The fox knows many things; the hedgehog one great thing." This saying is one of the few surviving fragments of his works, and Isaiah Berlin pointed out that "these dark words . . . may mean no more than that the fox, for all his cunning, is defeated by the hedgehog's one defence," or that we might see the hedgehog as an idealist who guides all her actions by a single overriding principle, whereas the fox is more of a pragmatist who pursues a variety of loosely related goals.[1]

We think Archilocus was really talking about people, of course, as Aesop did in his fables. For the purposes of this hack, we'll take the word "know" literally, and define "hedgehogs" as specialists (people who have narrow but deep knowledge) and "foxes" as generalists or comprehensivists (people with broad but shallow knowledge). The breadth of knowledge some "foxes" have is praiseworthy, and the depth of knowledge some "hedgehogs" have attained is astonishing: People have become experts in areas as diverse as doorknobs, medieval Dutch castles, and Esperanto coins and postage stamps.

However, is there — besides knowing little or nothing at all, of course — a feasible alternative to knowing a lot about one thing or a little about many things? We think so, and it's a path to success that's relatively overlooked compared to that of the fox or the hedgehog.

In Action

Why not become a *polyspecialist*? That's our word for someone who knows a lot about multiple things, and a little about even more. The emphasis of polyspecialism is neither on extreme depth in one subject nor on broad but shallow understanding of the whole world of human knowledge. Instead, the emphasis is on a deep understanding of several subjects together with a nodding acquaintance of many more, incidentally acquired during study.

Any individual area of a polyspecialist's study may be useful, but the real power lies in how those areas complement one another. As the Roman philosopher Seneca said, "It is better, of course, to know useless things than to know nothing." Several useless things taken together may generate one or two very useful things indeed. Seneca also said, anticipating twenty-first century polyspecialism,

> *Shun no toil to make yourself remarkable by some talent or other; yet do not devote yourself to one branch exclusively. Strive to get clear notions about all. Give up no science entirely; for science is but one.*[2]

In Bruce Sterling's terms (Hack 26, "Woo the Muse of the Odd"), a generalist is "well-rounded," but a polyspecialist strives to be "spiky," with narrow, deep spikes of skills and knowledge protruding in multiple directions. (Of course, few people have to try very hard to obtain wide, deep chasms of ignorance, so don't worry about those!) Such spikiness can be a boon to your career, and the cartoonist Scott Adams makes the case for the polyspecialist path admirably:

If you want an average successful life, it doesn't take much planning. Just stay out of trouble, go to school, and apply for jobs you might like. But if you want something extraordinary, you have two paths:

1. *Become the best at one specific thing.*

2. *Become very good (top 25%) at two or more things.*

The second strategy is fairly easy. Everyone has at least a few areas in which they could be in the top 25% with some effort. In my case, I can draw better than most people, but I'm hardly an artist. And I'm not any funnier than the average standup comedian who never makes it big, but I'm funnier than most people. The magic is that few people can draw well and write jokes. It's the combination of the two that makes what I do so rare. And when you add in my business background, suddenly I had a topic that few cartoonists could hope to understand without living it.[3]

Of course, this is a bit vague. If you are a programmer, what does it mean to be in "the top 25%"? The top 25% of the general population? The top 25% of all professional programmers? Of all Perl programmers? Of all Perl programmers who specialize in regular expressions? Cutting crosswise, the top 25% of programmers in any language who specialize in regular expressions?

We take the 25% number figuratively. Adams seems to be saying that his rule of thumb is that one way to succeed is to be pretty good at a number of mutually reinforcing skills, especially ones that don't usually go together, and if the skills work together, you don't have to be the best at any of them. That is a principle we can endorse.

Take a look at your current set of skills and areas of knowledge, particularly those which you've studied to more than an average degree and of which you have a reasonably deep grasp. Also look carefully at more unusual skills and knowledge you may have. It may help to list them on paper so you can see them side by side.

Once you have done that, look for synergy: How can two or more of them fit together?

- Are you fascinated by both aerospace and glacial melting? Perhaps one day you will launch satellites to study the polar ice caps.

- Are you a budding rock historian with an interest in the postal system? Perhaps you could establish a museum of rock and pop music paraphernalia that was given away and sold through the mail.

- Do you know how to field-strip a laser printer, add IPv6 addresses in your head, and also have an interest in diplomacy and foreign affairs? Perhaps you can rise to be the head of IT for the Council on Foreign Relations, or, if you're of an anti-establishment bent, create the next WikiLeaks.

When you see how your particular constellation of experience meshes, you may find a whole new direction or project for yourself — one for which you're a ready-made expert. You may even invent a whole new field of study.

How It Works

One might argue that Leonardo da Vinci was a good example of someone who had mastery of all knowledge, and was therefore neither a narrow specialist, a polyspecialist, nor a shallow generalist or comprehensivist. However, strictly apart from the question of Leonardo's native intelligence (which was very high), in his time, there was simply much less knowledge readily available. Given that just the *searchable* part of the World Wide Web circa 2001 contained 170 terabytes of information, equivalent to 17 Libraries of Congress (Hack 14, "Integrate Your Interests"), it's clear that it would take much more than a human lifetime to assimilate all the recorded information in the world, even if a single person could remember it all.

Further, given that no one can know everything in practice, it's clear that the alternatives include to know nothing, to know a lot about one thing, to know a little about many things, or to be a polyspecialist. We remain open to other logical possibilities, but it's fairly clear that, as Scott Adams says, "the magic" often happens when people can do at least two disparate things pretty well.

Once you grasp this idea, where it can take you is, as they say, limited only by your imagination and your interests.

In Real Life

Ron tends to be a polyspecialist. He is neither a superb programmer or computer scientist (compare Donald Knuth), nor a superb writer (such as Shakespeare or James Joyce). However, for a writer, he's a pretty good programmer; and for a programmer, he's a pretty good writer. This may seem like damningly faint praise, but it has served him well in a number of day jobs, where his title is usually *programmer writer* or *programming writer*. It's also helped with his books, which, you may notice, are sprinkled liberally with illustrative computer programs and scripts. As well, knowing how to write step-by-step procedural documentation has helped him write both mind hacks and game rules (game design being another of his areas of polyspecialization). Marty's experiences as a technical editor are similar; she's not even as strong a programmer as Ron, but she understands enough about how programming and technology in general work to be often regarded as "highly technical" compared to other editors on her teams. Meanwhile, her coder friends consider her a word whiz.

See Also

Although the following two books largely predate the web, they are still useful sources for getting a sense of the breadth of human knowledge overall, as well as how individuals specialize. The doorknob and medieval Dutch castles examples cited earlier were taken from the second book.

- Deborah M. Burek, Martin Connors, and Christa Brelin, *Organized Obsessions* (Detroit: Visible Ink Press, 1992).

- Henry Doering, editor, *Book of Buffs, Masters, Mavens and Uncommon Experts* (New York: World Almanac Publications, 1980).

Notes

1. Isaiah Berlin, *The Hedgehog and the Fox* (Chicago: Ivan R. Dee, Inc., 1993).
2. Lucius Annaeus Seneca, *Moral Letters to Lucilius*, letter 88, line 45.
3. "Career Advice," Scott Adams, *Dilbert.Blog*, March 2011, `http://dilbertblog.typepad.com/the_dilbert_blog/2007/07/career-advice.html`.

Hack 14: Integrate Your Interests

Use new software to cross-reference your interests and discover new web pages about them, and maybe even new friends who share them.

Have you ever felt as though you couldn't squeeze any more information out of the Internet on topics that interest you? That you've seen, read, heard, and watched everything the web has to offer on your hobbies, research, or occupation (`www.endoftheinternet.com/`)?

Of course, it's implausible to think you've seen everything. As of this writing, just the *searchable* part of the web contains more than 170 terabytes of information, equivalent to 17 standard *Libraries of Congress*.[1] The real problem, then, may be that rather than mining informational gold using search engines, you are sifting only the leaf mold and litter of the web's surface.

By way of analogy, hydrogen is the simplest and most common chemical element in the universe; hydrogen atoms are even more common than crummy websites. Fuse them in solar fire, however, and you can obtain the carbon atoms necessary for life, or the precious metal gold. Just as life comes from carbon, and carbon comes from hydrogen, the dross of the cosmos, with this hack you can take common ideas and fuse them using "interest integrator" software to generate extraordinary, unpredictable results.

If you seek an integrated philosophy instead of a loose grab bag of ideas and interests, this hack demonstrates how you can relate each of your interests to every other one.

The more you combine your interests and obsessions, the stronger and more diverse your conceptual framework becomes.

How It Works

To prepare for running this hack, you'll need to take the following steps:

1. Download the file archive for this chapter from the book's website, find the Perl script *ii* (pronounced "aye aye") in it, and then install it according to the section "How to Run the Programming Hacks" in the Preface.

2. Install the file `obsessions.txt` in your home directory. This is a version of Ron's own file of interests or "obsessions"; you can create your own according to the instructions that follow. In fact, you should! A file of someone else's interests won't do you any good except as an example.

3. Run the script. As the usage instructions in the script indicate, there are three main ways to do so:

   - Typing something like **ii chimp hilarious-consequences** searches Google for both terms.

   - Typing **ii chimp** searches for "chimp" plus a random obsession from the obsessions file.

   - Typing **ii** by itself combines two random obsessions from the obsessions file and then searches for the combination. This is the usual way to run the program, and the easiest.

A listing of the *ii* script follows:

```
#!/usr/bin/perl
# ii, Interest Integrator
# Ron Hale-Evans, rwhe@ludism.org
# 2009-07-15
$nargs = $#ARGV + 1;
srand;
# You may need to adjust the following values,
# depending on your environment
$home = $ENV{HOME};
$obsessions = "$home/obsessions.txt";
$browser = "firefox";
# Usage information
```

```
if ($nargs > 2)
{
    $two = "\"ii chimp hilarious-consequences\" googles both terms.";
    $one = "\"ii chimp\" googles \"chimp\" plus a random obsession.";
    $zero = "\"ii\" by itself googles two random obsessions.";
    die "usage:\n$two\n$one\n$zero\n";
}
elsif ($nargs == 2)
{
    $arg1 = $ARGV[0];
    $arg2 = $ARGV[1];
}
elsif ($nargs == 1)
{
    $arg1 = $ARGV[0];
    $arg2 = random_obsession();
}
else
{
    $arg1 = random_obsession();
    $arg2 = random_obsession();
}
$arg1 = munge($arg1);
$arg2 = munge($arg2);
$url = "http://www.google.com/search?num=100&q=$arg1+$arg2";
print "$url\n";
`$browser '$url'`;
sub random_obsession()
{
    open FILE, "<$obsessions" or die "Could not open obsessions.txt:
$!\n";
    rand($.) <1 and ($line=$_) while <FILE>;
    close FILE;
    return($line);
}
# Tweak the search terms so they can form part of a valid URL
sub munge($)
{
    my ($a) = @_;
    chomp($a);
    $a =~ s/\"/\%22/sgi;
    $a =~ s/\+/\%2B/sgi;
    $a =~ s/ /\+/sgi;
    return($a);
}
```

Each line in the obsessions.txt file is a valid Google query, formatted according to the rules on Google's help pages.[2] Specifically, you can use double quotes (") to delimit phrases, and the pipe symbol (|) to separate alternative versions of the same search term. Here is a short excerpt from the beginning of Ron's obsessions file so that you can see its syntax:

```
"3d chess"|"three dimensional chess"
"3d photo"|"stereo photo"|"stereo photography"|stereogram|stereoscope|
 "three dimensional photo"
4d|"fourth dimension"
"abductive inference"|"abductive logic"|"abductive reasoning"
"abstract game"
advaita|vedanta
agnosticism
"alan moore"
```

Of course, you can modify *ii* to query a search engine other than Google (see the section "Possible Improvements" later in this hack).

In Action

The more obsessions you have in your obsessions file, the better this hack will work for you. As of this writing, Ron has 231 distinct terms in his file. That makes $231 \times (231 - 1)$, or 53,130 unique combinations of interests that the script can use for a search. He expects to have reading material for a lot of rainy weekends to come.

Read the list of links output by the program *carefully*. Don't skip anything, and don't forget to take advantage of Google's search history feature. The script can produce high-quality results faster than you can absorb them, so it's good to be able to return to them.

You may find that you can stump Google. Sometimes just one page will be returned; this is a form of *googlewhacking*, a game where players see if they can devise a two-word search without quotation marks on Google that brings up exactly one result. (See `http://googlewhack.com/tally.pl` for more details and some other examples.) Certainly don't be surprised if your own pages come up. You might be the only person on the Web interested in that combination of topics.

Possible Improvements

The *ii* script is open source, so if you'd like to contribute improvements to the source code, here are some possible areas of interest:

- Add an option to pull a random word as one of the search terms, from a system dictionary such as `/usr/share/dict/words` on a Linux computer.

- Add an option to perform several searches at once. For example, perhaps **ii 5** would open five tabs in your web browser, each containing a separate *ii* search.

- Adapt *ii* to search other search engines or specific sites such as Delicious .com, with terms from the obsessions file. Depending on the site, the results might be very interesting, or they might not be as interesting as those from Google because the search space is smaller, and Google would lead you to a site like Delicious anyway.

In Real Life

Before the *ii* script was even finished, Ron was testing it with a small subset of the terms in his current `obsessions.txt` file. It happened to search for a combination of terms like **borges "fourth dimension"**, and he was delighted to find a review of a brand-new book called *The Unimaginable Mathematics of Borges' Library of Babel*. He ordered a copy and discovered that it hypothesized that the fictional Library of Babel written about by Jorge Luis Borges was a glome.[3] (A glome is a four-dimensional hypersphere; see Hack 43, "Enter the Fourth Dimension," for details.) Furthermore, there was a detailed combinatorial analysis of the library, which Borges said contains a random arrangement of every possible book. The whole experience was charming, because *ii* itself is like randomly dipping into the great Library of Babel that is the World Wide Web.

In the following examples, the whole command line is only given so that you can reproduce the search. Ron usually either types **ii** with no arguments or clicks a button on his menu bar that runs the script — a convenient thing to have if you begin to use *ii* a lot.

Very often, *ii* will take you to a web resource that discusses not only the conjunction of the two search-term concepts, but also many similar concepts of immediate interest. For example, **ii "abductive inference" "cognitive ergo-nomics"** leads to the fabulous Wikipedia Thinking Portal,[4] of which Ron was unaccountably ignorant before.

Similarly, **ii "barrington bayley" escher** leads to the MathFiction site,[5] which includes 765 works of math fiction in its index, and where you will learn that math fiction is to math as science fiction is to science. For example, Edwin Abbott's *Flatland* is a classic work of math fiction.

The search **ii "anthropic principle" lojban** leads to the *Speculative Grammarian*, a website devoted to satirical linguistics, and specifically to the hilarious article "Survey of Linguistic Evidence of Meta-Consciousness in Tier-19 Terran Primates," which reads like a blasphemous cross of Noam Chomsky, G. I. Gurdjieff, and *The Hitchhiker's Guide to the Galaxy*.

However, this hack is not without its dangers. Combining hard-science search terms with "soft stuff" often leads to crackpot results. Try the following if you would like to read some speculation that's less half-baked than gooey:

```
ii "fourth dimension" vedanta
ii "faster than light" meditation
```

Then again, if you enjoy reading that kind of thing, the hack can also provide you with hours of amusement.

See Also

- Edward de Bono, *Po: Beyond Yes and No* (Penguin Books, 1990). Readers of our other work may notice that the *ii* script works somewhat like Edward de Bono's word *po*. In fact, the script was even named *po* for a while, but Ron finally decided that *ii* would be less confusing.

Notes

1. "Information content of the surface web," Wolfram Alpha, accessed 15 July 2009, www91.wolframalpha.com/input/?i=information+content+of+the+su rface+web.

2. "Google Search Basics: More Search Help," Google, retrieved 15 July 2009, www.google.com/support/websearch/bin/answer .py?answer=136861#exceptions_punctuations.

3. William Goldbloom Bloch, *The Unimaginable Mathematics of Borges' Library of Babel* (Oxford: Oxford University Press, 2008).

4. Wikipedia Thinking Portal, Wikipedia, accessed 15 July 2009, http:// en.wikipedia.org/wiki/Portal:Thinking.

5. "Mathematical Fiction," Alex Kasman, accessed 15 July 2009. http:// kasmana.people.cofc.edu/MATHFICT/all.php.

Hack 15: Sift Your Ideas

Chad Urso McDaniel

We often aren't very good at making a choice from many similar options. Learn a technique that uses mini-decisions to enable the best options to rise to the top.

Most of us live in a world of options — from the mundane (which TV show to watch) to the significant (what to eat for lunch). Sometimes one of the options is the clear choice, but other times we are stymied by the task of choosing.

This problem is similar to that facing groups of people voting, whether it's for a political leader or a creative decision such as a club's T-shirt design. Methods used for voting systems can also be used by an individual to make decisions.

There is evidence that making choices can cause us a surprisingly high amount of stress.[1] Hopefully, this technique can reduce that.

In Action

This hack applies to situations in which you want to choose from a set of three or more options. You're going to divide the decision into several smaller sets of options and use the results of those choices to determine the winning, or final, option.

Let's say Herbert wants to see a movie by himself this afternoon, but he can't decide which one. Here's the list of movies he's interested in (with abbreviations), in no particular order:

- *Action Driver 2* (AD2)
- *Meet-Cute in Pittsburgh* (MCiP)
- *Surprise Ending Horror* (SEH)
- *Subtitled Smarty Pants* (SSP)

To help him decide, he transforms the preceding titles into a list of two-option choices following these rules:

1. To start, Herbert takes the first option in the list and copies it onto sequential lines a number of times equal to the number of options below it on the original list. In this case, he writes "AD2" three times because there are three other movies to choose among.

   - AD2
   - AD2
   - AD2

2. On the same lines, he writes alongside "AD2" each of the movies below AD2 in the original list, to create a comparison of each movie with AD2.

   - AD2 – MCiP
   - AD2 – SEH
   - AD2 – SSP

3. Below that, he writes the second option from the original list enough times for the items below it on the original list. In this case, there are two movies below MCiP.

   - AD2 – MCiP
   - AD2 – SEH
   - AD2 – SSP

- MCiP
- MCiP

4. Alongside these new "MCiP" lines, he writes the options below it in the original list.

   - AD2 – MCiP
   - AD2 – SEH
   - AD2 – SSP
   - MCiP – SEH
   - MCiP – SSP

5. Continuing with the third item from the original list, he continues the process by writing one line with "SEH."

   - AD2 – MCiP
   - AD2 – SEH
   - AD2 – SSP
   - MCiP – SEH
   - MCiP – SSP
   - SEH

6. When there is only one item left, he adds the final item in the original list to the final line with the next-to-last item.

   - AD2 – MCiP
   - AD2 – SEH
   - AD2 – SSP
   - MCiP – SEH
   - MCiP – SSP
   - SEH – SSP

Herbert stops when he finishes with the second-to-last line in the original list. This same process would continue with longer lists, but Herbert is done in this example.

Herbert now has six comparisons between pairs of movies. For each pair, he chooses his preference:

- **AD2** – MCiP
- AD2 – **SEH**
- AD2 – **SSP**

- MCiP – **SEH**
- MCiP – **SSP**
- **SEH** – SSP

For a given pair (if you are Herbert), it may be that you don't favor either option over the other. In that case, leave the pair with no choice and the rest of the technique will still work out. Before doing that, you may want to try checking "coin-flip clarity": Assign one option to heads and the other to tails. Flip a coin and decide if you are happy with the result or if you wished for a specific result before the coin landed. If so, then you have your clear choice.

Herbert goes back to the original list and scores each movie according to how many times it wins a two-item comparison:

Action Driver 2 (AD2)	1
Meet-Cute in Pittsburgh (MCiP)	0
Surprise Ending Horror (SEH)	3
Subtitled Smarty Pants (SSP)	2

The final scores represent how many times the option "beat" an opposing option. In this case, *Action Driver 2* was chosen over only one other option, and *Surprise Ending Horror* was favored over every other option. It is possible for a tie to occur. In that case, try the coin flip clarity mentioned above, except in this scenario you can actually let the coin decide if you truly don't care.

The winning option is *Surprise Ending Horror* with a score of 3. It also seems Herbert really doesn't want to see the romantic comedy *Meet-Cute in Pittsburgh*, perhaps due to lack of company.

How It Works

This technique is known as *pairwise comparison* and is related to decision-making theories about fair elections when there is more than one candidate. It was first invented by Nicolas de Caritat, marquis de Condorcet, in 1785. He was a mathematician and philosopher trying to make things fair in group decision making, like juries and elections. In the 1900s, mathematicians analyzed and enhanced the concept of pairwise comparison.

Pairwise comparison works for election results because the desired outcome is to find a clear winner, not to rank all of the options from best to worst. The strict rule in such a pairwise comparison is that the winner must have beat all the other opponents, but in this hack about personal choice, determining the most wins is sufficient.[2]

Pairwise comparison is also related to psychological theories about how people make choices: Choosing between many options is typically more difficult than choosing between two options. Your brain can choose between two items much more simply and quickly than it can analyze and rank a whole list at once — in fact, it can usually handle many such pairs of options in less time than it takes to arrange a larger group.

Pairwise comparison can also be used with groups of people. In that case, each person makes his or her own choices between the pairs, and then everyone's choices are counted at the final step. Do this by creating the list of pairwise options for each person (or share one list), and then count up all of the wins across every person.

This method of generating pairs of options guarantees that every combination is present. It also *assumes* that the order of the comparison is not important (i.e., comparing A to B is the same as comparing B to A). If you have n options, then the list of pairs will have $[n \times (n-1)] / 2$ comparisons.

You can use a table rather than the lists, but I think lists are easier overall. Table 15-1 shows an example of a table using Herbert's movie options.

Table 15-1: Herbert's Movie Choices

	AD2	MCIP	SEH	SSP
AD2	X	X	X	X
MCiP	AD2	X	X	X
SEH	SEH	SEH	X	X
SSP	SSP	SSP	SEH	X

In Real Life

I often suffer from indecision when trying to determine the best choice. I regularly use this technique for my media choices, such as which video game I feel like playing or which book I want to read. We are faced with so many media options these days that simply having favorites doesn't work anymore because we have so many favorites.

I can now implement the pairwise comparison technique very quickly, and I often do three-option decisions in my head. Sometimes I don't even need to complete the individual choices because the process reveals to me that I already had a clear preference and didn't realize it.

See Also

- http://en.wikipedia.org/wiki/Condorcet_method#Pairwise_counting_
  and_matrices

Notes

1. Sheena S. Iyengar, "Sheena S. Iyengar," accessed June 2, 2011,
   www.columbia.edu/~ss957/index.shtml.
2. Kenneth J. Arrow, *Social Choice and Individual Values* (New Haven: Yale
   University Press, 1951, 2nd ed. 1963).

Hack 16: Ask the Hive Mind

Chad Urso McDaniel

Across the web, people share what interests them and what they prefer and like, as well as their personal funds of knowledge. We know more collectively than we do individually. This is the phenomenon of the Hive Mind. Learn how its honey is collected.

The web presents us with a tremendous amount of choice and many, many options. Often, trying to find something ("Which wiper blades fit my car?") or solve a problem ("How can I make it stop raining on my parade?") is more about finding your way than choosing among options.

The web is also full of opinions and suggestions. The most apparent of these are reviews and ratings you can find on shopping, restaurant, and entertainment sites. These may look like random shouts from the masses and a mere average of everyone's opinion, but they contain some hidden subtlety. There are also communities on the web that offer a tremendously better signal-to-noise ratio when you want advice. Some even have experts who answer questions that are posted on the site.

There is *much* more going on than the opinions that users volunteer, too. For example, shopping websites are constantly analyzing how users search, select, and buy products. This information is correlated by recommendation engines to show future shoppers products they are more likely to buy. By knowing more about how these recommendations work, you can better use them to harness the subtle opinions of thousands of people.

In Action

The rest of this hack describes approaches to various kinds of decision making, from the most passive to the most active, and ranging from shopping to open-ended questions. The best approaches to take for a given decision vary according to the problem.

Automated Recommendation Systems

Almost every major online retailer presents suggestions for products they think you might like. Their intent is to reveal products that you haven't realized yet that you would love to buy. These recommendations range from the very broad ("best sellers") to the very specific ("People who bought *Action Driver* also bought *Action Driver 2*") and personal ("You bought peanut butter last month, so you might want to buy it again this month"). The more specific and personal the recommendation message, the more likely it will be meaningful and useful for you. Look for words like "people," "customers," and "you" to help determine this.

Sometimes recommendation systems will indicate what percentage of shoppers bought one product instead of another. This can be useful if you keep in mind that such information is most relevant to product categories with a lot of similarity, such as appliances or furniture, but *not* for products that are *not* very similar, such as books, movies, and other media.

Reviews and Ratings

Pretty much every online retailer provides user reviews and ratings. When you read reviews, remember that generally people with the most positive or negative opinions will post reviews. Reviews one notch below most favorable often avoid this bias, so you can often find more useful information from a four-star review than a five-star review, for example. If a site allows you to mark a review as useful or not, do so and be honest. It's a small contribution you can make to the overall quality of the web.

Average ratings (usually represented by stars) are usually featured very prominently and often influence which items you see first when browsing. It may seem that it would be easy for malicious users to abuse these ratings, but there are many techniques at work behind the scenes to ensure that these are more than just simple averages. (More on that later in the "How It Works" section.) Generally, they mean what they say. One way that average ratings sometimes don't give an honest average, however, is when recent events have drastically changed public opinion, because the average rating generally does not weigh recent reviews higher than those in the past.

Question and Answer Forums

Often, you aren't interested in buying a product or consuming media. You have a problem or question and would like suggestions and solutions from someone who knows what they are talking about. Finding discussion forums and Q&A-specific websites is relatively easy. What can be difficult is deciding whether you can trust the people there to assess their own knowledge: Do they really have expertise in what they are saying? Ideally, you would ask an honest plumber about a problem with your kitchen sink, for example.

Yahoo! Answers (http://answers.yahoo.com/) is probably the largest online Q&A service. It contains answers for a tremendous variety of questions, and it is often the case that someone has already asked your question. It can be difficult to sort through the answers, though, as many devolve into forum discussions with jokes and debates. If there's a top-rated or "Chosen by Asker" answer, then that's usually the signal in the noise.

Ask MetaFilter (http://ask.metafilter.com/) is a website with answers well above the Internet average in quality. Two major reasons for this are that all members must pay a small fee before joining, and the community has a strong policy of self-policing to remove advertising and other inappropriate content. The members are skewed toward young and geeky, so consider that when you read the answers they provide.

Aardvark (http://vark.com/) is a very different service. It analyzes key topics in your question and tries to find people to answer who are close in your social network in terms of e-mail, instant messaging, and Facebook. Interaction with Aardvark is more real-time, using instant messaging and mobile devices to connect question askers with potential answerers. This means that askers get answers quickly, and it also offers the opportunity for dialogue, to ask for clarification or thank someone for an answer. If you're an Aardvark member, you can choose which topics you're willing to answer questions about, how often the service asks you to answer a question, and other details. You can even request that the service send you a copy of answers provided by someone else for a question you couldn't answer.

There are also Q&A services with actual experts who provide answers. Two of these are the MadSci Network and AskPhilosophers. The MadSci Network website (http://madsci.org/) features a very broad collection of answers across almost every field of science. The questions and answers are fully moderated, and the answers are provided by Network member scientists. It's geared primarily toward students, so the community is open to basic science questions in addition to more esoteric topics. You don't have to be working on a report for school to ask questions. The archive, while taking you back to some late-1990s web design, is a tremendous resource of science information for nonscientists.

AskPhilosophers (www.askphilosophers.org/) describes its mission as follows: "On the one hand, everyone confronts philosophical issues throughout his or her life. But on the other, very few have the opportunity to learn about philosophy. . . AskPhilosophers aims to bridge this gap by putting the skills and knowledge of trained philosophers at the service of the general public." The answers are provided by practicing philosophers, almost all of whom are teaching professors in the Western philosophical tradition. The topics vary greatly and the answers are often grounded in everyday practicality. Some questions provide multiple answers demonstrating different views and philosophies.

NOTE A general rule for asking questions on any forum: Search before asking! The Internet is a big place and there is an increasingly good chance that someone had the same problem that you do and posted it publicly.

How It Works

The hive mind has many subtleties and is rapidly evolving on the web. Let's look at some of the secret mechanisms inside. You may be familiar with what these resources look like, but you might not realize what kind of math is involved in their design, or that the theories they're based on predate the technology by many years.

Automated Recommendation Systems

Shopping sites track every search, product view, and purchase. A tremendous amount of data is logged every day about what real people are doing on websites as they shop.

Many statistical and analytical algorithms are applied to this data to identify patterns. The most common is *conditional probability*. Conditional probability can help answer questions such as "If a person buys an apple, what is the chance that they will buy a banana or orange or durian?" Knowing the answer to this question enables that algorithm to choose which fruit to recommend to someone who just bought an apple on the website. If a fruit is recommended arbitrarily, then the shopper is more likely to find the recommendations uninteresting and ignore them, which wastes a sales opportunity.

Using the notation A for the event of someone buying an apple and B for the event of someone buying a banana, the conditional probability is expressed as $P(B|A)$ and is read as "the probability that someone bought a banana given that they bought an apple." The back-end servers on shopping sites gather all the shopping logs, count the number of times apples were bought and the number of times apples and bananas were bought together, and then use these values to calculate the conditional probability.

Making the logical assumption that past shopping behavior is indicative of future shopping behavior, the website can use these calculations to make recommendations. When a shopper buys an apple on the website, the server generates a list of the top products with high conditional probability with apple purchases and shows those to the shopper. Other factors, such as what products shoppers view in the same session as buying an item, can refine the results even further.

Reviews and Ratings

Several techniques are employed to help increase the overall quality of reviews and ratings.

Product ratings are usually averaged using a technique known as *Bayesian averaging* (named after Thomas Bayes (1702-1761), who also developed the theory underlying conditional probability). Instead of a simple average, Bayesian averaging includes several artificial ratings that represent the site-wide average review score. This draws both very high ratings and very low ratings toward the middle when there are only a few ratings.

As the number of ratings increases, the Bayesian average approaches the simple average (mean). For example, consider a new whisk introduced on Stir .com that so far only has two reviews submitted on a five-star scale: one rating 1 and another rating 2. The average (mean) rating is 1.5. The Bayesian average may throw in five ratings of 3 to every product's average, resulting in an average of 2.6 for the whisk in this example. This helps smooth the opinions of a few people and reduces the impact of competitors submitting artificially low ratings, shills who artificially increase ratings, or other possible dishonest ratings. If it truly is a bad whisk, the score will be lowered as more ratings are added. Alternatively, some sites simply don't show the average rating until the total number of ratings reaches a threshold, which provides a clearer average as well.

The impact of dishonestly favorable or unfavorable written reviews can also be reduced by several other techniques, such as requiring users to be registered for a week or so before posting. Displaying how many reviews a user has written can give other users a clue about the quality of a review, as this is usually an indicator of overall competence and care when writing reviews.

Question and Answer Forums

Q&A systems have a lot in common with review and rating systems, because they all deal with people submitting their ideas and opinions, with all of the vagueness and trust issues related to that. Good systems implement internal ratings metrics to measure the usefulness of a person's contributions. Sometimes this rating is shown and you'll see that some users are described as "Top Contributors" or have a level associated with them. Q&A systems often also limit the number of questions and answers new users can submit, to reduce spam and moderate the kinds of questions that newbies often ask.

Some systems measure how well a user seems to do answering questions about specific topics, and will favor that user for future answers related to similar topics. This enables the concepts of trust and expertise to grow out of the question and answer format. Many Q&A systems do this explicitly by allowing users to rate answers and allowing answerers to specify which topics they are knowledgeable about. Aardvark adds an implicit system based on the social network, trust relationships, and your public information on the Internet, such as blog posts.

Some services are heavily moderated and provide answers only from selected members. This helps to ensure the quality and accuracy of the answers, with the trade-off of longer response time and less total breadth of knowledge.

In Real Life

On several occasions I have used automated recommendations to help me shop for gifts. To do this, I visit a shopping site with the gift recipient in mind. I'll first browse products that I know they like. I then look at the recommendations offered to me, and I often find gift ideas for the recipient that they didn't need to ask for and which match their interests well. This has helped me surprise friends who have assumed every gift they receive will come from their online wish list.

I find that Aardvark is very good for tips when visiting a city. I can type questions like "What's that newish really good Italian scratch pizzeria in San Francisco?" and get an answer to this vague question in three minutes. Part of the reason for this is that Aardvark recognizes "San Francisco" in the question and routes it to people on my network who know the city. This has helped tremendously because I love good pizza and once had only a few hours before my flight home.

See Also

- Want to try your hand at developing a recommendation system? Check out RecLab: http://code.richrelevance.com/reclab/. (Note that Chad, the author of this hack, is an employee of RichRelevance.)

- Barry Schwartz, *The Paradox of Choice: Why More Is Less* (New York: HarperCollins, 2005). Useful for its examination of the problems associated with too many options.

- Sheena Iyengar, *The Art of Choosing* (New York: Twelve, 2010). More interesting research into making decisions and the stresses it causes.

■ Damon Horowitz and Sepandar D. Kamvar, "The Anatomy of a Large-Scale Social Search Engine," `http://vark.com/aardvarkFinalWWW2010 .pdf` (April 2011). Goes into detail about how to route questions through a social network.

Hack 17: Write Magnificent Notes

Lion Kimbro

Maximally develop your thoughts with an advanced, seventh-generation note-taking system.

You may be working one day — writing a computer program, filling out a form, or taking a hammer from your garage to your living room — and suddenly be inspired with an idea — for a tool, for a new way of organizing things, or just a beautiful idea. Is it a good idea? What can you add to the idea? What more does it need? By writing down the vision, you can attach further notes, contacts, references, and developments of the idea. Or perhaps you may notice a pattern in life, involving how groups of people work, or your very own mind. To develop these ideas further, keep notes on them. As you read fantasy stories, news articles, or books, you may find out more. Keep notes!

This hack is about novel ways of keeping such notes for the purpose of developing thoughts. As a side benefit, it can help you remember things, get into a reflective state of mind, record phone numbers, and log events, but the techniques described here are mainly geared toward the goal of progressively developing thoughts.

The following list outlines the features that I have found to be most important in a notekeeping system that aims to develop thought:

■ **Speed in writing:** You need to be able to write new entries quickly.

■ **Speed in finding:** You need to be able to quickly find what is in your notebook. If you can't readily find your previous thoughts on a subject, you'll find it difficult to extend them.

■ **Proximity:** You need to be able to find related thoughts quickly, and the easiest way to do that is to look on the same page, or one not too many pages away.

■ **Scalability:** You need to be able to quickly find what is in your notebook even after a thousand pages of notes, even after two years of notekeeping.

■ **Adaptability:** Your life is a living thing, and living things change. Your notes reflect your life. You want a system that is able to change gracefully along with the changes in your life.

- **Comfort:** When you are developing ideas, it is important that your interaction with your medium occurs smoothly and naturally.

- **Ability to accommodate pictures and diagrams:** Many of our thoughts are most naturally expressed graphically. For me, the ability to express an idea in pictures, diagrams, shapes, and schematics is absolutely necessary.

- **Portability, durability, and security:** You need to be able to carry a useful collection of your notes with you at all times. Because you want your notes to last for a long time, they should be able to weather the elements. You also need sensitive notes to be safe from prying eyes, and protected against being lost forever.

The notebook system I share here meets the majority of these demands. It is a *paper-based system*, rather than a computerized system; this is not because I have any strong feelings against technology, but because I strongly prefer being able to handwrite and hand-draw my notes. Tablet computer screens don't have the fidelity of resolution yet to capture the detail of even casual drawing and handwriting, nor have they eliminated perceptible drawing latency. Try to write or sketch on a tablet as you do on paper, and you'll see what I mean. Although it's possible to compensate somewhat by "zooming," I find that I lose concentration when perpetually zooming and unzooming the medium. I know, because I've tried all of this — I really want it to work! And one day it will, but that day is not today.

As a paper-based system, my method loses out on security — a big problem. However, there is no ideal solution. I have opted to trade security for comfort and convenience, as well as an easy capacity for pictures and diagrams. On the whole, I have found this to be my favorite notekeeping system, integrating the best aspects of a decade of experimentation.

In Action

This notekeeping strategy has three essential parts:

- **Open space:** Leave open spaces, providing room for emergence. Distribute notes across the book.

- **Emergent structure:** Work with what is forming. Attach new notes to preexisting, related notes.

- **Indexes:** Make indexes as you go, to quickly find what you need when you return.

A Basic Framework

My recommendations for the basic note-taking framework include the following:

- A multicolor fine-tip pen
- A notebook about the size of your hand
- Roughly 120 leaves of relatively thick paper

I use and recommend the Sarasa line of replaceable gel ink pens, manufactured by Zebra Pen (www.zebrapen.com). The Sarasa 3+ pen comes with red, blue, and black ink, and a pencil and eraser as well. The fine tip is 0.5 mm, which makes it possible to pack a lot of detail into small spaces just about anywhere. Moreover, the line is utterly solid and even. Buy plenty of replacement gel sticks, because you'll likely rip through ink, and you won't want to stop in the middle of an idea because your ink runs out. I recently discovered the Sarasa 4 pen line, which supports four colors (though no pencil), so you can use green ink as well. Conventional four-color pens are too thick and result in an uneven line.

I like a notebook about the size of my outstretched hand. It's light and easy to carry around. You'll want a lot of pages, especially with this technique; 120 leaves gives you 240 pages, which is plenty of room to seed a great many ideas, and 160 leaves (320 pages) is even better. It can be difficult, but try to find college-ruled pages; you can fit much more in the same amount of space. Artists will find value in unruled pages, but when I use unruled pages I find that I cannot write both neatly and small; either I must write larger (sacrificing information density, and thus proximity), or my writing ends up going in many different directions, and I inefficiently use space.

When you have your gear together, there is one very important thing that you must do: You must number the notebook's pages. This is not optional — numbering pages is a must. If you don't number the pages, this hack won't work. Unfortunately, most notebooks aren't sold with prenumbered pages, so if you can't find one, you'll have to number the pages yourself.

There are no tricks to it — it's just 1, 2, 3, 4, 5, etc. You can save a lot of time by numbering the right-side pages first, and then the left-side pages. Try to position and flip pages so that the writing hand isn't moving away from its basic position much. I'm right-handed, and I number the left side by putting the notebook face down, lifting up the pages as one mass with my left hand, and then "flipping" pages down, so that my right hand can write the number onto each page. I look at the number on the opposite side to know what to write. It's okay to miss some of the pages as you flip — you can just add them as you use the notebook. It's faster to miss a few than to rearrange your hands to get the one you missed. When you're done, you have a fully prepared notebook. Great!

Now let's get back to our three core ideas: open space, emergent structure, and indexes. Open spaces distribute notes across the book, and leave room for emergence. Emergent structure works with what is forming, and attaches notes to preexisting related notes. Indexes enable you to navigate the mental terrain.

Open Spaces and Emergent Structure

In most journaling systems, you would write the first entry on page 1, then the next on page 2, then the next on page 3, and so on, front to back. Perhaps you would make partitions ("This subject for the next 20 pages"), and the partitions would follow one after the other. *The system described here is very different.*

In this system, it is very important that when you are about to write, you first ask yourself: "Do I already have something like this in the notebook? If so, where?"

If you have something that is *somewhat* related but also somewhat different, put the new entry within 3–10 pages of the prior entry. If it is *closely* related, put it just 1 or 2 pages away. If it is grossly unrelated, keep the new note far away — perhaps 20–40 pages away from anything else. Just plop it anywhere in the book. If what you are adding is merely a detail, put it right next to the closest point, on the very page. For example, if my friend Ron Hale-Evans is mentioned in my notes, I might jot his phone number right beneath where I used his name.

When you're done working like this, you'll find that your notes seamlessly bleed into one another by topic, subject, and association. Your thoughts are almost magically located near other, related thoughts, and you'll make serendipitous discoveries. When you share ideas with others through the notebook, you'll find relevant and related materials side-by-side.

The image I want you to form is of filling up your whole notebook evenly, over time, rather than going from front to back. Your first entry may be on page, say, 40. Your second entry may be on page 107. Your third entry may be on page 176. Your fourth entry may be on page 43, if it's related to the first. Your fifth may be on page 10. You distribute your pages — you do not write front to back.

Leave open spaces. As they fill in, you will start to get a sense of relatedness and structure. Some of the seeds will die. Some will expand enormously, and even outgrow the boundaries around them. You don't know beforehand which is which (which is why adaptability is important), so just let them die or grow, and let your notes adapt to what is forming.

When you want to develop an idea already on a page, write the development on the same page where you originally recorded the idea, if possible. Barring that, put it on a nearby page, and add a pointer to it near the original idea.

Feel free to mentally hold "partitions" in your mind, but also feel free to break them later. You might think, "I anticipate 20 pages of material here, because this is of great interest to me"; then eight days later, you might think, "That didn't turn out to be as important as I thought it would be. I'm just going to reserve three or four pages for that."

Part of the beauty of this system is that it grows and adapts gracefully with you. When your book is full, you will find that it has a terrain and geology that match the experiences of your life, and that the contents of your book smoothly transition from subject to subject.

There's something else you need, though: an index.

The Index

Make an index in the back of your book, just as described in Hack 7, "Write in Your Books." I have found good value in five pages of index: A–F, G–L, M–R, S–X, Y–Z–123. (The numbers are for numbered index entries, for example, "311," "42," "4G technology," and so on. You can place these entries first in your index instead; it doesn't much matter.) This works well (erring on the side of insufficient space) for a 240-page notebook. Six pages may be better. Given the spelling patterns of English, you might want to give C and S more space (look at "C" in Figure 17-1), join J with K into JK, join U with V into UV, and join X, Y, and Z into XYZ. This way, you can save a page without losing anything. If you're taking notes in another language, you can adapt your index similarly to fit the letter distribution in that language.

When you write an idea in your notebook, think of two to five words that you'd use to get back to this idea. They could be names of people to show the idea to, names of people who inspired the idea, names of the parts of the idea — any words that should bring you back to that page. You're not looking for the "right" keywords for that idea; they should reflect your own thinking and your own associations to work best. Add the words to the index, if they're not already there, and point them back to the text.

You may find that your index is getting crowded. You can help prevent this early on as you record index entries by subdividing the first-letter index entries by the second letter. Try to add your words such that they are roughly entered in alphabetical order.

Sometimes, you may want a more fine-grained index. For example, you probably don't want to overload the letter S just because you have a project with index entries like "Saturday House Plans," "Saturday House Calendar," "Saturday House 3 Documents," "Saturday House Reactable," "Saturday House Location Search," "Saturday House Activity Ideas," and so on. Just make a special separate index for that subject and put it next to your related notes. You can make a small index on half a page. Then, put an entry for "Saturday House Index" (or whatever) into your main index.

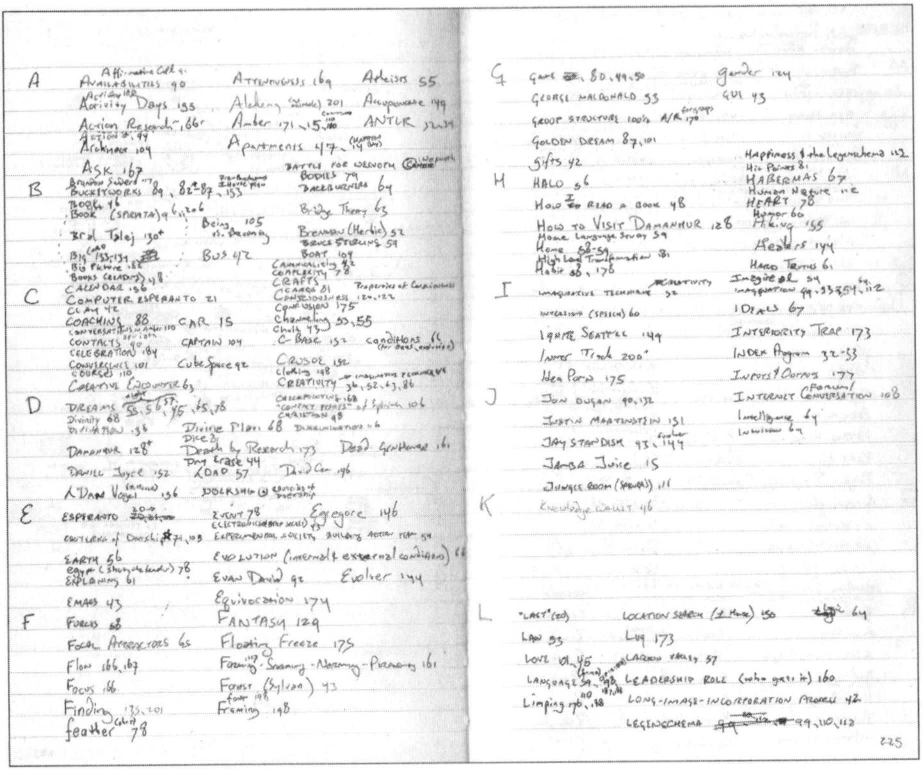

Figure 17-1: Index example

There are other ways of organizing your contents as well. You can keep a two-page visual index, a conceptual map of contents. I have found it valuable to reserve two pages for a "life index." It tracks a map, something like a labyrinth, representing the period of my life while I kept the notebook, calling out major events, interactions with people, and movies seen. There are page numbers pointing to details; for example, I took a trip to Bucketworks from April 17–19, and my insights from that trip cross pages 82–89. (See Hack 5, "Recall Long-Ago Events" for a similar idea.)

Then there is my *reverse table of contents*, which associates page numbers to contents (rather than contents to page numbers). Figure 17-2 shows one of my RTOCs.

For example, pages 20–27 are notes on Esperanto. You can also see the Bucketworks trip I mentioned earlier — pages 82–89, as specified. Notice that thoughts about dreams and broad ideas are next to the thoughts from Bucketworks. This is an example of how blending naturally develops when you apply open spaces and allow for emergent structures.

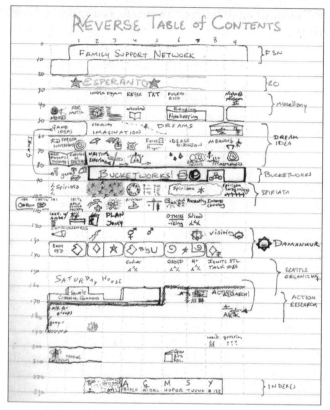

Figure 17-2: Reverse table of contents

It is my sincere hope and belief that more thought will be given in our society to exploring visual indexes.

Additional Ideas

Reserve two to four pages for quickly jotted notes, one-line seeds of ideas that you need to get out and record in a hurry, which you may or may not flesh out later. I realize that I'm only giving a paragraph to this idea, but I consider it to be very important: The best ideas strike at bizarre times, and you need a space to capture them: These reserved pages are that space. Keep it dense and pack the ideas in. Do make index entries for these brief thoughts. You can specially number these ideas for quick access straight from the index. For example, 42:13 can refer to "idea #13 on page 42," or S13 can refer to "quickly-jotted note #13."

Sticky notes are good emergency devices until you can add an idea to the notebook later.

Reserve a page (and its other side) for testing inks. This way, you can see how the ink will interact with the paper, determine whether an ink is really waterproof, and check which inks will bleed through to the other side. You want to avoid that, of course, and everything depends on the combination of pen plus paper.

Do not strive to completely fill your notebook! Rather, occupy 70–80% of the pages, and then start a new notebook. Revisit (and extend) the prior notebook when you have fresh insights into the older subject matter. Because of the unique way in which older content is revisited in this system, few pages are ever truly "done," and you will find that the remaining 20–30% of content is filled in even as you begin putting new thoughts into the new notebook.

Finally, my last word of advice is to layer, layer, and layer. Do not be a neatnik. When you're done, you'll have many layers of evaluation and development. It's amazing, almost magical when you put ideas next to related ideas, on the same page, and return to it later — everything comes back to you all at once.

How It Works

Proximity — things being near related things — results from the open space and emergent structure. We also get adaptability in the same stroke.

The index makes it possible to find things quickly. When you're using open structure, it can take a little bit of time to figure out where you want to put something, but with the index, that time is greatly shortened. Indexes scale beautifully, as Delicious.com and other tagging systems have successfully demonstrated, and I have found this system to be no exception. I am presently working on software to combine indexes from multiple notebooks.

Because the system is paper-based, it comes very naturally to most people, and you have full access to pictures and diagrams: You're not locked into text. It's also very portable, and has a very long battery life. Unfortunately, it's not very secure, but I'd rather risk losing the highest quality notes than be insured against losing lower-quality notes — and there's always a copy shop for backup.

In Real Life

Figure 17-3 shows two pages from one of my notebooks. This section describes how they developed into their present form.

Notice the page numbers in the lower-left and lower-right corners. Note the use of images and pictures; you often don't need a lengthy explanation, because you understand your own pictures.

The page on the right began by being about "meaning." I was using the page as a collection device, for collecting my various thoughts about meaning. I began with the image of a meaning hierarchy, and pieces in a story. Over time, I expanded that into an image of wholes and parts. When I talk with people about meaning, I open up to this page, so I can show them "this is what I mean."

It's like a miniature presentation. I also added a quote that a friend gave me: "The whole is greater than the sum of its parts, *and* the part is greater than its role in the whole."

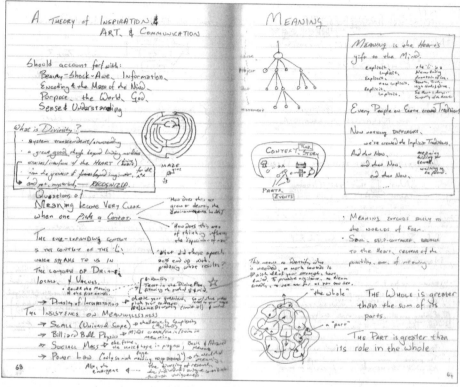

Figure 17-3: Notebook pages

Later, the left page took shape. I was having some initial thoughts on a theory of inspiration, art, and communication, and I drew up an outline of what such an account would look like.

A little more thought came to me, but much later; the discussion on meaning was going much further. I had a radically different take on meaning: "Meaning is the heart's gift to the mind." It was clearly about meaning, but page 70 was already taken up with thoughts on "What would a nondogmatic theology be?" Therefore, I sectioned off a part of the page for this particular development, in the top-right corner.

Challenges to the concept of meaning arose — one of my friends told me, "It doesn't mean anything that it doesn't mean anything." My response was visceral: "Questions of meaning become very clear, once one picks a context." Because

I was running out of space on the right side, I simply used the halfway mark on the left side of the page. Page 68 was originally going to be about a theory of inspiration and art, but thoughts just weren't coming. But that's what open spaces and emergent structure is all about: You don't know ahead of time what will develop, and what won't. Therefore, I repurposed part of the page in the service of a discussion on meaning.

With time, even more notes about meaning were added, as well as responses to common critiques of the concept of meaning. The challenges were written in black, the responses in blue. You can see that even more detail arose, and text got smaller and smaller.

Finally, much later, a concept related to the art theory arose: What does "divinity" signify? Thankfully, there was still a bit of space — I had only used half the page.

I call this way of developing a page "layering," or "selective attachment." The layers are the different parts of the story added over time.

In traditional notebooks, you enter text in a linear manner from the first page to the last page, one page at a time. That's good for developing a sense of "when," but it's not very helpful for revisiting subjects and developing an idea. The concept here is to develop a question or an idea like a seed, over time. Putting related ideas next to related ideas is essential to this process.

Beyond the individual sentences and images, the subjects here blend from one to the other. Pages 66 and 67 are about ideals. Page 68 is about inspiration, and page 69 is about meaning. Page 70 is about nondogmatism, and page 71 is about "doership." This was not a preplanned structure; it arose out of selective attachment and granting myself open spaces. These ideas all contribute to one another, and I've found incredible value in having related ideas share space. I hope you will find great value with these techniques as well.

See Also

- "How to Make a Complete Map of Every Thought You Think," Lion Kimbro, 2003, www.speakeasy.org/~lion/nb/.

  This book, which I wrote in 2003 describing my fourth-generation note-keeping system, received a lot of attention. I do not recommend following it, but it contains some valuable ideas related to visualization and capturing thought. What you are reading in this hack is my seventh-generation notekeeping system.

- CommunityWiki (`communitywiki.org/`) and MeatballWiki `www.usemod.`
`com/cgi-bin/mb.pl`).

These two wikis have developed practices for ordering information socially, with a wiki. Unfortunately, the older pages of these two sites are not ordered very neatly, because we were naïve and overly prolific. But we have learned, and new pages are neatly structured by comparison — for example, the PageMaintainerSeries. If you're interested in the subject of keeping notes socially with others, or developing thought socially with others, I invite you to come talk with us. We're always happy to share what we have learned.

Time Management

Time management may seem like a dry topic unsuited to a book of fun mind hacks, but unless you have time to advance your plans, you have nothing, not even the capacity to read this book. It's a limited resource that can slip away all too easily, leaving you wondering why you don't have more to show for it.

This chapter demonstrates how to get control of your time with innovative techniques such as keeping all your appointments in your head (Hack 18, "Keep a Mental Datebook"), keeping time with new kinds of clocks and calendars (Hack 19, "Tell Time Who's Boss," and Hack 20, "Meet MET"), knowing when it's better to organize your life with a streamlined time-management system (Hack 21, "Get Control of Yourself"), and when you'll be more productive by simply blowing it all off (Hack 24, "Knock Off Work").

Hack 18: Keep a Mental Datebook

Create an appointment book in your head so you need never miss a meeting or class again. You can implement this hack with your favorite mnemonic systems; our example builds on existing memory hacks to demonstrate how they can be combined into a custom system.

This advanced hack explains how to combine several other hacks into a custom memory system to remember your appointments or other important events in the week ahead. It builds on other mnemonic systems, including the Dominic

System, the Major System, the Number-Shape System, and the Journey System. You can learn about these systems from sources such as the Mentat Wiki that are freely available online; we'll cite relevant URLs in the following discussion.

There are two main points to this hack. The first is to teach you how to create a mental datebook containing your schedule, and always have that information available, closer than your fingertips. You can combine the various memory systems exactly as described in this hack, and you will have a functional mental datebook.

However, the way the datebook is set up below might not be to your taste, and the same may be true for many of the other hacks in this book. Therefore, the second point of this hack is to serve as a working model for how to combine and customize hacks, whether they come from this book, from the Mentat Wiki, or from anywhere else. It's a useful skill to have, akin to combining the interfaces in a software development kit to write your own application, or building your own creation out of individual LEGO bricks. As just one example, you could modify this hack slightly to create a mental address book.

In Action

Our running example involves remembering a team meeting on Monday at 3:00 P.M. in room 2233 of your office building. You will need to remember four facts about each appointment: the day it's on (Monday), at what time it occurs (3:00 p.m.), its location (room 2233), and what it's about or with whom you're meeting (it's a team meeting). Let's address each of these separately.

Fact 1: The Day of the Week

There are various methods you can use to remember the day of your meeting; this is where customization starts. For example, if you use the Number-Shape System, you would number the days and use shapes to remember the day of the meeting. If you numbered Monday as 1, Tuesday as 2, and so on, you would remember Monday with a candle, which is in the shape of the number 1. (You can see a quick overview of this system at the Mentat Wiki: www.ludism.org/ mentat/NumberShapeSystem.) Ron prefers to use the mild synesthesia he seems to have with numbers, days of the week, and so on, to remember the fact that the meeting is on Monday. Monday always seems gray to him — literally. Table 18-1 shows Ron's color associations for the days of the week. If you experience weekdays as having colors too, your colors are almost certainly different, so you'll have to make your own table.

Table 18-1: Synesthetic Associations with Days of the Week

DAY	COLOR	OBJECT
Monday	Gray	Ash
Tuesday	Yellow	Banana
Wednesday	Purple	Grape
Thursday	Brown	Chocolate
Friday	Green	Green bean
Saturday	Red	Apple
Sunday	Argent (silver/white)	Dove

We've also assigned an object to each color for mnemonic purposes. For example, yellow (Tuesday) is represented by a banana. Monday, the day of the meeting, is gray, so it's represented by ashes. To make this more vivid, we chose to visualize the ashes as being in a crematorium urn. This image is perhaps a bit morbid, but that's what makes it memorable. However, this hack is all about customization, so if the image disgusts or depresses you, substitute another image — such as a huge, elaborate ashtray like the kind you sometimes find in hotel lobbies.

Fact 2: The Time

It's really easy to remember the clock time of a meeting if you use the Dominic System, which is optimized for memorizing four-digit numbers. (Again, see the Mentat Wiki for a quick look at the Dominic System: www.ludism.org/mentat/DominicSystem.) The Dominic System uses an easy-to-remember number-to-letter conversion and the initials of memorable people to create vivid mnemonic images. Each two-digit number is associated with a person, and each person has a signature action. If you're memorizing a four-digit number, the first two letters represent a memorable person, and the second two digits represent the action associated with another memorable person. For example, 8015 becomes HOAE, which becomes Santa Claus (HO!) writing on a blackboard (the action of AE, Albert Einstein).

To remember the time of your appointment, first convert the time from a 12-hour clock to 24-hour time. For example, 3:00 P.M. is 15:00 on a 24-hour clock.

Next, convert the 24-hour clock time (15:00) to letters of the alphabet according to the Dominic System (AEOO). You can remember this four-digit string with the character and associated action in your personal version of the Dominic System. For example, ours is Albert Einstein (AE) knocking something over like Dennis the Menace (OO = "oh oh!"). What Einstein is knocking over is the urn of ashes.

If this system seems complicated, realize that you only need 24 people and two actions (00 and 30) to remember most appointments. In fact, you could probably get away with 12 people, because most appointments occur between 8:00 AM and 8:00 PM.

If you prefer the Major System (www.ludism.org/mentat/MajorSystem) to the Dominic System, you might remember a ToweL (15) protecting some DaiSieS (100, so "fifteen hundred") from some ashes blowing by (Monday).

Fact 3: Location

You must also remember where your meeting will take place. If it's somewhere you know well, such as your office, you can simply visualize the mnemonic scene as taking place there — for example, Albert Einstein knocking over an urn of ashes in your office.

If where you have to meet has an address such as a room number or street address, you need to be a bit more creative. If you're meeting in room 2233, you can remember it with another Dominic System character — in this case, Bilbo Baggins (BB = 22), twirling a cane and waddling like Charlie Chaplin (CC = 33).

Now our image is of Albert Einstein knocking over an urn of ashes onto Bilbo Baggins, who is twirling a cane and waddling.

Fact 4: What You're Doing

You might not need to remember this fourth fact about your appointment. For example, if you're meeting someone at the Museum of Glass in Tacoma, chances are good that you're going to spend the day looking at glass art, so remembering the location is probably sufficient. However, you may have a more specific objective at the appointment. In our running example, you have a team meeting at work. In that case, you can visualize a sports team or a team of horses to represent that fact. Since Ron doesn't follow sports, he would imagine a team of horses.

Putting It All Together

The final mnemonic image of a team meeting at 3:00 p.m. on Monday in room 2233 is as follows:

Albert Einstein (AE = 15) knocks over (OO = 00) an urn of ashes (gray = Monday) onto Bilbo Baggins (BB = 22), who's waddling and twirling a cane like Charlie Chaplin (CC = 33). The ashes blow into the eyes of a team of horses in the room (team meeting), and they stampede into the hallway.

When you try to recall what you have to do on Monday, remember the central image of ashes. You'll remember the image for your team meeting, and will be able to decode the time and place it occurs, as well as what you'll be doing. This may seem like a lot of work to remember a meeting, but with practice and habit, it will become easy.

In Real Life

As explained, the mental datebook is an advanced hack, and you can hack the hack to your heart's delight.

Maybe you don't want to associate colors or shapes with weekdays. You could use a "memory palace" system (www.ludism.org/mentat/MemoryPalace) or a memory dungeon (Hack 2, "Build a Memory Dungeon") and associate each day with a room or other location.

If you're worried that by using the Dominic System twice, you'll conflate the meeting time (15:00 in our example) with the location (room 2233), notice that 22:00 is 10:00 P.M., long past office hours for most workers, and few people would meet at 33 minutes past the hour anyway. Still, hack the hack however you like. You can try using the Dominic System for the time and the Major System for the location, or the reverse.

If seven days isn't enough look-ahead for you, try setting up a mental "43 folders" tickler file system (http://wiki.43folders.com/index.php/Tickler_file), for the potentially 31 days in the upcoming month, plus the 12 months in the upcoming year.

See Also

Although we had heard of such systems before, Mark S. D'Arcy's article "How to Remember Appointments — The Mental Diary," (www.buildyourmemory .com/diary.php) is the first place we ever saw a mental datebook described in detail. Its author uses the Major System, but Ron prefers the Dominic System, so he started tinkering, and this hack is the result.

Hack 19: Tell Time Who's Boss

Tired of punching your 24-hour clock and watching the days roll by on your 12-month calendar? You can reorganize your personal time and open your mind to the vastness of cosmic time by experimenting with other clocks and calendars.

Time extends from the distant past to the distant future, further in both directions than our minds can grasp. Clocks and calendars were invented to divide time into pieces that we can understand and use in ways that we find meaningful. To begin to measure the span of time, it would be useful to have a clock that accurately ticked off the number of seconds since the Big Bang. Of course, that will never happen. Nonetheless, it can be useful to remember that the ways we measure and manage time are arbitrary. You can get some sense of what time is really like outside of the clock and calendar time you're accustomed to if you design, program, or just use enough different — and preferably wildly contradictory — clocks and calendars. You may be able to understand and manage your practical timekeeping better as well by expanding how you approach it.

In Action

This section describes various clocks and calendars with which you can experiment, and what you might gain from considering them.

Universal Time

Universal time (UT) is a type of timekeeping system that can be used uniformly all over the world, no matter which time zone you're in. The most widely used version of universal time is Coordinated Universal Time (UTC), which is a more accurate version of the older Greenwich Mean Time (GMT). Midnight in UTC starts at midnight at the Prime Meridian, 0 degrees longitude, which runs through the Royal Greenwich Observatory in Greenwich, England.

There are many advantages to UT, starting with astronomical observations, and extending to travel and telecommunications in an increasingly globally aware world. It would be hard to imagine how the Internet would function without some form of UT; just check the header on one of your e-mail messages and you'll see the time when you received the message in UTC. Your computer almost certainly works with UTC internally and displays the time in your local time zone for your benefit.

Knowing the time in UTC can be very useful. For example, it's usually easier to calculate directly from UTC to a friend's time zone than indirectly from your own. If your watch or phone has a second-time-zone feature, there's probably no more useful time zone you can set it to than UTC or GMT.

The International Standards Organization has created an extension of UTC named *ISO 8601* (www.cl.cam.ac.uk/~mgk25/iso-time.html). Its advantage over UTC is that it expresses not only the time, but also the date, and can do so in a very flexible way. For example, the current time as I write this, October 18, 2009, 8:37 P.M., Pacific Standard Time, can be expressed in ISO 8601 in several ways:

- 2009-10-19 03:37Z (October 19, 2009, 3:37 A.M., UTC)

- 2009-W43-1 (week 43, day 1 of 2009)

- 2009-292   (day 292 of 2009)

You can find your current ISO 8601 date and time on the ISO 8601 page of Wikipedia (http://en.wikipedia.org/wiki/ISO_8601).[1]

ISO 8601 is a rich standard that provides an unambiguous way to express time zones, durations, intervals, repeating intervals, and abbreviations. In addition, it's "big-endian," which for our purposes means that it's easy for computers to sort ISO 8601 timestamps. So, for example, if you have a podcast, date your episodes with ISO 8601, and you and your fans will have no trouble storing your shows in order.

Decimal Time

Decimal time is any timekeeping system based mainly on the number 10, rather than the numbers 12, 24, and 60. You may have heard of the *French Revolutionary Calendar*, which was used for about a dozen years in post-revolutionary France in the late 1700s. After the Revolution, France had big ideas about the benefits of decimal systems; they developed the decimal calendar along with what became the modern metric system of weights and measures. The calendar had 12 months of three 10-day weeks. Days had 10 hours, each with 100 minutes of 100 seconds each. Although much of the metric system is obviously still in use today, the French metric timekeeping system didn't catch on, partly because it was adopted mainly for ideological, rather than practical, reasons.

However, there is a form of decimal time in wide, current use: the *fractional day*. This is simply the number of hours past midnight divided by 24, extended to any precision. Thus:

- Midnight = 0.00
- 6:00 A.M. = 0.25
- Noon = 0.50
- 6:00 P.M. = 0.75

And so on. Computers often use fractional days internally, and astronomers and other scientists use them, too. Roughly speaking, astronomers add a fractional day based on UTC's zero meridian, to the integral part of the Julian day (see below).

In combination with some form of Julian day, fractional days make it easy to calculate time intervals. For example, which time interval is easier to calculate: 7:22 A.M. to 2:08 P.M. or 0.31 to 0.59? Both are the same interval, but the latter requires only simple subtraction, whereas the former requires twiddling multiples of 60.

NOTE Here's a trick Ron discovered to make mentally converting conventional clock time to a rough fractional day easier: Multiply the hour of the day by four, and then add a little. For example, 7:00 P.M. is 19:00 hours. 19 x 4 = 76, so the day fraction is probably something like 0.78. A calculator tells us that 19/24 is 0.792, so that's pretty close! This trick relies on the concept of *aliquot parts*, or exact divisors; 25 and 4 are both aliquot parts of 100.

Swatch Internet Time is a form of decimal time introduced in the late 1990s by the Swatch Corporation, a watch manufacturer. It was an attempt to create a kind of universal time for the Internet (www.timeanddate.com/time/internettime .html). In Swatch Internet Time, the basic unit is a *.beat*, or a thousandth of a day, so @000 is midnight and @500 is noon (the @ sign merely indicates that the three-digit number is a .beat).

It might have caught on if it had used Greenwich as its prime meridian, like UTC. Then it would have been equivalent to the fractional day part of a modified Julian day (see below), and could have been easily calculated from UTC. Instead, Swatch chose Biel, Switzerland (the site of their corporate headquarters), one time zone east of Greenwich, so that midnight in Greenwich was @042 in .beats. Choosing promotion over compatibility, the company ensured that Swatch Internet Time stayed in the realm of publicity stunt, rather than become a viable standard.

Some experimenters have used a kind of modified .beat among themselves, with the prime meridian in Greenwich.[2] If you can still find and set a watch that keeps Swatch Internet Time, it may at least be useful to help track fractional time.

Julian Days, a form of decimal time used by astronomers, roughly represent the number of days since noon at the Greenwich Meridian on January 1, 4713 B.C.). This may seem like an arbitrary date, but the sixteenth-century French scholar Joseph Justus Scaliger chose it because it is the most recent date on which three important calendrical cycles coincided. It is conveniently before the beginning of recorded history, which is generally agreed today to begin in the fourth millennium B.C.E. Thus, negative Julian days are not required for any historical date.

As we write this, it's Julian day number 2455123. A fractional time is also usually added, making this 2455123.651 if we use the time given above (20:37 PST on October 18, 2009 or 03:37 on the "next day" in UTC).

Because a Julian day starts at noon UTC, rather than midnight, it's always half a day ahead of UT. Because its epoch (the time and day it starts) is almost 7,000 years ago, it tends to be rather a long number. For both these reasons, the system of *Modified Julian Days* was introduced. A modified Julian day is a Julian day minus 2400000.5. The Julian day above (2455123.651) becomes 55123.151, so let's say it's 55123.2 right now.[3]

Remind you of anything? Someone once remarked that Modified Julian Days, or MJDs, are the closest thing we have to Star Trek's "stardates." *Truncated Julian Days* as defined by the National Institute of Standards and Technology (NIST) are even more so; their integral part is four digits long, and can be calculated by lopping off the first digit of an MJD. They are convenient for telling time — Ron once wrote a TJD "stardate" clock and kept it running for a few months on his netbook — but as they repeat every 27 years or so, TJDs alone might be somewhat ambiguous, even within a single human lifetime.

Julian days of all sorts are useful, however. If you want to calculate the duration between the first walk on the moon (July 21, 1969, 02:39:33 UTC) and the inauguration of President Barack Obama (January 20, 2009, 17:00:00 UTC), you can subtract 1969 from 2009, about 40 years. If you want to know the answer with great precision, however, MJDs are invaluable. Simple subtraction of 40423.11 from 54851.71 equals 14,428.60 days.

The linear quality of MJDs or TJDs might also make them useful for a kind of Mission Elapsed Time (Hack 20, "Meet MET").

Offbeat Clocks and Calendars

The *28-Hour Day* proposal would divide our 168-hour week into six 28-hour periods, rather than seven 24-hour periods (see www.dbeat.com/28). Assuming the first "day" began on what we normally consider midnight on Monday, it would end at 4:00 A.M. Tuesday, the next "day" would end at 8:00 A.M. Wednesday, and so on, every day ending four hours later in the "real" solar day. The claim is that this scheme would have various benefits, including helping people to sleep longer and varying each day's amounts of light and darkness in an interesting way, with lots of light on the weekend.

This scheme has been on the Web since the late 1990s, and *xkcd*, a pillar of geek culture, published a comic strip to publicize it (http://xkcd.com/320). However, Ron is inclined to think it's a hoax, partly because it's too silly to be adopted widely, but primarily because the web link that reads "Serious proponents of the 28-hour day share their views here" has returned an HTTP 404 (not found) error since 1999. Nevertheless, people *do* discuss it seriously, and it may be the alternative time scheme most familiar to geeks.

The *World Calendar* (www.theworldcalendar.org), designed in 1930, is perpetual, meaning it doesn't change from year to year. It always begins on Sunday, January 1, and every quarter has three months, with a total of 91 days (or 13 weeks). It would make arcane calendrical calculations obsolete.

The World Calendar was considered by the United Nations, but despite its convenience, religious objections were raised related to Sabbath days drifting out of sync with the calendar because of intercalary days (such as leap days), so the U.S. pressured the United Nations not to study it further.

The *Darian Calendar for Mars* (http://pweb.jps.net/~tgangale/mars/converter/calendar_clock.htm) is one of the best-constructed and best-known Martian calendars — that is, calendars for use on the planet Mars. Martian days, known to astronomers as *sols*, are about 24 hours and 40 minutes long.

The Martian year has about 668 sols, so it's long enough for 24 months of about 28 sols each. As I write this, it's Sol Saturni (that is, Saturday) 21 Vrishika, with only seven more days left in the year 212. In eight days, or sols, it will be 1 Sagittarius, 213, the Martian New Year, which is the first day of spring. It will be spring for roughly the next six months on Mars in the northern hemisphere. Because Martian timekeeping is well understood, and people like to play with new ideas for Martian clocks and calendars, the preceding website contains information about hundreds of others.

Of course, time is time everywhere, but one of the surest ways to vault out of Earthly timekeeping considerations — and thereby gain a wider viewpoint — is to develop a clock and calendar for another world. As Lance Latham points out, because you can't rely on comfortable Earthly constants like 365, 24, and 60, developing a calendar for another planet can be a self-test for understanding calendrical concepts.[3] After considering the Martian Time schemes, why not try designing a calendar for Saturn; one of the moons of Jupiter, such as Europa; or the asteroid Ceres?

Remember, just as with constructed languages like Esperanto and Klingon, at least half the fun of clocks and calendars comes from tinkering and designing your own. If engineering an interplanetary calendar seems like a big step, a smaller one might be sketching a more rational global calendar than the Gregorian one we use now, like the World Calendar.

How It Works

This hack works in a couple of different ways. The first way is cognitive ergonomics, discussed at length in Hack 40, "Notate Wisely," and Hack 39, "Notate Personally." By parceling the infinite linear extent of second after second into imaginable units like years and hours, clocks and calendars enable us to get a better, easier handle on time and thereby tell time who's boss, at least within our own lifetimes.

However, cognitive ergonomics has a price, and that price is cognitive lock-in. If the only calendar you use is Gregorian, you might start thinking that the world will end when the "odometer" turns over in A.D. 1000 or 2000. As I write this, there's an industry devoted to convincing people that the world will end on December 21, 2012 in our calendar because that's the ancient Mayan calendar's odometer date.

Calendars can also make time so easy to cope with that it almost seems cozy, small enough that it might have begun around 4000 B.C., for example. But time is like some immense alien god. It's very big, to put it mildly, and it doesn't give a fig, not to mention a date, about you. If you are either frightened or smug because of some calendar-related belief, soak yourself in as many clocks and calendars as possible until you see how partial and arbitrary they are, and the immensity of time and the cosmos opens up for you once again. You'll be freed to take a more rational view of what time is and how it works, change your relationship with it, and possibly find new ways to meter it and manage it in your own life.

In Real Life

Goaded by Robert Anton Wilson's article "How to Live Eleven Days in 24 Hours" (www.kelsung.com/calendar/RAW.htm), in which he describes his own multical-endar system, Ron wrote a Macintosh application several years ago that explored clocks and calendar systems he had never seen implemented in software before, such as Tolkien's Elvish calendar, the World Calendar, stardates, the Bahá'í calendar, and a few he had seen before, such as Tolkien's Hobbit calendar and Swatch Internet Time.

The more calendars Ron added, the more he realized that they all depended on a kind of interlanguage, an Esperanto of time, which in the case of the application was the Julian day. No matter what date you gave the program, it needed to convert it to a single number on a number line before it could convert it back to Bahá'í, or the Elvish calendar, with its six seasons.

> **NOTE** Linux and Unix computers have a similar "number line" called *Unix Time*, which is the number of seconds since January 1, 1970. Right now, that time is 1255941734. If you have a Linux or Unix computer, type date +%s from the command line to check the current Unix time.

No matter which clocks or calendars you use to make time seem like home, the underlying reality is that time is vast; if you want to have any hope of grasping it, you need to think less cyclically and more linearly. When humankind ventures farther into space and we establish permanent bases on the moon and Mars, as well as the International Space Station, the utter arbitrariness of our present calendars will become obvious.

However, cyclical time measurement has its uses. To start expanding your time sense, you can try switching from the Gregorian calendar and 24-hour clock to other cycles. Scientists who worked on the Martian rovers Spirit and Opportunity worked by a Martian clock to capitalize on Martian sunlight hours. Because the Martian day is almost 25 hours long, their work day skipped forward almost an hour every Earth day. In essence, though not specifics, they were performing a 28-Hour Day experiment.

Coordinating time on two planets is bad enough. Imagine living in a civilization that must coordinate research and business all over the solar system. How many clocks and calendars would we need then? Wouldn't it be better to use a universal linear measure such as Julian Days, or one even less tied to Earth, perhaps a straight count of seconds such as a modified version of Unix Time?

No matter what system works for such a scenario, it will require thinking about time in a different and more flexible way.

See Also

- Charles Stross, *Glasshouse* (New York: Ace Books, 2006). Science fiction novel in which our transhuman descendants live in an interstellar civilization that tracks time by the kilosecond (about 15 minutes), hundred kiloseconds (about a day), megasecond (about a week and a half), and so on.
- Hack 40, "Notate Wisely," discusses a similar system based on Planck units, fundamental physical units of mass, length, and time.

Notes

1. http://web.archive.org/web/20021207210935/www.universal-time .org/udtprinciples.htm
2. http://web.archive.org/web/20080504033508/http://www.artefakt .com/projects/ibeat/
3. Lance Latham, *Standard C Date/Time Library: Programming the World's Calendars and Clocks* (Lawrence, KS, USA: R&D Books, 1998).

Hack 20: Meet MET

Use the clock NASA uses to deal with unforeseen hiccups and emergencies in your daily schedule.

Mission Elapsed Time (MET) is the time that has elapsed since the beginning of a project or "mission." For example, if we tell you our MET is 5/22:09:17, you know it has been 5 days, 22 hours, 9 minutes, and 17 seconds since our project started. NASA uses MET on all its flights to minimize the confusion caused by flexible launch times. In this hack, we'll explore the ways you can make the concept of Mission Elapsed Time work for you.

In Action

NASA's own explanation of Mission Elapsed Time (http://web.archive.org/ web/20070718124711/http://science.nasa.gov/Realtime/Rocket_Sci/clocks/ time-met.html) can hardly be improved upon, so we'll steal from it in this section with an extremely simple example.

We live about a three-hour drive from our favorite bookstore, Powell's City of Books in Portland, Oregon. When we visit, we sometimes take our dogs along. If we were to plan an itinerary for a trip to Powell's, it might look like this:

8:00 A.M. – Leave home.

8:15 A.M. – Gas up the car and get a soda.

10:00 A.M. – Stop at a rest area to stretch and walk the dogs.

11:45 A.M. – Arrive at Powell's.

However, we never know when we're going to leave, because we usually sleep late on weekends and there are frequently last-minute delays such as gathering up a few last books to sell or receiving an unexpected phone call. NASA would say we have a long launch window for our trip. Thus, an actual trip to Powell's might look more like this, in ordinary clock time:

11:47 A.M. – Leave home.

12:02 P.M. – Gas up the car and get a soda.

1:47 P.M. – Stop at a rest area to stretch and walk the dogs.

3:32 P.M. – Arrive at Powell's.

However, it might be easier to build an itinerary around MET, which is relative, rather than absolute, clock time:

0:00 – Leave home.

0:15 – Gas up the car and get a soda.

2:00 – Stop at a rest area to stretch and walk the dogs.

3:45 – Arrive at Powell's.

If we set our clocks to use MET — by using the stopwatch function of our phones, for example — we can stick to our schedule without recalculation. Of course, NASA must take into account astronomical events, such as the orbit of the moon and planets, which NASA can't change. You also may find that there are events during a project whose times you cannot change, such as important meetings.

MET is similar to a form of relative timekeeping with which you may be more familiar: scheduling actions backward from a fixed-time event. NASA uses this too; MET is a positive number, but you may have heard expressions such as "T minus one hour" to designate one hour before launch time, the same idea in negative-number form. It's also common in planning for trips and weddings. You may find it useful to incorporate both positive and negative relative time-keeping in your own schedule if you have fixed-time events. We talk about how one might address fixed events with a computer in the "In Real Life" section.

How It Works

As explained, Mission Elapsed Time is useful because it enables you to schedule events relative to the start of a project, rather than at a specific absolute clock time. Imagine an MET timer app for your smartphone. If your mission were simply considered to be your day, you could tap the app to start it when you got up, and it could remind you to do all the things you need to do, but in a more flexible way than if you entered them as ordinary alarms, one by one. It would be similar to apps that remind you to avoid repetitive stress injury by resting your hands, but much more powerful. It could also remind you to do the following:

- Walk your dog.
- Exercise.
- Stand up straight.
- Smile.
- Go to bed (always a problem for Ron to remember).

You could program it with any periodic reminder you wanted (Hack 52, "Metabehave Yourself"). It would be useful for trips and travel, as we've seen. It could play sound files to alert you to tasks, or vibrate to remind you to read the screen. It might be useful when you have a set amount of time that you can spend among a number of tasks, and you want to make sure you get to them all. For example, you might have only Saturday afternoon to clean your house, but you want to ensure that you clean three critical rooms and not leave any room out entirely, even if you don't clean them all as thoroughly as you could. You might set your MET timer like this:

0:00 – Living room

1:00 – Bedrooms

2:45 – Kitchen

As of 2011, there are already Mission Elapsed Time apps for iPhone and Android, but they only show you the MET for NASA's latest space missions — which is great, of course, but we want an MET app for our own missions!

In Real Life

Ron wrote a simple Perl script, met.pl, which you can use as an MET timer to set elapsed-time alarms on your laptop or desktop computer. It takes a flat text file as its input. Figure 20-1 is a file for the Mission to Powell's featured earlier in the "In Action" section of this hack.

```
000/00:00:00,Leave home
000/00:15:00,Gas up the car
000/02:00:00,Walk the dogs at a rest stop
000/03:45:00,Arrive at Powell's
```

Figure 20-1: powells.txt

Whenever MET is equal to or greater than the elapsed time specified for one of the events in the file, met.pl will display the message for that event (such as "Gas up car") until it's time to display the message for the next event ("Walk the dogs at a rest stop").

WARNING   You must specify the events in your text file in the right order, or unpredictable things will happen. Fortunately, if you write the time in the correct MET format, you can enter events in any order, then sort them later with the sort feature of your text editor or word processor.

This Perl script is basically a proof of concept. Ways that it could be improved include the following:

1. Add alarms for fixed-time events, such as meetings.

2. Add a graphical interface.

3. Add the capability to play sound files or run arbitrary commands or programs.

4. Enable nudging alarms forward or backward in time while the program is running.

5. Enable setting repeating alarms with just one entry in the text file . This would make it like a more flexible Motivaider device, as in Hack 52, "Metabehave Yourself".

6. Enable accepting input on-the-fly, acting as a kind of MET-based journal.

7. Port it to a smartphone, such as Android or iPhone, as described in "How It Works."

8. Give it the capability to interface with a Twitter feed, blog, or SMS.

None of these improvements is particularly difficult, but all of them together would create a powerful time-management tool. For example, the first item (adding fixed-time events) would probably require adding the capability first to specify events with times in UTC format (Hack 19, "Tell Time Who's Boss"), and then reading the events in the text file into an array at run time and sorting them by which happens first. If you're a programmer of moderate ability, like Ron, this is probably a few hours of work. (And why UTC? Consider what happens if you're traveling not to a local bookstore but to another time zone.)

An MET timer such as met.pl (Figure 20-2) is like a GPS device for your time, or an exoself (Hack 31, "Mine the Future"), because you tell it to tell you what to do, and when.

```perl
#!/usr/bin/perl
# met.pl
# Ron Hale-Evans, rwhe@ludism.org

use Time::HiRes qw(gettimeofday tv_interval);

$t0 = [gettimeofday];
$minute = 60;
$hour = 60 * $minute;
$day = 24 * $hour;

$in_file = $ARGV[0];
open (IN_FILE, "< ./$in_file")
    or die "Couldn't open input file: $!\n";

$i = 0;

while (<IN_FILE>)
{
    chomp;
    s/(\d\d\d)\/(\d\d)\:(\d\d)\:(\d\d)\,(.*)/{$fdays = $1; $fhours = $2;
$fminutes = $3; $fseconds = $4; $objective = $5}/sie;
    $fraw = $fdays * $day + $fhours * $hour + $fminutes * $minute +
$fseconds;

    $rawtimes[$i] = $fraw;
    $objectives[$i] = $objective;
    $i++;
}

$maxraw = $rawtimes[$i-1];

# Clean up.
close IN_FILE;

$objective = "";
$i = 0;

while (true)
{
    $curtime = [gettimeofday];
    $met = tv_interval($t0, $curtime);
    $raw = int($met);

    $met_days = int ($met / $day);
```

```
$met = $met - $met_days * $day;

$met_hours = int($met / $hour);
$met = $met - $met_hours * $hour;

$met_minutes = int($met / $minute);
$met = $met - $met_minutes * $minute;

$met_seconds = int($met);
$met = 0;

if ($raw >= $rawtimes[$i])
{
  $objective = $objectives[$i];
  $i++;
}

# Clear screen
system("clear");

print "MET: ";
printf ("%03s:%02s:%02s:%02s\n",$met_days, $met_hours, $met_minutes,
$met_seconds);
print "$objective\n";

if ($raw >= $maxraw)
{
    exit;
}
else
{
    sleep 1;
}
}
```

Figure 20-2: met.pl

Hack 21: Get Control of Yourself

Matthew Cornell, M.S.

Lost control of your life? Get back in the driver's seat with Jetpack, the pocket-sized system for managing your work and freeing up your brain for better things.

With so much to do in our hyperkinetic lives, one of the most empowering practices we can adopt is a solid personal system for being more productive. In reality, all of us use *some* kind of workflow method — it might be sticky notes plastered around our monitors, a stale set of stained and crumpled to-do lists, or a paper "piling system" — but they're usually not as effective as a well thought-out method is. The good news is that for most of us there is room for big improvement in how efficiently we get our work done. Beyond becoming more productive, you may find that once you get a handle on your work and life, you'll feel less stressed and more mentally turned-on.

This hack details Jetpack, a straightforward system for organizing your work. The primary influence on these techniques is David Allen's seminal time-management book, *Getting Things Done*.[1] We first mix that in, combining the ideas with other classic self-management practices, and then simplify everything. We follow that with some short, real-life examples.

In Action

The key concept of this hack is changing the way you think about how work flows through your life, and how you structure it. The goal is to create a tight system in which incoming demands are turned into executable work. You'll do this by breaking it down into four stages:

1. **Capture** all incoming *attention tokens* into a small number of inboxes.

2. **Empty** your inboxes daily using the *5 D's*.

3. **Work** during the day solely from your calendar and two lists: Tasks and Waiting.

4. **Review** your Projects list every week, along with your calendar, Tasks list, and Waiting list.

Notice that only four organizing artifacts are involved: a calendar and three lists.

- **Calendar:** Essentially a chronologically organized set of time-sensitive tasks and reminders. You can use a datebook, a calendar on your phone or computer, or whatever else can mark time for you.

- **Tasks:** A master list of bite-sized activities from all projects, plus individual "stand alone" activities like errands.

- **Waiting:** A list of delegated work that you can follow up on if necessary. It captures who, what, and when.

- **Projects:** A comprehensive list of large activities that require multiple tasks to accomplish.

NOTE The tools you need are dead simple. Everyone has a calendar, and almost anything can serve as a list, including paper, a simple text file, or the Tasks feature of Microsoft Outlook, Gmail, or whatever else you use for your integrated "one-stop shop" for e-mail, calendar, and contacts.

Each stage requires distinct types of activities, skills, and thinking, and should not be mixed. Importantly, each stage represents legitimate work, and none of them can be skipped. This is a major shift for most people, who usually jump between tasks in an unorganized manner.

Let's look at each one, and then pull them together with some examples.

Capture into Inboxes

Work arrives in everybody's lives in the form of tokens representing things that need your attention. These are any items containing information that haven't been run through your system, and therefore haven't had executable work extracted from them. Most typical are e-mail messages, voicemails, and paper such as memos (including "honey-do's"), snail mail, articles to read, or notes to yourself. "Physical" things can qualify too, like dead batteries or the cool gadget you ordered that just arrived in the mail. This leads to a rule:

Rule #1: Everything needing your attention goes into inboxes.

E-mail and voicemail are always collecting for you automatically, so you may only need to set up a system for handling physical things. Do this by getting a set of stacking trays, putting them on your desk within easy reach, and training yourself and everyone else to use them and not anything else. Not your chair, not your desk, not your kitchen table, and not taped to the back of your dog. No exceptions. Collecting everything in one approved place instead of all over puts you in good shape for the next stage.

Empty Your Inboxes

Now that you've set up inboxes, you need to empty them so that you can figure out your responsibilities for each token needing attention. The rule is:

Rule #2: Empty all of your inboxes every day.

Otherwise, how can you ensure that when you have some time available you are making the best choice regarding what to do? The principle at play here is that work arrives unstructured. (If it arrives structured, you're probably either in school or in a nursing home. In both cases, you're better off learning a different hack.)

You perform this act of "sense making" in a principled manner by running through each item one at a time, extracting from it everything that calls for action, then moving the item to an appropriate place. Sit down with your inboxes, your calendar, your Tasks list, and your Waiting list. Use the *5 D's* mnemonic to process the items: Delete, Deposit, Delegate, Do, and Defer. Take a hard look at each item one at a time and ask the following questions in order. Refer to Figure 21-1 as you go through each step.

- **Delete:** Can I junk it? If yes, then trash it with a flourish and move on to the next item. Otherwise, ask:

- **Deposit:** Is it something I don't need to take action on but that I need to keep around? If yes, then file it and go to the next token. If it needs action, ask:

- **Delegate:** Can I get some other poor fool to do this? (Remember, you're too busy to do everything yourself. Plus, if you've configured your world correctly, then people do the work they're the best at.) If yes, then pass it along and track it on the Waiting list. Just make a short single-line entry that says what it is, who it went to, and the current date. This enables you to follow up. If you can't delegate, ask:

- **Do:** Is it possible to do it right now in a few minutes? Getting small tasks out of the way immediately helps to prevent your lists from getting cluttered with minutiae. Typical examples are making a quick e-mail reply or paying a bill online. If it's too big to do now, then you'll have to do it later.

- **Defer:** Finally, is this time- or date-specific? If yes, then put it on your calendar. If not, then put it on your Tasks list.

In this system, the calendar is sacrosanct — use it only for action or information that is relevant on a specific day. A good test for this is to ask if you'll sink yourself if you don't act on it sometime during the day (or at an exact time, for appointments). Everything on your calendar should carry the answer "yes." This includes reminders, such as the server is down, a co-worker is on vacation, or that it's time to review a project's milestones or reassess an issue.

Don't worry if this sounds like a lot. After a little practice you'll get the knack of this thinking, and it'll become ninja-like second nature.

NOTE Solid methods for self-management should include a "Not Doing" list. Perhaps surprisingly, tracking items that you are *not* going to do in your life is important to freeing your mind of them. This decision must be made explicitly and honestly, factoring in the many things you've already said you *will* do. You should review that list once in a while to decide the fate of its items: resuscitate to your inbox, keep it on life support, or kill it for good.

Focusing on what you don't do turns out to be an important success strategy for businesses as well. See Jim Collins' classic book *Good to Great* for more information.

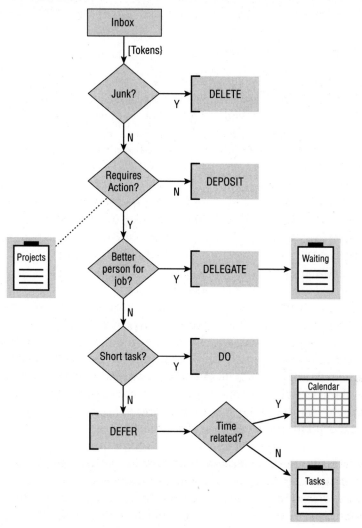

Figure 21-1: 5 D's processing diagram

When you're going through your inbox, keep in mind this rule:

Rule #3: *Process inbox items in order, one item at a time, with no skipping or putting back — and, except for small items, no doing!*

The reasoning here is that emptying is decision time. You don't get to put it off to think about later; you have to front-load the decision-making. Otherwise, your lists will be a turnoff because some items will feel unreasonably heavy, and you'll find yourself procrastinating.

> **NOTE** An issue that comes up is what to do with the actual e-mail or piece of paper that you need to keep around until you get to its associated deferred task. A simple solution is to create "Pending" folders for both e-mail and paper. Move the item in question into those folders so you can find it later when you need it to do the task. This trick gets them out of the inbox but keeps them within reach.

Note a subtlety, though: not all work is of the same scope or complexity. Typically, you'll have a mixture of five-minute tasks (e.g., make a phone call), hour-long project work (e.g., sketch a plan), and large multi-step undertakings (e.g., organize a conference). You can address this with the following rule:

Rule #4: *Break big jobs down into projects.*

In this system, a *project* is anything that takes more than one step to accomplish. It is essentially just a list of tasks, ordered in a logical way, and associated with whatever planning materials you need to keep it moving ahead. You keep track of projects on your Projects list, which has one line for each project in your life, expressed as a few key words. We don't mix projects and actions on the same list because our minds tend to avoid bigger demands, given a choice. Tasks are the units of operational execution, and have a correspondingly small granularity. Projects are for longer-term thinking, and enable you to work at the "forest" level, rather than the "trees" level (the task perspective).

During the emptying stage, when you come across something to defer that is clearly a project, you should take a moment to decompose it by doing two things. First, add the name of the project to your Projects list. Don't go overboard trying to capture everything that the project involves; just write a short description on one line.

> **NOTE** If your brain starts cooking the project on high while you are emptying your inbox, then do a five-minute project planning session on a blank sheet of paper. That should give you some mental relief until it's time to do the project's next task. Stick to five minutes, though, or you'll blow the time you should be using to empty your inbox.

Second, pull out *one* concrete task from the project and put it on your Tasks list right now. You do this because of the following ironclad rule:

Rule #5: Every project must have its next task listed on the Tasks list.

The idea is that your Tasks list operates as a master list that includes concrete, executable tasks mixed together from all of your projects. Having each project represented on the Tasks list ensures that you can move all your projects ahead simultaneously.

Which of the project's possible tasks should you choose? Pick one that's small, concrete, and doesn't depend on anything else. In other words, it should be one that, if you had a chunk of time right now along with all the necessary tools, nothing would prevent you from doing. It is this one that is entered on the Tasks list. If more than one is possible, then just pick one at random. When it's time to check the task off, you will activate another from that project, and so on until it is completed.

At this point you know how to empty your inboxes, extracting bite-size chunks of executable work units into your lists and calendar. This gets you ready for the next step, where you make principled, mature decisions about what to do when you next have a chunk of time, even five minutes, to get something useful done. This, we hope, will be more effective than consulting Nostradamus or the Magic 8 Ball to figure out what you should do next.

Work Your System

All your work in steps 1–2 has put *you* in the master control center — your calendar and lists — for working smart during the day. You'll make this pay off by following the next rule:

Rule #6: During the day, work exclusively from your calendar, then your Tasks and Waiting lists.

This means no exceptions, short of truly urgent work. Not from your e-mail dinger, your phone ringer, your buddy dropping by to show you an article, or mental dialog from your fascinating inner world. This is usually a very new habit, but with practice you can switch over to letting your system guide you regarding what you should do with your time.

To do this:

- **Check your calendar:** During the day you'll be checking your calendar to see what's up. You check the calendar first, and regularly, because the activity there is time-sensitive and you have to deal with it that day.

- **Choose from your Tasks list:** Between appointments you'll fit in work from your Tasks list. To choose, match up the task with how much time you have, your brainpower at the moment, and your priorities. Mix and match to give yourself some variety.

- **Scan your Waiting list:** Sometime during the day you should scan your Waiting list for anything that's gotten stale enough to warrant a follow-up.

Review Your System

As with any well-tuned system, you have to maintain it regularly. Do it by following this rule:

Rule #7: *Your system must be comprehensive and current.*

Otherwise, you can't trust that it's up to date, and therefore that you're making the best possible decisions regarding which work to tackle next. That's why you should look at your calendar and lists regularly (once a week should do) to check for anything that's missing (think back on the week's activities for ideas) or that's been checked off. It's also a good time to see if any of your tasks are stale, and to do some soul searching to determine if, and why, anything is stuck.

> **NOTE** If you have time, it's a great practice to do a "brain dump" once a week. You simply grab a sheet of paper and start writing down all the material swirling in your head. Don't edit or organize, just go for quantity. The more you write, the better you'll feel. When you are done, toss it into your inbox, where it becomes just another attention token. Most people find that getting things off their mind like this reduces stress and helps free up the gray matter.

Now that you have the idea, it's time to see the system in action.

In Real Life

Let's summarize the workflow. During the day, stuff is flowing into your inboxes with minimal effort on your part. E-mail and voicemail are completely autonomous, but you may need some new habits to get your paper flow tightened up. You know where your e-mail and voicemail boxes are, and you're putting your physical mail and other physical tokens into your inbox and nowhere else.

Once per day you empty all of your inboxes. You probably won't do them all at once, and most people prefer to empty their voicemail and e-mail a handful of times each day, but the new habit is to empty them consciously, completely, and a limited number of times per day, instead of every five minutes.

When you're not emptying inboxes, you are working from your calendar (because those things will expire that day) and then fitting in items from your Tasks list. Finally, you'll check what you are waiting for on your Waiting list, and do necessary follow-ups.

This whole system puts you in tiptop shape for making great choices about how to spend your time. It's usually much tighter and more efficient than *ad hoc* methods that people come up with on their own.

To get a little simulated practice, pretend the following items have shown up in your e-mail inbox. Here's how you might process each one:

- **Message from the boss asking for a quick project status:** You can reply in a minute, so do so, and then archive the message to its project folder. Done!

- **Message from a partner asking to order equipment:** You can order in two minutes (let's say online ordering is fast), so order it right then, make an entry on your Waiting list to remind you that you're waiting for the equipment to arrive, and then move the e-mail to the Pending folder in case you need to follow up if the equipment is late or you have a problem with it. You'll also use it to let your partner know when the order has arrived.

- **Message asking for a quarterly report:** This will take longer than two minutes, but it can be done in one sitting (an hour or less). Since it's not date-related (that is, it should be done as soon as possible), make an entry on your Tasks list.

- **Message setting up a meeting for next week:** The proposed date is OK, so reply to confirm, put the appointment on your calendar, and then delete the message.

- **Message asking to arrange a conference on a specific date:** This is a complex multi-step task, so first add an entry to the Projects list. Then pull out a reasonable starting task (e.g., "research conference venues") and add it to the Tasks list. Next, put the date on your calendar (perhaps with some "see the train a-comin'" reminder points one and two months prior, for example), and then finally move the message into a new e-mail project folder you create for messages and attachments related to that conference.

How It Works

Having a coherent system to structure your work is immediately helpful at the practical, rubber-meets-the-road level because you are more efficient and can get more done in less time. It also provides some farther-reaching benefits. For one, consistently practicing this method has a way of lowering stress because you don't have to keep track of things in your head. If you've ever had trouble falling asleep because all the things you need to do are spinning around your head (e.g., the dripping faucet, the insurance claim problem, etc.) you'll see the value of an efficient system that helps you get your work done.

A related benefit is that it can free up your brainpower and creativity because you no longer waste mental CPU cycles on processing things needing attention inefficiently in the subconscious, rather than keeping the mind empty of all but what you're doing in the moment. You might be surprised by how effortlessly ideas and solutions start coming to you.

A good system can also help you avoid procrastination because when you are switching to a new task, you don't have to think long and hard about what to do next. Within 15 seconds you can pick something and then just "point and shoot." This works partly because you've broken down tasks into bite-size pieces that won't seem overwhelming. You've also reduced the significant energy that decision-making takes by front-loading it at emptying time. For an in-depth analysis of the costs of decisions, see the fascinating book *The Paradox of Choice: Why More Is Less*, by Barry Schwartz (New York: Ecco, 2003).

The Seven Rules Reference

Rule #1: Everything needing your attention goes into inboxes.

Rule #2: Empty all of your inboxes every day.

Rule #3: Process inbox items in order, one item at a time, with no skipping or putting back — and, except for small items, no doing!

Rule #4: Break big jobs down into projects.

Rule #5: Every project must have its next task listed on the Tasks list.

Rule #6: During the day, work exclusively from your calendar, then your Tasks and Waiting lists.

Rule #7: Your system must be comprehensive and current.

See Also

■ Richard Koch, *The 80-20 Principle* (New York: Doubleday, 2008). This is the definitive guide to not simply doing things more efficiently, but being more *effective*. He describes an idea called the "Pareto principle," which observes that not all causes have the same significance. Astonishingly, often a small minority (the "vital few") have a far greater impact than most other things (the "trivial many"). In the typical relationship, 20% of things you do account for 80% of the results, but those numbers are misleading because they do not need to sum to 100. Actual relationships might be 80-10 or 90-30, for example. Koch lists fascinating examples, such as 20% of criminals account for 80% of crime, 20% of motorists cause 80% of accidents, or 20% of your clothes will be worn 80% of the time.

■ Patrick Lencioni, *Death by Meeting* (San Francisco: Jossey-Bass, 2004). Meetings are the bane of many organizations. This book provides an original perspective on how to make them more effective, including identifying four specific types of meetings, when to use which type, and how to run them well.

■ The starting point for a Getting Things Done community is the public forum at www.davidco.com/forum/forumdisplay.php?5-PUBLIC-Discuss-Getting-Things-Done. The folks there are knowledgeable and eager to help newcomers. For related blogs, check out *Zen Habits* at http://zenhabits .net/ and *Productivity501* at www.productivity501.com/.

Notes

1. David Allen, *Getting Things Done: The Art of Stress-Free Productivity* (New York: Penguin Books, 2002). Allen's work is a tight and refreshing take on classic time-management ideas, along with a dose of Zen. It is detailed, rigorous, and highly comprehensive, and it is now the de facto standard for implementing a reliable self-management system. There is a large community of helpful practitioners, and tools galore. Some are listed below in the "See Also" section.

Hack 22: Locate Lost Items

Professor Solomon

Did you know that most lost objects are found within half a meter of where they were lost? Learn a simple algorithm to find items when you lose them.

We all lose things. It's a universal problem, intrinsic to being human, or at least to having possessions. It's also an age-old problem; Neanderthals probably misplaced objects. No one is immune from this dismaying — and sometimes disastrous — occurrence.

Every day, millions of objects are misplaced in the United States alone. Among them are wallets, purses, jewelry, car keys, tools, hats, eyeglasses, theater tickets, documents — you name it. The monetary value of lost or misplaced objects can be estimated at $50 million dollars per day. Of course, many of these are later found; what's even more troubling is the productivity permanently lost looking for missing objects, which can be estimated at $1.5 billion every year, just in the U.S.[1]

Most of those objects could have been found easily, within minutes, by following a method: specifically, the following twelve principles for finding lost objects.

How It Works

The twelve principles are a set of precepts designed to lead you *directly* to your missing object. Like most people, I've had years of painful experience constantly misplacing things, often items that were crucial to my daily functioning, such as car keys or eyeglasses. It was ridiculous, but then it dawned on me that lost objects can be found easily if one is prepared to conduct a systematic search — that is to say, to follow a set of fundamental guidelines. These guidelines evolved from my years of losing and, when lucky, finding.

In Action

The first three principles are preparatory. They are designed to prepare you for the actual search. Don't start looking for the object until you're ready to do so; this is absolutely critical. Here are those initial principles:

1. Don't look for it.

   Your basic instinct is to immediately start looking for the object, to search for it in a random fashion, to start rummaging about. You must resist this urge. It's what I call the *basic blunder*. As urgently as you may need the object, restrain yourself. Don't look for it yet. Wait until you have some idea *where* to look.

2. It's not lost, *you* are.

   Let's face it — the problem is not really with the object, but with ourselves. There are no missing objects, only unsystematic searchers. Once you accept that fact — once you admit to yourself that you are the problem — you're on your way to finding your lost object.

3. Remember the Three C's.

   The key to a successful search is the proper state of mind, and you must attain that state before beginning the search, which means paying attention to the following "Three C's":

   - **Comfort:** Make yourself physically comfortable. Sit in a comfortable chair. Take off your shoes. Loosen up.
   - **Calmness:** The misplacement has disrupted your day, and you're probably seething with negative thoughts. Empty your mind of such thoughts. Relax and breathe deeply.
   - **Confidence:** Tell yourself that it's going to be a breeze, the easiest thing in the world. You're just minutes away from finding that object.

   All right! Now you're ready to begin a *systematic* search. Principles four through twelve are designed to physically lead you to the missing object. Go through them step by step until the object is found.

4. It's where it's supposed to be.

Amazingly, things are often right where they're supposed to be. Is there a place where your coat, for example, is normally kept? If so, look there first. You may have actually hung it up as usual, or someone in your household may have done so for you.

5. Remember domestic drift.

   If your object isn't in the place it's supposed to be, it may be where it was last used. I call this situation *domestic drift*. Where in the house were you last using that screwdriver?

6. You're looking right at it.

   It's possible to look directly at a missing object and not see it because of the agitated state of mind that often accompanies a misplacement. Your object may be staring you in the face, but you are so upset with yourself that you don't perceive it. But, hey, what's with the agitation? Go back to the Three C's and get calm, then check out what's right in front of you.

7. Consider the camouflage effect.

   Sometimes a missing object is indeed where it's supposed to be, or where you last remember having it, but it has become *hidden from view*. Something — a newspaper, a package, a sombrero — has inadvertently been placed on top of it, rendering it invisible. Look under stuff.

8. Think back.

   Actually, you probably know where the object is, because you're the one who left it there. However, the memory has sunk into the murky depths of your brain. Retrieve that memory. Think back, and it may rise to the surface.

9. Look once, look well.

   Don't run around in circles, looking again and again in the same place. If it wasn't there the first time, it won't be there the second — assuming, of course, that your first look was thorough. Be sure to make it so.

10. Check the Eureka Zone.

    I have found that many objects are in the immediate vicinity of where you figured they were. However, they have undergone a displacement — a slight shift in location that has rendered them invisible. For example, a book on a shelf may have been shoved behind other books.

    Objects often "wander" in this fashion, but in my experience they tend to travel no more than 18 inches from their original location. I call this circle with a radius of 18 inches the *Eureka Zone*. Determine the Eureka Zone of your missing object, and then search that zone meticulously.

> **NOTE** You can make a *Eureka Stik* to measure Eureka Zones from a 12-inch ruler and a printable attachment (`www.professorsolomon.com/eureka-stik` `.html`). Alternatively, remember that there are 18 inches in a cubit, which for most people is the distance from their elbow to the tip of their middle finger. (See Hack 39, "Notate Personally" for more "anthropic units.")

11. Tail thyself.

    Put on your deerstalker cap and fire up your meerschaum pipe, for you're about to follow your own trail like Sherlock Holmes. Physically retrace your steps, starting from the place where you last recall having the object. Proceed slowly and deliberately, and keep a sharp eye out. You may find a pleasant surprise along the way.

12. It wasn't you.

    When all else has failed, explore the possibility that your object hasn't been misplaced — it's been misappropriated. Someone has borrowed it and failed to inform you. And it's probably someone you know well, such as a spouse, a sibling, a roommate, or child. Approach that person and pleasantly inquire.

That's it. By now, you've probably been reunited with your missing object. Once a Loser, you've become a Finder.

In Real Life

Here's a real-life example of the twelve principles.

My friend Larry lost a bunch of checks. He had arrived at his bank, parked, and looked for the checks, which were made out to his business and which he intended to deposit. They were nowhere to be found. Panicking, he clawed through his pockets and rummaged around the car, pawing through the glove compartment, poking about beneath the seat. Nothing!

At that point he decided to apply the twelve principles (to which I had introduced him). He had already, he realized, violated principle one: "Don't look for it." But maybe it wasn't too late. So he began by applying the Three C's — adjusting the car seat to make himself comfortable, taking deep breaths to calm himself, and assuring himself that he was going to find those checks.

Next, he applied principle six: "You're looking right at it." Alas, the dashboard was empty.

Then he remembered principle eight: "Think back." Settling back in the seat, he allowed his recent memories to surface, and he recalled how earlier, at home, he had gathered together both the checks and some letters to be mailed at the post office. Oh, no — he must have dropped everything into the mailbox!

Larry drove back to the post office, and they allowed him to look through the hamper in the back room. The checks weren't there.

Returning to his car, Larry continued to think back, and he recalled something else. After his initial stop at the post office, he had scooped up the trash in his car — bags, wrappers, newspapers — and thrown it all away while in a parking lot. Could the checks have been in with that trash? Larry was soon hopping into the trash bin in that parking lot, a bin into which he might have deposited his checks. Sure enough, there they were. He climbed out of the bin in triumph.

When he related this to me, I congratulated Larry on his successful use of my method. Of course, he might have found his checks faster if he had stayed calm, started with the first principle, and proceeded through the other eleven principles methodically.

See Also

- Robert C. Metzger, *Debugging by Thinking: A Multi-Disciplinary Approach* (Boston: Digital Press, 2003). The author compares the problem-solving methods of Sherlock Holmes, Lord Peter Wimsey, and Professor Solomon, and applies them to debugging computer software. Eye-opening for coders!

- "The Man with the Twisted Lip" by Sir Arthur Conan Doyle. Sherlock Holmes applies the 3 C's. Available in The Adventures of Sherlock Holmes, www.gutenberg.org/etext/1661.

- "The Purloined Letter" by Edgar Allan Poe. A classic expression of Principle Six: "You're Looking Right at It." www.gutenberg.org/etext/2148.

- For additional finder's tips, download my book (it's free) at www.professorsolomon.com.

Notes

1. These figures come from order-of-magnitude estimates made by Ron. There are 300 million people in the U.S. If even 1% of them misplace an object on a given day, that's 3 million people. Let's round this up to 5 million; we can round down later. If each of these people loses one object with an average value of $10, that's $50 million worth of objects lost a day, or about $15 billion lost annually (rounding down quite a bit). If each of these people spends just 10 minutes looking for the object, that's 50 million minutes of wasted time, or about a million hours, rounding up. If each

person's time is worth just $5 an hour (rounding down from the Federal minimum wage of $7.25), that's $5 million of lost productivity every day, or about $1.5 billion annually.

Hack 23: Huffman-Code Your Life

Make your life and thought more efficient by making more frequently used items and ideas smaller, more accessible, or otherwise easier to use.

Huffman coding is a kind of data compression discovered by information theorist David Huffman in 1951. It can be used to compress any set of symbols that occur with varying probability, such as letters of the alphabet.

For the purposes of this hack, the most salient feature of Huffman coding is that more common, probable, or frequently used characters are encoded more efficiently. For a glimpse of this principle in action, consider Morse code, which doesn't use Huffman coding, but does anticipate it. The two most commonly used letters in English, "e" and "t," are represented by a compact and easy-to-remember single dot and single dash, respectively (· and -). Conversely, "q," which is used much less often in English, must make do with two dashes, a dot, and another dash (- - · -). This is harder to remember, harder to transmit, and harder to transcribe. It doesn't matter much, though, because you seldom need to send a *q*, compared to an *e* or a *t*.

A similar idea, but in this case implemented in a dynamic, rather than a static way, is the Recent Calls menu on many mobile phones. The most recent phone number you have called, or that has called you, goes to the top of the menu and is removed from lower down the list if necessary. The second most-recent call then becomes the second item in the list, and so on. Because the Recent Calls menu is only 10 or 20 items long, seldom-used numbers eventually "drop off" the bottom of the menu. Nevertheless, because most people usually call a few numbers over and over (immediate family, close friends, coworkers), the Recent Calls menu is very convenient. Indeed, we've heard some people remark that they never use their phone's address book features, and rely exclusively on their Recent Calls menus.

In Action

Huffman-coding your life means generalizing the principle just outlined, whether statically or dynamically. We'll examine it in several different contexts, including how to file paper documents, store everyday clothing, pack for a trip, and make your kitchen more efficient.

The Noguchi Filing System

Some paper filing systems file items alphabetically, some by subject matter, others by a combination of both. Much like the Recent Calls menu on your mobile phone, the Noguchi Filing System, developed by Noguchi Yukio in 1993,[1] places your most frequently used files at the left of a row of such files for easy access.

Whenever you use a file in this system, simply return it to the left of the row. Thus, most of the items you need to access will always be among the first few files.

Occasionally, you will need to dig a little deeper for an older file. These files won't be too much farther to the right, and they will be easy to find because of date and contextual cues provided by surrounding files.

Ancient files that you haven't accessed in a long time (such as your 1999 tax forms) "fall off" the rightmost, oldest end of the row and are archived in long-term storage with similar files (in this case, perhaps in a box labeled "1999").

The original Noguchi system has a number of other interesting features, such as using cropped, dated, and color-coded manila envelopes, rather than folders, to store documents, but the time-sort aspect is the most innovative and interesting feature.

Organizing Your Clothes

Making your most frequently worn items of clothing most accessible is probably something you do to some degree anyway, so it serves to illustrate Huffman coding in everyday life very well. You might place underwear and socks, which are worn every day, in your top dresser drawers. In-season shirts and pants might go into lower drawers. Less frequently worn items (dress pants, clothes for yard work, travel clothes) might go into progressively less convenient locations, and winter clothes can be stored in a trunk in the garage in the summer. With a little thought about Huffman coding and considering what you wear frequently, you might find ways to arrange your clothes that are even more efficient.

Packing for a Trip

Of course, similar principles apply to packing for a trip. For example, don't bury medication you take several times a day at the bottom of your backpack under a pile of dirty laundry. However, a slightly different Huffman-based principle also applies, in terms of bulk and weight rather than accessibility.

Packing Huffman-style in this case means also making sure that items you use frequently (toothbrush, cell phone, laptop) are small and light. Conversely, items you will only use once (such as food and water) and items you will not have to carry long (such as a gift for your hosts) can be heavier or bulkier.

Of course, you can always put the frequently used, light objects in your carry-on luggage, and that gift for your hosts, which is heavy and which you won't need until you get there, in your checked luggage. The latter is the equivalent of items "falling off the end of" your Recent Calls menu or a row of Noguchi files.

Organizing Your Kitchen

Huffman-coding your kitchen can save you a lot of time and energy. Placing your pots and pans near the stove is pretty obvious, but consider where you store your utensils. Instead of sorting them by type, wouldn't it make sense to have a drawer that contains only the most frequently used utensils? Instead of filling the drawer with all the stirring spoons or spatulas, fill it with your favorite spoon, favorite spatula, favorite tongs, can opener, and so on, storing the other spoons and spatulas in a secondary drawer. If you have friends over to eat regularly, think about using the cabinets and drawers closest to the entrance of the kitchen to store your everyday flatware and dinnerware. That way, people who need a plate or fork can duck in and grab it without disturbing someone cooking and without rummaging through all the cabinets.

Consider doing the same with your pantry, placing often-used items like peanut butter or cans of soup and tuna on the most accessible shelves and using higher shelves for items you use less often, like that can of baby corn you bought on a whim and plan to use in something someday. Likewise, place a small box on your seasoning shelf to hold the spices you use most — salt, pepper, onion powder, curry, or whatever you enjoy — so that when you're cooking you can quickly grab the item you need without digging everything out. (If you use a spice rack, you can similarly arrange the containers, putting your most frequently used items closest to your stove.)

How It Works

The basic principles of Huffman coding, in the loose sense we're using here, may seem obvious. After all, don't you normally carry your medication in your carry-on bag and the cast-metal bookends for your hosts in your checked luggage, and not the other way around?

What's important is the ability to generalize this principle to anything you can imagine. In addition to the examples described in the preceding section, consider applying the Huffman principle to these areas of life:

- office
- workshop
- library or bookshelves
- other collections, such as board games or DVDs
- web browser bookmarks

In Real Life

When you become aware of what we're calling Huffman coding, you begin looking for it, or ways to implement it, *everywhere*. For example, Ron was recently wishing his new Android had a Recent Apps menu and was about to search the Android Market for a Recent Apps app, when he accidentally discovered how to call up such a menu by long-pressing the Home button below the screen.

Ron's method of studying paper books is also very similar to the Noguchi system. He keeps a pile of books on his nightstand. When he feels like reading one, he pulls it out of the pile and reads a chapter or two. When he's finished, he drops the book on the top of the pile.

As he acquires more books, the pile grows higher and more unsteady, until he is forced to winnow it. He carries the books he is no longer interested in at the moment back to the library, where first they enter another pile and finally are shelved.

This may seem like an inefficient way to get any kind of serious reading done, but Ron has been completing a book or more per week for a couple of decades, as well as dipping into and skimming many more. He can also usually find the references for whatever he's currently working on within a few minutes.

See Also

- "Power law," Wikipedia contributors, accessed April 14, 2011, http://en.wikipedia.org/w/index.php?title=Power_law&oldid=421458465.

Notes

1. "The Noguchi Filing System," William Lise, accessed April 14, 2011, http://replay.waybackmachine.org/20051224/http://www.lise.jp/honyaku/noguchi.html.

Hack 24: Knock Off Work

Accomplish impressive amounts of work by simply doing things that are more fun and superficially less important.

It may sound unbelievable, but procrastinating on important tasks may actually be useful, if you do it thoughtfully. You can accomplish many things that are fun, urgent, and truly important by postponing other things that are boring and only apparently urgent or important. The technique we will explore for doing this is called *structured procrastination*, a term coined by John Perry, a Stanford professor of philosophy, in the mid-1990s (www.structuredprocrastination.com/).

Based on an informal survey, it seems that many people have invented structured procrastination independently. This hack can't hope to rival the charm and clarity of Perry's presentation, so we urge you to read the original piece on his site. It's written somewhat tongue in cheek, but in our experience, the technique does work, although there is a certain inevitable quantum of *Sturm und Drang* involved.

In Action

The following is a brief, four-step program describing how to engage in structured procrastination. It may seem like there's not much to it, but it can help you become — or at least gain a reputation as — a highly productive person.

1. Choose a task that seems to be enormously important or urgent or both, but actually isn't. We'll call this your *scare task*. For example, you might choose writing a doctoral thesis with a deadline three years in the future. It might seem you should get started right away, but there is probably room for a bit of creative dawdling.

   Sometimes your scare task is not of your choosing, such as filling out your federal income tax forms. You could make good use of such a task anyway. It's all grist for the ever-cycling structured procrastination mill, which, as you shall see, is powered by Escher's waterfall.

2. Ignore this task in favor of other, more immediately rewarding tasks, such as designing idiosyncratic crossword puzzles or fleshing out a constructed world you've been imagining since childhood. (We suspect Middle-earth was created during stolen moments in Tolkien's life as a triumph of structured procrastination.)

3. As you complete various other more interesting tasks, the deadline on your notionally more important task will be preparing to fly by. However, you will have created a pile of crossword puzzles you'll be proud to submit to Will Shortz, or a conworld that's so rich and real the inhabitants have actually attained sapience and now worship you as their god.

4. Return to step 1 and select a new scare task that will make the old one look like playing hooky at the mall. Then do the old one, if it hasn't already resolved itself of its own accord. (See "In Real Life," below, for an example of a "must-do" task that evaporated.) This should now be much easier, because not only does it seem less daunting than the new scare task, but living with it awhile has probably lessened your dread somewhat. Letting

it percolate in the back of your mind has probably given you some new ideas about how to tackle it (Hack 58, "Retreat and Reboot"), and moreover the tasks you've been doing all along have increased your momentum and confidence.

How It Works

There are a couple of keys to this hack:

- Accept that you will procrastinate, and be ready for it by having appropriate and productive things to work on when you do, instead of believing you'll never procrastinate or that you can eliminate doing so. These tasks can break a mental block and get you moving again, doing something instead of feeling sick and scared, or surfing bad daytime TV.

- Learn to discern what is really important and urgent from what only seems so. If you delay a task, will it significantly affect you or anyone else? If so, how badly? Does your deadline have any flexibility? And so on. You must have actual clarity about these issues, at least long enough to safely fool yourself about them.

John Perry says structured procrastination works because "one is in effect constantly perpetrating a pyramid scheme on oneself. . . This is not a problem, because virtually all procrastinators have excellent self-deceptive skills also." There is a certain amount of truth to this, but we think the pyramid metaphor misses an important aspect of the technique, although Perry himself probably didn't miss it. Metaphorically, the currency in this pyramid scheme is not real money. The ever-bigger and ever-more-important tasks you must keep putting at the top of your pyramid of priorities are not in fact bigger and more important, or at least not as much as you tell yourself. It's enough that they only *seem* more important at the time. Thus, rather than a pyramid scheme, we think a better metaphor would be a conceptual version of the ever-rising Penrose staircase illusion (see Figure 24-1) or the auditory Shepard tone (http://en.wikipedia.org/wiki/Shepard_tone).

In Real Life

Ron has used structured procrastination for many years with good effect. Here's an example from several years ago, minus some identifying details.

Ron was working as a technical writer in a small software department. Much of the writing consisted of editing and rewriting the engineers' hasty and sloppy notes to turn them into documentation fit for the public. However, he enjoyed much more the task of writing programs that automated the documentation process. It gave him a chance to be creative about combining his writing and coding skills.

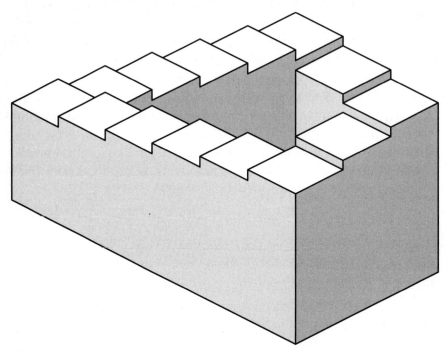

Figure 24-1: Penrose staircase

He was also occasionally persuaded (or ordered) to do software testing, although he hated it. One day Ron was asked to test some new microcontroller software. He didn't want to, so he signed up as the last person on the list. Meanwhile, he focused on automating the documentation. The engineers and the testers themselves took turns passing the microcontroller around, and by the time it was Ron's turn, they had found so many bugs that they decided it was more useful to fix them than test it anymore. He ended up not having to test the microcontroller, and instead spent all his time during this round of tests doing the fun and creative work he preferred. Furthermore, the documentation had never looked better, and he received a number of compliments about it.

NOTE Be aware that this technique is like playing Tetris. You can't do it forever. You may be the world champion Tetris player, but eventually your screen is going to fill up with little squares, and you're going to have to come clean with yourself about what your real priorities are so you can take care of any actually important business you've been putting off. That's OK; take a little time to make sure you're not late for a class or doctor appointment and haven't spent all your lunch money on quarters. Then you can go back to playing Tetris.

See Also

- Humorist Robert Benchley's essay "How to Get Things Done" (`http://hackvan.com/etext/how-to-get-things-done-despite-procrastination.txt`) is the source of the quotation, "Anyone can do any amount of work, provided it isn't the work he is supposed to be doing at that moment," and anticipates John Perry's essay by about 50 years.
- "The Art of Productive Procrastination," Saul Griffith, *Make:* Vol. 25. This short article contains a number of useful techniques similar to structured procrastination.

tivity and Productivity

Creativity and productivity: making new stuff and getting work done go hand-in-hand. You can even use your creativity to make stuff that will help you get work done more productively (Hack 28, "Turn a Job Into a Game," and Hack 29, "Scrumble for Glory"). The worker and the artist should be friends.

That said, because there are already so many productivity tips in Chapter 4, "Time Management," this chapter tilts a bit toward the creativity side. You'll learn how to write a revolutionary manifesto for fun and prophecy (Hack 25, "Manifest Yourself"), find inspiration from the past (Hack 30, "Salvage a Vintage Hack") and from possible futures (Hack 31, "Mine the Future"), dare to be creative (Hack 34, "Don't Know What You're Doing"), and why it's OK if the result is weird (Hack 26, "Woo the Muse of the Odd") or even downright bad (Hack 27, "Seek Bad Examples," and Hack 33, "Make Happy Mistakes").

We had a lot of fun with this chapter. It's hard to be creative without having fun, so we hope you have at least as much fun with these hacks, and we hope you'll import some of that creative zest to wherever you need to get work done.

Hack 25: Manifest Yourself

Writing a manifesto — yes, like the Communist Manifesto, the Cluetrain Manifesto, or the Surrealist Manifesto — can crystallize your intentions about a creative project and light its fuse. Stop trying so hard to be cool, and get fired up.

A manifesto is a person or group's statement of their philosophy, especially their principles and what they intend to do about them. Sometimes this is not very nice, which is why manifestos have a bad name among some people. Mostly, however, manifestos are simply forceful and heartfelt; they can be extremely useful to produce and to have, and they're definitely fun to write!

Manifestos can be artistic, political, religious, or ethical in nature. They go by many names; for example, political manifestos are often called *platforms* (such as the Democratic National Platform in the U.S.), and religious manifestos are sometimes called *creeds* or *credos*, such as the Apostles' Creed in Christianity.

A manifesto can clarify and sharpen your views — sharpen like a bayonet. They can fill you with purpose and charge your work with feeling. Why not write your own?

In Action

Manifestos are like position papers, but usually with much more emotional language. They roughly fall into two types:

- The first type attempts to persuade others about the rightness of a philosophical position. The Communist Manifesto (www.gutenberg.org/etext/61) might be considered one of these.

- The second type preaches to the converted, attempting to circle the wagons, rally the troops, and strengthen their faith, if you will permit an extremely mixed metaphor. Arguably, Tristan Tzara's 1918 Dada Manifesto (www.391.org/manifestos/19180323tristantzara_dadamanifesto.htm) can be considered an example of this type.

The first thing you need to do when writing a manifesto is decide which type yours will be. Type 1 tends to be more reasonable, but Type 2 can use more colorfully vituperative language and can be more fun to write.

Once you've decided who your audience is, just start writing and really let go. State what you believe. State what you are, and what you're not. State what you hate and who you disagree with. State the purpose of what you want to do, and what evil forces you hope to defeat with your efforts. Sketch the bright new world you hope to bring forth. For once, let go of irony and intellectual detachment and let yourself be as dramatic, unfair, selfish, and flamboyant as you need to be. One of the great strengths of the excess of Type 2 manifestos is that it helps you break free of the compulsion to be objective and intellectualized, which can hinder your style if you're trying to do something creative. There will be time enough to regain your adult composure later; for now, give voice to the fist-shaking teenager inside, and bring along the spray paint and staple guns.

Anyone can write a manifesto just by stating their views in a coherent way, but before you get started, you might want to read a few well-known manifestos to improve your style of fulmination and your understanding of manifesto mechanics.

Artistic Manifestos

■ The Ambient Music Manifesto

    `www.ele-mental.org/ele_ment/said&did/eno_ambient.html`

■ The Manifesto of the Futurist Programmers

    `www.graficaobscura.com/future/futman.html`

Political Manifestos

■ The Cluetrain Manifesto

    `www.cluetrain.com/`

■ The GNU Manifesto

    `www.gnu.org/gnu/manifesto.html`

Ethical Manifestos

■ The Hedonistic Imperative

    `www.hedweb.com/`

■ The Universal Declaration of Human Rights

    `www.ohchr.org/en/udhr/pages/introduction.aspx`

How It Works

In this case, how it works is quite simple. Deciding to write your views down, all at the same time and all in one place, forces you to really examine them and pin them down in a way you can articulate. Having to explain them to someone — the whole world — means you'll probably learn more about them yourself.

The main key, however, lies in what makes your statement a manifesto: putting yourself into a shamelessly passionate and biased mindset, using dramatic and forceful language, and daring to take up space in the ideosphere to metaphorically shout your beliefs from soapboxes and the rooftops with conviction. Focusing on yourself and what you believe, and fully committing to it, can give your work a thrust and edge that it never has when you work from a "cool" place of objectivity or detachment. It can infuse your viewpoint with a level of feeling and energy you may have thought you had lost forever, or never let yourself tap into before. Setting your thoughts in order is useful, but drumming up the feeling and belief to set them on fire is something else.

In Real Life

Between his last book and this one, Ron spent some time working on a book of board games. The project eventually succumbed to its sheer scope; he and his co-author had close to 200 submissions and no way to adequately playtest them. Had it been published, it would have been called Games Unboxed, and it contained a number of board and card games you could play with stuff around the house.

Why would people want to waste time on a board game made of toothpicks and pennies when they could play Cranium, Settlers of Catan, or YourCity-opoly, not to mention *Halo 3* or *World of Warcraft*? Ron had some strong feelings about that question, and it was to answer it that he sat down to write "The Unboxed Games Manifesto", a slightly updated version of which can be found in Appendix A. Please take a few minutes to read it.

See Also

- You can find interesting collections of manifestos at `http://Manifestos .net` and `http://ChangeThis.com`.
- David Wahl's "Write a Manifesto: Creativity Tip" (`www .creativecreativity.com/2007/04/write_a_manifes.html`) is an excellent short piece on why and how to write a manifesto.

Hack 26: Woo the Muse of the Odd

By focusing on the weird in your work and in yourself, you can break new ground, and have a lot more fun doing it.

Lafcadio Hearn, the nineteenth-century fantasy writer, vowed to draw attention to his writing by emphasizing the exotic and outré in his work. He must have done something right, because Amazon's page for him currently shows 54 books available for sale by or about him. We can attest he could certainly write a good Japanese ghost story: exotic, yet with enough historical context for a twenty-first-century Westerner to grasp. His fantasy most reminds us of his approximate contemporary Lord Dunsany, and that's a high compliment. Hearn wrote in an 1883 letter:

By purchasing queer books and following odd subjects I have been able to give myself the air of knowing more than I do; but none of my work would bear the scrutiny of a specialist; I would like, however, to show you my library. It cost me only about $2,000; but every volume is queer. Knowing that I have nothing resembling genius, and that any ordinary talent must be supplemented with some sort of curious study in order to place it above the mediocre line, I am striving to woo the Muse of the Odd, and hope to succeed in thus attracting some little attention.[1]

Perhaps by following strange avenues, you too can increase the appeal of your work. That is a good reason, but we will examine others: Weirdness helps you learn, helps you focus, sets the rules for your work and the work of others, and refines your unique aesthetic.

In Action

Let's explore in more depth these reasons to be weird and do weird work.

Weirdness Helps You Learn

Weird projects are more fun to work on. You learn better if you're not afraid to try some absurd or silly things. Even when you are taking baby steps in learning an art, a craft, or a science, try making your creations offbeat.

When Ron was learning model rocketry in junior high school, the first rocket he built accidentally blew up. The second rocket he built committed suicide at his command. The Suicide I, as it was called, did not have a parachute by design. The nose cone was glued into place and the clip holding the engine was loosened so that when the engine attempted to eject the parachute by expelling gas into the body of the rocket, the engine would eject itself instead. The nose of the rocket then became the heaviest part and it swung down to point at the earth. The rocket then plummeted straight down, embedding itself nose-first six inches into the ground.

It was enormously satisfying for a 12-year-old boy, and almost as satisfying when he built a clone as a demo for a friend a few years ago. Ron learned more about how to control the rocket, and the physics involved, than he would have by building a more conventional project, and the humor and perversity of making a rocket that would destroy itself was irresistible. It led to his motto, "No science without madness!"

Recently, as an attempt to explore robotics, he designed (but has not yet built) a LEGO Mindstorms NXT robot with stereo hearing that would chase his Pomeranian dog, Humphrey, when he barked. Like the Suicide I, the design served no immediate purpose other than fun — it probably wouldn't even teach

Humphrey not to bark so much. However, Ron is more motivated to build it than any stock robot from a LEGO instruction book; it's next on the agenda when he becomes obsessed with LEGO robots again. Thus, he's motivated to learn because of his weird design.

The Weird Are Pioneers

If your work is strange enough, it may constitute a new field, form, or medium. To some degree, that means you get to define the rules for the new field, and therefore your work will be its paradigm. As science fiction writer R. A. Lafferty put it in his story "Selenium Ghosts of the Eighteen Seventies":

The earliest art in a new field is always the freshest and is often the best. Homer composed the first and freshest, and probably the best, epic poetry. Whatever cave man did the first painting, it remains among the freshest as well as the best paintings ever done. Aeschylus composed the first and best tragic dramas, Euclid invented the first and best of the artful mathematics (we speak here of mathematics as an art without being concerned with its accuracy or practicality). . .

Of course, not everyone can simply clap their hands and invent something that's never been done before. Lafferty's passage is written in hindsight and (we think) somewhat jokingly. But at least don't worry about making your work fit into an established field or discipline. Strike out and break new ground, whether on this planet or another.

Weird Is Its Own Aesthetic

We speak about this elsewhere in the book, and won't recapitulate it here. However, it's worth noting that the weird and the bad have in common that they're shunned by people who prefer the conventionally good or even mediocre — that is, most people. Thus, by spending time acquainting yourself with the weird and the bad, you give yourself the freedom to develop aesthetically in ways that most people never will. This will change you, provide you with fresh angles in your personality and encourage you to put them into your work even when they don't exactly fit expectations. It will make your work lively and original, setting it apart from the conventional.

As science fiction writer Bruce Sterling said in his address to the Computer Game Developers Conference in 1991, which reminded the world of the phrase "woo the Muse of the Odd":

Don't become a well-rounded person. Well-rounded people are smooth and dull. Become a thoroughly spiky person. Grow spikes from every angle. Stick in their throats like a pufferfish.[2]

Well-rounded art is smooth, sweet, and dull. Many people like that, but many others want a bit of novelty, at least. Too much and you might catch in their throats as Sterling suggests, of course. Some few will still be able to swallow your work, however; some people of refined taste *like* pufferfish. They will be your audience. They will be your people. Pufferfish is considered one of the greatest delicacies in Japan. Perhaps Lafcadio would appreciate the irony.

Ron has a kind of mathematical inequality that shows his aesthetic priorities. Perhaps it will speak to you:

Innovative success > innovative failure > conventional success > conventional failure.

In this scheme of things, innovative failure is preferable to everything except innovative success, and conventional failure is the least preferred of all. However, sometimes even conventional failure has its place. See Hack 27, "Seek Bad Examples," for suggestions on making the most of both innovative and conventional flops.

Accepting Your Weirdness Enables You to Focus

Most of this hack has been about the benefits of doing weird things and freeing yourself to make things that are weird, but now we're going to shade into the benefits of simply *being* weird. If one can avoid the opposite extreme of becoming a self-obsessed dilettante, letting one's freak flag fly concentrates the mind wonderfully.

Mindhacker contributor John Braley used to play in chess tournaments at a high level, ranked as an International Master. He sometimes found that in high-pressure tournaments — and almost only then — he would feel compelled to engage in OCD-style behavior, such as touching every other linoleum tile in a long hallway with his foot.

When John allowed himself to succumb to what he thought of as weird, superstitious behavior, it became a kind of outlet for his stress; not worrying about it let him focus on his game and play better, in his own estimation. Perhaps this is akin to the technique of "ubiquitous capture," which means getting everything obsessing you down, onto paper or into computer memory, out into the world, anywhere but in your head, so you can retain "mind like water."

It's hard to be weird, but it's even harder not to be, if you are.

In Real Life

Here are a few pioneers to whet your weird and inspire you to make your own. We'll let Bruce Sterling have the last word:

Follow your weird, ladies and gentlemen. Forget trying to pass for normal. Follow your geekdom. Embrace your nerditude ... don't read Shakespeare. Read Webster's revenge plays. Don't read Homer and Aristotle. Read Herodotus where he's off talking about Egyptian women having public sex with goats. If you want to read about myth don't read Joseph Campbell, read about convulsive religion, read about voodoo and the Millerites and the Munster Anabaptists. There are hundreds of years of extremities, there are vast legacies of mutants. There have always been geeks. There will always be geeks. Become the apotheosis of geek. Learn who your spiritual ancestors were. You didn't come here from nowhere. There are reasons why you're here. Learn those reasons. Learn about the stuff that was buried because it was too experimental or embarrassing or inexplicable or uncomfortable or dangerous.[3]

If you're interested in weird art and media, the following table provides pointers to many examples of it. The "See Also" and "Notes" sections provide further references.

FORM	EXEMPLAR
Mystery Novels	Harry Stephen Keeler
Science Fiction	R. A. Lafferty, Philip K. Dick, Barrington Bayley, Robert Anton Wilson
Fantasy	Avram Davidson
Poetry	Ben Marcus
Interactive Fiction	For a Change; The Gostak
Cuisine	Molecular gastronomy
Comics	*Tales of the Beanworld*
Opera	*The Forest*, by David Byrne; *VALIS*, by Tod Machover
Game Design	See `www.ludism.org/scwiki/IslandOfMisfitGames`
Conlangs/ Languages	Artlangs, `http://en.wikipedia.org/wiki/Artistic_language`
Travel	*Lonely Planet Guide to Experimental Travel*. Also, "Weird" and "Curiosities" books, such as *Washington Curiosities*, by Harriet Baskas
Web	The Wikipedia Unusual Articles Page (see Hack 55, "Take the One-Question IQ Test")
Computer Programming	Esoteric languages: `http://esolangs.org/wiki/Language_list`
Music	John Cage; *Re/Search: Incredibly Strange Music*; Tuvan throat singing (of course, it's not weird to Tuvans, but it did wonders for Nobel-winning physicist Richard Feynman)

See Also

- Maria Bustillos, *Dorkismo: the Macho of the Dork* (Los Angeles: Accidental Books, 2008). This is one of the best books we know on living life as a geek and letting live. If you're weird and you're sick of trying to be cool, we couldn't recommend this book more highly.

- Lafcadio Hearn, *Kwaidan: Stories and Studies of Strange Things* (www .gutenberg.org/ebooks/1210). One of Hearn's better-known collections; probably a good place to start if you want to read him.

Notes

1. Lafcadio Hearn to W. D. O'Connor, 1883. *The Life and Letters of Lafcadio Hearn, Volume 1*, pp. 290-91.
2. "The Wonderful Power of Storytelling," Bruce Sterling, March 1991, https://w2.eff.org/Misc/Publications/Bruce_Sterling/comp_game_designers.article.
3. Ibid.

Hack 27: Seek Bad Examples

Let others make your mistakes for you by experiencing their astoundingly bad works, and take courage from the fact that few works are so bad that they have no merit at all.

We presume you know how to find good examples of art, culture, and technology, and that you're taking the time to experience and analyze them. It's easy to find inspiration and guidance from the best, and it's crucial to see how things are done well when you're learning how to do them. However, the power of this hack comes from being able to compare the good with the bad, and to broaden your thinking beyond the conventional by seeing the broad spectrum of human creativity, instead of only a few shades.

War isn't peace, freedom isn't slavery, and ignorance isn't strength, but sometimes things are so bad they're good. You can learn from others' mistakes in a variety of ways, and you can find the grain of goodness in the worst work. Go forth into the sewers of human culture, and be not afraid.

In Action

There are ways to learn from bad examples. Here are some reasons we've found to seek them. You may find other reasons as you go along, but this is some of the gold we've panned out of all that muck.

Hone Your Individual Aesthetic Sense

Most people have definite ideas of what constitutes good art. Some have even been taught institutionalized standards of aesthetic taste — what's widely considered to be "good" and "bad." However, there are many different *kinds* of goodness, and little work is so bad that it holds no interest for its own sake.

Looking at bad examples objectively and appreciating them on their own terms can help you build an individual aesthetic and refine real knowledge about what you like and don't like, as opposed to what you're told you should like. You'll also gain a richer understanding about why you like it. It's possible to wrestle bad art onto neutral conceptual ground far from cultural norms, and analyze it objectively. This can help you tune your aesthetic sense in ways that are more sophisticated and more individual than merely considering whether something is in good taste, whether it fits accepted standards, or simply whether you like it.

For this reason, it's important to look at original sources of bad art and not just satire of them. Satire already has a viewpoint, so it doesn't always enable you to develop your own views freely. You can learn things directly from bad art, and you can learn things from satire of it, but they're different things.

Avoid Mistakes

Avoiding mistakes is, of course, the main reason most people seek out bad examples. For instance, you were probably introduced to some examples of bad writing in school, but we propose that most of those examples were probably merely mediocre, not truly bad.

Truly bad art and culture often have a naively humorous quality to them that leads people to seek them out as entertainment. In the 1990s, the TV show *Mystery Science Theater 3000* capitalized on the abundance of bad movies by satirizing a new movie every week with sarcastic voice-overs. Almost 200 films were "MSTed," and the writers and cast members of the show are still in business today with the show's offshoots RiffTrax and Cinematic Titanic.

What few people realize is that MST3K and its offspring are excellent coursework in filmmaking. We've learned a lot from watching the show; often enough, a snarky comment from one of the characters identified a bit of cinema that we wouldn't have noticed consciously as bad filmmaking, but we could clearly see as such when it was highlighted. For example, during the movie *Santa Claus Conquers the Martians*, the film's actors wander off-screen, leaving the camera lingering on an empty set for several seconds, the cinematic equivalent of radio "dead air." The catcalls of the MST3K cast made us sit up and pay attention to why that moment didn't work.

After MST3K became a cult classic in its own right, fans began MSTing other noncinematic artworks, from science fiction novellas (*The Eye of Argon*[1]) to text adventure computer games (*Detective*[2]), often with the characters from the TV show offering the commentary.

Why not try your own hand at MSTing? It needn't be as elaborate as interpolating snarky comments into interactive fiction source code, as with *Detective*. It can be as simple as talking back to the screen the next time you watch a bad movie at home with your friends. After all, that's probably how the phenomenon started in the first place.

To sum up, satire shouldn't be the only way you experience bad art, but it can be invaluable in teaching you how to avoid its pitfalls yourself.

Learn How to Be Funny

Because so much bad culture is funny, you can learn a lot about how to be funny yourself by imitating it. If your work isn't meant to be comic, then you don't need to know these things; otherwise, bad art is comedy platinum, and a great place to learn the craft. It's a classic source, and many comedy masters have mined it through the years.

Bad art tends not to be self-conscious, so its mistakes are big and clear — the kinds of mistakes a self-conscious artist would notice and self-edit out. From bad art you can learn verbosity, pomposity, writing in offensive dialect and baby talk, sexism, lugubrious and melodramatic subject matter such as famous maritime disasters, bathos, histrionics, humorlessness, banality, moralizing, self-importance, and technical incompetence, such as being unable to make verse rhyme or scan. Of course, all of these characteristics are unintentional on the part of the bad artists, but you can make them yours and use them intentionally for comic effect.

By way of example, here's an excerpt from a Hale-Evans family favorite poem, "The Happy Little Cripple," by James Whitcomb Riley (approximately 1890):

> I'm thist a little cripple boy, an' never goin' to grow
> An' get a great big man at all! — 'cause Aunty told me so.
> When I was thist a baby onc't, I falled out of the bed
> An' got "The Curv'ture of the Spine" — 'at 's what the Doctor said.
> I never had no Mother nen — fer my Pa runned away
> An' dassn't come back here no more — 'cause he was drunk one day
> An' stobbed a man in thish-ere town, an' couldn't pay his fine!
> An' nen my Ma she died — an' I got "Curv'ture of the Spine!"
>
> I'm nine years old! An' you can't guess how much I weigh, I bet! —
> Last birthday I weighed thirty-three! — An' I weigh thirty yet!
> I'm awful little fer my size — I'm purt' nigh littler 'nan
> Some babies is! — an' neighbors all calls me "The Little Man!"

An' Doc one time he laughed an' said: "I 'spect, first thing you know,
You'll have a little spike-tail coat an' travel with a show!"
An' nen I laughed — till I looked round an' Aunty was a-cryin' —
Sometimes she acts like that, 'cause I got "Curv'ture of the Spine."[3]

It goes on like this for several stanzas. In 1912, a Victor Talking Machine recording was made of Riley reading this poem. We have two questions. First, would anyone care to wager on whether he read it in falsetto? Second, have you ever written anything this funny?

You can also learn to create good art using the techniques of bad art. Probably the best-known example of this is "The Most Unwanted Song" by the artistic duo Komar and Melamid (http://awp.diaart.org/km/musiccd.html). They polled the public to discover which musical forms and elements irritated the most people, and created a piece of music with composer Dave Soldier that incorporated as many of them as possible. The result is a 25-minute song that rapidly swerves from an operatic soprano rapping cowboy lyrics while "Tumbleweeds" plays in the background, to a children's chorus singing about less popular holidays such as Veterans Day, to bagpipes.

Nevertheless, people seem to overwhelmingly prefer it to the same artists' "The Most Wanted Song," a bland piece reminiscent of Céline Dion. The enduring question is why peoples' reaction to the engineered art is so different from what might be projected: Is it because they think the bad song is funny? Is it because they like its idiosyncratic quality? Is it because taste doesn't really scale from individual to broad cultural terms exactly? That's why "The Most Unwanted Song" is real art and a real exploration of aesthetics and humanity, and while it's hilarious, it's not merely funny. Komar and Melamid have continued to explore these questions in visual art, producing "Most Wanted" and "Least Wanted" paintings for several countries around the world (http://awp.diaart.org/km/).

Appreciate Artistic Passion, Commitment, and Integrity

1940s mystery writer Harry Stephen Keeler's novels are ripe for ridicule and criticism. They're filled with many of the faults listed in the last section, such as offensive dialect, opaque verbosity, and sometimes bizarre subject matter such as human skulls and sex with circus freaks. Nonetheless, Keeler is an original. There's no other writer like him. He has a unique, powerful voice, and he invented complex writing techniques such as "webwork plotting" that are still imitated today, and not necessarily for comic effect. For a more modern example of webwork plotting, see *Keyhole Factory* by William Gillespie (http://www.spinelessbooks.com/keyholefactory/index.html). You can also learn more about Keeler, if you're interested, from the Harry Stephen Keeler Society (http://site.xavier.edu/polt/keeler/).

So it is with bad artists like Keeler and many others. Their unique obsessions and innovative techniques mean that while they may be bad, they're not *merely* bad. If an artist's work is spectacularly bad, it's unconventional, and therefore it's probably creative and even innovative despite its faults. You can learn what a certain kind of artistic courage looks like from bad artists, and what it can be like to sharpen and strengthen an artistic idea and then follow through to make it real, no matter what. It takes a great deal of vision and commitment to buck convention and criticism and make something truly bad. When you find bad art, someone stepped outside of good taste and made what they made anyway, with passion and conviction. To some extent, the whole field of "outsider art" is based on this idea, and the "legitimate" art world has begun to recognize that there's merit to work that falls outside traditional standards.

The Muse of the Odd (Hack 26, "Woo the Muse of the Odd") as well as the Muse of the Bad has touched these artists, and you can learn from them. Despite missteps, horrifying failures, and unintentional humor, this is often what the cutting edge looks like; as with science and technology, artistic breakthrough is often preceded and surrounded by failure.

In Real Life

If you're interested in bad culture, the following table provides pointers to examples of bad writing, bad art, bad science, and more. The "See Also" and "Notes" sections provide further references.

FORM	EXEMPLAR
Mystery Fiction	Harry Stephen Keeler
Science Fiction	Lionel Fanthorpe
Heroic Fantasy	*The Eye of Argon*
Painting	The Museum of Bad Art
Film	Ed Wood, Roger Corman
Poetry (Bad Poets)	William McGonagall, Julia A. Moore, Amanda McKittrick Ros
Poetry (Collections)	*The Stuffed Owl*, *Pegasus Descending*, *Very Bad Poetry*, *In Search of the World's Worst Writers*
Translation	*English As She Is Spoke*
RPG	*The World of Synnibarr*
Interactive Fiction	*Detective*
Cuisine	Corporate promotional cookbooks in the mode of *The Joy of Jell-O*
Physics	*TimeCube.com*
Superhero Comics	Fletcher Hanks
Orchestral Performance	The Portland Sinfonia
Operatic Vocals	Florence Foster Jenkins

See Also

- Stephen Waller and Stephen Pile, *The Book of Heroic Failures* (Harlow: Pearson Education in association with Penguin, 2000). Pile writes, "People do not widely realize that to be really bad at something requires skill, dedication and intense originality of vision."

Notes

1. The Eye of Argon: `www.bmsc.washington.edu/people/merritt/books/Eye_of_Argon.html`.

2. Detective: `http://ifdb.tads.org/viewgame?id=imopnqh4llwkvfne`.

3. *Riley Child Rhymes*, James Whitcomb Riley: `www.gutenberg.org/ebooks/9777`.

Hack 28: Turn a Job into a Game

Mary Poppins had it right when she said, "You find the fun, and snap! The job's a game." In this hack, we'll survey some of the many resources that can make painful activities pleasurable, from housework to exercise.

You don't need to be a "zero work" (`www.whywork.org`) activist to recognize that sometimes work isn't, well, fun. If you're a gamer, or know one, the solution is obvious: Turn the work into a game. This hack contains eight mini-hacks and two complete games that will help you game the dreariest job.

In Action

The following games employ a variety of tricks to help you do (and enjoy) the tedious and frustrating things you have to do, ranging from the chance and surprise of the Honey Do Jar, Project Deck, and FitDeck, to the rigor of StickK, from the imaginal "augmented reality" of Chore Wars, Scrumble, and metaphorming, to the alphabetic weirdness of Oulipo Groceries.

The Honey Do Jar

The Honey Do Jar is a fixture of many American households. You've probably heard of it already; if you haven't, you might want to try it — many, many people have found it useful. It consists of a jar full of little slips of paper on which a less-handy member of the household has written job requests for a handier one: "Honey, do this; honey, do that." Often enough, these household members are two spouses, and a typical slip might request that the handy spouse put up curtains or fix a leaky toilet.

The main benefit of a Honey Do Jar over an ordinary to-do list is that the jar provides surprise and variety. A common variant suggested to improve follow-through and general use of the jar is adding slips that specify fun things to do instead of chores. That way, you're gambling: You might draw a chore, but you might luck out and draw some fun instead.

ProD Yourself with the Project Deck

The Project Deck, or ProD, is an improvement on the Honey Do Jar that was developed by David Westbrook. It's a deck of cards you make yourself describing creative projects to work on. You shuffle the deck and deal yourself a project at random.

The ProD is basically a Honey Do Jar in card deck form, with a couple of extra features. One is that it's you who creates the ProD, not your spouse or partner. Another is that the tasks in the ProD are things that you ostensibly *want* to do, making the ProD more useful for overcoming resistance to your projects that may result from perfectionism, fear, confusion, or some other mental hurdle.

To create a ProD, begin with a stack of index cards or other small blank cards. On one side of each, write a creative project that you want to undertake but that you feel unmotivated to do for some reason. Every morning when you get up, draw a card from the ProD; that project is the one you will either begin or continue working on. Now get to work, and enjoy!

The ProD can also help you determine which of your projects are the most important to you. If after drawing a card you realize that you'd rather work on another project, then do so. Don't stifle your creativity in service to your motivational tool.

FitDeck

The FitDeck (http://fitdeck.com) is like a Project Deck for physical exercise. It's a beautifully produced *game system* (set of components with which you can play more than one game, like a regular deck of cards) that's commercially available in several versions. The original, generic adult FitDeck has been renamed the Bodyweight Deck; Figure 28-1 shows a card from this deck. FitDeck Junior is the children's equivalent of the Bodyweight deck. There are also specialized decks for yoga and Pilates, as well as expansion sets with exercises that can be performed under specific circumstances such as office environments.

SQUATS
Wide

LOWER BODY

12 18 24
BEG INT ADV

• Stand with feet wider than shoulder-width apart
• As you squat, raise arms straight out in front for balance
• Continue to squat down until thighs are parallel to floor
• Return to starting position
Tip: Do not allow knees to go forward of toes

Figure 28-1: Squats card from the FitDeck Bodyweight deck

Each FitDeck card shows the name of an exercise, such as Squats or Push Ups; a "suit" such as Upper Body, Middle Body, Lower Body, or Full Body; a number of repetitions or number of seconds to perform the exercise for Beginner, Intermediate, or Advanced levels; and instructions about how to perform the exercise, with illustrations.

Although all these features, such as the suits, provide great "hooks" for card games, most of the games suggested by the FitDeck designers — apart from "draw five random cards and do the exercises," which does add variety — are on the level of children's games like Simon Says, War, and 52 Pickup. However, the "In Real Life" section at the end of this hack contains rules for a silly but more strategic game for the FitDeck called Make Frank's Monsters Fit.

StickK

StickK (http://stickk.com/), pronounced "stick," is a website that pares turning a job into a game to its core. It works by betting and leveraging personal aversion. You provide a stake, say a few hundred dollars, and bet that you can complete a task such as writing your thesis in a given time, or that you can consistently perform a task, such as doing ten push-ups a day. If you succeed, you get your money back; if you fail, a neutral referee will approve the disbursal of your money to a destination you find personally repugnant: a "foe" (a person you dislike), or an "anti-charity" (such as the NRA if you're a liberal, or the Clinton Presidential Library if you're a conservative). Since you presumably don't want this to happen — a *lot* — it's sound behavioral economics (Hack 52, "Metabehave Yourself").

Chore Wars

Chore Wars (`http://chorewars.com`) is an online game system that enables the members of a household to track the chores they do with experience points, gold pieces, treasures, monsters, and in general all the accoutrements of role-playing games with a medieval fantasy setting, such as Dungeons & Dragons. A typical chore might be recorded as an adventure with the title "taking out the garbage," and a reward of 30 experience points and 50 gold pieces. Larger one-time tasks can be designated as special quests, and any adventure can contain unusual features like monsters or magical artifacts.

To reiterate, Chore Wars is not so much a game as a *game system*. Your household will need to make its own rules regarding how it tracks chores and what the rewards will be within the Chore Wars system. In the "In Real Life" section below, we recount the steps the Hale-Evans household, aka the Order of Seekers of Order, went through in developing its own rules, and append the actual rules by which we play.

Scrumble

Scrumble is another productivity game with a medieval fantasy setting, this time combining the agile programming methodology of the *scrum* with the Viking drinking ritual of the *sumble*. There's a whole hack in this book devoted to Scrumble; for more information, see Hack 29, "Scrumble for Glory."

Metaphorming

The object of metaphorming is to reinterpret your environment in a way that makes you happier and more productive. It's a variant of the ancient kid's game Let's Pretend, and a less-structured version of Chore Wars and Scrumble.

Here's an example of metaphormation: If you're trying to get work done in a crowded environment filled with chatter, you can remind yourself that the first permanent Mars colony will probably have dozens or hundreds of people living in crowded conditions too, and yet who would fail to volunteer to be part of it? Thus, by reimagining your work environment as a Mars colony, you recontextualize the problems and add a little adventure. With only a tiny temporary suspension of disbelief, you can make work more pleasant for yourself and make yourself more productive.

Anthony Judge, in his brief article "Reinventing Your Metaphoric Habitat" (www.laetusinpraesens.org/musings/methab92.php), suggests that a bureaucracy can be "reconfigured imaginatively as the Court of Louis XIV — replete with courtiers, courtesans, and people pissing in the corners." Similarly, the excellent book *Playful Perception*[1] suggests pretending that garbage cans are alive and that you can feed them by picking up litter, or that washing dishes is your hobby and you are a kind of dishwashing connoisseur. The possibilities are coterminous with your imagination.

Oulipo Groceries

The game of Oulipo Groceries, designed by Marty on a day when she could no longer face the mundane chore of grocery shopping as she knew it, is named after a French literary collective called the Oulipo, short for *Ouvroir de littérature potentielle*, or Workshop of Potential Literature. The Oulipo compel themselves to explore the weirder fringes of literature — by, for example, writing novels without the letter E, and palindromes almost 10,000 words long, among other feats.

The Oulipo Groceries game is meant to compel you to explore the weirder fringes of your grocery store in a similar way, by introducing constraints into your grocery shopping. It's also meant to push you into seeing and thinking about your familiar store and products in a new way. You're encouraged to design your own constraints, but here are a few to start you off, in increasing order of rigor:

- Shop at a new store.
- Buy only items you've never bought before, such as new types of food or new brands. You'd be surprised at all the things you've never noticed at your usual store — look above and below eye level.
- Only buy items that have a certain letter in them, such as T or P. To make this even harder, only buy items that begin with a certain letter. You may have to think creatively about what the name of an item might be.
- Only buy items with packaging that contains a certain color, such as yellow.
- Shop at separate stores for different kinds of groceries: produce at one, meat at another, canned goods at another, and so on. This forces you to focus on each type of food. If you're at a store to buy produce, you'll look closely at the produce. Similarly, when you're deciding which store to use for produce, you'll think carefully about which store offers the best.
- Only buy items that do not contain the letter E.

How It Works

As with many of the other "metahacks" in this book, how this hack works depends to a large extent on how you implement it.

In general, harnessing competitiveness, rewards, and fun increases participation in, and lowers resistance to, tasks you might otherwise resist doing because they're dull or mildly unpleasant. Also, many parts of this hack depend on the principle of *metabehavior*, or changing your behavior with behavior. For example, because games often require keeping score, they're ideal for tracking your behavior, a key concept of metabehavior. The version of Chore Wars described below depends on tracking your behavior, with the understanding that your personal commitment will be reflected by your pocket money for a given week; that is, it will be proportional to how much work you do — you are literally being paid for your effort. Scrumble works more or less the same way, but emphasizes public commitment. StickK is almost entirely based on public commitment, as well as negative monetary consequences for reneging.

All this is what game designers call *mechanics*, but the *themes* of these games shouldn't be discounted, either. Chore Wars and Scrumble, for example, enable role-playing in a goofy quasi-medieval setting, which in itself is more fun for many people (or there wouldn't be such booming business for Renaissance fairs). Metaphorming is more free-form, and works not only because it makes your everyday world a little more fun and imaginative, but also because it changes your expectations to fit a new set of circumstances.

Make Frank's Monsters Fit works because the theme and the mechanics work well together. While you're toning your upper, middle, and lower body according to which FitDeck cards you draw, you can imagine those parts of your body being brought to life galvanically as part of a monster.

In Real Life

Here are two real-life examples of games we've developed and used to turn jobs into games.

Chore Wars: Hale-Evans Edition

Here's a detailed example of how we used Chore Wars to make chores around the Hale-Evans household quite a bit more fun, as well as get them done more consistently. Our system evolved over several months; we're including a lot of detail about our development process so you can see how we did it. Perhaps you'll find it useful, or maybe you'll come up with one that suits your household better. If you're not interested in game design, feel free to skip or skim this section, but if you're interested in gamifying your life, read on!

We tried Chore Wars when it was released to the Web by Kevan Davis in 2007, but we fell victim to experience-point inflation and a general lack of direction. We decided that for our second attempt at Chore Wars, we would approach it as game designers and carefully develop a rigorous set of rules for our own Chore Wars game.

One ground rule we established early on, because of our previous bad experience, was that all changes to the game had to be made by unanimous consent. Previously, we had both added chores and set rules and rates at our own discretion, which led to a lot of disagreement and some distrust that the other player was trying to exploit the system.

This time, we decided that our game should have real-world rewards tracked by experience points (XP) or gold pieces (GP). The rewards didn't have to be expensive, but they should be *something*. Gold pieces seemed like a natural game element for this, because you can spend them and zero out the score for each new week, unlike experience points, which accumulate. We decided that GP awarded in Chore Wars should be payable in U.S. dollars as real-world "pocket money," a personal allowance paid to us by the household after we contributed what we earned to the joint budget.

The Chore Wars site explicitly recommends setting XP for most chores to equal the number of minutes it takes to do the chore, with a variable number of GP and treasure, perhaps redeemable for outside rewards. As a first pass, we calculated what Chore Wars would pay if we billed chores at 0.1 GP per minute, or 6 GP per hour. Then we learned that the Washington state minimum wage in January 2009 was $8.55 per hour. Paying ourselves a little better than minimum wage for chores, $9.00 per hour, would come to $0.15 per minute. Ten hours of chores would come to $90. A couple of days later, Marty suggested making chores worth a flat $10 per hour, with 15 minutes as the smallest billable unit of time, mainly to streamline calculation. Fifteen minutes would equal 15 XP as Chore Wars suggests, but 25 GP, so 1 GP would be worth $0.10. We started filling out the templates for adventures (that is, chores) with XP and GP values, but agreed we would determine empirically how much each was worth, with a timer.

Less than a week of playing Chore Wars later, it was clear that we couldn't budget monetary rewards at $10 per hour without a cap, because the pocket money that the household would owe us could well exceed the pocket money budget in a given week, and might fluctuate far too much, making it hard to plan. Therefore, Ron proposed that a fixed amount of pocket money should be allotted each week in the budget, and that we each receive a percentage of it based on how many GP we earned separately. Thus, if $100 of pocket money were available in a week, and Marty earned 60 GP while Ron earned 40 GP, Marty would be paid $60 of the pocket money and Ron would be paid the remaining $40. Similarly, if $200 of pocket money were available, Marty would be paid $120, and Ron would be paid $80. This would enable us to budget a relatively constant amount of pocket money, and to establish a variable exchange rate between GP and dollars, depending on the supply of each. Moreover, the system could remain the same whether the household budget happened to be tight or flush at any given time.

This change might sound complicated, but it was a watershed in making the system workable and practical. It made the system more viable within a reasonable household budget and flexible enough to follow changes in factors like household income. It also changed the focus of the game from getting paid directly for work to learning how to divide the household work equitably.

At one point, Ron was earning a lot of GP for cataloging our library on LibraryThing (www.librarything.com). The library contains several thousand books, so this was time-consuming but satisfying, even pleasant work, and it was a lot more important to Ron than to Marty. We initially agreed that library cataloging should be compensated in GP at half the normal reward, or 50 GP per hour. Later, we decided that cataloging should be compensated normally, but limited to three paid hours per week. This decision came partly because cataloging can expand to enormous numbers of hours, and would allow Ron to easily tip the balance of work in any given week by focusing on it at the exclusion of more important but onerous jobs, such as taking out the garbage.

Similarly, Marty insisted that computer maintenance should be at half the normal rate. Most computers in the house run free and open-source software at Ron's insistence, and Marty contends that this means he must spend more time on keeping the computers running smoothly. It's also very "lumpy" work — often nothing needs to be done, but occasionally it can suddenly use up many hours without warning, which makes it difficult to plan. Ron disagrees that it takes more time to maintain computers running open-source software, but does agree that it can pose a planning problem, and knows how to pick his battles. In any case, truly heroic maintenance can be added as a quest.

Most of the Chore Wars game design occurred while Ron was unemployed. At one point, however, he was about to start a new full-time technical writing contract, more than an hour's commute away, and we needed to decide how to reevaluate our time spent on chores. We needed to find a way to compensate for the fact that Ron now had much less available time to spend on chores, because Marty (who currently doesn't work outside the house) would have both more flexible free time and easier access to the house to do the chores. We also wanted to acknowledge that Ron would be contributing a lot of time and work to the household good by working the job, and it would be equitable for Marty to take on more of the housework in return. We tried several complicated formulas to compensate, but eventually settled for simply doubling Ron's GP before we calculated the weekly totals, making his time within the game "worth" roughly twice as much. This seemed fair to both of us and works well in practice.

We created a spreadsheet for the rest of the year, and now all we had to do was plug in our respective GP totals each week and how much total pocket money was available that week, and we instantly found out how much pocket money we each got for the week. Now, every Sunday morning, in order to zero out our score for the new week, we spend our GP in Chore Wars, recording how many real dollars we're buying with them, usually with trash-talk that makes us laugh, such as "Martania spent 1050gp on a $72.41-size can of whupass for Ronaldo and his $77.59 of suck." Then we transfer the money online from our joint checking account to our individual accounts, and a new week begins for the Order of the Seekers of Order.

If you're designing your own game for Chore Wars, you might consider personifying extra difficult tasks as monsters to be killed during special quests (one-shot adventures), or using individual treasures won during adventures, such as crowns or magic swords, as a kind of coupon to be redeemed for gifts or favors later.

You can find the spreadsheet for the Chore Wars rules we use at the website for this book (see the Introduction).

The Rules: Hale-Evans Chore Wars

1. Players are competing to gain the largest portion of the pocket money allotted to the household for the week.

2. Players gain experience at the rate of 1 XP per minute for a task of normal difficulty.

3. Players gain gold pieces at a rate of 25 gold pieces for 15 minutes of a task of normal difficulty, with a minimum of 15 minutes.

4. Players are rewarded with a portion of the total available pocket money corresponding to the proportion of the total GP they have earned.

5. How much a task is worth in XP and GP may be changed by agreement of the players: doubled if it's especially onerous, or halved if it's especially pleasant. Players can also agree to cap the weekly number of hours for which a pleasant task will be compensated.

6. If one or more of the players has a full-time outside job while one or more other players works at home, the GP earned by the players with full-time jobs are valued at twice the rate of that earned by the players who work at home.

Make Frank's Monsters Fit

Make Frank's Monsters Fit is a FitDeck game for 2–4 players by Tim Schutz of tjgames.com (http://tjgames.com). There is also a sequel, aptly called Make Frank's Monsters Fit 2.

The Story

Frank Einstein has been making monsters for years at his monster factory. In the factory, there are three worktables so that up to three monsters can be built at nearly the same time. Some say he has it down to a science; Frank says, "It's easy! Just put the parts together in the right order and then add some life and exercise."

The one thing Frank is serious about is quality control. Frank knows that if, at any time, there are three of the same body parts on the three different tables without a complete monster being made, or a monster is completed but not brought to life, those parts have been out long enough to spoil and must be tossed away. . . and this does not make Frank happy. What makes Frank happy is when everything comes together and a monster is made. Frank's motto is "A fit monster is a good monster." Frank's fit monsters are always good at their jobs, whether that means helping around the house or terrorizing a village.

To play the game, you need the following:

- A FitDeck that has the Upper Body, Middle Body, and Lower Body suits, plus one additional suit (preferably Full Body). The best decks to use with this game are the Bodyweight Deck and FitDeck Junior. If you're using the Bodyweight Deck, randomly remove two cards from every suit except Full Body, to make the deck a bit more balanced.

- Some kind of tokens for scoring. These can be pennies, paper clips, poker chips, or any other small item. About 50 or so would be good.

Setting Up the Game

Decide where to play the game; you'll need enough room to lay out cards in a 3 × 3 grid of nine spaces. Cards will be played to the table on this imaginary board, described in Table 28-1.

Table 28-1: The Imaginary Board

Upper Body	Upper Body	Upper Body
Middle Body	Middle Body	Middle Body
Lower Body	Lower Body	Lower Body

Give each player three scoring tokens and place the rest of the tokens on the table to make the bank. Players should keep their own scoring tokens separate from each other. Deal three cards face down to each player; cards in your hand are kept hidden. Place the rest of the deck face down where everyone can reach it to draw cards, and leave a spot for a discard pile. Pick a player to go first, and get ready to make monsters!

Playing the Game

In Make Frank's Monsters Fit, players take turns. On a turn, each player should take the following actions.

At the beginning of your turn, check whether all three cards in your hand are the same body part suit. If they are, you can (if you want) show everyone that they're all the same, and then discard two cards and replace them with two new cards. If all three of your cards have the same suit after you draw the new cards, you can repeat this action until you have more than one suit.

Next, play an Upper Body, Middle Body, or Lower Body card onto any empty space on the board that matches that body part. This may complete a monster, but it may not.

If you have completed a monster with all three body parts in the same column, you can then play a Full Body card, if you have one. The Full Body card brings the monster to life.

If you bring the monster to life, remove the three body part cards that make up that monster from the board, and add the Full Body card. Next, select one of these four cards for yourself, and then the other players each randomly take one of the remaining cards. Now everyone does the exercise on the card they have; each player can decide at what level to do the exercise (Beginning, Intermediate, or Advanced).

After everyone has done the exercise, all the players receive from the bank some tokens depending on the level they successfully achieved: one token for Beginner, two tokens for Intermediate, and three tokens for Advanced. The player who made the monster gets one bonus token and keeps the card he selected, placing it face down in front of himself to hold until the game ends. (This card may be worth bonus points later.) The other three cards are placed into the discard pile.

If you didn't bring a monster to life, check the board. If you completed a lifeless monster, or if you placed the third of a particular body part onto the tables (one row is full), the parts are spoiled, and must be discarded. You must pay one scoring token to the bank, then remove those cards from the board and discard them. If you have no tokens, you pay nothing, but you must still discard the spoiled body parts. If there are both three of the same body part and a completed monster, select one to remove (either a row or a column of cards).

You can now (if you want) discard one card in your hand.

Finally, draw enough cards to refill your hand to three. If the draw deck is depleted, reshuffle the discard pile to make a new draw deck.

Play through the deck twice. The game ends when a player can't draw enough cards to fill her hand, after the second time through the deck.

Scoring the Game at the End

When the card play is completed, players with bonus cards that they received from making a monster can use these cards to earn bonus scoring tokens. Players can earn up to three extra scoring tokens per card by repeating the exercises on the card. To earn the bonus, select a card from your bonus card pile, do the exercise, and earn one token for Beginner level, two tokens for Intermediate, and three tokens for Advanced. Discard that card after doing the exercise. You can perform the exercise on each of your bonus cards at any level to score the bonus once. You don't have to do all bonus cards if you don't want to — you can just discard a bonus card (or several) and earn no bonus from those cards.

After everyone is done, add up your scoring tokens: The player with the most scoring tokens wins.

See Also

- Jane McGonigal, *Reality Is Broken: Why Games Make Us Better and How They Can Change the World* (New York: Penguin Press, 2011). This is a comprehensive survey of the theory and practice of gamification, why games are good for you, and why we should all play more, including detailed studies of a number of the emerging phenomenon of *alternate-reality games* (ARGs), which reinterpret reality to make it more fun — including Chore Wars. (Scrumble, from Hack 29, "Scrumble for Glory," is another ARG by McGonigal's definition.) Find out more at http://realityisbroken.org/.

- Dave Gray, Sunni Brown, and James Macanufo, *Gamestorming: A Playbook for Innovators, Rulebreakers, and Changemakers* (Sebastopol, CA, USA: O'Reilly Media, 2010). Also recommended, this book takes a different approach. Less theory and more practice, it's a collection of rules for games you can play in the workplace, to generate ideas, solve problems, resolve conflicts, and generally make your job a more fun and creative place to work. Learn more about it at www.gogamestorm.com/.

Notes

1. Herbert L. Leff, Ph.D, *Playful Perception: Choosing How to Experience Your World* (Burlington, VT USA: Waterfront Books, Inc., 1984).

Hack 29: Scrumble for Glory

Scrumble is a special case of turning a job into a game. It's a role-playing game with a practical purpose: to help you accomplish things that are important to you.

This productivity hack combines the agile software development framework of the *scrum* (www.softhouse.se/Uploades/Scrum_eng_webb.pdf) with the ancient Viking drinking ritual of the *sumble* (www.altx.com/interzones/violet/sumble.html). It's a lightweight role-playing game or *alternate-reality game* set in Virtual Valhalla, the home of those who are virtually Norse gods. You are a god or demigod who swears mighty oaths, and then fulfills them. You meet periodically in *scrumble* to hoist your mighty virtual flagon to the principles and heroes that have inspired you, brag about your accomplishments since the last scrumble round, and pledge to accomplish great deeds by the next one.

Because anything can happen in Virtual Valhalla, whether you're playing face-to-face or online, you can be any character you want, and toast with any drink. When someone passes you the virtual drinking horn, it magically becomes any vessel you desire, and the lite beer, chocolate milk, or stale office coffee you're really drinking — or even your empty hand — can become Olympian ambrosia, the sacred Soma, or Château Lafitte-Rothschild 1945.

Sound too much like Dungeons & Dragons? There's at least one big difference: the only things you have to take seriously in Scrumble are your promises.

In Action

The actions in a typical game of Scrumble are as follows:

1. Choose the first Scrumblegiver.
2. Write the Great Tale.
3. Make toasts, boasts, and oaths.
4. Fulfill oaths.
5. Calculate scores.
6. Meet again later to repeat steps 3 through 5.

Choose the First Scrumblegiver

The Scrumblegiver is a kind of master of ceremonies chosen from among the players. The first Scrumblegiver is chosen by consensus, and is usually either the project leader or the player who initiated the scrumble.

The Scrumblegiver has several duties:

- Remind the other players when a round is starting and encourage them to participate.
- Lead the toasts.

- Coordinate the deeds in the Great Tale.
- Challenge other players to ensure they pledge oaths that are neither trivial nor impossible.
- Determine when the round is over.
- Calculate player scores and determine the new Scrumblegiver. (If the project is such that having a constantly changing Scrumblegiver would disrupt it, the latter action may be omitted and the Scrumblegiver may stay the same.)

Write the Great Tale

Before the game proper begins, players take part in a planning session in which a Great Tale is written. The first Scrumblegiver leads this effort. The Great Tale should incorporate a high-level, long-range view of the whole project, including the final goal and important milestones, as well as a description of how the goal is to be reached. The goal of the scrumble is to make the Great Tale and its many lesser tales, one for each player or subproject, come gloriously true.

A tale should be written in the past tense, as if it has already happened. For example, a simple lesser tale from a Great Tale about writing an anthology of board game rules might read "The game Dimension Meta has been rewritten, illustrated, laid out, and is ready for publication." This tale requires four deeds:

1. Rewrite the game.
2. Illustrate it.
3. Lay it out.
4. Check that it's ready for publication.

Make Toasts, Boasts, and Oaths

There are four simple phases to this action:

1. Toast a god or principle you believe in.
2. Toast a hero, a person who embodies those principles.
3. Boast about one or more of your accomplishments.
4. Swear an oath that you'll accomplish one or more specific deeds.

A deed represents a specific task you intend to complete before the next round. Usually, it's a task in the Great Tale or one of its lesser tales, the next step you need to take on your part of the project. For every deed you accomplish by the next scrumble round, you gain one point of honor. For every deed you fail to accomplish, you lose one point of honor, The more outrageous your tipple in

Virtual Valhalla, the better; honor your principles and heroes by getting creative and thinking up drinks that are worthy of their stature.

In a synchronous environment, such as a face-to-face setting, telephone call, or chat session, all players can perform the same phase, and then move on to the next phase together — each player toasts a principle, then each toasts a hero, and so on. In an asynchronous environment, such as e-mail, it saves time if the Scrumblegiver performs all four phases in one message, then the other players send messages with their own four phases.

- **Toasts to principles:** At ancient sumbles, pagan gods such as Odin and Thor were toasted during this first phase. Twenty-first century scrumblers will probably prefer to toast the principles such gods represent, such as wisdom and courage, respectively.

  Lift your glass to a principle that inspires you in your work and other actions.

- **Toasts to heroes:** Lift your glass to a hero who inspires you in your work and other actions, preferably one who embodies the principle you just toasted.

- **Boasts:** Lift your glass to yourself, to celebrate an accomplishment that you have achieved since the last round. You may also boast and celebrate the adventures of another player, as a reward for her prowess.

  During this phase, the Scrumblegiver boasts the deeds of the other players since the last round of the game, as well as their scores, and names the new Scrumblegiver.

- **Oaths:** Lift your glass and pledge an oath that clearly states a deed you will accomplish before the next round. You may swear as many oaths as you are confident you can fulfill.

  When everyone is finished swearing oaths, the Scrumblegiver declares that the round is over, and announces the time and place of the next round.

Fulfill Oaths

Between rounds, the players try to fulfill the oaths they have sworn. Note that by participating in a scrumble, you are bound to make every reasonable effort to help the other players fulfill their oaths as well as fulfilling your own. You're all working together on the same Great Tale, after all.

Calculate Scores

Just before the next round begins, the Scrumblegiver calculates player scores and determines the new Scrumblegiver. Scoring is simple. Every time a player fulfills an oath, he receives one point of honor. Whenever he fails, he loses one. At her discretion, a Scrumblegiver may award a point of honor to a player for a mighty deed the player performed on the previous round, even if that player neglected to pledge it beforehand.

The Scrumblegiver determines who the next Scrumblegiver will be — namely, the player with the most honor. If there is a tie for most honor, the old Scrumblegiver may freely choose the next one from among those tied. While the role of Scrumblegiver can change from round to round, it's not unusual for it to belong to the same player several rounds in a row, or even for the whole game.

Repeat

Players meet again for another round at the time and place announced. When they do, they repeat steps 3, 4, and 5, making more toasts, boasts, and oaths and cheering on their fellow heroes. Players should continue doing so until completion of the project.

How It Works

Scrumble works by *turning a job into a game*, and particularly through *applied behavior analysis* (Hack 52, "Metabehave Yourself").

- Oaths work through the mechanism of *making commitments.*
- Honor and rewards work (but to a limited extent, especially online) through *operant conditioning.*
- Toasts work because they inspire the players and act as *reminders* of ideals they would like to live up to, bringing meaning to what might otherwise be pretty mundane work.

You may find that the hardest part of playing Scrumble is getting your co-workers to try it in the first place, but once people play, they tend to keep playing.

In Real Life

Here is a lightly edited transcript of an actual round of Scrumble that was played as part of the writing of *Mindhacker.*

Cast of characters

Limbic: Jonathan Davis (-1 point of honor)

Lion: Lion Kimbro (1 point)

Martania: Marty Hale-Evans (not actively scrumbling, but occasionally mentioned)

Stormhair Rainbowbeard: Ron Hale-Evans (2 points; Scrumblegiver)

Yatima Fatima: John Braley (0 points)

We'll start in the middle of Scrumble Round 2, with the e-mailed or Twittered boasts, toasts, and oaths of everyone but the Scrumblegiver.

Limbic writes:

I, Limbic, lift a cup of beetroot juice to toast the principle of Hilaritas — a true key to happiness: www.theatlantic.com/doc/200906/happiness.

I lift this test-tube of stem-cell nutrient soup to the Laughing Buddha, who asks "What are you taking too seriously?"

I, Limbic, have caused a storm in hell with the brilliance of the latest edit of the "Take a Semantic Pause" hack submitted today.

I lift this vat of Portuguese wine to toast my oath that I will submit my next edit before the deadline set by Martania and Stormhair.

Lion writes:

We meet again at the glorious table!

I, Lion Kimbro, do toast, with this cup of my father's wine, that glorious living unfolding Rose; she sits in the future, whispering encouragement onward.

I toast Walt Disney, who inspired a world of animators, makers, and countless children and adults.

I boast that a brief time ago, I did write my draft on marginalia, and in so doing, did liberate many from the tyranny of untouchable books.

And mark my words: by Sunday night, I will supply PNG images to extend my chapter, and complete the second draft. Further, I boast that the outline of another chapter still shall follow!

May they who reign at the end of the age give me the strength and constancy I require, to fulfill what is written.

Yatima writes:

I, Yatima Fatima, brandish this very used plastic Snapple bottle of icy unfiltered Seattle tap water from the Tolt River Wilderness to the high/low minded/instinctual principle/ trick: where there is chaos introject order — where order, chaos.

And I raise this lovely sixth-grade-ceramics-class mug, vibrant with strawberry kefir (kefirs, keefir, kephir, kewra, talai, mudu kekiya, milkkefir, búlgaros) to Lani Guinier — nobody's choice but mine for Supreme Court Justice.

And I brag with this Mandarin Orange Slices tin can of canned fruit syrup that I was able to initiate my own virgin scrumble (this very one) before the end of Woden's day and that it probably is taking me longer to write it than any scrumble ever, heretofore, written.

Before I succumb to the ravens of time, I swear (but not on Earth, for it is god's Ottoman), that before Thor's day is done I will have addressed some issues in the 3D hack's Google document, while adding data, and beginning my draft. Make it so say we all.

Stormhair announces Scrumble Round 3, and writes:

I, Stormhair Rainbowbeard, Scrumblegiver, toast the principle of persistence with this 128-ounce Super Big Gulp of coffee-flavored 1,3,7-trimethylxanthine, trimethyl xanthine, theine, methyltheobromine, for it is only persistence and coffee that have gotten me through the last few hellweeks of trying to restore the Mentat Wiki and four others from backup, while working full time, commuting three hours a day, and desperately trying to write Mindhacker *as well.*

And I, Stormhair Rainbowbeard, Scrumblegiver, toast every human being, alive or dead, who has ever made it through a day- or week-long meditation retreat through the principle of persistence, with her legs falling asleep, and back aching, and brain falling asleep, and mind aching, without screaming. I toast them all — and all sentient beings — with this demitasse of green tea.

And I, Stormhair Rainbowbeard, Scrumblegiver, boast with this Leyden jar of white lightning, which contains every color of the rainbow in my mighty beard, that I have fulfilled two of the three oaths I swore at the last scrumble: (1) to comment on all hacks submitted to me, and (2) to submit two hack drafts to Martania ("Mediate Your Environment" and "Roll the Mental Dice"). However, I failed at my oath to write a Great Tale, with a lesser tale for everyone in the Scrumble. Thus:

> *Previous score = 2*
>
> *Fulfilling two oaths = +2*
>
> *Failing one oath = -1*
>
> *Total = 3*

And I boast that although I have not completed many hacks since the last scrumble, yet I broadly continue to add material to existing hacks, and shall continue to do so.

And I boast that my comrade-in-arms Yatima has fulfilled his oath to address issues in the "Enter the Third Dimension" hack, adding material, and beginning his draft, before the end of Thor's day, 28 May. One point of honor to Yatima, for a total of 1!

And I boast that my comrade-in-arms Limbic has completed a draft of his "Take a Semantic Pause" hack. Alas, he didn't boast he would do so beforehand, but I am hereby awarding Limbic a point for his doughty efforts. He's just had bad timing, failing to pledge his deeds before he does them. He's back up to 0.

And I weep into my cup that Lion scores -2 this round, for a total of -1, for failing to fulfill his two oaths, of (1) providing graphics for his marginalia hack and completing the second draft, and (2) submitting the draft of a second hack. I note that part of the problem was Google Docs, which was down when Lion had time to work on his hacks, although the current scrumble round was extended for just that reason. I also declare that he can retroactively change his -1 honor to a 0 or 1 if he actually did his work offline while Google Docs was down, and can get it to me soon.

Thus, the scores are as follows:

> *Stormhair = 3 (continues to be Scrumblegiver)*
>
> *Yatima = 1*
>
> *Limbic = 0*
>
> *Lion = -1*

Finally, I, Stormhair Rainbowbeard, Scrumblegiver, swear by this goblet of Iw HIq, *or Klingon blood wine (because I'm on a conlang kick), that I shall do the following mighty deeds by the next scrumble round:*

1. *Because I failed to last time, I will write a Great Tale, with a lesser tale for everyone partaking in the scrumble.*

2. *I will submit at least three hack drafts to Martania, whether new or revised, per her previous comments.*

3. *I will transcribe all of my notes for the book from the month of May, and then remain current.*

4. *I will create a page for* Mindhacker *on the Mentat Wiki.*

5. *I will pester everyone who has agreed to scrumble but has not yet joined us at the feasting table.*

6. *I will upgrade my new netbook, which just returned after a 10-day keyboard repair, to Ubuntu Netbook Remix, so that it is a worthy tool for writing on the road, and does not hang on an hourly basis, as it does with the factory-installed OS.*

All drink! Skål!
Play, and work, continue. . .

See Also

The following science fiction novels describe characters drinking fantastic concoctions in virtual environments and were a direct influence on Scrumble.

- The uploaded characters in the science fiction novel *Accelerando* by Charles Stross (www.antipope.org/charlie/blog-static/fiction/accelerando/accelerando-intro.html) drink live jellyfish in margaritas at one point, modifying their virtual biology to make the act pleasurable.

- Chapter 8 of Greg Egan's science fiction novel *Permutation City* depicts a billionaire who has been uploaded into a virtual reality after death, and pours himself a tumbler of pure Confidence and Optimism in a moment of depression.

Hack 30: Salvage a Vintage Hack

The DIY and Maker movements are full of people who resurrect old technologies, often because the conditions that made them obsolete no longer apply. The next time you're up against a tangled technological problem, you may find your solution in the pages of a Popular Mechanics *from the turn of the* last century.

In the early twenty-first century, with an abundance of computing power and high-quality electronic and mechanical components available, sometimes the high-tech solution is nevertheless the wrong one. Maybe you can't find the right software for what you want to do, and it's too expensive or time-consuming to write your own. Maybe a high-tech solution is overkill, like building a particle beam cannon to kill a gnat. Or maybe the high-tech solution has a drastically negative effect on the environment, like that particle beam cannon in the middle of a meadow.

Instead, try ransacking the libraries and trash cans of your forebears and salvage a vintage hack. Vintage hacks have the advantages of being quick, dirty, and cheap. By "dirty" we don't mean that they aren't green — they're often greener than their high-tech alternatives by far. Consider whether a calculator or an abacus produces more waste, both in production and after it breaks. Instead, by "dirty" we mean that while a vintage hack may not solve your whole problem, it may solve the important 80% of your problem with only 20% of the time, effort, and materials. In other cases, a vintage hack can sometimes produce a complete and elegant solution.

Many people, such as the Steampunk movement, salvage vintage hacks for fun. We've heard it observed that as Western societies grow richer, with a higher level of technology and more leisure time, they tend to adopt hobbies that used to be considered tedious jobs, such as candlemaking. Philosopher of technology Kevin Kelly has pointed out that more stone hand tools are being flint knapped today — about 1.5 million a year — than there were during the Neolithic, when people made them for survival.[1] Nothing says you can't wield your vintage hack with a neo-Neolithic or steampunk sense of style, but the point here is to use low tech because it's fast, it's cheap, and, most important, *it works.*

One final advantage of vintage hacks is that they tend to get your hands dirty. If you live in your head as much as many geeks do, that can only be good.

In Action

Every hack is different, so the *metahack* of salvaging a vintage hack will take a different form every time you use it. It might mean dumpster-diving for recyclable materials, pillaging ideas from old magazines, using an ASCII solution like a flat-text file instead of an application with a complex GUI, or employing any other kind of quick-and-dirty, low-tech physical solution instead of a shiny digital or ready-made plastic one.

Most of the hacks in this book have low-tech counterparts. Even such a seemingly computer-dependent hack as Hack 4, "Space Your Repetitions," can be performed by hand with flash cards using an algorithm such as LogFlash.[2]

Can a Vintage Hack Help You?

To discover whether you can benefit from a vintage hack, ask yourself whether the usual solution to your problem is too expensive, either in money, time, and effort, or some other factor such as environmental impact. If the answer is yes, how did people solve or cope with the problem before the unaffordable solution was invented, or how do they cope in places where resources are scarce? For example, your modern, high-tech solution to combat summer heat might be air conditioning. However, sometimes placing a wet towel in front of a window fan for evaporative cooling is better than an air conditioner — if you haven't got the money for an air conditioner, or your windows won't accommodate one (http://lifehacker.com/5313401/hang-a-damp-towel-to-cool-a-hot-house).

You might be able to afford the high-tech solution, but it often pays to consider a vintage hack anyway. High-tech solutions aren't preferable by default, and you'll want to weigh the advantages and disadvantages of using a lower-tech solution. For example, even though prices for LED lamps are rapidly dropping, you probably want candlelight for your romantic dinner.

Where to Find Vintage Hacks

There are many places to find these hacks, both online and off. Because vintage hacks tend to be old (by definition), information about them is often in the public domain. Try searching the following sources if you decide you want to find a vintage hack to salvage:

- *Make*: magazine (http://makezine.makezine.com/), from O'Reilly Media, is a must-read for anyone interested in the Maker and DIY (Do It Yourself) movements, and vintage hacks. Their online blog is a fantastic, searchable source of material.

- The *Make*: blog (http://blog.makezine.com/) often links to material from *Instructables* (www.instructables.com/), an online archive of thousands of

DIY articles posted by people from all over the world. Marty recently built Ron a dash mount for his GPS device with little more than an Instructable, a pair of scissors, and a sponge from a convenience store (www.instructables.com/id/Car_Dash_Camera_Mount/).

- The Dead Media Project (http://web.archive.org/web/2008/http://www.deadmedia.org/) has catalogued hundreds of antique forms of communication, from carrier pigeon to Gopher. The project itself is unfortunately also dead, but the archives are still available.

- Victor Papanek's 1971 book *Design for the Real World: Human Ecology and Social Change* is short on hard design information, but it provides plenty of inspiration for people trying to do more with less, especially in developing countries. Designs in the book include a candle-powered radio made from a tin can and only one transistor, which was built for less than nine cents in 1966 dollars.

- Foxfire (www.foxfire.org/) is a project founded in 1966 to preserve the vanishing lore of the Southern Appalachia region of the United States. It produced a series of anthologies called the *Foxfire Book*. Over the years, the books, which run to 12 volumes, have explained lost arts such as building a log cabin, moonshining, butchering a hog, washing clothes in an iron pot, making a dulcimer, and our favorite, the toys and games of Appalachia.

- *507 Mechanical Movements* (http://builders.reprap.org/2008/09/507-mechanical-movements.html): Looking for a unique linkage for your LEGO bot? This freely available 1868 book has about 500 of them. Tim Schutz, who designed the Make Frank's Monsters Fit game (Hack 28, "Turn a Job Into a Game"), says this book is almost a hack in itself, and he is considering designing a board game around it.

- Thanks to Google Books, *Popular Mechanics* (www.popularmechanics.com/technology/upgrade/4295362.html) has a complete archive online stretching back to around 1902. This is an extremely rich vein of information for vintage hacks from such eras as the Great Depression.

How It Works

How any particular vintage hack works depends on the hack, of course. However, the metahack of salvaging vintage hacks works because vintage hacks are proven, working about as well today as they worked yesterday or 100 years ago, or as well as they work in another part of the world. It only requires changing your expectations.

Paradoxically, people often find these antique hacks to be surprising, which may be an advantage in addition to their relative cheapness and speed. Aesthetic

surprise is a feature of the delightful home-brewed eight-track Walkman (www
.instructables.com/id/8-Track-Walkman-Pod-thing-Retro-tech/), and tactical surprise was the result of a radio built from barbed wire and tree bark (among
other components) by the inmates of a World War II POW camp (blog.makezine
.com/archive/2009/07/japanese_pow_camp_radio.html). In this regard, it's
useful to remember Johnny Mnemonic's Law: "If they think you're crude, go
technical; if they think you're technical, go crude."[3]

It's also useful to remember that as high technology advances, low technology
advances along with it. What people consider disposable today, such as an old
boom box, would have been the basis for a technological revolution a century
or two ago. As Bruce Sterling — another seminal cyberpunk author who loves
low tech — has written, "Any sufficiently advanced garbage is indistinguish-
able from magic."[4]

In Real Life

This section provides several examples of salvaging vintage hacks, because
every vintage hack is different. The following examples are only jumping-off
points for your own creativity, of course, but you might be tickled to learn the
answers to the following questions:

- When is paper better than a word processor?
- How can you make a model of a rhombic dodecahedron with drinking
  straws instead of CAD/CAM?
- Why did a leading architecture firm build its own offices without air
  conditioning?
- Since when is a Roomba low tech?

Draw on the Power of Paper

Paper has many advantages over digital technology. For example, paper books
from centuries, even millennia, ago can still be read today, whereas retrieving
a file from a floppy disk only a few years old can be a challenge — assuming
the data is even intact, which is not a foregone conclusion. In his science fiction
novel *Glasshouse*[5], Charles Stross envisions a future in which historians know
more about our distant ancestors than they do about the twentieth and twenty-
first centuries, because we foolishly kept our records on fragile magnetic and
optical media.

Ron doesn't like to write in front of a computer, and works much faster and
more freely writing by hand. This book, indeed this hack, was assembled in
Google Docs, Microsoft Word, and OpenOffice.org, and then post-processed

for Wiley's page layout and publication software, but it started as shorthand notes (Hack 47, "Streamline Your Shorthand") in his "catch," which is mainly a stack of index cards held together with an elastic hairband. The first drafts were mostly written from these notes on a clipboard with letter paper, something Ron could do even while carpooling. Only then were they transcribed into Google Docs, sometimes by way of GNU Emacs, an ASCII text editor *par excellence*. If you write, try this technique sometime — copying and pasting is fast when you're writing in a word processor, but drawing an arrow on paper where the text should go is even faster.

If you love paper, you're in good company. Vladimir Nabokov wrote some of the finest novels in the English language on stacks of index cards. Robert Pirsig, author of *Zen and the Art of Motorcycle Maintenance*, maintained the outline of his elaborate metaphysical philosophy on thousands of such cards — or at least his alter ego did, in his autobiographical novel *Lila* (http://members.optusnet.com.au/~charles57/Creative/Idea_Recording/lila.htm). P. G. Wodehouse tracked the rococo plots of his Jeeves and Wooster novels on loose pages covering virtually all four walls of his workroom.[6]

Maybe these writers could have benefited from a software assist. For example, perhaps Pirsig could have maintained his metaphysics better on a wiki. But if you seriously think that software as such — wiki, word processor, or whatever — can make you a better writer than Nabokov or Wodehouse with their heaps of paper, we beg you to read *Pale Fire* or *The Code of the Woosters* and prayerfully reconsider. They were doing something right, and while using similar techniques may not grant you their talent, it might elevate your own a bit.

Paper can be useful in everyday life too. One of Ron's co-workers was often late to meetings because her Palm PDA did not sync with Outlook on Windows. Paper syncs with everything, and Ron never missed a meeting at that gig because he tracked meeting locations in his work notebook, a steno pad.

We discovered while rewriting this hack that Ron's co-worker was fired. We hope she's not using that PDA to submit her resume to Monster.

3D Modeling

When you're working with three-dimensional objects (Hack 42, "Enter the Third Dimension"), CAD/CAM software may be useful, but unfortunately it engages only the sense of sight. However, physical 3D models can potentially engage all of your senses, especially touch and proprioception. Moreover, they're truly 3D and not just a projection or flattening from 3D into 2D. Both of these factors enable your brain to understand the objects more easily. As for four-dimensional objects (Hack 43, "Enter the Fourth Dimension"), it's hard enough to understand their three-dimensional representations without having to flatten them further into 2D on a screen.

3D modeling material doesn't need to be expensive. *Steven Caney's Ultimate Building Book*[7] explains literally dozens of ways to build 3D models, most of which rely on recycled materials.

Alphabet Buildings

To save energy and reduce the environmental impact of their new office building, the Weber Thompson architecture firm in Seattle reclaimed a mode of architecture from the early twentieth century called *alphabet buildings*. These buildings are so named because when seen from above, they often look like a letter of the alphabet, such as H, K, O, or U. The Weber Thompson building itself looks like an O.

Alphabet buildings have no air conditioning; the hollow spaces in their centers usually contain courtyards onto which workers can open windows to regulate the temperature of their offices. In an age of costly energy, this passive cooling makes sense. In the temperate Pacific Northwest, it might get uncomfortably warm in these buildings only a couple of days a year. On those days, workers wear shorts — or go home early. The company saves enough money by not running complex and inefficient HVAC systems that they can afford to give everyone the afternoon off when necessary.[8]

Insect Robots and BEAM

Despite decades of hand-waving and predictions that artificial intelligence will be here any day now, we still have nothing like human-equivalent AI. But in 2011, we do have functioning robots, including home robots such as the Roomba, and battlefield robots such as the PackBot.

Both of these robots derive from the work of Rodney Brooks, who developed "insect robots" in the early 1990s, abandoning any attempt to build consciousness or complex cognition into them, and instead focusing on behavior (Hack 52, "Metabehave Yourself"). Insect robots run simple, thoughtless subroutines. A typical insect robot might walk forward until it hits an obstacle, at which time a routine to lift the robot's legs takes over. Once past the obstacle, the "walk forward" routine resumes. Your Roomba works in a similar way. It has no mental map of your living room; it just vacuums until it bumps into something, then backs up, spins around, and moves on.

Although Brooks's robots use only a fraction of the computational power of traditional robots, when physicist Mark Tilden saw Brooks speak, he was inspired to build robots with practically none. This was the origin of BEAM robotics (Biology, Electronics, Aesthetics, and Mechanics). BEAM robots are usually built from electronic junk that's just lying around, like old VCRs, and which as a rule don't even contain microprocessors.[9] In this, they were partly inspired by the 1948 "tortoise robots" of William Grey Walter, which were built with vacuum tubes. (www.extremenxt.com/walter.htm) *That's* a vintage hack.

You wouldn't think a device as simple as a vacuum-tube turtle could exhibit complex behaviors, but the tortoises could autonomously seek or hide from light, and dock with a home base to recharge like a modern Roomba. Thanks to the "subsumption architecture" pioneered by Brooks and continued by Tilden, in which simple behavior is layered on simple behavior, the tortoises' memetic descendants can behave in very complex ways indeed.

See Also

For more information about the splendor of paper, we refer you to the ongoing discussion on the original wiki, "Is anything better than paper?": http://c2.com/cgi/wiki?IsAnythingBetterThanPaper.

Notes

1. "Surprising Continuity of Ancient Technologies." Kevin Kelly, *The Technium*, accessed 24 July 2009, http://www.kk.org/thetechnium/archives/2007/02/surprising_cont.php.

2. "Overview of the Flash Process," Bob LeChevalier and Nora LeChevalier, 1992, http://www.lojban.org/files/software/flashman.txt.

3. William Gibson, "Johnny Mnemonic," *Burning Chrome* (New York: Arbor House, 1986).

4. Bruce Sterling, "Ivory Tower," *Futures from Nature*, ed. by Henry Gee (New York: TOR, 2007).

5. Charles Stross, *Glasshouse* (New York: Ace Books, 2006).

6. Douglas Adams, "Introduction to Sunset at Blandings," in *The Salmon of Doubt: Hitchhiking the Galaxy One Last Time* (New York: Harmony Books, 2002).

7. Steven Caney, *Steven Caney's Ultimate Building Book* (Philadelphia, PA, USA: Running Press Kids, 2006).

8. "The Rise and Fall of the Air Conditioner," Joshua McNichols, www.kuow.org/program.php?id=17477.

9. David Hrinkiw and Mark Tilden. *JunkBots, Bugbots, and Bots on Wheels: Building Simple Robots with BEAM Technology.* (New York: McGraw-Hill Osborne Media, 2002).

Hack 31: Mine the Future

Obtaining ideas from the imagined futures of science fiction is like having a time machine, with the advantage of being less likely to destroy the universe through paradox.

Science fiction is full of ideas. Some are ideas for hardware, such as ion drives for space travel. These can be inspirations for long-term technological design. Other ideas are about social innovations that require no technology in the conventional sense. These can be tried out today, in our world.

This may seem obvious at first, but the degree to which science fiction has already changed the world — and still can — may not be obvious. For example, did you know that mobile phones were directly inspired by *Star Trek* communicators? Martin Cooper, former chief engineer at Motorola and sometimes called "the inventor of the cell phone," said in an interview[1] that his team was well aware of communicators, and in fact regarded them as an "objective." Flip phones even have a similar form factor.

In this hack, we're not advocating that you "steal someone's ideas," but do as Martin Cooper did: Take a fantastic idea from science fiction and make it real, giving full credit to its source.

In Action

In the memorable phrase of science fiction author, editor, and anthologist Pamela Sargent[2], "Science fiction is the literature of ideas." This isn't because other genres don't contain ideas, but because ideas are typically the crux of science fiction, sometimes to the detriment of characterization, plot, style, and so on. (See Hack 26, "Woo the Muse of the Odd," and Hack 27, "Seek Bad Examples.") Of course, for the purposes of this hack, that is science fiction's strength.

Sargent goes on to say,

Alone among our present genres it can show us a world which does not exist, has not existed, but which could come into being. It can show us alternatives, many of which might be opposite to our presuppositions. It can mirror our thoughts, fears, and hopes about the future in terms of literary experience.

A work of science fiction often springs from a central idea. Optimally, the author tries to extrapolate from that idea as accurately as possible. Good science fiction can be like the best thought experiments in physics or philosophy, such as Einstein's imagining himself to be sitting on a photon, traveling at the speed of light. Bad science fiction stacks the deck and loads the dice in the thought experiment, and the result often reveals the author's biases, or amounts to propaganda. Try to read more objective science fiction if you're scouting for ideas.

Of course, it's harder to take that medicine than to prescribe it, but here are a few tips, without singling out any books or authors:

- All else being equal, if the fiction you're reading relies heavily on magic, it's probably not useful as a source of technological ideas.

- If the author seems to want to promote an agenda, political or otherwise, the story is probably constructed to do exactly that and not to explore practical possibilities. This is not to say it can't have a viewpoint, but beware of work where this takes a front seat.

- Generally speaking, the less the world described by the author could plausibly be derived from the real world, the fewer ideas that bear on the real world it will have to offer.

The hardware ideas in science fiction might not be possible right now, but you can work towards them in the long term. For example, the aerospace pioneer Robert Goddard was inspired to develop some of the first rockets by the novel *The War of the Worlds* by H. G. Wells, and Russian aerospace pioneer Konstantin Tsiolkovsky was inspired by Jules Verne's *From the Earth to the Moon*.[3] Many decades later, the first space shuttle orbiter ever built was named the *Enterprise*. And now, thanks in part to the vision of H. G. Wells, space travel is not only possible, but approaching routine with the advent of commercial space agencies like Virgin Galactic, the first company to offer reservations on flights into space to the paying public.

Science fiction's social innovations usually appear in so-called soft, social science fiction, in which the technology comes from anthropology, psychology, and so on. For example, the political philosophy of Odonianism described in Ursula K. LeGuin's *The Dispossessed*[4] appears to be an extreme kind of anarcho-syndicalism. Some people live like this now, and you can probably find them (www.ic.org). In LeGuin's novel, however, the philosophy is adopted by a whole planet, and you can join LeGuin in speculating about how that would work. Conversely, if your tastes run more to anarchocapitalism, you could do worse than study the MYOB from Eric Frank Russell's novel *And Then There Were None* (www.abelard.org/e-f-russell.php).

To be inspired by science fiction, however, you have to know how to find inspirational science fiction. One of the best ways to find science fiction that contains interesting ideas is to obtain some good science fiction reference works, such as *The Encyclopedia of Science Fiction*, by John Clute and Peter Nicholls,[5] or *Brave New Words: The Oxford Dictionary of Science Fiction*, by Jeff Prucher.[6] Look up topics of interest, read their entries, and then seek out and read the works cited. Here are some sample topics from *Brave New Words*:

- cryostasis
- matter transmitter

- space elevator
- needle gun

While the *Encyclopedia* has some similar entries, most of them are authors and titles, so it's better to look up a word or concept in *Brave New Words* and then cross-reference the author or title in the *Encyclopedia*.

This process is particularly helpful if you're looking for inspiration on a specific topic or in a specific field; these works can cross-reference you right to the books that contain the kind of ideas you're looking for. You can also browse them, of course, to come across interesting ideas by chance and then follow them up for more inspiration.

In Real Life

The ideas described in this section come from science fiction, but they can all be implemented to some degree today in the real world. In fact, they are some of Ron's favorite science fictional ideas, and every one of them has had a profound effect on his life.

The Mentat

Frank Herbert's concept of the *mentat*, from his *Dune* novels,[7] has influenced Ron a great deal, but because we've written about it elsewhere, this section just highlights some implications it has had for him. This book wouldn't exist without the mentat concept, for one.

The mentat deliberately, systematically, and comprehensively hones skills like those of an autistic savant, to become a kind of human computer (in the *Dune* universe, electronic computers are under religious interdiction). On the hunch that a lot of people are interested in feats of memory, mental calculation, and so on, Ron created the Mentat Wiki (www.ludism.org/mentat). This led to a book deal, and the successful publication of our first book made it easier to find an agent and sign a contract to publish *Mindhacker*. Thus, you're holding one of the practical upshots of the mentat idea: a book that promotes the ethic of becoming a better thinker. We don't know yet what the readership of *Mindhacker* will be, but our first book has sold tens of thousands of copies. If you count pirated copies, borrowing from friends and libraries, and so on, possibly hundreds of thousands of people have been influenced to become better thinkers because of Herbert's original idea of the mentat and our attempt to embody it.

The Asarya

Just as Frank Herbert's concept of the mentat inspired the Mentat Wiki and our first book, so David Zindell's concept of the *asarya* from his *Requiem for Homo Sapiens* series,[8] which has a lot in common with Herbert's *Dune* series, inspired

Mindhacker. Danlo wi Soli Ringess, the slightly transhuman protagonist of the *Requiem*, aspires to become an asarya, which Zindell defines as a "completely evolved man (or woman) who could look upon the universe just as it is and affirm every aspect of creation no matter how flawed or terrible."

Similarly, a lot of the hacks in this book are "asarya hacks," meant to help you say yes to your world, and to learn the basic human skill of wanting what you have. Among the asarya hacks are Hack 27, "Seek Bad Examples;" Hack 28, "Turn a Job Into a Game;" Hack 50, "Acquire a Taste;" Hack 59, "Get Used to Losing;" and Hack 60, "Trust Your Intelligence (and Everyone Else's)."

IDIC

The IDIC (http://en.wikipedia.org/wiki/File:STVulcanIDIC.jpg) is a symbol from the fictional race of Vulcans on *Star Trek*. The acronym stands for the English phrase "Infinite Diversity in Infinite Combinations." (The Vulcans have their own name for it.) It has three components: a triangle, a circle, and a small gem.

A long scene from an early version of the script for the original series episode "Is There In Truth No Beauty?"introduced the symbol and the philosophy (http://forums.startreknewvoyages.com/index.php?topic=4481.0):

SPOCK (nods): Indeed. Perhaps even with those years on Vulcan, you missed the true symbology.

(indicates medallion)

The triangle and the circle. . . . different shapes, materials, textures . . . represent any two diverse things which come together to create here . . . truth or beauty.

There was more. The actors protested because they felt the IDIC was a merchandising gimmick, and most of the speech was cut. Nevertheless, fans adopted both the symbol and the philosophy, an appreciation for the synergy that occurs when dissimilar things meet.

While the IDIC could just be taken as a fertility symbol, it ties into much more, some of which is described in this book. One can think of the IDIC as a kind of *Taijitu* or yin-yang symbol that emphasizes diversity, rather than nonduality. It's an icon for the digital age. Some of Ron's associations with it include the following:

- The Laws of Form (Hack 40, "Notate Wisely"), because the IDIC shows how things arise from the combination of just two elements (0 and 1 or space and distinction).
- The *Tao Te Ching*, because of this related passage:

The Tao begot one.

One begot two.

Two begot three.

And three begot the ten thousand things.

The ten thousand things carry yin and embrace yang.

They achieve harmony by combining these forces.

- The combinatorial literature of the French literary group, the Oulipo.
- The Jorge Luis Borges story "The Library of Babel."

So what if the IDIC is corny? Make your own meaning for it and don't be afraid to take it lightly while you're taking it seriously.

The Exoself, the Mediator, and the Outlook

The exoself is a kind of "outboard brain" described by Greg Egan in several of his science fiction novels. It's much like a highly advanced internal smartphone. You program it, and it programs you, maintaining, structuring, and changing your mind at your command.

Because the exoself and its components are mainly software, we can have better-than-pretend versions of them right now or sooner. The world's first to-do list, probably in cuneiform, was a kind of exoself. There have been increasingly sophisticated versions ever since, from the Franklin Planner (http://store .franklinplanner.com) to Emacs Org Mode (http://orgmode.org/), and countless smartphone apps. Egan is imagining this kind of technology perfected and brought "on board" again.

Another of Egan's outboard brain components is the mediator, the subject of Hack 49, "Mediate Your Environment." It helps manage the interface between your brain and the outside world. The augmented reality smartphone apps that are currently appearing (in 2011), such as those that can translate the language of street signs on the fly, are also examples of mediator-style technology.

Whereas the mediator is a kind of communication device, the outlook might be thought of as security software, like an antivirus application or a firewall. Its purpose is to maintain the integrity of your personality, or to change it to one you prefer — a happier one, for example. Common wisdom has it that it takes only 70 years to transition from bright-eyed baby to "you kids get off my lawn!" How much worse would the problems be for people with life spans of millions of years, as in some science fiction?

The outlook plays a part in this book, too. Hack 52, "Metabehave Yourself," talks about creating reminders for yourself about how you want to behave, such as a picture of Gandhi in your cube at work. The IDIC can also serve as a kind of static, physical outlook. Ron sometimes wears an IDIC himself, not too conspicuously, to remind him of his ideas and ideals: all of the ones mentioned earlier, plus Stoicism, so akin to Vulcan philosophy, and Gene Roddenberry's futurism and humanism.

The exoself user is in some ways the opposite of the mentat described at the beginning of this section. The mentat mandates that nothing be used beyond the computing power of the bare human brain, whereas the exoself user is a cyborg.

Whether you obtain inspiration from technology in hard science fiction or try to implement social innovations in the here and now from soft science fiction, we hope you can see how science fiction can be a rich mine of ideas that might one day change the world.

Notes

1. *How William Shatner Changed the World*, DVD, (Woodland Hills, CA, USA: Allumination Filmworks, 2007).

2. Pamela Sargent, *More Women of Wonder: Science Fiction Novelettes By Women*, (New York: Vintage Books, 1976).

3. John Anthony McCrossan, *Books and Reading in the Lives of Notable Americans: A Biographical Sourcebook*, `www.russianspaceweb.com/tsiolkovsky_bio.html`

4. Ursula K. LeGuin, *The Dispossessed* (New York: Harper & Row, 1974).

5. John Clute and Peter Nicholls, *The Encyclopedia of Science Fiction* (New York: St. Martin's Press, 1993).

6. Jeff Prucher, *Brave New Words: The Oxford Dictionary of Science Fiction* (New York: Oxford University Press, 2007).

7. Frank Herbert, *Dune* (London: New English Library, 1972).

8. David Zindell, *The Broken God, The Wild,* and *War In Heaven* (New York: Bantam Books, 1994, 1996, and 1998).

Hack 32: Dare to Do No Permanent Damage

When faced with an opportunity that carries risk, use the rule of No Permanent Damage and roll on to profit and glory.

The inspiration for this hack comes from magicians Penn and Teller, who write about it in their book *How to Play with Your Food*. The heart of the idea is recognizing that rational fears are important and useful, while irrational fears often keep you from doing things that may profit you, give you an interesting experience, get respect from your friends, and generally make a name for yourself and live your life out to its edges. The problem is learning how to differentiate between rational and irrational fears, let the rational ones help you to remove real danger, and dispel the irrational ones. The rule of NPD can help you do it.

In Action

Obviously, magicians rely constantly on the rule of NPD. (Penn and Teller cite Houdini as an example of someone who worked it relentlessly.) In practice, the rule has two parts: Both respecting rational fear and discarding irrational fear are important to performing stunts and illusions as well as to many decisions in your life, like taking a new job, riding a roller coaster, eating strange food, or performing karaoke. Using knowledge to remove actual danger enables you to act on your respect for rational fears, and it also helps you to let go of fears that don't relate to real danger. This translates to three steps in applying the rule of NPD:

1. Determine what fears are grounded in reality because of real danger of permanent damage.

2. Find ways to remove real dangers.

3. If and when all real dangers are eradicated, dismiss irrational fears and proceed.

So how do you assess real danger? At base, anything that can actually kill you carries real danger. You don't want to be maimed either, or even break a leg. However, people fear many things that do *not* inflict real or permanent damage. Being disgusted, having to clean up a mess or replace a broken object (as long as it's not a priceless heirloom), getting dirty or tearing clothes — none of these cause real or permanent damage. Perhaps most important, embarrassment and looking foolish do not cause permanent damage. All of these can be inconvenient, but most of the time they're not as bad as people expect or fear. Examine each fear, ask yourself what is the worst that could happen, and see if you can find real danger among them.

To take the preceding examples, riding a roller coaster can carry real danger. However, most modern rides are extremely safe, as long as you follow the rules laid out by the designer. They only look dangerous. You can proceed to the second item, removing real danger, by making sure you fit into the seat properly and use all restraints correctly, so that they close and latch securely. Also, of course, follow any other rules, such as not riding coasters that warn against certain health problems such as heart ailments if you have those problems. If all of those measures are in place, there's no rational reason to give in to your other fears, so you may as well push through them and go for it.

Similarly, eating exotic food may be dangerous if you have food allergies. However, food that's simply unfamiliar or that consists of items you wouldn't normally find appetizing (such as insects) is probably not dangerous — after all, people in another culture eat it with gusto, and with no ill effects. Remove real danger by ensuring that you know there's nothing in the dish that will set off your known allergies, and then dig in.

Finally, consider that karaoke mic. Embarrassment most certainly doesn't cause permanent damage, so there's really no way to hurt yourself in a serious way by doing karaoke. You may pull it off spectacularly, winning the admiration of your friends and nearby strangers. Perhaps there's a certain amount of risk if you're singing in front of someone with whom you need to maintain a professional reputation, or a date you want to impress. However, it's worth considering that showing a fun side can make you look even better to your business associates (if they're the type who would go to a karaoke bar at all) and even if you don't sing as well as you hope, you might benefit by showing your bravery and that you're willing to join in with the team on an activity. The date, too, may be impressed by your courage, may be charmed if you do well, or may find your failure endearing and have interesting ways of comforting you.

Even a large decision like taking a new job carries relatively little danger of permanent damage. It seems as though changing jobs can ruin your life if it goes wrong, but in fact that's almost never true. Even a job that doesn't work out can give you an opportunity to gain new skills while you're in it, or help you prove to yourself whether that option is as great as it seemed, letting you clear the uncertainty about it out of your mind. Make sure you have a Plan B that will prevent you from becoming homeless, and give it a try. If it works out, your life has taken an interesting turn and you haven't missed out by listening to irrational fear. If not, you've gathered new information and new experiences, which is what living should be about.

Again, understanding the difference between real danger and the appearance of danger is an illusionist's stock-in-trade. You may not want to become a professional magician, but being able to bring a little magic wherever you go can be a wonderful thing. With some preparation, you can even learn a well-thought-out stunt or two and make it look casual and spontaneous, as well as exciting. This is what the professionals do, and having such a social tool can profit you in untold ways by making you absolutely unforgettable.

How It Works

What's important in this hack is to both respect rational fear and disrespect irrational fear, using your knowledge to assess risk clearly and override emotional reactions. It's not about dispelling fear completely and being foolhardy; fear has an important evolutionary purpose when it helps you to identify danger. However, fear can be attached to many things that don't warrant true caution, through over-imagination, bad experiences, and so on. The skill of respecting true danger and determining how to avoid it frees you to confront and dispel the fears that keep you from risk-taking that can really pay off.

The bugaboo that seems to grab most people is the fear of embarrassment. Many people miss out on a plethora of interesting and unfamiliar experiences simply because they're afraid to look foolish. Yet everyone looks foolish from time to time, so anyone watching can probably sympathize. We fear that onlookers will make fun of us, although this rarely actually happens after middle school. In fact, your audience is more likely to be thrilled if you succeed, be touched if you fail, and respect you for having tried something difficult. It's a no-lose situation. Once you wrap your mind around this, it becomes easier and easier to dismiss that fear.

In Real Life

We've already talked about many ways that the rule of NPD can apply in your everyday life, and you've seen how it's crucial to stage magic. Another group who lives by the rule of NPD is professional athletes, and none more than race car drivers. Auto racing can be legitimately dangerous, but modern racing is far less dangerous than it appears. Considering the real perils of racing has led to the development of high-tech safety equipment that greatly reduces the chance that drivers will be killed or seriously injured, even if they experience a crash. Professional drivers rely on highly skilled pit crews who make sure that all the necessary equipment is present and working properly, and that everyone on the track follows established rules and procedures scrupulously. Thinking through everything that could go wrong and acting on those fearful contingencies enables engineers and other professionals to reduce actual danger to a bare minimum, which means the crews and drivers can overcome any remaining fear to go out and confidently put their all into the races that provide an exciting show, and, possibly, immortality in the annals of the sport.

Hack 33: Make Happy Mistakes

Everyone makes mistakes. Learn to take advantage of your good ones.

It's often said that we should learn from our mistakes, and while that's generally good advice, it's not quite what this hack is about.[1] Instead, we'll be discussing how to recognize serendipity when it occurs — when your "mistake" is the right answer.

We'll also examine how more than one mind hack has come from a happy mistake, including a streamlined way to count to more than 1 million on your fingers, which is completely explained in the "In Real Life" section.

In Action

Clearly, many questions have only one answer, and it's always easier when procedures provide the results you want and expect. However, many people apply this expectation too broadly, and therefore miss an innovation or improvement that may be masquerading as a failure or imperfect example of something else. Although we may forget it, many of us actually learn this principle as children: A cygnet makes an awfully funny-looking duckling. The trick is to remember to look at what's really there and recognize the swan for what it is.

This requires open-ended thinking and approaching processes with an objective view. Instead of thinking of a linear process whereby you follow a procedure that "should" produce an expected result, or a question that has a specific correct answer, think of doing something and then observing the result. It may be the result you expected, but don't assume that the unexpected is automatically incorrect.

If you want to take a more systematic, objective approach, you can turn to the scientific method (Hack 54, "Think, Try, Learn"). Observe and record the results of your efforts. However, rather than just conclude you failed when something you did doesn't work out as planned, perform some post-"failure" analysis to see if anything can be salvaged, and whether your unexpected results might point the way to an improved solution. Ask yourself not only:

- *where* you failed,
- *how* you failed, and
- *why* you failed, but also
- *whether* you failed at all.

This sort of analysis corresponds to the Learn phase of the Think, Try, Learn process. The next step would be returning to the Think phase, to design an experiment to test the validity of your proposed better solution.

How It Works

People make mistakes for many reasons. Sometimes, one of these reasons is that the mistake is actually a more natural answer, even an obvious innovation. However, recognition of the innovation may be blocked because a certain way of doing things has been so taken for granted, so institutionalized, that although it may be obvious to an outsider that there is a better way to do things, it's not at all obvious to people inside the system (and sometimes "the system" is your own mind). In such a situation, your unconscious mind may process information or recognize reality faster than your conscious mind does, and override your intentions, producing the supposed mistake.

Natural selection functions by capitalizing on serendipitous mistakes. Most genetic mutations, or mistakes, are genuine failures that decrease the fitness of the organism and its descendants, if it has any. On occasion, however, a mutation occurs that works better in an organism's environment than the status quo. Organisms that inherit that happy mistake often go on to out-reproduce organisms that don't have it, and the mutation spreads.

Evolution can occur with ideas, or *memes*, as well as with genes. Ideas reproduce by being communicated; often a miscommunication produces invalid information, but sometimes it can produce a positive mutation, so to speak. You can think of this hack as memetic evolution, or, because your conscious effort enters into the selection process, a kind of memetic engineering.

In Real Life

There are many examples of recontextualizing and taking advantage of a happy mistake in the history of science. One is Alexander Fleming's discovery of penicillin. He accidentally let some mold enter a petri dish containing a culture of bacteria. When Fleming discovered that the mold could kill the bacteria, he worked to develop the first drug effective against such killers as *staphylococcus* bacteria and syphilis, with happy results for the world. Another famous example is Charles Goodyear's invention of the vulcanization process for curing rubber, which he found during his research when a sample of a certain mixture of rubber and sulphur was "carelessly brought into contact with a hot stove."

Ron can think of at least two occasions when making a happy mistake helped him substantially in creating or refining mind hacks. While they aren't nearly as important as the discovery of antibiotics or vulcanization, they may be a little more helpful as examples.

The Hotel Dominic Mistake

The first occasion on which a happy mistake helped create a mind hack was Ron's development of the Hotel Dominic system (www.ludism.org/mentat/ DominicSystem), which – in theory! – enables memorization and retention of 10,000 memory items or more, such as elements on the periodic table, world capitals, vocabulary words, bones of the body, and so on.

Ron developed the Hotel Dominic at a time when he was still learning the original Dominic System of mnemonics but didn't fully understand it. He was using the two-digit numeric codes of the Dominic System as a series of "loci" or "places" (as in Hack 2, "Build a Memory Dungeon"), whereas the "proper" use would have been to employ the Dominic System to memorize number strings, such as credit card numbers or phone numbers, and to store those in the places of a more orthodox memory journey like the memory dungeon.

Because Ron was already using the Dominic System the wrong way, and because the Dominic System is especially well-suited to memorizing four-digit numbers, it occurred to him that he could use the 10,000 four-digit numbers available (0000 to 9999) as places in an enormous imaginary hotel of 100 floors with 100 rooms each. He named this the Hotel Dominic in honor of the original system's inventor, Dominic O'Brien, and it became the basis for one of the hacks in our first book.

The Counting-to-a-Zillion Mistake

Another serendipitous creative leap came when Ron was interviewed on the local NPR station to promote our first book. One of the hacks in the book that consistently got the most attention was about counting to large numbers (about 1 million) on one's fingers. The basic idea for the hack came from a page on the Mentat Wiki called Phyabin (www.ludism.org/mentat/PhysioArithmetics), written by someone under a pseudonym.

Phyabin requires the person counting to use each finger to represent two distinct binary numbers at the same time. The technique is to first raise and lower fingers from the right thumb through the right pinky, to the left thumb through the left pinky for the values 1 through 512, and then repeat the whole sequence by curling and straightening the same fingers for the values 1,024 through 524,288.

If this sounds complicated, it is — much more complicated than it needs to be. In retrospect, it's so unnatural that it was perfectly natural for Ron to respond off-handedly (and mistakenly) that the hack uses base four, not base two, when the show's host asked him about it. In considering why he misspoke, Ron realized that the system works even better if you consider it in terms of base four instead of base two and use each finger to represent only one number.

The "mistake" of treating each finger as one base-four digit makes the system teachable in a few minutes to anyone who understands the concept of number bases (see Table 33-1).

Table 33-1: Simplified Positions for Counting to a Zillion on Your Fingers

BASE-4 DIGIT	BASE-2 EQUIVALENT	FINGER POSITION	VISUAL REPRESENTATION
0	00	straight, down	
1	01	straight, up	
2	10	curled, down	
3	11	curled, up	

In addition, while writing up this hack from memory, Ron forgot the order of fingers in Phyabin and again assumed that what seemed most simple and natural to him was correct. In this case, he looked at his hands and assumed his rightmost finger (right pinky) was the low digit and his leftmost finger (left pinky) was the high digit, just as if one were reading a base-four number off a page in a book or on a computer display.

Thanks to these two simplifying happy mistakes, you now have everything you need to count as high as 1,048,575 (4^{10}-1) on your fingers. The original hack took about seven pages of explanation, with six tables and four illustrations of hand positions.

NOTE The advantage of being able to read the number off your fingers from left to right should be obvious. However, if you find it tiring to flex your right pinky every time you add one to the number, you can retain the new base-four encoding but return to the Phyabin finger ordering, starting with the right thumb as low bit, which is more dexterous than the pinky in most people.

This very hack would probably not exist were it not for Ron's mistake on NPR; after the show, he thought about the Latin phrase *felix culpa* or "happy fault," which occurs in various forms throughout *Finnegans Wake*, one of his favorite books. He was spurred to develop this hack.

Notes

1. Alina Tugend, *Better by Mistake: The Unexpected Benefits of Being Wrong* (New York: Riverhead, 2011). A pretty good book on how to learn from mistakes, including actual examples of the medical checklists mentioned in Hack 1, "Remember to Remember."

Hack 34: Don't Know What You're Doing

Regain your creative spark and your artistic voice by letting go of control, silencing inner critics, and focusing on process rather than product.

Humans create as naturally as breathing. People throughout time and in all places draw, tell stories, and perform plays and rituals. Small children do it without instruction or thinking about it, instinctively, but somehow we lose the ability to do this without fear. As we grow older, we're taught that it's proper to spend our time working, or at least being "productive," and that creativity is only productive if you make something useful, exceptional, or otherwise objectively valuable.

Many creative projects die before being born because the uncertainty of a clean page is so frightening. Thinking about whether you have any talent, how to make something people will like, what it should look or sound like, and why you have any right to "waste" time and materials is a certain way to never actually create anything.

To move forward, you must learn to tolerate, and even enjoy, not really knowing what you're doing or going to do, and to be willing to let the process take you for a ride. You have to focus on the motion and action, rather than the resulting object. You have to understand that your creativity isn't wholly in your control, that it's a function of yourself and the world, and your relationship with the world. You have to further understand that you don't go through the process of making art to come out with a "good product" at the end, but for the fun and transcendental experience itself. What you actually make is a postcard you send yourself from the road.

This is true of any creative pursuit. You can create as you move through the world, going back to doing it as naturally as breathing — that's the origin of the word "inspiration," after all — by giving yourself space and time, and being in that space and time. Lynda Barry describes it this way in her book *What It Is* (Drawn and Quarterly, 2008):

> *What do drawing, singing, dancing, music making, handwriting, story writing, acting, remembering, and even dreaming all have in common? They come about when a certain person in a certain place in a certain time arranges certain uncertainties into certain form. The time for it is always with us, though we say, "I do not have that kind of time. The kind of time I have is not for this, but for that. I wish I had that kind of time." But if you had that kind of time — would you do it? Would you give it a try? A kind of doing both takes and gives time — makes live the dead hours inside us.*

In Action

The creativity exercises in this hack are meant to help you with a few tasks. One is to help you recognize what's stopping you from creating, so that you can effectively fight it. Another is to help you learn how to think about making art as a process instead of a means to the end of creating an object, and to get out of your own way. There are many, many other paths to these ends; these are only a few to set you on the road.

The Inner Critic

Before you move into the creative activities, it's helpful to learn about things that often stop you. One of the most powerful is the inner critic, the embodiment of an emotional force that inhibits you from creating. Most of us have multiple inner critics who wheedle, heckle, browbeat, and discourage us, from a vantage point inside our heads. Some might resemble a disapproving professor who doesn't think you're smart enough, or a parent who doesn't want to clean up your mess, or an arts columnist who thinks your work is trite and derivative. Sometimes inner critics can even seem friendly at a first glance, such as an aunt who thinks you'd be happier spending time with your kids, or a coach who exhorts you to be strong and ignore your emotional life in favor of getting "real" work done.

Your inner critics defend the status quo; they don't know anything about art or creativity, but they know that creating is upsetting and they want you to stop doing it. The inner critic will compare your representation to consensus reality and judge its "accuracy." What it doesn't understand is that art is not about accuracy or representation, but about filtering; it's your individual viewpoint that gives life to your art and makes it unique in the world, but your inner critics want to make you shut up and conform. The inner critic has a lot of investment in shutting you down, it's heartless, and because it lives in your head, it knows how to manipulate your emotions very well. No wonder it can scare you into never letting your real self out.

One of the primary ways to start disarming inner critics is to know the enemy. Draw your inner critics and write descriptions of them. Don't think too hard about this or try to be clever; capture whatever comes to mind and think about it later. Make a WANTED poster and a rap sheet. You usually have more than one inner critic, so draw them all. You need to know these voices and faces so you can recognize them the next time they come after you. Once you know who they are, practice telling them off.

Usually there are points in time and particular experiences when inner critics arise and form. You can help weaken their hold by understanding where they came from. Here's a possible map to points you may not recall consciously: Draw some simple things, an apple, a dog, a car. Then, look at the drawings as if someone else did them, and try to determine how old the artist might be. You may need help from someone else to be objective about this, so ask a friend who doesn't know you drew them. That age may reflect an experience when something froze in you artistically; use it as a clue to think what that experience might have been.

Keep Moving

Creativity is motion. When we spend too much time planning, evaluating, editing, and judging before we've even done anything, we've frozen, and it's hard to move again. We become focused on planning and executing the perfect sequence of actions that will produce a good, or at least acceptable, result on the first try. Successful artists and writers know, however, that drafts are key. The way to make something great is to produce and produce, then choose and edit later. Many people learned this in school writing papers (although many of us who were decent writers were lazy and still only produced one draft); others have learned how to do this since the advent of digital cameras, which make it easy for us to shoot 20 pictures of something and then select the best one.

Our writer friend Jay believes that everyone must write "a thousand pages of crap" before producing something that works, so the faster you produce those pages, the sooner you start doing things you like better. Realize that not everything you make must matter, and that making stuff that doesn't matter is also part of the process. If you have an idea for a story, write the same story five times; if you write about a memory, try writing it from five different viewpoints or interpretations. If you draw or paint, keep adding and fill up your paper to the edges. Start over and fill up another page or two. Doing works of small scope can help you warm up to this. Write haiku or nanofiction (stories of exactly 55 words); make quick sketches and abstract shapes.

Once you've made a lot of stuff, you can start choosing and focusing, and even recombining. Pick your favorites, or favorite parts. Maybe it seems clear that the start of one story actually works better with the end of another. Reshape a painting, cutting the canvas or paper into a different shape to focus on a part you like or cutting away something that doesn't add to the whole. You can even start drawing and painting on it again, glue other pieces to it, or glue it to another painting.

Don't be afraid to "waste" resources, whether that means time or supplies. If it makes you feel better, use inexpensive supplies meant for kids: newsprint, tempera and watercolor paint, chalk, crayons. Think about how much you might spend on going to the movies (considering tickets, refreshments, and so on), and then spend an evening with the supplies you bought with the same money. If you like to build sculptures, use objects from your recycle bin. Don't be afraid to spend a little to let your mind and hands consume creative "food" any more than you'd worry about giving your body a snack or a good meal. Experiment to see what kind of line you like to make; some people like pens, others pencils, crayon, brushes with ink, brushes with paint — find what feels good and makes you excited when you use it.

Practice keeping your hands and pen (crayon, pencil, brush, or whatever) moving. Lynda Barry suggests setting a timer for five or ten minutes and seeing if you can keep from stopping while you fill paper with writing and drawing, alternating if necessary. If you get stuck, draw spirals or shapes, or write the alphabet, as long as you keep moving. If you'd rather write, try "freewriting" for a set period of time, simply writing words down continuously, whether they're story, nonsense, or a stream of your thoughts at the moment, anything. To remember how to draw in motion the way kids do, illustrate a story as some-one reads it to you. Don't try to capture scenes in the story; draw the action and keep changing the same drawing so that it evolves as the story progresses.

Let Go of Control

If you think you can't draw without thinking it through first, remember the drawing we call doodling. Everyone submits to the urge to draw freely in cer-tain circumstances, but we dismiss this by calling it a silly name and saying it doesn't count. Doodling happens when your mind is elsewhere and your body is stuck in a place, such as a meeting or waiting on hold on the phone. It's mindless, aimless, motion-based, and all your own. I'll bet you know in the back of your mind that you return to the same shapes and patterns every time you have a chance to doodle. This is the last bastion of the free drawing inside you.

Try making doodle-type drawing meaningful. Get together with a friend and try to have a conversation via doodling. Take a pencil and start by drawing a shape on a piece of paper. Then give the pencil to your friend so that he or she can respond. Trade the pencil back and forth, altering the shapes, adding new ones, and seeing if you can understand without actually talking. When you both think you're done, you can discuss it if you want. What were you talking about? Is it an argument? Is it a story? If so, then try to write the story in words.

Understand that you don't have to constantly judge and control to create. Gather up some paper and paint, crayons, or whatever you enjoy, put on some music that you find interesting, then blindfold yourself and start painting. You might feel silly, but don't pay attention to the inner critic that's telling you it's silly. You might make a little mess, but don't listen to the inner critic telling you that you're not allowed — you're a grown-up and can clean up after yourself. Paint and draw blind for the space of a song, and then see what happened, what was sent through you onto the paper. Try it again, and again.

Collage is a great form for intuitive creation. Start with one of your blind-painted pieces and start adding to it. Alternatively, page through old magazines quickly and cut out images and words that catch your attention. Layer pieces, paint around and over them, emphasize and alter images with chalk or crayons. If something just seems like it needs some red, put some red on there. Keep going and don't try too hard to "make it look good." If you're more interested in writing, use the random words and images you found to write a story. Pick three words and one picture and go. Is the picture what you see? Who are you in that scene? What don't you see that might be behind you or to the side? Try using the same words and pictures to write a romantic story, a murder mystery, an alternative history, a science fiction story.

Get out of your own way and watch what happens. Don't be afraid to love what you make, although an inner critic may tell you that it's egotistical to do that. When you see that you aren't the maker, but the transmitter, of art — when you understand that when you create, you form a channel for the world to pass through, filtered by who and where you are in the moment — you'll be able to see that it's okay to enjoy that ride and appreciate the results.

Moments of shock in your life cause natural motion and disorientation, and they often renew your vision. If you move to a new location, change your relationship, have children, or undergo some other major life change, it changes how you see the world and shakes up a lot of your old, set patterns of relating to it. This can be a great source of fresh insight, so use it!

Artistic Kin

What visual art sings to you? Do you have an author who amazes you by expressing just what you'd say and how you'd say it, "if only you could write"? These artists are your "artistic kin." You recognize, even unconsciously, a shared view or aesthetic; what you love in their work is something that resonates with part of you, and that is likely to be part of your authentic work as well.

You can learn about yourself and your voice by studying what your artistic kin do. When you've produced some drawing or writing of your own, start reading or going to museums and checking art books to find work that looks similar to yours in certain ways. Start keeping a collection of stories and passages, or pictures, that evoke an emotional response in you or remind you of something you've made. Compare and identify the similarities, and how their work differs from yours. Note well: The purpose of this is not to mimic other creators or judge the "quality" of your work against theirs. It's to identify what belongs to you and to sharpen your vision of it, by looking at it next to similar work. It is also to help you see yourself in the company of these makers and take support from their virtual fellowship.

How It Works

Drawing comes naturally to children. Translating our experiences and what we see into pictures seems to be a basic human urge. For kids, drawing is an activity unto itself, a sort of do-it-yourself animation, something that happens in the moment as we think and tell stories. There's a direct line from mind to pencil, and we draw suspended in the moment, for the adventure of seeing what happens next or what appears on the paper.

As we get older, we learn that no activity is acceptable unless it's productive. Spending our time "playing" and "using up materials for no good purpose" is no longer supported or encouraged. We learn that working is what we should spend most of our time on, and even our nonwork time should be spent in "productive" pursuits. The focus shifts from doing something for joy or pleasure, or because it's fun and interesting, to the results we get from what we do, and whether it was "worth" spending time and money (in the form of materials) on. We judge the process by judging the product; if we don't find the product "valuable" in some way, the process has been a waste.

This is inimical to true creativity, but the next step is even worse. We start performing a cost-benefit analysis ahead of time, judging that we "have no talent" or skill, thus anything we make won't be very good, so there's no reason to make anything. We edit and critique our imagined project until we convince ourselves that there's no point to making it in the first place. We imagine giving ourselves a little gold star for being so sensible and saving all that wasted time and money! Over time we succeed in cutting ourselves off from those "childish" activities and the thoughts and feelings that drive them. If we do create, we try to make something good enough to justify the expenditure, but our efforts fall victim to our internalized criticism and reinforce our notion that we might as well not bother. Many of us nonetheless still carry that innate human urge to create, which won't be extinguished, and we find ourselves stuck, unable to know how to move forward, afraid of being foolish and of the critical voices in our heads, disconnected from the driving force of real self-expression, and aching to follow the urge again.

To reconnect with the joy and satisfaction of making art, we have to relearn how to think of it as a process and stop thinking about judging the object that may result from it. A piece of art should be a by-product of the adventure of making it, not the goal. To recapture the adventure that making art should be, you need to become comfortable with not planning out everything you'll do before you start, not knowing what will happen next, not necessarily being "good" at it — with being a little out of control.

In her wonderful graphic essay "Two Questions," Lynda Barry discusses the process of disconnecting from a child's experience of drawing to an adult's mannered fearfulness, and eventually reconnecting. The two questions referred to in the title are "is it good?" and "does it suck?" Learning to ask those questions is how we disconnect from authenticity. When we ask "is it good," we look for approval through making "good" art and follow someone else's standards to please them and get rewards. When we ask "does it suck," we learn to internalize inhibiting criticism and start changing and editing what we do to avoid negative feelings when someone tells us our art is "bad." We try to do only what is "good" and eliminate what is "bad," reacting to outside feedback rather than acting from our own instincts. Through it all, something inside knows that what we're doing is taking us further from ourselves, and that something is wrong, but we may not be able to pinpoint the problem or how to solve it. Only when we let go of solving it, when we can confidently answer "I don't know" to both questions and give ourselves back over to the mystery and free-fall excitement of creating without judgment, do we find our voices again.

This is not to say that there is no value to artistic discernment, or the editorial eye. We don't believe that *everything* made is great art. However, we think that most people exercise too much criticism and put the activities in the wrong order. *Editing should be applied after creativity happens, not before it starts.* To apply it to a potential creative act is to shut that act down and prevent it from happening, or from happening in a way that connects to personal truth. Sapping creative endeavor of personal truth drains it of vitality, authenticity, and originality, and even of the pleasure and enrichment that the creator can get from the act.

Because all of us have a past full of experiences connected to creativity, and because we all have inner critics, many readers will decide ahead of time that these techniques and exercises are silly and that they won't work. Because these techniques develop intuitive sense and are meant to stimulate action, they aren't easy to convey on a static page of text; conveying what you can expect to experience if you try them is impossible. You can only take the risk and jump, and see what happens to you.

In Real Life

We can't overestimate the influence of our teacher, Vedika Dietrich, on our understanding of these principles. Many of the exercises in this hack are adapted from her classes on intuitive creativity; Ron has taken her course on intuitive writing, and Marty has taken two courses of intuitive visual art with her.

Marty, in particular, found these courses life-changing. She has struggled all her life with the urge to create and the conflicts inherent in trying to do so, damage from inner critics, war with Lynda Barry's two questions, and more. By the time she reached Vedika's class, she had almost completely shut down her creativity. Through working with Vedika, she not only regained some equilibrium and new insight about how she creates and why she doesn't create as much as she'd like, but created art that frankly astonished her. She evaluates art differently when she sees it now, and the act of creating inspires her again, bringing her new insights about herself and the world that carry over into all areas of her life.

See Also

- If you happen to live in the Seattle area, you can take Vedika Dietrich's courses yourself. Visit her website at www.artsurgery.com to find her current course schedule, artistic manifesto, and more.

- Lynda Barry, *What It Is* (Montreal: Drawn and Quarterly, 2008) and *Picture This* (Montreal: Drawn and Quarterly, 2010). These books contain some of the ideas and techniques from Ms. Barry's course "Writing the Unthinkable," told in a combination of collage, story, autobiography, and suggested exercises. Marty has been a fan of Lynda Barry for decades, and she finds them beautiful, mind-blowing, and unfailingly inspirational.

- Danny Gregory, *The Creative License: Giving Yourself Permission to Be the Artist You Truly Are* (New York: Hyperion, 2006). Another take on how to reconnect with authenticity and pleasure in creativity, with advice and drawing/writing suggestions to follow.

- Dean Nimmer, *Art from Intuition: Overcoming Your Fears and Obstacles to Making Art* (New York : Watson-Guptill Publications, 2008). A different set of very practical, step-by-step instructions for following a course of exercises to develop freer, more intuitive art.

■ David Bayles and Ted Orland, *Art and Fear: Observations on the Perils (and Rewards) of Artmaking* (Santa Cruz, CA: Image Continuum Press, 1993). A classic exploration of the psychology of creative blockage.

Hack 35: Ratchet

The Roman poet Ovid wrote, "Add little to little and there will be a big pile." In many areas of life, from board games to the board of directors, a spectacular "win" is not as important as a steady gain-and-maintain.

In terms of tools such as socket wrenches, ratcheting refers to mechanisms that move in only one direction, usually in a series of small incremental steps. In the sense we'll be using it in this hack, ratcheting refers to accumulating things and accomplishments so that you add to them consistently, even if it's only a little at a time, and avoid depleting them.

Money is an example of something that can go either way. Generally, we both earn and spend money constantly. However, we're taught from childhood that if we start saving some, even a few dollars per week, it will add up to a substantial amount over time if we don't touch it. The trick is to keep putting away that little bit and find ways to keep yourself from spending it.

No one can steal your having written a book or having composed a song from you. Your accomplishments only accumulate. Someone might sue you for the royalties from your song or (as happened to Ron once) even claim to have written your book. However, your accomplishments will remain.

In Action

Here are some ways you can try to ratchet your life toward a gigantic pile of goodness.

Blog

As many writers have realized, if you have anything at all interesting to say, writing frequent blog posts is a great way to develop a body of work and keep your writing fingers limber. It's also a way to attract some attention to your writing, as long as you don't write exclusively about your cat, what you ate for lunch, or how long it has been since you last blogged. Even writing about those things can bring you attention, however, if you do it well and consistently. Over time, if you consistently keep adding to your pile of blog posts, you accumulate work and readership, bit by bit. Many writers have parlayed this into book deals and more.

Save

Your mom and dad told you to add a dollar to your piggybank out of your allowance every week, and they were right. Saving even a tiny bit of money every week adds up, and eventually you can accumulate enough to invest and let the money multiply itself while you're ratcheting more into the system.

Many employers offer an option to route some of your earnings into savings before you even get it in your paycheck — you never have a chance to touch it, much less spend it. This can be very useful if you don't trust yourself to faithfully remember to sock your bit away every time. Some companies enable you to put the money into a retirement account before taxes, matching the funds to a prescribed amount. Many people don't take advantage of this, thinking that they can't afford to save enough to make it worthwhile. If this is you, rethink your position; any money saved is money you'll have later, and matching funds are free money! Typically, it's hard to withdraw money from such accounts without a penalty, which is another bonus; once you accumulate a little more, consider investing in a CD or other short-term investment to make it even harder for you to weaken and spend it.

In addition, if you've put your saved money into a bank account or certain other investments, it automatically takes advantage of another classic ratcheting mechanism: interest. If you look at it as a separate amount, the interest paid on many investments seems like a tiny amount, almost not enough to even think about. If it's consistently added every month, however, it can turn into a substantial amount. Furthermore, compounded interest is a percentage of what you've added, so the amount added to your account adds to the amount of interest you get — it's interest on your interest, a double ratchet, so to speak.

Read and Learn

You can't unread a book, however much you might wish you could in some cases. That makes reading ideal for ratcheting.

Any time you finish a book, log it and keep a careful record of what you've read so far for the year. You might be pleasantly surprised by how much you read, or unpleasantly surprised by how much of it was trashy entertainment. Either way, it's a record of the knowledge and experience you've accumulated, bit by bit. Thinking about reading as ratcheting and seeing the "balance sheet" of what you're stockpiling in your head may even change how you choose your reading material. For help with making a lifetime reading plan, see Hack 6, "Establish Your Canon."

Why not try implementing a hack a week from this book or another book of hacks you find useful, such as *The Lifehacker Guide to Working Smarter, Faster, and Better* by Gina Trapani and Adam Pash (Wiley, 2011)? Many people are daunted by reading the whole book at once, thinking they could never learn all of the techniques. However, taken one at a time, many of them aren't very hard. Little by little, you'll be adding to your skills and making your mind a little stronger and more agile, and that will translate to benefits in other parts of your life.

Use Small Time

The next time you have half an hour, or even 15 minutes, with little to do, consider how to fill it. You could ignore it, or you could use it to exercise, clean off a tabletop or fold a pile of laundry, read an article, or sort your mail (see Hack 21, "Get Control of Yourself"). Each task seems small, but over time you'll end up with a fitter body, a cleaner house, more interesting conversation, and a better handle on your personal affairs. Make the habit of looking for small tasks to fill odd bits of time when you're waiting for something or between other tasks. Keep a list if necessary, and be ready so that you don't have to waste the time, when it arrives, thinking about what to do.

How It Works

How it works, in this case, is fairly straightforward: Little bits add up to a larger quantity over time. The main challenge is often believing this simple idea. While it's quite obvious when you consider it abstractly, it's easy to dismiss it in real life. We often look at a few dollars, or a page or two of writing, or 20 minutes of physical exercise, as being trivial or unworthy of consideration. By dismissing the importance of these smaller items, we throw away the possibility of obtaining the large aggregate we could achieve if we were patient and consistent in our actions.

Often, the key is to remove the control from our hands or our conscious decision making. By implementing techniques in your life that will control the small bits for you (e.g., diverting a small stream of money automatically, or setting up a blog that reminds you to write), you can painlessly make progress on accumulating something considerable. (See the "Organizing Your Environment" section of Hack 52, "Metabehave Yourself," for more about this kind of technique.)

In Real Life

We often think about life in terms of board games because some of our profoundest life lessons have come from them. Games can teach you about careful resource management, seeing the big picture, planning, timing — and ratcheting.

One important lesson on ratcheting came to Ron when he was studying an article on strategy in auction games such as Modern Art or Dream Factory (not his strong suit). The article's author wrote that some players of auction games typically won't make an offer if they think the other player would be getting a better deal. However, he pointed out, the question is not whether any particular person is getting a better deal than you are in a particular transaction. The question is whether *you* are getting "a little something," such as a few victory points, on *every* turn. Win by ratcheting.

Marty has had a similar experience in improving her Scrabble game. In her case, she realized the relationship between the idea of ratcheting and the game concept of *tempo*, meaning that in order to win a game, you usually need to mind the pace of the game and ensure that you don't fall behind the other players too far, even if you haven't had an opportunity to make a big winning score yet. By focusing on keeping pace, you're ready to benefit when the big score arrives. Furthermore, you can draw ahead (or consolidate a lead) by simply ensuring that you score even a few points more than your opponent on every word.

It is said that if you're lucky, you'll live about 30,000 days. Over 23,000 of those will be spent as an adult. If you write one page a day as an adult, you'll have written enough for about 75 300-page books. Science fiction writer Gene Wolfe was able to write his award-winning, four-volume masterpiece, *The Book of the New Sun*, over several years because he ratcheted. He was employed full-time as an industrial engineer at the time, and a good one too — he designed the device that makes Pringle's potato chips. For 20 years, Wolfe arose at 5:00 a.m. to write for an hour before he went to his day job. He now writes full-time.

Geek icon Jonathan Coulton changed his career from computer programmer to professional recording artist when he recorded a song every week for a year with his "Thing a Week" project. He posted these songs on his website, and over the course of the year he accumulated a portfolio of songs and a fan base, as word spread about the project and more people visited his site to listen to the songs each week. Because he was releasing one song a week, rather than a book a year, and he had a viral boost from the Internet, Coulton was able to quit his day job even faster than Wolfe was.

Certainly Gene Wolfe and Jonathan Coulton have talent and skill, but what tipped the scale was their willingness to ratchet rather than waiting until they could stop everything else to focus on a big project. Although we're nowhere near as successful as Wolfe or Coulton, the book you're holding is also the result of ratcheting. From the initial establishment of the Mentat Wiki and the work of many contributors there, to our first book, to *Mindhacker*, there has been a long, slow, hack-by-hack accumulation of content and technique.

You too can do this! What ability do you have that you can exercise once a day or once a week to produce something that grows into a valuable asset?

See Also

- Robert Maurer, *One Small Step Can Change Your Life: The Kaizen Way*, (New York: Workman, 2004).

Math and Logic

Math and logic: Many of us both love them and hate them simultaneously. If you're math-phobic, you might try to get along by avoiding them as much as possible, but we hope these hacks can help you learn to let them into your life a little more. Mathematics and logic are critical skill sets for clear thinking (Hack 38, "Think Clearly about Simple Errors") and solving real-world problems (Hack 41, "Engineer Your Results"), as well as expanding your understanding of the physical world (Hack 42, "Enter the Third Dimension").

Math and logic can help you have fun, too. You can learn simple techniques to roll dice in your head (Hack 36, "Roll the Mental Dice") so you can play games on car trips and other places where real dice would be inconvenient, and hone your logic skills with games in which you play detective (Hack 37, "Abduct Your Conclusions").

Some people think the world is made of math. Whether or not that's true, it certainly seems to follow mathematical and logical laws, and it always pays to understand the rules for the world in which you live. Breaking those laws can have powerful consequences, so don't get busted — ignorance of the law is definitely no excuse!

Hack 36: Roll the Mental Dice

You need a random number, but you don't have dice handy. Generate random numbers as large as you want by rolling dice in your head.

Quick! You need a way to generate random numbers using just your brain, because you're playing in the pool, driving, falling asleep, or doing something else that makes it difficult to roll physical dice. Maybe you're playing games (board, role-playing, or purely mental) or breaking out of a rut by making decisions randomly. Don't panic — you can use simple math on random words from your surroundings to quickly create random numbers, just about anytime and anywhere.

In Action

For each of these procedures, you'll need to be able to come up with a short random word, either spontaneously or from the environment. To get one, check nearby signs or reading material, ask a friend or passerby, or do anything similar that seems good to you. You'll also need to know or work out the number value of each letter, corresponding to its place in the alphabet: A=1, B=2, C=3, and so on through Z=26.

Flipping a Coin in Your Head

You can quickly simulate some coin flips or obtain some binary (base-2) digits by summing the letter values of a word and checking whether the result is odd or even. An even result can be considered tails or 0. An odd result can be considered heads or 1. For example, you can get a coin flip from the word "tie" as follows:

```
T=20, I=9, E=5.
20 + 9 + 5 = 34.
```

34 is even, so the result is either tails or 0, depending on whether you need a coin flip or a binary digit (bit), respectively.

The d6 Method

To emulate a six-sided die, follow this procedure:

1. Find a short word, such as "cat."
2. Sum the numerical values of the letters in the word: C=3, A=1, T=20, and then 3 + 1 + 20 = 24.
3. Calculate the number modulo 9 (see the section "How It Works" for the procedure).

If the remainder is a 0, 7, or 8, which will happen one-third of the time, discard it and try a new word. Otherwise, the remainder will be a pseudo-random number from 1 through 6. Congratulations! This is your six-sided die roll. (The result for the word "cat" is 6.)

The d10 Method

To emulate a ten-sided die, or find a base-10 digit from 0 to 9, follow this procedure:

1. Find a random short word, such as "gnu."
2. Sum the numerical values of the letters in the word: G=7, N=14, U=21, and then 7 + 14 + 21 = 42.
3. Calculate the number modulo 11 (see the section "How It Works" for the procedure).

If your remainder is 10, which will happen less than 10% of the time, discard it and try a new word. Otherwise, the remainder will be a pseudo-random number from 0 through 9, your virtual ten-sided die roll. (The result for the word "gnu" is 9.)

To simulate sizes of dice other than d6 or d10, you can use the d10 method to generate base-10 digits, which you can then string together to make as large a number as you need. For example, mentally rolling a d10 twice will get you two base-10 digits, with which you can emulate percentile dice by using one number for each digit (00–99). If you need a die with a size between a d10 and d100, let's say a d80, then roll the larger die (d100) and discard any values over 80. If you need a d800, then first roll a d1000 and then discard any values over 800, and so on (www.boardgamegeek.com/geeklist/7467/item/119405).

> **WARNING** You can't just add dice together to get the result you want, such as adding two d6s together to try to get a d12. The distribution of numbers (how often each comes up) will be wrong. On a fair d12, each number from 1 through 12 comes up just as often as the others. On two d6s added together, some numbers, such as 7, will come up much more often, because they can result from so many combinations (1+6, 2+5, 3+4, 4+3, 5+2, and 6+1), whereas a 1 can *never* be rolled because the smallest number possible on two dice is 2 (1+1). This imbalance is the basis of a lot of dice games, such as craps.

How It Works

The number theory behind modulo mathematics is not important for this hack. You only need to understand that modulo 9, explained below, produces integers from 0 through 8; modulo 11, also explained below, produces integers from 0 through 10. Both of these procedures generate integers in a fairly unpredictable way and with a uniform distribution. These two key features enable you to simulate six-sided dice, ten-sided dice, coin flips, and ultimately dice of any size you like with effectively random (or random enough) results.

The Modulo Operation

Calculating with the modulo operation means getting the remainder of one number when it is divided by another number, called the modulus. Thus, 64 modulo 5 (or 64 mod 5 for short) equals 4, because 64/5 = 12 with a remainder of 4. The remainder is the number that will simulate your die roll.

If the number being divided is less than the modulus, the result is 0 with the first number as a remainder. Thus, 3/8 = 0 with a remainder of 3, so 3 mod 8 = 3.

Modulo 9

There is an easy shortcut for calculating a number modulo 9. Sum the digits of the number, and keep doing so until you have a single digit. If the digit is 9, treat it as 0. The result is the original number modulo 9.

Examples:

```
429 mod 9
4 + 2 + 9 = 15
1 + 5 = 6
```

Therefore, 429 mod 9 = 6.

```
9396 mod 9
9 + 3 + 9 + 6 = 27
2 + 7 = 9 (same as 0)
```

Similarly, 9396 mod 9 = 0.

Modulo 11

Calculating a number modulo 11 is almost as easy as calculating one using modulo 9, with a little practice:

1. Sum all the digits in odd places (ones, hundreds, ten thousands, and so on — see below); call the result the *odds*.
2. Sum all the digits in even places (tens, thousands, hundred thousands, and so on); call the result the *evens*.
3. Subtract the evens from the odds.
4. If the result is greater than 10, as when calculating a number modulo 9, repeat the preceding steps until you have a number less than or equal to 10. If you get a number less than 0, keep adding 11 to it until you have a number from 0 to 10 inclusive. The final result is the original number modulo 11.

Examples:

```
5417 modulo 11

4 3 2 1 (places)
5 4 1 7
```

1. The odd places contain 7 (in place 1, counting from the right) and 4 (in place 3). 7 + 4 = 11. We call this sum the *odds*.
2. The even places contain 1 (in place 2) and 5 (in place 4). 1 + 5 = 6. We call this sum the *evens*.
3. Subtract the evens from the odds: 11 - 6 = 5.
4. Thus, 5417 mod 11 = 5.

```
9396 modulo 11

4 3 2 1 (places)
9 3 9 6
```

1. 6 + 3 = 9 (the odds)
2. 9 + 9 = 18 (the evens)
3. 9 - 18 = -9 (the odds minus the evens)
4. -9 + 11 = 2. Thus, 9396 mod 11 = 2.

In Real Life

This hack can help you with everything from playing board games to selecting pizza toppings, but your friends are going to get bored and restless if you take a long time to calculate a "die roll," so practice is essential. To use this hack quickly, it particularly helps to memorize the values of the most common letters of the alphabet. Then you can count backwards and forwards from them to find the values you need. For example, T is 20, so S is 19 and U is 21. It's also especially helpful to memorize the values of the vowels.

A three-letter word will always generate a number that is two digits long at most; ZZZ, the highest possible three-letter "word," has a value of 78 (3 × 26). This makes three-letter words especially useful for the d10 method, because to calculate modulo 11, you simply subtract the left digit of the sum of the letter values from the right one. (The "left digit" of a one-digit number is 0.)

Another way to improve the quality of the results is to be even more creative about finding your initial "word." Take the first or last few letters of long words from your environment (such as "nce" from "performance"), or the second, third, and fourth letters, or the first letter of three consecutive words, and so on. This provides a wider range of possible results, because including non-word letter sequences provides a larger pool of letter combinations. Using uncommon combinations also makes it harder to cheat by suggesting common words. For example, so many people suggest "cat" to Ron when he asks for a three-letter word that he always asks for another word, because he know its result by heart (see above).

Hack 37: Abduct Your Conclusions

Most people know about deductive logic, and most scientists understand the role of inductive logic in science. Now learn about the neglected step-sibling of deduction and induction, abduction.

Sir Arthur Conan Doyle's great fictional detective Sherlock Holmes was fond of saying he came to his conclusions through a process of deduction, but this is not strictly true. Holmes's method is not deduction for the most part; deduction takes a general rule and follows it to a specific conclusion. More often, Holmes would use a form of logical inference first described by his real-life American contemporary, the philosopher Charles Sanders Peirce. This form of logic is used in police work, science, and medicine to generate explanations for unexplained phenomena, and is known by various names, such as *inference to the best explanation, retroduction,* and *abduction.* We use the latter term, which was coined by Peirce, in this hack.

A particularly good example of Holmes's use of abduction comes from *The Sign of Four:*

> *[Holmes] answered, leaning back luxuriously in his arm-chair, and sending up thick blue wreaths from his pipe. "For example, observation shows me that you have been to the Wigmore Street Post-Office this morning. . ."*
>
> *"Right!" said [Watson]. ". . . But I confess that I don't see how you arrived at it. It was a sudden impulse upon my part, and I have mentioned it to no one."*
>
> *"It is simplicity itself. . . Observation tells me that you have a little reddish mould adhering to your instep. Just opposite the Seymour Street Office they have taken up the pavement and thrown up some earth which lies in such a way that it is difficult to avoid treading in it in entering. The earth is of this peculiar reddish tint which is found, as far as I know, nowhere else in the neighborhood."*[1]

Conan Doyle understood abductive reasoning well enough to make a career of writing fiction about it, but he alternated between calling abduction "deduction" and using other terms like "observation," as in this passage. Of course, Peirce's term was quite new when Conan Doyle was writing, and there's no reason to believe Conan Doyle was aware of it. Similarly, you may understand abduction instinctively, because you've learned it in school science labs or seen people walking through the steps on TV shows. However, like many people, you may not have known what it's called, or how it differs from induction and deduction. (Many people conflate these terms and apply them incorrectly, so it's not surprising that there's a great deal of confusion about them.) Please bear with this explanation, because you may have to unlearn some of what you think you know about it!

As you'll see, one of the main differences between deduction and abduction is that abduction and induction are forms of *defeasible reasoning*. More science than math, they do not always come up with the right answer, even when done correctly. By contrast, proper deduction is airtight, like arithmetic. For example, one common use of deduction is to rule out all alternative possibilities in a limited domain, as in a game of Clue. As Holmes might say, "Haven't I told you, Watson, that once you have eliminated the impossible, whatever remains, however improbable, must be the truth? It was Colonel Mustard in the library with the lead pipe!"

In Action

Let's examine the three main types of logical inference, from the most familiar, deduction, through induction, to the least familiar, abduction.

Deduction

Deduction is the process of moving from fact to fact by a step-by-step logical process. In a typical deductive syllogism, or logical argument, the first step is a general law, the second step is a particular fact, and the third step is a conclusion arrived at by combining steps 1 and 2 in a logical way. If the first two steps, or premises, are correct, and the reasoning process itself is sound, then the third step, the conclusion, must also be correct.

The classical example of a syllogism is as follows:

1. All men are mortal.

2. Socrates is a man.

3. Socrates is mortal.

In the nineteenth century, Charles Sanders Peirce created a thought experiment for trying out all three kinds of logical reasoning we're interested in. It's usually called the *beanbag model* today. He wrote:

Suppose I enter a room and there find a number of bags, containing different kinds of beans. On the table there is a handful of white beans and, after some searching, I find one of the bags contains white beans only.[2]

Peirce's example of deductive reasoning uses the beanbag model as follows:

1. All the beans in this bag are white.
2. These beans are from this bag.
3. These beans are white.

Of course, this conclusion is about as surprising as the "discovery" that Socrates could die. This is one reason we need defeasible methods of reasoning like induction and abduction, which are riskier but offer potentially larger rewards. On the other hand, because of its rigor, deduction enables useful error checking. If steps 1 and 2 are true, then step 3 logically follows. Otherwise, if the beans you have in step 3 are not white, then you know that either step 1 or step 2 is not true, or both. Either some of the beans in the bag are not white, or the beans you have did not come from the bag.

Notice how our deductions move from the general (all men are mortal; all of the beans in this bag are white) to the particular (Socrates is mortal; these beans are white).

Induction

By contrast, induction is often said to reason from the particular to the general, or from observations to laws. The discovery of the general law $E = mc^2$ from many particular observations in physics was at least partly the result of inductive reasoning. Instead of reasoning 1, 2, 3 as deduction does, induction reasons backwards — 3, 2, 1.

Here's how induction works in the domain of the mortality of Socrates. From now on, we'll mark the parts of our syllogisms with Peirce's names for them: *law, hypothesis,* and *observation*:

3. **Observation:** Socrates is mortal. (And Leonardo is mortal. And Shakespeare is mortal. And Fred, Ethel, Lucy, Ricky. . .)
2. **Hypothesis:** Socrates and the others are men. (In the old-fashioned sense of "human," of course.)
1. **Law:** All men are mortal.

This upside-down syllogism mirrors what humankind has induced to its sorrow over the millennia. Its beanbag counterpart is as follows:

3. **Observation:** These beans are white. (And so are these beans. These too.)
2. **Hypothesis:** These beans are from this bag.
1. **Law:** All the beans in this bag are white.

This is a useful conclusion to draw, no matter whether you're betting on the color of the next bean from the bag, or looking for a source of more white beans for soup. Of course, induction is defeasible, and therefore prone to errors from overgeneralization. You might reasonably assume that someone filled the bag with white beans, but maybe a brown one slipped in by accident.

Abduction

Finally, abduction is the kind of reasoning performed by a physician diagnosing your illness, or by Sherlock Holmes solving a crime. Instead of reasoning forward (1, 2, 3) like deduction, or backward (3, 2, 1) like induction, abduction reasons "sideways" (1, 3, 2), from a general *law* and a particular result or *observation* to a *hypothesis* which is to be tested further, usually with the scientific method. For example,

1. **Law:** All men are mortal.
3. **Observation:** Socrates is mortal.
2. **Hypothesis:** Socrates is a man.

The hypothesis that Socrates is a man is hardly surprising to us, but it might have been to his contemporaries; many humans in classical times were worshipped as gods, and Socrates himself claimed to be guided by a divine inner voice.[3]

Slightly more practically, abductively reversing steps 2 and 3 in Peirce's beanbag example nets us the following:

1. **Law:** All the beans in this bag are white.
3. **Observation:** These beans are white.
2. **Hypothesis:** These beans are from this bag.

This is a useful hypothesis, of the sort that might help you solve a crime, cure a disease, or both, in the case of a corporate malefactor that has tainted all the white beans with *E. coli*. The main problem is that reasoning this way seems counterintuitive, at least until you remember the model of a roomful of beanbags, all containing different kinds of bean — and, more important, that what you're after with abduction is a plausible, testable hypothesis, never airtight truth.

As explained, abduction is not an infallible method of reasoning; it is defeasible. Not only is it prone to logical fallacy, just as with deduction and induction, but even abductive reasoning that is logically correct can arrive at a conclusion that is *factually* incorrect. For instance, although the beanbag example above is a formally correct example of abductive inference, unless we have done an exhaustive search of the beanbag room, one of the other bags might contain a few white beans, and we might have drawn some of those. Even if we *have* done an exhaustive search of the room and found no other white beans, our beans might have come from another room!

Ultimately, all abductive inference can do is establish a testable hypothesis based on probabilities. However, because this is the basis of the scientific method and therefore most twenty-first century knowledge, that might just be sufficient.

In Real Life

For an even more concrete example of everyday abductive reasoning, consider this sequence:

1. **Law:** Our house has two rambunctious dogs, and there are often ice cream cartons in the garbage.

3. **Observation:** Tonight we came home to shredded ice cream cartons all over the living room.

2. **Hypothesis:** The dogs got into the garbage.

Now it's time to test the hypothesis against various other bits of evidence. We would expect to see ice cream on our dogs' whiskers, as well as other items that were in the garbage strewn around the scene of the crime. If we don't find these things, it may be time to consider that our hypothesis has been *falsified* and look for some other reason the ice cream cartons have been strewn around. A break-in, perhaps? Or maybe we're just slobs.

Let's compare the deductive and inductive versions of the ice-crime. On the one hand, if Ron knows the general state of affairs in the household (step 1) and Marty tells him on the phone that the dogs got into the garbage (step 2), it's not much of a leap to *deduce* that there are ice cream cartons all over (step 3). On the other hand, for a pet sitter who enters our house and observes that there are shredded ice cream cartons all over (step 3), and has other reason to believe that the dogs got into the garbage (step 2), such as catching them in the act, it would be entirely reasonable to *induce* the general law that we like ice cream and our dogs are rambunctious (step 1).

The moral of this hack is that there are at least three types of reasoning, and they run from the best known, deduction, which attempts to find a particular result, and reasons 1, 2, 3 using the model above; to the less known but still commonly used form of logic called induction, which attempts to formulate a general law and reasons backwards 3, 2, 1; to their neglected sibling abduction, which attempts to generate a plausible hypothesis and reasons "sideways" 1, 3, 2.

To get along in everyday life, you probably use a combination of all three types of logical tool, and you probably seldom consider it consciously. Now that you know what they're called and how they work, you can choose the best tools for the job with thoughtful discrimination.

See Also

- Bruce Thompson's "Types of Argumentation: Retroduction" (http:// web.archive.org/web/20080126071042/http://www.cuyamaca.net/ brucethompson/Fallacies/retroduction.asp) is a unique survey of the logical fallacies possible in abductive reasoning.

- *Sherlock Holmes, Consulting Detective* and *Crack the Case* are out-of-print board games with a detective theme that exercise abductive reasoning. Used copies may often be found for sale on BoardGameGeek (www .boardgamegeek.com/).

- "Lateral thinking puzzle" books usually offer the same kind of stimulation in a less structured way.

- Raymond Smullyan's books of "retrograde analysis" chess problems, *The Chess Mysteries of Sherlock Holmes* and *The Chess Mysteries of the Arabian Knights*, provide abductive reasoning exercises in one of their purest forms.

Notes

1. Arthur Conan Doyle, *The Sign of Four* (Project Gutenberg, 2008). Accessible at www.gutenberg.org/etext/2097.

2. Charles S. Peirce, Nathan Houser, and Christian J. W. Kloesel, *The Essential Peirce: Selected Philosophical Writings* (Bloomington: Indiana University Press, 1992).

3. Plato, *Apology*, trans. Benjamin Jowett, (Project Gutenberg, 1999). Accessible at www.gutenberg.org/etext/1656.

Hack 38: Think Clearly about Simple Errors

Strange but true: Many people frequently "flip the sign" on reality and logic, conflating true with false and existence with nonexistence. This defect, and a few others, can be unlearned. Here are the basics.

There are many errors you can make in everyday reasoning. You can find lists of logical fallacies in books on critical thinking, such as *ad hominem* arguments, circular logic, and so on. However, there are some mental errors you seldom hear about except in lists of mistakes made by software developers. These problems are actually extremely common outside the world of software development, and can have consequences ranging from missing a flight to merely making you look like a fool — or worse.

In Action

People make many kinds of mistakes, but we're only going to talk about three of the most common: sign flips, off-by-one errors, and a particular kind of off-by-one error called a *fencepost error*. Most of these errors involve small numbers, like 0, 1, 2, and -1, so we'll also discuss the problems people have thinking about small numbers in general.

Sign Flip

You may think of opposites, such as black and white, as worlds apart, but they usually have more in common with each other than with almost anything else. For example, black and white are both extremes of the same continuum; you can change black into white and back, but you can't change either into a kitchen table. People say "it's a black-and-white situation" to signify that the situation has stark differences, but a better phrase might be "it's a black-and-*wet* situation."

Just like Tweedledum and Tweedledee in *Through the Looking Glass*, opposites may be at war but still very difficult to tell apart. Opposites are frenemies, not enemies! Because people don't realize how similar opposites really are — the phrase "complete opposites" usually indicates maximal distinction — they're often fooled into substituting one member of a pair for the other. To express difference, it's better to think in terms of ideas that are completely independent, like the x and y axes in Cartesian space, rather than just the positive and negative sides of a single axis. As Ian Stewart and Jack Cohen wrote of another pair of twins in their science fiction novel, *Wheelers*:

> And if anyone ever needed evidence that the phrase "identical twins" was a misnomer, the Odingo girls were living proof . . . mentally, they were not so much opposites as orthogonal — their thoughts ran at right angles to each other. It had made them a powerful team on the rare occasions when they had joined forces. Orthogonal vectors span the largest dimensional subspaces.[1]

Because opposites are so similar, it's easy to mistakenly convert one into the other with a single word, or even a single character (-1 is not the same as 1).

The common expression "cheap at half the price" is a sign flip. If something costs 10 dollars, it's not surprising that it's cheap at five. The expression should be "cheap at twice the price" — if it would still be a good deal at 20 dollars, the asking price of 10 is naturally a bargain. For similar reasons, the expression "I could care less" is a sign flip too; people usually mean, "I couldn't care less."

Here's a simple way to fight sign flips in speech and writing. Count the number of times the word "not" or another form of negation is used in a statement. If the number is even (think double negatives in English), they cancel out, and the result is affirmation (yes). If the number is odd, then all but one of them cancel out, and the result is negation (no).

To take an extreme example, if your significant other should find you telling him you don't not not not not not not not not love him (nine instances of the word "not" plus an "n't" is an even number, meaning you do love him), he can relax, but if he tells you he doesn't not not not not not not not not not not love you (10 nots and an n't mean one is left, hence love is negated), maybe it's time for you to find an online dating site.

Yes, the love-me, love-me-not example is silly, but notice how easy it is to determine whether a sentence is an affirmation or a negation by simply counting, thereby overcoming the human short-term memory limit when all those *not*s pile up. This is similar to what computer programmers do, not only when they have a complicated series of negations, but more commonly when they need to use a lot of parentheses: The number of right parentheses must equal the number of left parentheses. Not enough closing parentheses and the code they are structuring has been "left open"; too many right parentheses will also generate an error. Thus, programmers get into the habit of counting parentheses as they go.

Sign flips also occur in a more literal sense when people consider numbers. A common example is calculating the time in a distant time zone: Do you add several hours or subtract them? Even if you regularly convert mentally from your current time zone to a different one, such as where your parents live or where a particular business office is located, it's easy to make this slip if you're not careful.

Off-By-One Error

An off-by-one error (also known as an OBOE) happens when you either add or subtract 1 by mistake when working with a number. For example, you might tell your carpool buddy you'll pick him up at 8:00 a.m. but mean 9:00. Thinking an important flight is at 11:00 when it's really at 10:00 could mean anything from the loss of several hundred dollars of nonrefundable airfare, to having to take an unwanted "staycation," to the loss of a business contract.

Sometimes an off-by-one error occurs because someone means "less than" instead of "less than or equal to" or the reverse; the same goes for "greater than" and "greater than or equal to." A harmless example in everyday life occurs when someone says "no one can play golf as well as I can," meaning everyone in the world is less of a golf player than he is. Even if the speaker really is the best golf player in the world by some objective standard, he has forgotten that there's one person in the world he's not counting. Of course, he's equal to himself, so he should have said, "no one *else* can play golf as well as I can," meaning everyone in the world is less than *or equal to* him at golf, including himself.

Fencepost Error

The fencepost error is a special kind of OBOE. Consider the problem of building a fence along a road. You need to cover 30 feet of road, planting a fencepost every 10 feet. How many fenceposts will you need to plant?

If you said three, you committed a fencepost error. You need four, as shown in Figure 38-1.

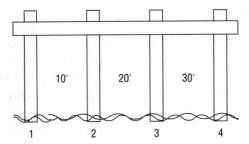

Figure 38-1: Fenceposts

This kind of problem comes up all the time in software development when iterating over a number of items, such as when counting items in an inventory. It's thought to have first been described by Vitruvius in the first century B.C.E.[2]

Some fencepost errors and other OBOEs in real life come from conflating *one-based* counting with *zero-based* counting. For example, we count birthdays and anniversaries with zero-based counting. A first birthday or anniversary is not the day something begins, which is the beginning of its first year, but instead occurs at the *end* of its first year, when it turns one. (The day you're born is technically your *zeroth* birthday.) Your second year starts with your first birthday, and so on. This mistake is particularly clear when people describe organizations and businesses: "Johnson's Tires is in its twenty-seventh year of serving the community!" If they mean the business is 27 years old, their twenty-seventh year actually happened when it was 26.

Zero-based counting was also the reason for the debate about when the third millennium "really" began. There was no year 0 in the Common Era. The calendar moved directly from 1 B.C.E to 1 C.E. (1 B.C. to 1 A.D.). Thus, the first millennium began with the year 1, the second millennium began with the year 1001, and the third millennium began with the year 2001. Many people, including Douglas Adams, saw this kind of precision as pedantry (www.douglasadams.com/dna/pedants.html). We saw it as an excuse to celebrate two years in a row.

General Problems with Small Numbers

Be aware that the errors described above are part of a broad class of roughly similar problems that occur when people don't reason clearly about small numbers like 0, 1, and 2. Perhaps these numbers don't seem important because they're so small, but they are some of the most important numbers in mathematics, and we use them every day in real life.

NOTE In some areas of mathematics, such as computer science, Boolean values (i.e., true and false) are represented by numbers such as 1 and 0 or -1, respectively. In such a case, a sign flip is really a "small number error" like OBOEs and fencepost errors; it may even be caused by an OBOE.

In some ways, it seems easier for most people to reason about large numbers than small ones. They talk about not being able to "grasp" mathematical concepts that are too "fiddly." Do they experience small numbers as too small and "slippery" to manipulate, in an almost synesthetic way? At times when trying and failing to grasp some slippery concept, Ron has felt a visceral squirmy sensation all over, akin to the times he's tried to retrieve a part he dropped in a tight space, such as inside a computer.

If people do feel physically uncomfortable when reasoning about small numbers, it's not surprising they avoid doing it as much as possible. It's hard to say what's going on here, but it may be a fruitful area to study.

How It Works

Kruger and Dunning (1999) showed that when people are unable to perform certain tasks, such as mathematical operations, they also often lack the "metacognitive" ability to think about their own thinking and determine how competent or incompetent they really are.[3] This can cause them to overestimate their own competence and make mistakes of which they're not even aware. In a world where people find reasoning about "simple errors" difficult — *simple* is not the same as *easy* — sign flips, off-by-one errors, and the like are pervasive but invisible.

The universal human tendency to flip the sign on things was deftly satirized by the comedy troupe Kids in the Hall with a sketch in which a character is compelled by voices in his head that repeatedly warn, "Never pour salt in your eyes!" As the warning repeats over and over, however, the character begins to hear the opposite command, and ends up pouring salt in his eyes. Don't laugh (OK, laugh) — a recent study showed that corrections to misinformation from political figures (like the correction "Switzerland does *not* have a nuclear arsenal") sometimes backfire in the same way, reinforcing the original misinformation ("Switzerland *does* have a nuclear arsenal!").[4] Of course, this tendency is used to great effect by propagandists: "Our office would like to make it absolutely clear that we categorically deny that we have any evidence that Senator Louseback wears rubber pants to bed every night for reasons that could well threaten our national security."

In Real Life

Ron has never missed a flight because he was confused about when it was leaving, but an OBOE similar to the carpool example did happen to him recently. His boss on a new job scheduled an early morning meeting and he said he would be there. However, the driver for his new carpool had a doctor appointment on that day and had told him he would pick Ron up at 8:30 when he really meant 9:30. Ron ended up getting in late, so the meeting had to be rescheduled, which ended up causing a chain reaction in other people's schedules. Not an auspicious start for a new job! However, all this could have been avoided if both his carpool driver and he had remembered the possibility of an OBOE or some other simple error and had been more careful to double-check their rendezvous time, instead of assuming they understood each other.

Because so many people do make simple errors, there are also times when *not* doing so will get you into trouble, ranging from fruitless arguments about when the third millennium began, to the brink of shoplifting charges. Here's an example of a general error in reasoning about small numbers: We were shopping in a store we'll refer to only as Ginormous Electronics, when we came across a "buy one, get one free" offer on diet cola. There was also a hand-lettered sign that read "Limit 2 Free." We reasoned that to get two bottles free, we would have to buy two bottles, for a total of four (two paid for and two free), so we stuck four bottles in the cart. This led to an extended contretemps in which four store personnel who couldn't follow our reasoning, including two clerks, a manager, and a security guard, all assumed we were trying to get away with something by putting more than two bottles into our cart. What the sign should have said, of course — what it was supposed to mean — was "Limit 1 Free," or better, "Limit 2 Bottles Total."

Simple errors mostly occur because people don't know they can occur. To crib from the title of Kruger and Dunning's study, some people are "unskilled and unaware of it." Becoming aware of these common errors and understanding how to correct them when you recognize them is the first step toward being able to avoid them.

See Also

- Read "The Ghost Not," by Allen G. Carter (www.buildfreedom.com/ content/reciprocality/r2/index.html), and then read Hack 60, "Trust Your Intelligence (and Everyone Else's)" for balance.

- Thomas E. Kida, *Don't Believe Everything You Think: The 6 Basic Mistakes We Make in Thinking* (Amhurst, NY, USA: Prometheus Books, 2006). A good popular book on human error that cites recent research and doesn't rehash the usual list of logical fallacies.

Notes

1. Ian Stewart and Jack Cohen, *Wheelers* (New York: Warner Books, 2000).

2. Robert K. Moniot, "Who first described the 'fence-post error' ?," accessed 11 July 2009, www.dsm.fordham.edu/~moniot/Opinions/ fencepost-error-history.shtml.

3. "Unskilled and Unaware of It: How Difficulties in Recognizing One's Own Incompetence Lead to Inflated Self-Assessments," Justin Kruger and David Dunning, 1999, accessed June 2011, http://citeseerx.ist .psu.edu/viewdoc/download?doi=10.1.1.64.2655&rep=rep1&type=pdf.

4. "When Corrections Fail: The persistence of political misperceptions," Brendan Nyhan and Jason Reifler, 2009, accessed June 2011, http:// geofaculty.org:16080/figures/Rood_Climate_Change_AOSS480_ Documents/Nyhan_Belief_Facts_Politics_PoliticalBehavior_2010.pdf.

Hack 39: Notate Personally

If you're American, do you really know how far a kilometer is? If you're not, do you know how far a mile is? Why settle for measuring in feet, pounds, meters, and kilos, when you can get a better understanding of size by measuring in terms of things you already know, like your own body?

It's useful to have a sense of common units of measure, but it can still be difficult to really grasp how big something is. To help with that you can invent your own units of measure and customize the ones with which you think. You'll increase your own numeracy, or mathematical literacy, and you'll also be able to measure and estimate easily at a moment's notice.

Historical examples of customized units of measure include the cubit, the span, and the smoot. They can be useful to measure size, distance, weight, and time in a way you can intuitively understand.

In Action

When you devise your own units of measure, it's often useful to distinguish between *natural units*, which are based on universal physical constants such as *c* (the speed of light), and *anthropic units*, or "human" units, which are based on human physiology or culture. One anthropic unit based on human physiology is the *cubit*. This is the distance between the elbow and the tip of the middle finger, which is about 18 inches. Anthropic units like the cubit are not only familiar, they're also convenient, since your "ruler" is literally always within arm's reach.

Since this hack is about personalizing units of measurement to make them more meaningful to you, we'll focus on anthropic units rather than natural ones. Natural units are discussed more fully in Hack 40, "Notate Wisely."

It's useful to know the size of parts of your body in standard units, and we encourage you to learn the measurements of your own body in this way. For example, Ron's span, or the distance from the tip of his thumb to the tip of his little finger with hand outstretched, is about 9.25 inches; the width of his index finger is a centimeter, or about 0.4 inches. The width of his netbook computer is about the same as his span minus half the width of his index finger: 9.25 minus 0.2 inches equals 9.05 inches, and a ruler tells us that the width of his netbook is actually 9 inches. Not bad!

Here are some other anthropic measurements you may find helpful:

- A U.S. dollar bill is very close to 6 inches long, making it useful for measurement in feet when a ruler or tape measure isn't available. It's also roughly 2.5 inches wide. A U.S. quarter is one inch in diameter.

- A *pace* is the distance between where your heel leaves the ground and where it strikes the ground again, making it convenient to count paces: Just count the number of times that heel strikes the ground. A *mile* was originally defined in ancient Rome as a thousand paces (the word *mile* comes from the Latin word for one thousand.)

- A large bag of sugar usually weighs five pounds in the U.S. If you know what it's like to lift a bag of sugar, you may have a better idea of what it would be like to carry a three-pound laptop around the next time you're purchasing a computer.

Of course, people have had fun with anthropic measurements. When we lived in Boston, we frequently traversed the Harvard Bridge, which crosses the Charles River between Boston and Cambridge near the campus of MIT. The bridge is marked off in *smoots*. A smoot is equal to the height of 1958 MIT fraternity pledge Oliver R. Smoot — five feet, seven inches, or about 1.7 meters. The bridge is marked off every 10 smoots, and the Cambridge Police use the markings to estimate accident locations. Thus, even silly units of measure can prove important through usage and custom.

Both Google Calculator (www.google.com/intl/en/help/features .html#calculator) and WolframAlpha (www.wolframalpha.com) can calculate in smoots. Of course, MIT graduates have probably infiltrated both high-tech companies, and MIT students love a good inside joke.

How It Works

The principle behind this hack is much the same as the one behind Hack 40, "Notate Wisely": *cognitive ergonomics,* or making notation fit the human mind, rather than the other way around. Using cognitive ergonomics clarifies your thinking by enabling you to reason in ways that are either more convenient or more objectively related to the situation at hand.

In this case, we take cognitive ergonomics a little further. Customizing units of measure for your unique cognitive style is like taking an already comfortable ergonomic office chair and adding a pillow that suits your own anatomy. Now it's just right.

Of course, it's important to use standard notation if you want to communicate with others or work precisely, but it's useful to use custom notation and units to help your own mind grasp an idea more clearly, or if you need a quick and convenient way to estimate.

In Real Life

Ron's first encounter with customized units of measurement occurred when he was no more than four years old, and a big fan of *Popeye the Sailor* cartoons. Each cartoon was about 15 minutes long, and he often watched several in a single sitting. At that age, he had no real grasp of clock time, so when his family was going on a car trip — let's say from their New Jersey suburb to the Jersey shore — his parents found it was easier to quell the ceaseless cries of "Are we there yet?" from the back seat by telling him there were ten Popeye cartoons left to drive, rather than 2.5 hours. Ten Popeye cartoons! What could be better? This gave Ron a practical idea of how long the drive would be, and he felt better about it, cheered by the thought of the cartoons.

Of course, twenty-first-century kids often have real cartoons to entertain them in the back seats of their parents' cars. Whether this makes the cartoon as a unit of time and distance more or less relevant probably depends on the individual family. It hasn't completely lost its relevance even for Ron; when he's complaining about how long a car trip is taking, Marty will gently remind him he's no longer four by couching the remaining trip time in Popeye cartoons.

Today, he uses the "commute" as a measure of travel time. When he's not working from home, his one-way commute time is about 90 minutes. Thus, Portland, Oregon, is three hours away, or two commutes, whereas San Francisco is a 12-hour drive, or eight commutes. Knowing this helps him determine how many days it would take to drive to San Francisco by himself. He already drives two commutes in one day routinely (one to work and one back) and could probably double that (for four commutes in a day) without undue stress or strain, especially if he weren't doing anything else. He could probably drive eight commutes in one day if there were an emergency, but it would be stressful and unpleasant. Thus, he'd want to allot two days to drive to San Francisco alone, allowing six hours of driving, or four commutes, per day of the trip.

See Also

- Marcus Weeks, *How Many Elephants in a Blue Whale?*: *Measuring What You Don't Know in Terms of What You Do* (New York: Puzzlewright, 2010). This beautifully-illustrated book is a *tour de force* in notating personally.

Hack 40: Notate Wisely

The invention of the numeral zero was a huge leap forward for mathematics, even though the facts of arithmetic didn't change. Similarly, there are some little-known notations today, such as the Laws of Form, that can help clarify your thinking.

Any sufficiently powerful notation system can notate or measure the same things as any comparable notation system. No reasonable person doubts that the imperial system of feet, gallons, pounds, and so on can measure exactly the same things as the metric system with its meters, liters, and kilograms. It's just that, United States tradition notwithstanding, the metric system is so much easier.

This ease of use comes from the *cognitive ergonomics* of the metric system. Its thoughtful, deliberate design amounts to a kind of power. In this hack, we'll touch on a few different ways to obtain and employ similar power. Our "In Real Life" case study examines how adopting the computer language LISP enabled one tech startup to vanquish its competitors.

Choose your notation system wisely, especially when working with logic, physics, or other fields in which small inaccuracies and deviations can make a big difference. While notation isn't everything, it's certainly something — if you care to doubt its power, try doing long division in Roman numerals.

In Action

This section examines how to leverage cognitive ergonomics, from measuring the universe in a more natural way, to some intuitive ways to study logic with which you might not be familiar, to cannily choosing computer languages for a project.

Natural Units

Natural units are units of measurement that depend on fundamental universal constants in physics, such as c, the speed of light. It's easy to confuse this term with *anthropic units* (Hack 39, "Notate Personally"), which rely on such basic personal measurements as the length of your stride or the breadth of your hand. While anthropic units are individualized and vary in absolute size depending on the person using them, natural units are extremely standardized and stable from person to person and even culture to culture, since they're based on phenomena that are highly unlikely to change.

By now, many people are aware that quantum theory claims our universe is "chunky" or "grainy" at the smallest level, rather than smooth and continuous. For example, there is thought to be a shortest possible length, roughly 1.616×10^{-35} meters. This is called the *Planck length*; it's about .00000000000000000001 of the diameter of a proton, and thus much too small for everyday use as a unit of measurement (www.alcyone.com/max/writing/essays/planck-units.html). However, if you multiplied it by exactly 10^{35}, you would have a basic length unit of 1.616 meters, optimized for daily use.

Science fiction writer Sean Williams imagines a whole range of such "Adjusted Planck Units" (http://seanwilliams.com/Excerpts/SITS%20appendix.htm), and they're fun to play with. However, the true advantage of natural units such as the Planck length is the ease they bring to certain kinds of scientific calculations. You might think of them as the universe's own "pace" and "handsbreadth."

Logic

Although modern logic, including predicate and propositional logic, is widely recognized to be a huge step forward over the Aristotelian "term logic" used in ancient and medieval times, its notation is a hodgepodge that has evolved and accreted over more than 100 years. Since the inception of modern logic, there have been several attempts to streamline and clarify the new notation. (Term logic is not completely obsolete; we use it to illustrate deduction, induction, and abduction in Hack 37, "Abduct Your Conclusions.")

The following sections examine two of these efforts. The Logic Alphabet is an effort to systematize and clarify the notation for logical connectives, and the Laws of Form are an attempt to create a completely new notation for all of logic, working from fundamentals.

The Logic Alphabet

The Logic Alphabet (www.logic-alphabet.net) is a simple, pedagogically useful way of representing the 16 basic logical relationships, such as AND, OR, NOT, and NAND (not-and). It was developed in the 1960s by independent scholar

Shea Zellweger, and graphically resembles J. R. R. Tolkien's "Tengwar" Elvish alphabet (http://at.mansbjorkman.net/tengwar.htm).

This is only partly a coincidence. Both Tengwar and the Logic Alphabet start with loops and stems resembling those in the lowercase Roman letters b, d, p, and q, but they use these features systematically. A stem in one position means one thing; on the other side of the loop, it means another. A long stem has one meaning; a short stem yet another. However, the Logical Alphabet is not an alphabet in the strictest sense. Whereas in the Tengwar alphabet the shapes of the letters have phonetic weight — they represent certain sounds — the shapes of the Logic Alphabet have a logical meaning.

When he started, Zellweger didn't realize that philosopher Charles Sanders Peirce (Hack 37, "Abduct Your Conclusions") had developed a similar system in 1902 (www.math.uic.edu/~kauffman/Peirce.pdf). Nevertheless, the Logic Alphabet in its present form is more practical and useful than Peirce's system. Because it has been Zellweger's life work, he has taken it much further than Peirce, with educational tools such as a "multiplication table for logic," mechanical devices called "flipsticks," and even ways to represent his system in 3D and 4D (Hack 43, "Enter the Fourth Dimension"). Many of Zellweger's visualizations of the "geometry of logic" are so attractive that they have drawn the attention of the art world.

NOTE Zellweger's 3D Logic Alphabet representation, the Logical Garnet, is a rhombic dodecahedron, the space-filling shape we explore in Hack 42, "Enter the Third Dimension."

The Laws of Form

The Laws of Form (www.lawsofform.org), as developed and explored in G. Spencer-Brown's 1969 book of the same name, encompass another new notation for logic and mathematics called the *calculus of distinctions*. This notation is mainly founded on the elaboration of spatial boundaries and similar distinctions, and needs only one kind of symbol to represent any logical expression. The symbol can be drawn in a number of different ways, but it's usually drawn as a plain circle like an O or an upside-down L. Individual symbols are nested or placed side-by-side to generate increasingly complex logical and mathematical expressions.

While most logicians think that the Laws of Form cannot express anything that ordinary logical notation can't, it does seem capable of expressing anything that ordinary notation can. Its strength and advantage over the usual notation lie in its extreme clarity and elegance (only one symbol!) and the intuitive understanding of logic that even non-logicians will have after giving it due study.

Note that Spencer-Brown was also anticipated by Charles Sanders Peirce, but once again, the later system is the more refined.

Computer Languages

Because a computer language is basically a notation for telling a computer what to do, choosing the correct language in which to write a software project is often crucial to its success. For example, the computer language Perl, in which many code examples for this book are written, is well known for enabling relatively rapid software development. However, it can appear so cryptic, even to the same programmer a few months later, that it's become jokingly known as a "write-only" language. A more recent scripting language, Python, fills a similar niche to Perl but is a little more finicky to code in. However, the very finickiness of writing code in Python — you must get all the indentation and other whitespace correct before your code will even run — means that many Python scripts are easier to read than Perl is, so it might be better for a large project where sharing code with other programmers is a priority.

It's also important to choose a language that suits the task for which the software is designed, if there's a clear difference. To compare Perl and Python again, both languages are probably equally powerful, in an absolute sense, at processing text with a feature called *regular expressions*. Perl's regular expressions are more compact and visually less "clunky" than Python's , but their compactness means they often look like gibberish to the uninitiated. While this might be a boon if you're trying to impress your boss, you might have trouble reading it later. Nevertheless, both Perl and Python can run text-processing circles around a simpler language like C, which has no regular expressions to speak of. That doesn't mean you can't process text with C — consider that many implementations of both the Perl and Python languages are themselves written in C because C is simpler and runs faster than either Perl or Python.

Every computer language, even some of the older ones like FORTRAN, have their proponents, so it's easy to get into a so-called "religious war" about which language is best. One thing is clear: As with other systems of notation, every computer language has its strengths and weaknesses, and is better for some purposes, less so for others. Also, while some languages may be equally good for a specific kind of application, some have clear advantages in terms of making the task of developing software faster and more efficient.

How It Works

Virtually every field of human endeavor has benefited from advances and improvements in notation, or the creation of a notation where none existed before. As well as spoken, written, and computer languages, and logic and mathematics, as we've discussed, there have been advances in sign languages, chemistry, timekeeping (Hack 19, "Tell Time Who's Boss"), music, and dance, among many others. It's even been suggested that money is a "value notation system," and voting is an "opinion notation system," so you can add the global economy and the democratic system of government to things we couldn't have without decent notation (www.gwu.edu/~rpsol/ASC%202005%20Conf/content/Paper/long.doc). Better notation leads to clearer thought.

A genuinely better notation might let you eat not only your competitors' lunch (see the next section), but your competitors themselves. Consider that spoken human language is a form of notation (a "first-order notation") that enabled our species, for good or ill, to dominate most of the other species on the planet. Written language, a "second-order notation" of spoken language, was another huge advance that enabled us to consolidate our dominance.

In Real Life

Programmer and investor Paul Graham wrote a well-known essay called "Beating the Averages" (www.paulgraham.com/avg.html) about developing one of the first online shopping server applications in 1995 for his company, Viaweb. He and his partner, Robert Morris, wrote it in the computer language LISP.

Any computer programmer reading this knows that LISP is an unorthodox choice for developing server software (the back-end software that runs on computers you access over the Net, such as Google and Amazon), but Graham argues that LISP offered extremely rapid development ("you can release software the minute it's done"), high-level coding ("we wouldn't need a big development team"), and several more arcane advantages such as enabling Viaweb to write programs that themselves wrote other programs.

Graham claims that these features of LISP gave him a permanent lead over his competition, who mainly programmed in C++ or Perl, and led to Yahoo! Shopping buying Viaweb in 1998. As of 2003, Yahoo! had about 20,000 customers using the software to create virtual storefronts.

Because Graham attributes Viaweb's success to his choice of the most appropriate notation (in this case, LISP), his conclusions are highly relevant to our study of choosing the right notation:

Everyone knows it's a mistake to write your whole program by hand in machine language. What's less often understood is that there is a more general principle here: that if you have a choice of several languages, it is, all other things being equal, a mistake to program in anything but the most powerful one. . . All languages are equally powerful in the sense of being Turing equivalent, but that's not the sense of the word programmers care about. . . The kind of power programmers care about may not be formally definable, but one way to explain it would be to say that it refers to features you could only get in the less powerful language by writing . . . the more powerful language in it.

In sum, never doubt that the right notation can make a difference, and never fail to notate wisely.

NOTE For more information on the concept of Turing equivalence, see Hack 60, "Trust Your Intelligence (and Everyone Else's)."

See Also

- David S. Oderberg's book *The Old New Logic: Essays on the Philosophy of Fred Sommers* is an examination of the recent attempt to rehabilitate and develop a new notation for Aristotelian term logic.
- Conrad Barski's book *Land of Lisp: Learn to Program in Lisp, One Game at a Time!* is recommended. If Paul Graham's account of eating his competitors' lunch thanks to LISP has made you hungry, this book is a fun way to learn more about the language. For dessert, try Graham's own book, *On LISP: Advanced Techniques for Common LISP*.

Hack 41: Engineer Your Results

Although mathematics, science, and engineering are related fields, the roles of mathematician, scientist, and engineer are often separate. Learn to bring them back together in your own thinking.

The popular view of mathematicians, to the extent that there is one, is that they operate by pure cogitation, deriving complex mathematical proofs from first principles merely by thinking about them very hard.

Although this may be true for a few mathematicians, it has seldom been the case for most of them. Mathematicians often engage in a number of exploratory and experimental activities even when in pursuit of an elegant, abstract proof. They may doodle, sketch, build 3D physical models of mathematical objects, simulate results with software, approximate with analog instruments, and do many other things to collect data that can stimulate their intuition.

Thus, there are many ways to explore a mathematical problem. This hack focuses on one especially simple and useful way, the *Monte Carlo method*.

In Action

Imagine drawing a square on the ground, then dividing it in half, and then in half again, at a 90-degree angle (see Figure 41-1).

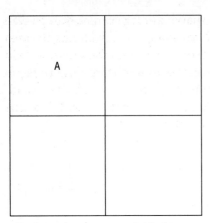

Figure 41-1: A square divided into quadrants

If you wanted to determine the proportion of the area of the quadrant marked *A* relative to that of the whole square, there are a couple of ways you could go about it. The first is to derive a simple geometrical proof, which would, of course, show the ratio to be ¼ or 0.25. Of course, most people don't need a proof for such a simple example; they can just see this fact. However, if you needed mathematical certainty, that's how you would go about it.

There is another way to calculate the proportion, less certain than a proof but enormously useful because it's widely applicable to situations where a proof is too hard, or at least too hard without further data. Imagine that you drop dried beans from a height onto the square so that they fall more or less randomly and equally all over it. Next, count the number of beans in quadrant *A*, and then divide that number by the number of beans that fell in the whole square. The resulting proportion might not be exactly 0.25 — it might be more like 0.2 or 0.3 — but if you perform this procedure enough times and take the average of the results, it will probably converge on 0.25.

This procedure is called a *Monte Carlo experiment*, after the famous casino in Monte Carlo, because it depends on chance. If you were to simulate the experiment with a computer by substituting coordinates from a random-number generator for dropping the beans, it would be called a *Monte Carlo simulation*.

A good definition of a Monte Carlo method is given by MathWorld: "Any method which solves a problem by generating suitable random numbers and observing that fraction of the numbers obeying some property or properties" (mathworld.wolfram.com/MonteCarloMethod.html). We solved the problem of the area of the quadrant by generating suitable random numbers (uniformly dropping beans onto the square or generating random coordinates with a computer) and observing that fraction of the numbers (roughly one-fourth) obeying some property or properties (falling within quadrant *A*).

This general procedure can be applied in many other ways, as you'll see in the "In Real Life" section. For now, please think about how you would go about determining what proportion of the square shape *B* in Figure 41-2 occupies. In this case, you can't just look at it and know the answer, and calculating the area conventionally would be tricky at best. However, just as with the square area in the first example, you may be able to ascertain the area by dropping beans on the square and counting how many fall within the irregular shape, then dividing by the number on the whole square (and repeating many times). It seems that dropping beans might be the best path to take after all!

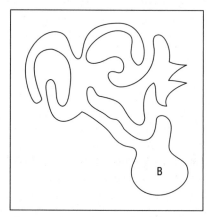

Figure 41-2: How much of the square does the squiggle occupy?

How It Works

People often think that they can reason facts about the world from a very limited basis. As an *epistemology*, or theory of knowledge, this position is called *rationalism*. You may be familiar with the dictum of the rationalist René Descartes, "I think, therefore I am." Descartes thought he could infer all human knowledge from this axiom, but this is a fairly pernicious belief. There's nothing wrong with reason, but it won't tell you everything you need to know about the world by itself. As Bertrand Russell said about an earlier philosopher, "Aristotle could have avoided the mistake of thinking that women have fewer teeth than men, by the simple device of asking Mrs. Aristotle to keep her mouth open while he counted." (www.panarchy.org/russell/rubbish.1943.html)

Empiricism is another theory of knowledge, and it can be thought of as "rationalism plus." In contrast to rationalism, empiricism requires checking reasoned ideas against observation. Empiricism is a cornerstone of the scientific method (Hack 54, "Think, Try, Learn"), and it has enabled enormous leaps forward in human understanding about the world, including the technological progress of the last few centuries.

Both Monte Carlo experiments and simulations are important aspects of the Monte Carlo method, but the Monte Carlo method is only one small screwdriver in the overstuffed toolbox of the new field of experimental mathematics. The early twenty-first century has seen this field burgeon because of ready access to powerful computers. Jonathan Borwein and Keith Devlin, in their 2009 introduction to experimental mathematics, *The Computer as Crucible*, define the field as follows:

> *Experimental mathematics is the use of a computer to run computations — sometimes no more than trial-and-error tests — to look for patterns, to identify particular numbers and sequences, to gather evidence in support of specific mathematical assertions that may themselves arise by computational means, including search. Like contemporary chemists — and before them the alchemists of old — who mix various substances together in a crucible and heat them to a high temperature to see what happens, today's experimental mathematician puts a hopefully potent mix of numbers, formulas, and algorithms into a computer in the hope that something of interest emerges.*[1]

John Barrow makes a good case that empiricism probably has a lot to offer mathematics in a fable in his book *Pi in the Sky*.[2] He writes about a science-fictional near future in which NASA intercepts a transmission of the mathematical knowledge of an advanced extraterrestrial civilization. At first, Earth's mathematicians are elated at the mathematical results received, which seem to be far beyond anything humans have ever been able to prove. When the aliens begin transmitting their methodology, however, Terran mathematicians become depressed:

> *The extraterrestrials' mathematics was not like ours at all. In fact, it was horrible. They saw mathematics as another branch of science in which all the facts were established by observation or experiment. They had used their fastest computers to check that every even number was equal to the sum of two prime numbers case by case through the first trillion examples. They found it so in every case and therefore regarded this as a general truth (which we call Goldbach's conjecture) established by experiment to a particular level of statistical confidence. . .*
>
> *In fact, their philosophy books had footnotes about a suggestion that had been made that they develop some way of ensuring that truths of mathematics held for all cases and not just the very large number tested by enumeration. But this approach rapidly became a backwater as mathematicians were unwilling to take a step backwards and redefine their subject in such a way that many of the results they regarded as true were no longer to be regarded as such. To give up their method of confirmation would be like fighting with one hand tied behind their back. So, it appears that they certainly knew about our method of proof, but it was just not competitive with their process of confirmation.*

Barrow's book was published in 1992. Ron bought his copy in 1998, and was astonished and delighted some 10 years later to learn that there are now mathematicians in real life who use this "horrible extraterrestrial" methodology, at least as an exploratory tool on the way to establishing conventional proofs.

The rationalist-versus-empiricist dispositional dichotomy in mathematics is sometimes framed as a battle between algebra and geometry. For example, Nicolas Bourbaki was the pseudonym for an influential school of French mathematicians who tended to opine that visualization had no place in mathematics, almost turning geometry, that most visual branch of mathematics, into a kind of algebra. However, Donald Coxeter reintroduced visualization into geometry, even personally making geometrical models of polyhedra and other polytopes out of cardboard and other materials (Hack 42, "Enter the Third Dimension").[3]

In the early twenty-first century, the pendulum seems to have swung from Bourbaki to Coxeter. We can only hope that students today are not told too often, as Ron was in high school calculus class, that drawing little pictures is all right for beginners but "real mathematicians don't visualize." Similarly, we hope that new empirical and experimental methods will continue to be introduced into mathematics, not to supplant rationalistic methods like proofs, but to supplement them as an equal partner.

Experimental mathematics itself is only one methodology for approaching math problems empirically, although it's an important one. Starting points for further explanation are provided at the end of this hack.

In Real Life

The Monte Carlo method has been very good to Ron. For example, he was able to impress one of his superiors in a small company he worked for by rapidly calculating the odds that three of the 11 people in the office shared a birthday.

Ron's secret weapon came from Monte Carlo. The literature on the so-called Birthday Paradox[4] is, if not overly complex, at least extensive, and he didn't want to plow through it for a bit of joking with his co-workers on Twitter. Far better to obtain a Perl one-liner that enabled a one-shot Monte Carlo approximation for specified values, insert the right values, and write a shell script around it that would let him call it a few hundred thousand times on his laptop. He sent the (approximately) right answer to his co-workers in a jiffy, looked like a math whiz, and was recruited to work on an important white paper a few days later. The paper went on to be widely cited in the Linux world (www.linuxfoundation.org/publications/estimatinglinux.php).

More recently, Ron was designing a deck of cards called the Kilodeck (www.ludism.org/tinfoil/Kilodeck). It's ten-dimensional in the sense that an ordinary deck of 52 cards is two-dimensional because every card can be described with just its suit and number. However, in addition to suit and number, the Kilodeck employs suit color, background color, border color, and five other attributes, or dimensions. Each attribute on a card can independently take one of two different values. For example, the suit of a card can be either circles or triangles, and the color of the suit can be either green or yellow. Thus, there are 2^{10}, or 1,024 cards, in the deck. Figure 41-3 shows two cards from the Kilodeck.

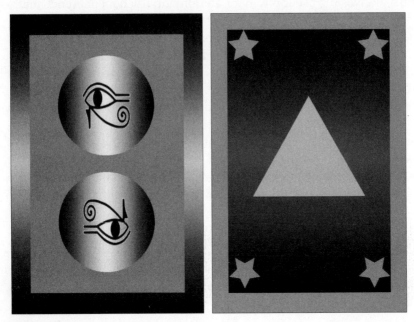

Figure 41-3: Two maximally different Kilodeck cards (some differences are lost due to printing in monochrome)

Ron was designing a game like 21 or Blackjack that could be played with the Kilodeck within an interactive fiction he was writing, much as the card game Double Fanucci is played within the classic interactive fiction Zork Zero (http://howell.seattle.wa.us/games/Fanucci/). He wanted to know two facts for a given number of cards:

1. How many attribute values would they share on average?
2. What were the odds that all the cards in the hand would share any attribute at all?

He couldn't derive equations that would enable him to calculate these values on the spot; his combinatorial chops were far too rusty. However, he was able to write a Monte Carlo simulation that would answer these questions approximately. The program shuffles a virtual 1,024-card Kilodeck, then "deals" as many cards as needed off the top. Each card is represented by a 10-bit binary number, and all bits in the same position in a hand of cards are compared.

A listing of the *kdeck.pl* script follows:

```perl
#!/usr/bin/perl -wall

$deckdimensions = 10;
```

```
$decksize = 2**$deckdimensions;

$minhand = 2;
$maxhand = 20;
$testcount = 20000;

for ($handsize=$minhand; $handsize<=$maxhand; $handsize++)
{
  $commontotal = 0;
  $positives = 0;

  for ($test = 1; $test <= $testcount; $test++)
  {
    # Shuffle up a Kilodeck
    for ($i=0; $i<$decksize; $i++)
    {
      $used[$i] = 0;
    }
    for ($i=0; $i<$decksize; $i++)
    {
      do
      {
        $r = int(rand($decksize));
        if ($used[$r] == 0)
        {
          $deck[$i] = $r;
          $used[$r] = 1;
          # Convert the Kilodeck to binary strings of attributes
          $binattribs[$i] = sprintf "%10.10b",$deck[$i];
        }
      } until ($used[$r] == 1);
    }


    # Sum all the bits in one dimension of the hand at a time;
    # the result is an array of sums called $attribsums
    $ncommonattribs = 0;
    for ($d = 0; $d<$deckdimensions; $d++)
    {
      $attribsums[$d] = 0;
      for ($c=0; $c<$handsize; $c++)
      {
        #print "$binattribs[$c]";
        $attribsums[$d] += substr($binattribs[$c],$d,1);
      }

      # Check whether every card in a hand shares any attributes by
      # comparing the sums to the number of cards in the hand.
      # If they're equal, that attribute is shared by all cards.
      # Also, dimensions that are all 0 are all shared too (duh).
      if (($attribsums[$d] == $handsize) || ($attribsums[$d] == 0))
```

```
          {
             $ncommonattribs++;
          }
          #print "N=$ncommonattribs\n";
       }

       # Increment the number of common attributes in this test run by the
       # number of common attributes in this hand
       $commontotal += $ncommonattribs;

       # If there are any common attributes among all cards, take note of
   the positive result
       if ($ncommonattribs > 0)
       {
          $positives++;
       }
    }

    # The average number of common attributes in this test run is
    # the number of common attributes in the entire run,
    # divided by the number of tests in this run
    $avg = $commontotal / $testcount;

    # The proportion of positive results (hands with at least some shared
    attributes)
    # is the number of positive results in this run divided by the number
    of tests
    $pospercent = 100 * $positives / $testcount;

    $suggscore = int (1 / ($positives / $testcount));

    print "Hand of $handsize cards:";
    print "  Average # of common attributes = $avg";
    print "  Probability they have at least 1 common attribute =
    $pospercent%";
    print "  Suggested score = $suggscore";
}
```

The final run of the program was 100,000 tests for each hand size of 2 through 19 cards. It worked very well. A couple of days later, Ron was able to induce the correct math from these Monte Carlo results and write a much shorter second program that provided exact results. What's more, he understood the reasons behind the math, something that would have taken him much longer without the Monte Carlo results to aim for.

A listing of the *kprobs.pl* script follows:

```
#!/usr/bin/perl

for ($c = 2; $c <= 20; $c++)
{
   $base = (2/(2**$c));
```

```
    $expected = $base*10;

    $probability = 1 - (1 - $base)**10;

    $score = 1/$probability;

    $probability*= 100;

    print "$c cards:\n";
    print "  Expected number of common attributes = $expected\n";
    print "  Probability of at least 1 common attribute =
$probability%\n";
    print "  Recommended score = $score\n";
}
```

The results from both programs are combined in Table 41-1.

Game designers and analysts have been using Monte Carlo methods since before computers have been widely available. Stanislaw Ulam, the father of the method, first conceived of it as a way to analyze games of Canfield card solitaire while recovering from an illness. He and his colleagues later applied it to problems in nuclear physics.[5]

Table 41-1: Kilodeck Probabilities

HAND SIZE	AVERAGE COMMON ATTRIBUTES (MONTE CARLO)	AVERAGE COMMON ATTRIBUTES (EXACT)	PROBABILITY OF AT LEAST ONE COMMON ATTRIBUTE (MONTE CARLO)	PROBABILITY OF AT LEAST ONE COMMON ATTRIBUTE (EXACT)
2	4.9895	5.0000	99.892%	99.9023%
3	2.4895	2.5000	94.278%	94.3686%
4	1.2422	1.2500	73.686%	73.6924%
5	0.6159	0.6250	47.160%	47.5540%
6	0.3092	0.3125	26.964%	27.2024%
7	0.1532	0.1563	14.357%	14.5709%
8	0.0767	0.0781	7.400%	7.5435%
9	0.0369	0.0391	3.622%	3.8383%
10	0.0194	0.0195	1.928%	1.9360%
11	0.0096	0.0098	0.952%	0.9723%
12	0.0043	0.0049	0.432%	0.4872%
13	0.0023	0.0024	0.227%	0.2439%
14	0.0011	0.0012	0.112%	0.1220%
15	0.0006	0.0006	0.060%	0.0610%

Continued

Table 41-1 *(continued)*

HAND SIZE	AVERAGE COMMON ATTRIBUTES (MONTE CARLO)	AVERAGE COMMON ATTRIBUTES (EXACT)	PROBABILITY OF AT LEAST ONE COMMON ATTRIBUTE (MONTE CARLO)	PROBABILITY OF AT LEAST ONE COMMON ATTRIBUTE (EXACT)
16	0.0002	0.0003	0.019%	0.0305%
17	0.0001	0.0002	0.009%	0.0153%
18	0.0001	0.0001	0.006%	0.0076%
19	0.0000	0.0000	0.001%	0.0038%

Backgammon experts performed some useful early analysis of the game's probabilities by playing thousands of games against themselves on real backgammon boards and counting the numbers of times various events occurred. Ron once did something similar by programming the computer board game engine Zillions of Games (http://zillionsofgames.com/) to play the simplistic commercial board game Dao against itself repeatedly for most of an afternoon. He returned to find that every single game was a draw, so tentatively concluded that with perfect play by both players, such would always be the result.

See Also

The following sources are good starting points for learning more about the many kinds of experimental and other empirical methods that can be applied to mathematical problems:

- Jonathan Borwein and Keith Devlin, *The Computer as Crucible: An Introduction to Experimental Mathematics* (Wellesley, MA, USA: A.K. Peters, Ltd., 2009). Cited above, this book is worth further general exploration. It's the best introduction to experimental mathematics that Ron has discovered. Monte Carlo methods are discussed but occupy only a few pages of this 158-page book.

- John Bryant and Chris Sangwin, *How Round Is Your Circle?: Where Engineering and Mathematics Meet* (Princeton, NJ, USA: Princeton University Press, 2008). In this hands-on book, the authors demonstrate how to solve various mathematical problems with physical devices you can build, including replicas of engineering devices from the Victorian era and earlier — imagine gadgets such as protractors, compasses, and slide rules, but much more sophisticated and less known today.

- Mark Levi, *The Mathematical Mechanic: Using Physical Reasoning to Solve Problems* (Princeton, NJ, USA: Princeton University Press, 2009). Levi's book shows how physics can be used to aid the discovery of mathematical proofs, theorems, and solutions. His demonstrations employ devices such as springs, soap bubbles, electric circuits, and bicycle wheels.

- "Ulam spiral," Wikipedia (March 2011) `http://en.wikipedia.org/w/index.php?title=Ulam_spiral&oldid=417955448`. The *prime spiral* is a fascinating mathematical phenomenon that seems to graphically show a kind of regularity in the distribution of prime numbers. It was discovered by Stanislaw Ulam while doodling at a meeting. (Yes, the same Stanislaw Ulam we mentioned earlier — he was apparently quite a guy.)

Notes

1. Jonathan Borwein and Keith Devlin, *The Computer as Crucible: An Introduction to Experimental Mathematics* (Wellesley, MA, USA: A.K. Peters, Ltd., 2009).

2. John Barrow. *Pi in the Sky: Counting, Thinking, and Being* (New York: Oxford University Press, 1992).

3. Siobhan Roberts, *King of Infinite Space: Donald Coxeter, the Man Who Saved Geometry* (New York: Walker & Company, 2006).

4. E. H. McKinney, "Generalized Birthday Problem," *American Mathematical Monthly* 73 (1966), 385–387.

5. Roger Eckhardt, "Stan Ulam, John von Neumann, and the Monte Carlo Method," *Los Alamos Science, Special Issue* 15 (1987): 131-137.

Hack 42: Enter the Third Dimension

John Braley and Ron Hale-Evans

Spatial aptitude can be enhanced with practice. Whether you rotate irregular, concave polyhedra in your mind's eye instead of counting sheep at night, or you can barely imagine a cube, this hack will help you improve your spatial visualization skills.

In school, many of us learned to think of geometry as a rarefied, abstract subject. Formal geometry is often taught almost as a branch of logic, dwelling on propositions and proofs. In addition, geometry in American schools often focuses on two-dimensional Euclidean logic. Because life is basically three-dimensional, this kind of geometry doesn't really exist in the universe in the abstract way we learned it. (See Hack 41, "Engineer Your Results," for more on what we call the "Bourbaki/Coxeter divide" in mathematics.) More to the point, we aren't taught to understand geometry in the ways that we experience it directly, so we end up blind to the structural underpinnings of much of the physical world.

You can gain many benefits by learning to think about geometry more directly and intuitively, exploratively and experimentally, and especially in the third dimension. Doing so can broaden your understanding of many other phenomena, such as architecture (use of space and structural strength), art, astronomy, chemistry (electron orbitals and the periodic table, crystallography, carbon bonds in organic chemistry), biology (the arrangement of cells in multicellular organisms, beehives, phyllotaxis or leaf arrangement in plants, the DNA double helix, virus protein shells), the structure of water in physics, and so on. You can observe how such things as crystals and plants are built; intuitively understanding three-dimensional geometry will help you understand why those structures work. Of course, 3D games and virtual worlds use a lot of 3D geometry as well.

If you're not convinced yet that direct three-dimensional visual apprehension and visualization of geometry is a useful skill, consider that it can help you in a number of areas of life, all the way from the earthly — understanding the geometric close packing of spheres will help you pack your car like Buckminster Fuller himself would have — to extraterrestrial scientific and engineering applications, such as understanding the innovative use of face-centered cubic packing of the airbags on the Mars Pathfinder lander (see Figure 42-1). 3D visualization may even help you understand human history. For example, the historically critical role of the alloy bronze was made possible by the cubic close packing of copper, with tin atoms mingled in its octahedral interstices. This arrangement made the copper less ductile, more rigid, and more able to be formed into tools and weapons, and arguably made the Bronze Age, and our civilization, possible.

Figure 42-1: Cubic packing of the airbags on the Mars Pathfinder lander[1]

The good news is that the quality of your spatial visualization is something that can be learned and improved. So read on!

In Action

There are numerous ways to enhance your 3D visualization skills. For example, you can sketch or draw 3D solids (as described later in the section "How It Works") on paper or using a 3D graphics program, of which there are many, such as Google SketchUp (http://sketchup.google.com). You can also visualize 3D shapes mentally without ever implementing them as 2D drawings or 3D models, as in the guided visualization that follows in the section "In Real Life." However, for the remainder of this section, in the interest of space (no pun intended), we'll talk about building and handling models of geometric shapes with 3D modeling sets, both the best commercially available set and one you can make at home.

Both of these sets have excellent texts to help you explore their geometries. Zometool (www.zometool.com/) has the *Zome Geometry* book,[2] which focuses on visualization and problem solving with classical geometry. Homemade sets can draw inspiration from *Steven Caney's Ultimate Building Book*, described later in the section "Hometool," which focuses more on engineering applications. The books guide you forward with information about what to build, how the pieces fit together to make complex shapes, and how to think about what you've built. Both books are aimed at kids, but there's plenty in them that even most well-educated adults could stand to learn (see Hack 12, "Study Kid Stuff").

Zometool

Probably the best commercial geometric modeling kit currently available is Zometool. Invented by solar and residential designer Steve Baer for use in architecture, Zometool is a "strut and ball" kit that excels at modeling certain kinds of 3D shapes, such as more common *polyhedra* (see Figure 42-2). It's also good at modeling certain higher-dimensional shapes (see Hack 43, "Enter the Fourth Dimension").

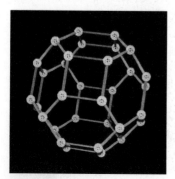

Figure 42-2: An irregular truncated octahedron built with Zometool

Zometool constructions have rigid joints with no moving parts. Zometool is not meant to build cars, trucks, or robots, only to explore geometry, and it's widely used for that purpose in schools and homeschools at all grade levels.

Note that Zometool cannot model every 3D geometric shape. For example, although you can come pretty close with a basic Zometool set, you can't technically build a regular tetrahedron without the advanced green struts expansion. (Every color of strut in Zome, including green, provides struts of different lengths and enables the balls to be connected at a different angle.) Since a "regtet" is one of the most basic 3D geometrical solids, and a basic component of many more complex shapes, if you buy a Zometool kit, the green struts are highly recommended.

Because Zometool is limited to the fixed angles built into the nodes and to the fixed lengths of the provided struts, you're somewhat constrained in what you can do. It's a bit like a computer's graphical user interface in the sense that a GUI generally constrains you by, for example, the menu options it offers. This can be frustrating for some people, but others will appreciate the guidance and find that it makes getting started easier. Either way, Zometool is a great and easy way to get started with 3D modeling and good for people who aren't as into the do-it-yourself ethic.

NOTE *Zome Geometry* does not ship with most Zome sets; you must usually buy it separately. However, the individual Zome kits come with instructional booklets that are quite interesting and should be enough to get you started working with Zometool.

Hometool

If you really want to get your hands dirty and model any shape you can think of, you'll have to build your own public domain, "unboxed" modeling set, what we might call "Hometool." Homemade systems allow for almost unlimited options and refinements; it's closer to the freedom that a command line offers, as opposed to a GUI.

If you want to learn about a variety of homemade modeling sets and pick the one that's best for whatever shape you're trying to visualize, *Steven Caney's Ultimate Building Book*, mentioned earlier, cannot be recommended highly enough.[3] Caney explains basic geometric principles from a concrete, real-world perspective, and describes how to build shapes with numerous building systems, including string and drinking straws, cotton swabs and rubber cement, PVC plastic pipe, coat hangers, and even day-old bagels. Ron's favorite system from Caney's book is "Clip Grippers and Straw Struts," in which drinking straws are held together with paper clips. It is very easy to build some fairly complicated structures comparatively rapidly with this system.

You can cut the struts for your set to any length and join them at any angle; the drawback is that you *must*. A good Zometool kit like Ron's, which costs a few hundred dollars, has about 1,200 prefab struts of various colors and lengths, and 400 balls. Because you can set your own price point on the materials you build with a Hometool set, if you're willing to cut 1,200 dowels or drinking straws, you can probably save yourself that few hundred, but it's certainly nice to have both options.

Unlike Zometool and similar commercial systems, homemade systems tend to have flexible joints and can help demonstrate important physics and engineering concepts such as triangulation, or building a shape with triangles in it to physically stabilize the structure. In fact, you may have some trouble creating a homemade system with which nontriangulated models can be readily constructed (another point for a prefab commercial system like Zometool).

NOTE If you're wondering why we're not recommending the most common building set, LEGO, for 3D visualization, it's because the LEGO bricks are, to some degree, like mere 3D computer graphics pixels, or *voxels*. To build a 3D shape with LEGO, you make a big, dumb pile of voxels. None of the geometry or structure of the shape is revealed. LEGO is great for plenty of other applications, though, such as learning robotics (see Hack 12, "Study Kid Stuff").

How It Works

Spatial aptitude can, in fact, be enhanced with practice, as studies have shown in which students exposed to simple 3D geometrical operations became significantly more adept at spatial visualization on later tests. In one study, about a thousand junior high school students were tested on spatial visualization skills both before and after partaking in exercises involving building (as in the "In Action" section earlier) and drawing solids made of cubes. They showed a significant increase in spatial visualization skills after the exercises.[4]

In another study, college undergraduates were treated to a weekly visualization session in which they mentally bisected 3D figures and drew their mental images of the resulting surfaces on paper. Once again, after the weekly sessions, the students performed significantly better on tests of spatial visualization than before.[5]

The latter finding is especially interesting because the mental visualization done by the students is similar to the one we offer in the following section. Perhaps there is an opportunity for someone to write a book of such guided spatial visualizations.

In Real Life

We've discussed building 3D models in "In Action" and drawing them to enhance your powers of visualization in "How It Works." Now, the following relatively challenging guided 3D visualization should help you feel more comfortable thinking about 3D shapes and transformations. There's nothing particularly special about the shapes we chose for it, but at the end of the visualization, you will probably feel more confident about understanding the geometric concept of *space filling*.

Take all the time you need, and feel free to double back on a step if necessary. If you don't get it right away, don't worry; turn to Appendix B, where you'll find graphics of some of the shapes and transformations, then return here and try again. Remember, skill in 3D visualization can be *learned*.

The visualization starts with the familiar shapes of cubes and gradually transforms them into less familiar rhombic dodecahedra. This might sound arcane, but part of the lesson here is how simple such a geometric concept really is.

You might want to make an audio recording of this visualization so you can listen to it with your eyes closed.

Visualization: From Cubes to Rhombic Dodecahedra

Imagine a grid of cubes filling space like a gray-and-white 3D checkerboard. Each gray cube is surrounded by six white cubes, with each white cube touching the gray cube on one of its faces. Each white cube is surrounded by six gray cubes in a similar way.

Now imagine a black point in the exact center of one of the white cubes, and that a black line extends from the center point to each corner of the white cube. There are eight corners, or vertices, on a cube, so eight black lines will extend from the center to the vertices. If you think about it, you will see that these eight black lines divide the cube into six pyramids. Each pyramid has four triangular faces, and a base that is one of the sides of the white cube. Its apex, or tip, is the central point of the cube.

Shift your focus over to an adjoining gray cube. Imagine that all of the white cubes that touch this gray cube have been subdivided into pyramids. You will see that the gray cube is now surrounded by six four-sided white pyramids, one for each face of the cube.

Imagine that these six white pyramids turn gray, and fuse with the gray cube to become a new shape. This new shape is called a *rhombic dodecahedron*. Notice that each of the triangles on the pyramids naturally fuses at its base with an adjacent triangle pointing in the opposite direction, to make a diamond shape, or rhombus. This means the dodecahedron has 12 sides instead of the 24 you might expect.

Now imagine that the white pyramids making up all of the white cubes throughout the grid turn gray and fuse with the gray cubes next to them. You will see that the white cubes have been completely "consumed." All that's left is a 3D grid of gray rhombic dodecahedra filling space, just as the gray-and-white checkerboard filled it before. Each rhombic dodecahedron is now filling the same space as two cubes did.

Notes

1. "Great Images in NASA," National Aeronautics and Space Administration, last modified August 16, 2004, http://dayton.hq.nasa.gov/IMAGES/LARGE/GPN-2000-000484.jpg.

2. George W. Hart, and Henri Picciotto. *Zome Geometry*: *Hands-On Learning with Zome Models* (Emeryville: Key Curriculum Press, 2001).

3. Steven Caney, *Steven Caney's Ultimate Building Book.* (Philadelphia: Running Press Kids, 2006).

4. David Ben-Chaim, Glenda Lappan, and Richard T. Houang, "The Effect of Instruction on Spatial Visualization Skills of Middle School Boys and Girls," *American Educational Research Journal*, 25 (March 20, 1988): 51–71.

5. T. R. Lord, "Enhancing the Visuo-Spatial Aptitude of Students," *Journal of Research in Science Teaching*, 22 (1985): 395–405.

Hack 43: Enter the Fourth Dimension

Paul Snyder

There is a fourth dimension, and we're not talking about time. Learning how to visualize four-dimensional objects is a kind of mental calisthenics like no other, and in this hack you'll learn several ways to do it.

If the three dimensions aren't enough for you (Hack 42, "Enter the Third Dimension"), why not try four on for size? In this hack, we'll look at ways to train your brain to visualize higher-dimensional objects.

In physics, time is often modeled as a fourth dimension, but one that is treated differently from the more familiar three spatial dimensions. For the purposes of this hack, though, we'll be exploring a fourth *Euclidean* dimension. By Euclidean, we just mean a new direction that behaves in the same way as directions in the ordinary, everyday space in which you seem to move, and that fits the axioms of Euclid's geometry: A straight line can connect any two points, parallel lines never meet, all triangles have angles that add up to 180°, and so on. The trick is that if you pick three directions that are 90° from each other in three-dimensional space (say, a line extending up through your head, a line straight out in front of you, and a line out to your right), this new direction is at a 90° angle from *all the other three directions*.

We won't try to provide rigorous definitions in this hack, and we'll keep the mathematics light. Instead, we'll focus on helping you to start developing a mental facility with 4D concepts, spaces, and objects, and we'll point you to more resources for further exploration.

Why bother to do all this? Mathematical equations frequently have many dimensions, but graphing more than three can be problematic, to say the least. Dimensions beyond the third are also essential to theories of modern physics. The techniques discussed in this hack won't get you all the way up to the ten (or more!) dimensions of superstring theory, but they might provide some interesting insights. Visualization can lead you to a new understanding of higher-dimensional equations and objects.

Beyond any utility, you can gain an appreciation for the beauty of *polytopes*, geometric figures similar to polyhedra. And, let's face it — it's fun to imagine where something might be if it's perpendicular to everything you know about, and how such a thing might act in ways you would find very strange. It's almost like understanding how magic would work.

In Action

To get your mind limbered up, it's useful to limit your viewpoint by imagining worlds where some of the dimensions that we normally take for granted don't exist (or if they do, they're as inaccessible to residents of those worlds as the fourth dimension is to us).

Nearly every modern introduction to the higher dimensions (including this one) owes a major debt to *Flatland: A Romance of Many Dimensions*, Edwin A. Abbot's classic stepping-stone to 4D insight.[1] If you've already spent some time exploring *Flatland* on your own, you can skip the warm-ups and jump straight to the exercises.

Analogy is one of the best tools for approaching the fourth dimension. You can think of each of these exercises as using a "dimensional ladder" of analogies. By starting from a low number of dimensions (either 0D or 1D) and progressively adding new directions, you can look at the leaps required between each of the familiar dimensions and try to extrapolate a similar step that might be required to reach higher spaces. Introductions to the fourth dimension using *tesseracts* (4D *hypercubes*, or higher-dimensional analogs of cubes) abound, so we'll take a slightly different approach and focus on the 4D *hypersphere* (sometimes called a *glome*).

We suggest several dimensional ladders for you to try out in the exercises that follow, so don't despair if the one of them seems to leave you hanging. By taking several different approaches, you can triangulate (or perhaps "4-simplex-ulate") on the ultimate goal.

Warm-Up 0: Contemplate Nothing

A mathematical point is something that is as close to nothing as possible (see Figure 43-1). It has no length, no width, no height, and a similar lack of extent in any other dimensions you might care to imagine. Imagine that this point is your entire world. In fact, let's call this place Pointworld.

●

Figure 43-1: A zero-dimensional point

Many things that we take for granted are impossible in Pointworld. There is no movement, as there is no dimension in which to move. There is no orientation, as there is nothing else to provide a reference point. There is no up or down, there is no left or right, and there is no forward or back. Even multiplicity is impossible, as there is only the Point. You cannot conceive of another point, as there is no place else for it to be.

This warm-up might seem simple at first, but it could provide decades of focus for meditation. When you are the Point, you are both everything and nothing. You occupy it entirely, but there is nothing to occupy.

Warm-Up 1: Go West, Young Point!

For this next warm-up, we will leave the cozy confines of Pointworld, stretch our non-existent legs, and climb the first rung of the dimensional ladder by adding one degree of freedom.

A mathematical line has one dimension. Similar to a point, a line has no depth or thickness, but it does allow us to have a concept of "direction." We'll pick one particular infinite line and call it Lineworld: a one-dimensional space, or *1-space*.

As you did in the previous warm-up, imagine what it might be like to live in a one-dimensional universe. One important thing to consider is that you would have length, so picture yourself as a *line segment*, rather than a point (see Figure 43-2). You have two ends — let's call them "forward" and "back." If you start to move in either direction, you can keep going until you meet an obstacle, but there is no way to move around obstacles. An obstacle in front of you will *always* be in front of you. You can't see past it, or inside it. There isn't even a way to turn around!

forward ◄———————●———————●————► back

Figure 43-2: A one-dimensional line

Contemplate what is still missing. There are no directions other than forward or backward, so left and right, up and down are all meaningless. Rotation is meaningless.

Now, change your perspective. Our choice of "forward" and "back" to describe the directions was completely arbitrary. Is there anything different if you think of them as left and right?

Change again, and think of the directions as up and down. Could Lineworld have gravity?

As you perform this warm-up, you'll undoubtedly find yourself slipping into three-dimensional thinking. Remember that the other two dimensions must not be considered. Keep ratcheting your perceptions back down to the point of view of a line segment.

You never miss what you have until it's gone.

Warm-Up 2: Get Flattened

Our next jump up the dimensional ladder is to a world much more expansive than the last: Planeworld. Try to visualize yourself in a world of your own with only two dimensions. You can move left and right, forward and back. We say that these two directions are *orthogonal* to each other; that is, a line oriented along the forward-back axis is at a 90° angle to a line oriented along the left-right axis. From a practical perspective, it doesn't matter exactly which direction the axes point.

The new axis gives you something else new: You can rotate! Note that you only have one possible rotation: Relative to the direction you consider "forward," you can only turn left or right.

Note that while you are in Planeworld, you are extremely limited in what you can see. If you are facing a geometric object like a triangle, remember that you are looking at it from the edge on. Don't think about thickness; there is technically no thickness in a 2D world. Rather, think about the way that light might shade the sides, or whether the sides are painted different colors. The only way to get a complete view of the triangle is to "walk" around it and look at it from every direction. You can enhance your perceptions by feeling the sharpness of the points and the smoothness of the sides, but the "inside" is invisible, and cannot be seen (see Figure 43-3).

Firmly keep any tendency to slip into three-dimensional thinking in check.

Now, let's turn this world on its side: Add gravity, and suddenly the Planeworld directions take on new meanings. You now have up, down, left, and right, but no forward or back. This vertical view of a two-dimensional world is described in A. K. Dewdney's marvelous tale of *The Planiverse*, which explores the lives of the residents of the disc-shaped world of Arde. Whereas *Flatland* is a parable, *The Planiverse* delves into the odd directions that biology and physics take in a 2D world.[2]

Spend some time imagining what it might be like if you couldn't even imagine a third dimension. Welcome to 2-space!

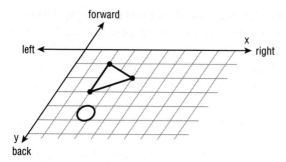

Figure 43-3: A two-dimensional plane. If you are a 2D creature (the circle) you can only see the sides of the triangle. Note that the *x* and *y* axes are 90° from each other, despite how they are drawn on the page with some perspective distortion.

Warm-Up 3: Drop in for a Visit

Next, we'll step up the dimension count by one again, bringing us to the familiar three. We won't go to Spaceworld just yet, but we'll start playing with some three-dimensional objects.

Take a plain, ordinary, three-dimensional sphere and a very sharp knife. Carefully slice it through the middle and look at the cuts you've made: The wide end of each hemisphere is a perfect circle. One way to think of a sphere is as an infinite number of circles of different sizes, stacked on top of each other. At the very bottom and the very top are single points. No matter which way you slice a sphere, the cross-section will always be a circle.

To make things a little more interesting, let's give the sphere some color: red at the top, blue at the bottom, and shading together to purple in the middle (see Figure 43-4). From a three-dimensional perspective, we'll place the sphere below Planeworld and let it rise up and pass through it. Let's see what happens when you imagine yourself as a two-dimensional creature watching this happen.

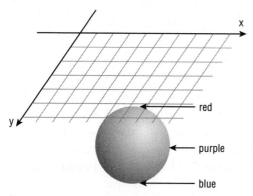

Figure 43-4: A sphere with a red "top" and a blue "bottom," floating "below" Planeworld

From your perspective, a single red point appears out of nowhere, and becomes a quickly growing red circle (see Figure 43-5). As the midpoint of the sphere nears, the circle grows more slowly and its color turns to purple, reaching its maximum size and purpleness at the diameter (see Figure 43-6) and then beginning to shrink, dwindling to a blue point and then popping out of existence (see Figure 43-7). From your 2D perspective, you can't see the entire circle, of course; all you can see is an edge-on view of the side closest to you.

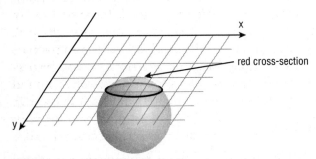

Figure 43-5: The top of the sphere intersects the plane, making a red circular cross-section.

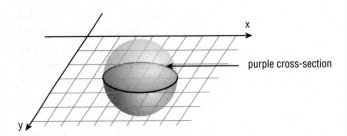

Figure 43-6: As the middle of the sphere intersects the plane, the cross-section grows and becomes purple.

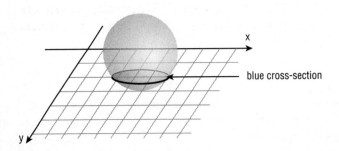

Figure 43-7: The sphere continues to rise and the color of the cross-section shifts to blue as it shrinks.

One key point to take from this warm-up is that a visitor from a higher dimension can only visit a lower in a form that fits the lower dimension. Any higher dimensional shape (such as the circle or sphere) that crosses Lineworld will be perceived by a resident as a line segment. Similarly, the 3D sphere visiting 2D Planeworld can only be seen as a 2D circle. Its higher-dimensional reality must be inferred from its seemingly impossible properties: the ability to change size or shape, and to appear and disappear by movements outside the context of the lower dimension.

A question to contemplate is this: Where did the visiting sphere come from? The third dimension is something exotic, completely outside the experience of a 2D being. Remembering the two axes of Planeworld (*forward-back/left-right*), a new direction is added, *up-down*, which is orthogonal to *both* of the other two.

Now, look around where you are sitting right now and let your consciousness expand to take in the 3D Spaceworld you are living in. You can rotate around all three axes, spinning, turning somersaults, rolling sideways. You can run forward, sidle sideways, and jump in the air. Surely there is no way for there to be *another* axis? After all, that would mean that a four-dimensional visitor could appear right in front of you, inside a closed room. . .

Exercise: Travels with a Hypersphere

A 4D *hyperplane* (we'll call it "Tetraworld," from the Greek word for "four") takes the three familiar spatial dimensions, and adds a fourth that is orthogonal (at 90°) to all of the other three. The directions along this axis are commonly called *ana* and *kata*, analogous to left and right, forward and back, and up and down. This is pretty hard to wrap your brain around, so let's take a sidelong climb up a different dimensional ladder in order to get a view of your first four-dimensional figure: the hypersphere.

The term hypersphere is a general one for any higher-dimensional analog of a sphere (which could be 4D, 5D, or 128D, as you like), so we'll call it a glome, which specifically indicates a 4D hypersphere.

For the bottom rung of our ladder, we need the 1D analog of a sphere. This is defined by picking a center point, and then taking all the points that are a certain distance away from it — let's say, one meter. In Lineworld, given a center point, there will be exactly two points that meet this definition, two meters apart from each other (see Figure 43-8).

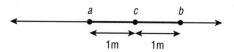

Figure 43-8: This 1D analog of a sphere is the two points *a* and *b* that are 1 meter from the center point *c* on a one-dimensional line.

That's not very exciting, so let's move up to Planeworld. We pick a center point, and then define a figure that is composed of all the points in the plane that are one meter away from it. With very little thought, you'll be able to see that this is a circle (see Figure 43-9).

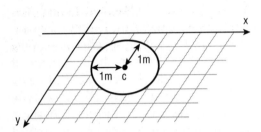

Figure 43-9: This circle, the 2D analog of a sphere, is all the points in a two-dimensional plane that are 1 meter from the center point c.

Our 3D sphere is, of course, a sphere: Picking a center point and taking all the points that are one meter from it, we get a hollow ball that is two meters in diameter (see Figure 43-10).

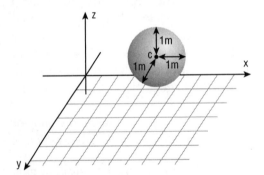

Figure 43-10: A 3D sphere is defined by all the points that are 1 meter away from the center point c in three-dimensional space.

I'm sure you can see where this is going by now: For a glome, go to a 4D hyperplane, pick a point, and define a figure that's one meter from this point in all four dimensions. By relating back to the steps above, you should be able to glimpse that you've got something that is, in some way, *rounder* than a sphere (just as the sphere is, in some way, rounder than a circle), but in a way that you can't directly perceive (see Figure 43-11).

So, as you sit here in Spaceland, imagine what might happen if a two-meter glome were to pass through our 3D world, right in front of you. The glome starts to the ana, and begins moving in the kata direction. As it intersects our 3-space, a tiny sphere will suddenly appear in front of you: It's a cross-section very near the end of the glome. As it keeps moving kata, the sphere will grow rapidly, slowing slightly as it nears its maximum diameter of two meters. (Hope you're in a big room!) It will then begin to shrink, slowly at first, then faster, until it disappears altogether, not even leaving a grin behind.

Hard to get a handle on? Let's try adding some color, to distinguish the different dimensions. Leave the glome where it is (to the kata of our world) and paint the ana end red and the kata end blue. Shade them together, so the midpoint is purple (see Figure 43-12).

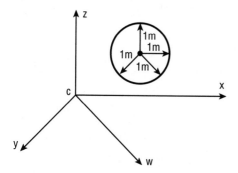

Figure 43-11: This *glome*, or 4D hypersphere, is made of all the points in four-dimensional space that are 1 meter from the center point *c*. Note that the *w* axis is 90° from the *x*, *y*, and *z* axes.

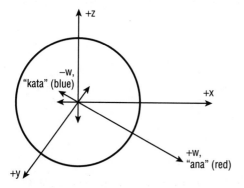

Figure 43-12: A glome. The colors are shaded along the *w* axis, from red at the *ana* end through purple in the middle, to blue at the *kata* end.

Now put the glome back in motion, this time moving from kata to ana. It shouldn't be too hard to see that the sphere that will seem to pop into existence will be red, shifting to purple as it gets bigger, and to blue as it shrinks away into nothing (see Figures 43-13 through 43-15).

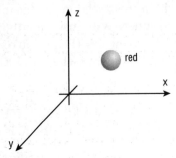

Figure 43-13: The glome from Figure 43-12 starts to pass through our 3-space, moving ana. As the ana end intersects, you see a red spherical cross-section.

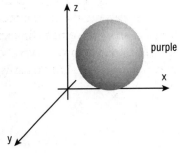

Figure 43-14: As the midpoint of the glome crosses our space, you see a large purple sphere.

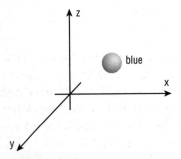

Figure 43-15: The cross-section shrinks and turns blue as the kata end becomes visible, then the glome finishes passing through this 3-space and seems to disappear.

Exercise: Suspend Your Disbelief

Let's try another way to create a glome: suspension. Both this construction and one in the next exercise are described in a very interesting paper by Mark Peterson on the cosmology of the Divine Comedy.[3]

Note one caveat: This suspension technique results in a "topological" hypersphere, rather than a geometric one. Topology is concerned with connectedness: From a topologist's perspective, a triangle, a square, and a circle are all identical, because by rearranging the connected points that make up the border of any of these figures, you can transform it into one of the others without making any cuts. We won't get too technical with the topology in this hack; just think of "inflating" the figures into a proper shape. For example, to inflate a triangle, imagine the sides beginning to bulge out, becoming more and more convex until they form a perfect circle.

This is, in fact, very close to the first step in the dimensional ladder of this new progression: Take a one-dimensional line segment, and place it in 2-space. Pick a point elsewhere in the plane (not in line with the segment) and connect the endpoints of the line to it. You can easily see that this forms a new figure: a triangle. This is the "suspension" method. Imagine the point above with the line segment hanging below like a hammock. Inflate your triangle to a pleasing rondure in order to make a circle (see Figure 43-16).

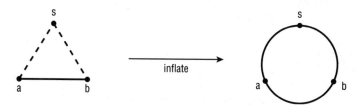

Figure 43-16: Suspend a line segment by its endpoints *a* and *b* from a point *s* and inflate to make a circle.

Move your circle into 3-space, flat in front of you, and pick a point above the circle. Next, connect every point around the edge of the circle to that point, so it is hanging from it like a pot-rack. The three-dimensional figure you've just defined is a cone. When you inflate it (so that the bottom of the cone sags down like a soup bowl and the angled surface of the top bulges out), you'll see it happens to be topologically equivalent to a sphere (see Figure 43-17).

Finally, we take our sphere over to Tetraworld. Pick a new point off to either ana or kata, and *connect every point on the surface of the sphere to that point*. It's important to remember that none of these lines will cross, and they'll all be perfectly straight, just like the top, angled section of the 3D cone (see Figure 43-18).

You know that you have a topological glome, but the real mental work will come in as you contemplate exactly *where* it gets rounder when you inflate it.

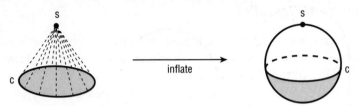

Figure 43-17: Suspend a circle *c* from a point *s* to make a cone, then inflate to make a sphere.

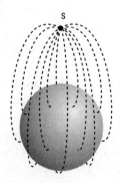

Figure 43-18: Make a glome by suspending a sphere from a point *s* in 4-space. Note that all the lines from *s* to the surface of the sphere are actually straight in 4-space. Inflate the figure four-dimensionally to round out the glome.

Exercise: Just Glue It

Here's another topological method for making a glome, and for this one, we'll introduce the concept of a *manifold*. A manifold is a topological space that acts Euclidean on a small scale but can have different properties on a large scale. For example, parallel lines might meet, or it might be impossible to move between two points. Again, we'll try to get just enough of the idea across so that you can explore some ramifications, and won't get too formal with the math.

Let's try another dimensional ladder, and revisit Lineworld. If Lineworld is a Euclidean line, it can extend forever, off into infinity. Note what the "neighborhood" of a point looks like: From this point you can move in either direction, without any interruption.

We'll now build a 1-manifold that acts like a line locally but actually wraps around. Take two line segments, and place them in 2D Planeworld. Bend each of them into a half-circle, touch the endpoints of one to the endpoints of the other, and glue them together: you've just formed a circle (see Figure 43-19).

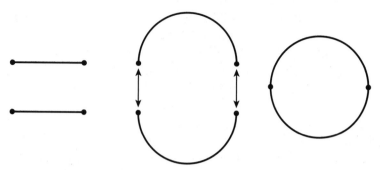

Figure 43-19: To make a circle from two line segments, bend them, then glue the endpoints together.

Now, pop down to your one-dimensional perspective, and visit the new, twisted version of Lineworld you've just created. If you are at any point on this circle's circumference, you can still move either direction, without interruption, just as if you were on a normal, Euclidean line. If you move far enough, though (all the way around the circle), you'll come back to where you were in the beginning! The world formed by the glued lines has become something distinctly non-Euclidean, as the line extended forever will eventually meet itself.

We now increase the dimensions by one, and repeat. Take two circles, and move them into 3D Spaceworld. We're now going to glue them together around the circumferences: Glue every point on the circumferences of one circle to a corresponding point on the other. As in the last exercise, inflate it a bit so you have a sphere rather than a saucer — this doesn't change anything topologically, it just helps make it look nice and tidy in your imagination (see Figure 43-20).

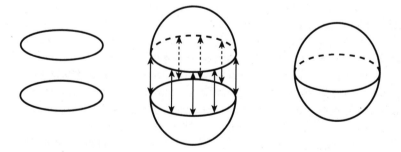

Figure 43-20: Make a sphere from two circles by bending them into hemispheres, then gluing together around the circumferences.

The surface of this sphere is a 2-manifold. Put on your 2D goggles, and imagine yourself as a Planeworld resident who's been moved to the surface of this sphere. It will still seem like a flat plane, but the world itself wraps around in all directions. If the world is big enough, you won't be able to detect the curvature just by looking. Conversely, if the world is small or you have a powerful enough telescope, you would be able to see yourself from behind.

Again, the last step is the real trick: Take two three-dimensional spheres, and move them to Tetraworld. Now, glue *every point on the surface of one sphere to a corresponding point on the surface of the other sphere.* Your new topological glome is pretty flat in the fourth dimension, so inflate it, with one sphere billowing out to kata, the other to ana (see Figure 43-21).

Now, drop in for a visit. Take your everyday, three-space self onto the 3-manifold that is the surface of the hypersphere, and see how far you can see. What happens if you fly forward forever? If the hypersphere is bigger than you could fly around in your lifetime, is there any way that you could detect the curvature?

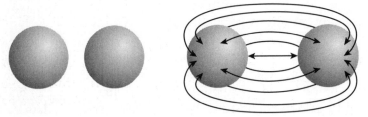

Figure 43-21: Glue the two spheres together in 4-space by connecting points on the surface of one sphere to matching points on the other. As with suspension, the figure needs to be inflated four-dimensionally to make a rounded glome.

Exercise: Rotate a Sphere

There's more than one way to skin a hypersphere, so let's try a new spin: The fourth dimension allows a whole new set of rotations. Rotations can also be used to construct a glome, so we'll clamber up a new dimensional ladder. In some ways, this is the hardest exercise to mentally model, because you're picturing movement in a higher dimension as well as shape. It may take you a few tries to grasp it.

Take a 1D line segment in a 2D plane, and hold down the 0D point in the center. Rotate the line segment around the point in two dimensions, and the endpoints trace a circle in the plane.

Now, take the 2D circle that you've just made, and move it into a 3D space. Hold down a 1D diameter (the longest line segment that crosses the circle), and spin the circle around it in the third dimension. The circumference of the circle will trace out the surface of a sphere. If you find this tricky to imagine, just think of standing a hoop upright and giving it a spin.

Here's the hard part: Take your new 3D sphere over to 4D Tetraworld and hold down a 2D great circle (a slice that passes through the midpoint of the sphere). Give the sphere a spin through the fourth dimension around that circle, and the surface of the sphere will trace a hypersphere in four-space.

Don't worry if you don't get it on the first try, or the fiftieth. Gaining an intuitive feel for how the fourth dimension works requires approaching the same idea from a lot of different directions.

An additional exercise to try: What would happen if the circle you are rotating around does not pass through the midpoint of the sphere? (Hint: Try it out with the line and the circle.)

Exercise: Spin a Hypersphere

In Lineworld, as you have observed, there is no such thing as rotation. You have just one *degree of freedom*: let's say, forward and backward. A degree of freedom is basically a direction in which you can move, whether it's an axis or a rotation. We'll take a mathematical approach, and start naming our axes. Traditionally, the single axis of Lineworld is called x.

Now consider Planeworld, with its two axes (x and a new, orthogonal axis, called y). This gives us two degrees of freedom: We can move along either axis, or both at once. Even more interestingly, we now also have a third degree of freedom: We can spin, as you saw in the last exercise. This rotation can be described as happening in the xy plane.

Spaceworld expands our options even further: Its z axis lets us move up and down, but we now have three different rotations available: Rotation in the xy plane, as before (commonly called *yaw*, imagine turning your head left and right); in the xz plane (*roll*, imagine tilting your head toward either shoulder); and in the yz plane (*pitch*, imagine looking upward and downward). Therefore, there are six degrees of freedom in 3-space: moving along the x, y, and z axes, and rotating in the xy, xz, and yz planes.

Now consider the degrees of freedom that Tetraworld's fourth (w) axis adds: In addition to sauntering back and forth, left and right, up and down, and now ana and kata (four degrees of freedom), there are six possible rotations, one for each pair of axes: to xy, xz, and yz, we add wx, wy, and wz. Ron has proposed new names for rotations in each of these planes: *wax*, *way*, and *waz* (though he does note that this makes the term *yaw* quite deceptive, and it might have to be renamed *yax* or *xay*). We can note another four-dimensional progression here: Each new dimension d we add increases the number of rotations possible by d-1. From these three new rotations in 4-space, plus the new w axis, we get four new degrees of freedom, for a total of ten!

We'll try two simple rotations, using the red-blue glome from the "Travels with a Hypersphere" exercise, earlier (refer to Figure 43-12). First, keep it aligned so that the red end is ana-most and the blue end is kata-most, and its midpoint is intersecting the 3-space you are in right now: You now have what looks like a two-meter, purple sphere floating before you.

Give it a spin in the xy plane as it floats in front of you; not much will happen, at least in terms of color changes (nor would it change if you were to spin in xz or yz, at least not yet). One key point is that these rotations are *parallel to a plane*, rather than *around an axis*. The latter makes sense in three-dimensional space, but not when you start moving into higher dimensions. This is a somewhat tricky point, so consider what happens when you rotate an ordinary sphere parallel to the xy plane (like the spinning of the Earth, where z is the "axis of rotation"). Every point on the surface except the topmost and bottommost has its x and y coordinates change, but the z coordinate of every point remains the same.

When you rotate parallel to the xy plane in 4-space, the w and z coordinates for a point do not change, but the x and y coordinates do. At the moment, a point's color is determined by its position on the w axis (redder toward positive w or ana, and bluer toward negative w or kata), but we're about to change that: Stop the xy rotation, and start a new rotation parallel to the wz plane — give it some *waz*. Rotate from ana (the positive w axis) toward up (the positive z axis). The spherical cross-section remains the same size in front of us, but the colors begin to change. The top begins to shade red, while the bottom shades blue. This continues until one end is bright red and the other is bright blue, and the colors that were once along the w axis are now along the z axis, As you continue to *waz* the sphere, shades then begin to shift back through purple, until the blue and red ends have switched. Try to keep in mind that you're merely looking at a 3D slice of this object, and the object itself isn't changing. The only difference is the part of it that you're looking at.

Our current glome, of course, is defined by shades from only two colors: at the start, one color at each end of the w axis. This makes it quite hard to visualize many of the rotations. Think about coloring the six points that mark the ends of each axis in a three-dimensional sphere, and imagining it as it rotates through 3-space. For a real mental workout, mark eight points on the axes of a glome with different colors, and try to work out the changing shades as it moves through each of the rotations. Take it easy at first, and just rotate through 90° in one plane at a time.

What happens to the shades if you move the glome so a different portion is intersecting your 3-space? How about if you spin it in two independent planes at the same time? (This last is a special rotation only possible in spaces with four or more dimensions, and is called a *Clifford rotation*.)

Exercise: Simple Is as Simple Does

The tesseract, which we mentioned earlier, is an example of a *polychoron*, or *4-polytope*. An *n*-polytope is simply an *n*-dimensional, "flat-sided" geometric figure. [More specifically, an *n*-polytope is bounded in *n*-space by a number of (*n*-1)-polytopes.] A 2-polytope is commonly called a polygon — for example, a square, a pentagon, or any other two-dimensional shape with a number of straight sides. A 3-polytope is a *polyhedron*, which could be a cube, an octahedron, a rhombic dodecahedron (see Hack 42, "Enter the Third Dimension"), a stellated rhombicuboctahedron, or something even more complex.

Let's try our hand at a polychoron, the most basic one possible: the 4-simplex. We'll work our way up the ladder from one dimension, as usual. First, imagine a one-dimensional line segment. As before, it has length, but no width or height. In Lineworld, there aren't many options. You can make the segment longer or shorter, but that's it. Therefore, move the line segment to Planeworld. Add a point in this new dimension, and connect the endpoints of the line segment to it. You've just created a triangle!

I'm sure you can see where this is going. As with our previous constructions, we move the triangle to Spaceworld, add a point in the new dimension, and connect the three corners of the triangles to it. This is a tetrahedron, which all Dungeons & Dragons players will recognize as the shape of a four-sided die. It looks like a pyramid with a triangular base.

Reviewing what we have so far: a line (a 1D figure) with two endpoints (0D); a triangle (a 2D figure) with three lines (1D) as its sides; and a tetrahedron (3D) with four triangles (2D) as its faces. If you were to guess that the next step would be a 4D figure with five tetrahedra as "sides," you'd be right!

Place your newly minted tetrahedron in Tetraworld. Pick a point off ana-ward, and connect the points at each corner of the tetrahedron to it. A projection of this figure all the way down onto 2-space will look a bit like a lopsided pentagram, but what you should focus on are the properties of this new figure. The new point can be combined with each of the triangular faces of the tetrahedron to make four new tetrahedra, and all five tetrahedra enclose a four-dimensional hyper-volume. All of the tetrahedra are on the "outside," and none of them intersect.

At this point, you may want to try out a polychoron modeling program (such as Stella 4D) and try manipulating and rotating a 4-simplex with the help of a computer before you jump straight into visualizing rotations and spatial intersections.

You're Only Getting Started

These exercises only scratch the hypersurface of the weird and wonderful complexity of four-dimensional figures and visualization.

For a bestiary of higher-dimensional objects, visit Jonathan Bower's marvelous catalog of uniform polychora (`www.polytope.net/hedrondude/polychora.htm`) — as of this writing, it lists 1,849 different polychora, as well as a large number of polytwisters (swirly, polytope-like objects). You can also explore a variety of unfolded polychora at Andrew Weimholt's site (`http://weimholt.com/andrew/polytope.shtml`).

For much deeper explorations of the topics covered in this hack, continue your reading with Jeffrey Weeks' *The Shape of Space*[4] or Chris McMullen's two-volume *The Visual Guide to Extra Dimensions*.[5] For yet another approach to 4D visualization using stereographic projections and animations (including the rendering of a hypersphere as a collection of interlocking, twisting equators called the *Hopf fibration*), watch the *Dimensions* film discussed below in the "In Real Life" section.

How It Works

Can humans really learn to visualize higher-dimensional objects and spaces? Or is our mental hardware wired to the topology of the everyday world that molded its development? Several studies are of particular interest, as they directly address this question.

Researchers at Princeton University examined the ability of subjects to perform *path integration* on a 4D maze. If you were to walk fifty feet north and fifty feet east, your capacity for path integration is what would prompt you to point southwest when asked to identify your starting point. Using a computer maze program to compare performance over time at path integration in virtual 4D mazes, four out of the five test participants demonstrated a "leap" in their performance levels after working with the maze program for a large number of runs. This leap corresponded to a level of ability that could not be explained simply by 3D spatial skills.[6]

Another study by the University of California has also suggested that practice can improve the ability to navigate through a virtual four-dimensional environment. Subjects searched through a multiroom virtual environment for a randomly positioned goal and returned to the home position. By the end of the trials, most of the participants had greatly improved their efficiency at the tasks.[7]

The University of Illinois used an immersive virtual reality chamber for a different sort of test. Participants were able to view different 3D cross-sections of randomly shaped 4-simplexes by walking along the w axis and observing how the visible slice changed. After studying the 4D object, participants were asked to estimate the distance between two points in 4-space. The results suggest that they were indeed using a basic level of 4D spatial ability, and were actually imagining objects as if they extended into a fourth dimension separate from the three familiar ones.[8]

These are small-scale studies and not conclusive, but they are suggestive. You can try some subjective experiments of your own using the visualizations and computer programs described in this hack.

In Real Life

Sadly, you probably won't be playing a game of hyperspherical basketball [9] or navigating a tesseract-shaped house[10] any time soon. Fortunately, there are many tools, games, and computer programs that can serve as windows into the four-dimensional world.

Fail to Go Insane with Hinton Cubes

Mathematician Charles H. Hinton (who coined the words *tesseract, ana,* and *kata*) developed a system of colored cubes to train his mind to think in 4D. This is a set of 81 cubes, each with differently colored faces. Eighty-one, as the alert reader may have noticed, is the number of cells in a $3 \times 3 \times 3 \times 3$ hypercube. The color codes of the cube are meant to help you gain an intuitive understanding of relationships in four-space — that is, what is "next to" what.

I first read about these cubes in the book *Mathematical Carnival* by Martin Gardner.[11] Gardner included a letter from a reader who wrote in about the dire consequences of working too closely with them, claiming they led to obsession. For many years, finding a copy of Hinton's original writings was devilishly difficult, leading to a certain Lovecraftian "Things Man Was Not Meant to Know" aura, with suggestions of pending insanity in the few mentions I found over the years.

Happily, the Internet Archive has scanned editions of his *A New Era of Thought* (first published in 1888)[12] and *The Fourth Dimension* (1904)[13], as both are out of print. You can now easily construct your own set of Hinton's cubes after the designs in *The Fourth Dimension* or other instructions online (www.scribd.com/doc/3046062/Hinton-Cubes).

I've played with a set of the cubes, but I didn't find them to be an exceptionally useful tool. Visualizing the folding and unfolding of a tesseract (or even watching a projected polychoron rotate on a computer screen) seems to be a much more direct route to the same ends.

I can also report that I haven't gone mad, or at least not any madder than I was before contemplating the cubes.

Build a Projection

Hack 42, "Enter the Third Dimension," suggests the use of the Zometool modeling kit to build three-dimensional models. While you can't build a four-dimensional model directly, you *can* build its projection in 3-space. One disadvantage of these projections is their rigidity, as you can only rotate them in the boring three dimensions of the everyday world. Even so, having an actual three-dimensional projection has distinct advantages over a two-dimensional drawing, not least of which is its tactile nature. You can turn it over in your hands and examine it from different angles. It can serve as a crutch, a stepping-off point for different visualization experiments, and a touchstone for when you lose track of all the different moving, rotating polytopes.

Expand Your Mind with Dimensions

For a brilliant and mind-blowing exploration of polychora, watch *Dimensions*, a free, nine-part mathematical film (www.dimensions-math.org). *Dimensions* has beautiful computer animations of stereographic projections of four-dimensional figures, and walks you from the second dimension up through polychora and the Hopf fibration. Even if you don't try any of the exercises in this hack, watch this video!

Visit Tetraspace

As you venture deeper into the fourth dimension, you'll find that many others have been blazing the trail for you. Garrett Jones's Tetraspace website (http://teamikaria.com/hddb/forum/) has forums that include many lively discussions about higher-dimensional matters. Browsing through the history of previous posts will give you many more ideas for visualization exercises, and you can post your own questions or theories.

Lean on Your Computer

Numerous programs are available that enable you to model and manipulate four-dimensional objects. Here are a couple to get you started:

- **Stella 4D** (www.software3d.com). One of the best tools for exploring polychora is Stella 4D, an expanded version of Software3D's Stella program for visualizing (and printing foldable) polyhedra. It's not cheap ($99 for a single-user license), but a free demo version is available.

- **Tesseract Trainer** (http://happypenguin.org/show?Tesseract%20Trainer). A web search will turn up many programs that enable you to manipulate 2D representations of a 3D projection of a tesseract. The one from Mushware is nice, can do a stereoscopic view, and has a free GPL version for Linux.

Play a Game

Computer games are another way to help tune your 4D intuition by manipulating higher-dimensional objects and moving through representations of four-space. Here are a few to check out:

- **4D Maze** (www.urticator.net/maze). Wander through a randomly generated four-dimensional maze.

- **Magic Cube 4D** (www.superliminal.com/cube/cube.htm). Solve a four-dimensional analog of a Rubik's Cube puzzle.

- **MagicCube5D** (www.gravitation3d.com/magiccube5d/). Are you worried that four dimensions might not be hardcore enough to impress your friends down at the mathematicians' pub? This five-dimensional Rubik's Cube puzzle will help you keep your street cred.

- **4dtris** (http://sourceforge.net/projects/dtris/). A variant of the popular block-dropping game, upping the usual number of dimensions by two. Fill up the game grid with hypercubes.

- **Adanaxis** (www.linuxgamingworld.com/?q=node/64). Exercise all ten degrees of four-dimensional freedom in this space shooter game. Fly a ship through 4D space and blast enemies.

- **Miegakure** (http://marctenbosch.com/miegakure/). This game is still in development, but we would be remiss not to mention it. Solve puzzles by moving objects ana and kata. The demo video shows a player interlocking two solid rings without cutting them, by first moving one into the fourth dimension.

See Also

- Dionys Burger, *Sphereland: A Fantasy About Curved Spaces and an Expanding Universe* (New York: Crowell, 1965).

- Norton Juster, *The Dot and the Line: A Romance in Lower Mathematics* (New York: Random House, 1963). See also the 1965 MGM short film, *The Dot and the Line*.

- Henry Parker Manning, *Geometry of Four Dimensions* (New York: MacMillan Company, 1914). Also freely available online (www.archive.org/details/geometryoffourdi033495mbp).

- Tony Robbin, Rudy v. B. Rucker, and Linda Dalrymple Henderson, *Fourfield: Computers, Art and the Fourth Dimension* (Boston: Little, Brown, 1992).

- Rudy v. B. Rucker, *Geometry, Relativity and the Fourth Dimension* (New York: Dover Publications, 1977).

- Rudy v. B. Rucker, *The Fourth Dimension: Toward a Geometry of Higher Reality* (Boston: Houghton Mifflin, 1984).

- Rudy v. B. Rucker, *Spaceland, A Novel of the Fourth Dimension* (New York: Tor, 2002).

- Ian Stewart, *Flatterland: Like Flatland Only More So* (Cambridge, Mass: Perseus Pub., 2001).

- The Glome Wiki (`www.ludism.org/glome/`), companion to the Mentat Wiki, focuses on both higher and lower dimensions.

Notes

1. Edwin A. Abbott and Ian Stewart, *The Annotated Flatland: A Romance of Many Dimensions* (Cambridge: Perseus, 2002).

2. A. K. Dewdney, *The Planiverse: Computer Contact with a Two-Dimensional World* (New York: Poseidon Press, 1984).

3. Mark A. Peterson, "Dante and the 3-Sphere," *American Journal of Physics* 47, no. 12 (1979): 1031–1035.

4. Jeffrey R. Weeks, *The Shape of Space: How to Visualize Surfaces and Three-Dimensional Manifolds* (New York: Marcel Dekker, 2002).

5. Chris McMullen, *The Visual Guide to Extra Dimensions* (CreateSpace, 2008).

6. T. N. Afflalo and M. S. A. Graziano, "Four-Dimensional Spatial Reasoning in Humans," *Journal of Experimental Psychology: Human Perception and Performance 34*, no. 5 (2008): 1066–1077. `www.princeton.edu/~graziano/Aflalo_08.pdf`

7. Gregory Seyranian, P. Colantoni, and Michael D'Zmura, "Navigation in Environments with Four Spatial Dimensions," *Perception 28*, Supplement 7 (1999).

8. Michael S. Ambinder, Ranxiao Frances Wang, James A. Crowell, George K. Francis, and Peter Brinkmann, "Human Four-Dimensional Spatial Intuition in Virtual Reality," *Psychonomic Bulletin & Review 16*, no. 5 (2009): 818–823. `www.springerlink.com/content/5m124881475810w4/`

9. Homer C. Nearing, Jr., "The Hyperspherical Basketball," collected in *The Sinister Researches of C. P. Ransom* (New York: Modern Literary Editions, 1954).

10. Robert A. Heinlein, " — And He Built a Crooked House — ," collected in *The Unpleasant Profession of Jonathan Hoag* (New York: Gnome Press, 1959).

11. Martin Gardner, *Mathematical Carnival: From Penny Puzzles, Card Shuffles and Tricks of Lightning Calculators to Roller Coaster Rides into the Fourth Dimension* (New York: Knopf, 1975).

12. Charles Howard Hinton, Alicia Boole Stott, and H. John Falk, A *New Era of Thought* (London: S. Sonnenschein & Co., 1888). www.archive.org/details/anewerathought00falkgoog

13. Charles Howard Hinton, *The Fourth Dimension* (London: Sonnenschein, 1904). www.archive.org/details/fourthdimension00hintarch

Communication

We all must communicate with one another, but what is the quality of our communication? In some ways, technology has provided us with the means to communicate more than ever before, constantly, and with more people. However, it has also meant that more of our communication is mediated and considered; it's less spontaneous, but we often apply more sophisticated expectations about communicating efficiently and effectively.

You can clarify your communication with some of this chapter's hacks (Hack 44, "Spell It Out," and Hack 48, "Communicate Multimodally") and communicate — or conceal — delicate shades of emotion with another (Hack 46, "Emote Precisely"). You will learn how to fit more communication into a medium with little bandwidth, such as a mobile phone text message, using a simplified and improved version of shorthand (Hack 47, "Streamline Your Shorthand"). This chapter will also show you how to create a kind of textual augmented reality that sands the rough edges of the Internet (Hack 49, "Mediate Your Environment").

John Donne famously said that no man is an island. However, in a sense, some people are islanders, by choice or accident; even when we communicate prolifically, we're often isolated in other ways from those with whom we're communicating. The more isolated you are, the more it can benefit you to use the techniques in this chapter to upgrade your message-in-a-bottle communication system to something a little more high-tech.

Hack 44: Spell It Out

Learn fingerspelling and the NATO phonetic alphabet — both often useful for disambiguation in noisy environments, and sometimes useful to conceal information as well.

The *NATO phonetic alphabet* uses unambiguous words to stand for each letter. Designed for speakers of many different languages, it's used to spell out words in voice messages and to convey critical information unambiguously in potentially dangerous settings such as air traffic control. You've probably heard of it even if you don't know what it's called; when you hear someone saying, "This is Charlie-Tango-Foxtrot zero-three-eight" as their call sign in a movie, they're using the NATO phonetic alphabet (or a similar variation).

Fingerspelling uses hand gestures to express letters of the alphabet. It's most commonly seen when it's used by the Deaf community to supplement sign language. The version we will explore in this hack is part of ASL, American Sign Language, and is known as the *American Manual Alphabet.*

Both the NATO phonetic alphabet and the American Manual Alphabet can be used by sighted and hearing people to clarify their speech in certain situations. For example, if you are talking to someone on a bad mobile phone connection, you can use the NATO alphabet to clarify what you're saying; if you were chatting with someone over Skype or face-to-face at a noisy party, you could perhaps use either or both.

We had both tried to learn both alphabets by rote on several occasions, without success. We needed a mnemonic, so we designed one that linked both alphabets together so that each reinforced the other in memory. In addition, there are pairs of letters that reinforce each other within the mnemonic system as well.

In Action

Table 44-1 shows both the NATO phonetic alphabet and fingerspelling equivalents for each letter of the Roman alphabet, followed by a mnemonic that joins the corresponding NATO and fingerspelling letters together and makes them easier to remember.

- There are several ways to use the table to learn the new alphabets: You can try to learn both alphabets straight through, saying the NATO letter and fingerspelling at the same time.

- When you think you have learned both alphabets from beginning to end, practice running through them backward.

- Try spelling the names of your friends, family, and pets in either or both alphabets. If you can't remember the fingerspelling for a letter, the NATO version may jog your memory, and vice versa.

- Converse with a friend using the alphabets. At first, you might want to limit yourself to chat and text abbreviations. (Oscar Mike Golf! Lima Oscar Lima!) Because these abbreviations are already an efficient way to communicate, they're useful for this hack.

- You can also conceal information with these alphabets. More people seem to know the NATO alphabet than fingerspelling, but even the former can be useful around children and animals. For example, we refer to our dogs Humphrey and Bridget as "Hotel" and "Bravo," respectively, if we don't want to catch the dogs' attention.

- You can also use these alphabets to create code words and safe words in a relationship (see Hack 57, "Take a Semantic Pause").

- If you want to virtually guarantee that no one but you and your unbearably geeky buddies will have any idea Whiskey Tango Foxtrot you're saying, try combining this hack with the Lojban attitudinals from Hack 46, "Emote Precisely."

Table 44-1: Mnemonics for NATO and Fingerspelling Alphabets

LETTER	NATO PHONETIC ALPHABET	AMERICAN MANUAL ALPHABET	MNEMONIC	NOTES
A	Alfa		The ALPHA male raises his fist in triumph.	Note international spelling of "Alfa." Most languages do not pronounce "PH" as "F."
B	Bravo		Hand ready to clap BRAVO!	
C	Charlie		The director CHARLIE Chaplin adjusts the lens of his movie camera.	See also OSCAR.

Continued

Table 44-1 *(continued)*

LETTER	NATO PHONETIC ALPHABET	AMERICAN MANUAL ALPHABET	MNEMONIC	NOTES
D	Delta		"That's a DELTA plane up there!"	
E	Echo		The stone you threw into the cave made an ECHO.	Hand position resembles holding a stone.
F	Foxtrot		The judge in the dance contest thought your FOXTROT was *magnifique*!	See also TANGO.
G	Golf		"GOLF? This way to the links, madam."	
H	Hotel		Don't forget your HOTEL key.	Hand position resembles a key.
I	India		Lift your pinky when you sip a cup of Darjeeling tea from INDIA.	
J	Juliett		JULIET asks Romeo for a "pinky swear" that he'll keep their night together secret.	See also ROMEO. Note international spelling of "Juliett."

LETTER	NATO PHONETIC ALPHABET	AMERICAN MANUAL ALPHABET	MNEMONIC	NOTES
K	Kilo		A KILO is about two pounds.	Hand position for the number two.
L	Lima		"The hard fact is, you're a loser if you don't eat your LIMA beans."	Hand position resembles the "L for loser" sign.
M	Mike		Your roommate told you to put your thumb-MIKE away or she'd cut it off.	Note also that the three fingers together resemble the letter M.
N	November		The month of NOVEMBER contains the date 11/11, which silly people consider super-spooky.	Hand position resembles the characters "11/11." Note also that two fingers together resemble the letter N.
O	Oscar		The lens of the camera for Charlie Chaplin's OSCAR-winning film.	See also CHARLIE.
P	Papa		When PAPA snaps his fingers, you'd better pay attention.	

Continued

Table 44-1 *(continued)*

LETTER	NATO PHONETIC ALPHABET	AMERICAN MANUAL ALPHABET	MNEMONIC	NOTES
Q	Quebec		If you go birdwatching in QUEBEC, you'll see Canada geese.	Hand position looks like the head of a goose.
R	Romeo		ROMEO says, "Juliet, I'll never kiss and tell — honest!"	In some cultures, people cross their fingers when they're lying. See also JULIETT.
S	Sierra		They came to blows over the Treasure of the SIERRA Madre.	Hand position looks like a fist ready to punch someone.
T	Tango		The judge in the dance contest gave your TANGO the evil eye.	In some cultures, this hand position is a gesture to ward off the "evil eye." See also FOXTROT.
U	Uniform		A good Boy Scout always wears a UNIFORM.	Hand position resembles the Boy Scout salute.

LETTER	NATO PHONETIC ALPHABET	AMERICAN MANUAL ALPHABET	MNEMONIC	NOTES
V	Victor		V for VICTOR-y.	Hand position is traditional gesture of victory.
W	Whiskey		Three fingers of WHISKEY is quite a drink!	
X	X-ray		"Doctor, I broke my finger and now I need an X-RAY!"	
Y	Yankee		"I tried to hang loose, but those Vermont YANKEEs can't surf!"	Hand position resembles surfers' "hang loose" gesture.
Z	Zulu		The clock was set to ZULU Time. The pendulum went tick-tock.	Hand gesture moves back and forth like a pendulum. Zulu Time is another name for Greenwich time.

How It Works

A means of communication, such as a cell phone connection or a crowded dance floor, is called a *channel* in information theory. An inefficient or imperfect channel — one that does not convey all of the *signal* piped through it — is called a *noisy* channel. In the real world, all channels are more or less noisy.

The NATO phonetic alphabet (and fingerspelling, if you have visual contact) works by increasing the *redundancy* of the signal transmitted, thereby giving the intended recipient more chances to correctly decode it. If you say the letter "B," the recipient may hear it as "P" or "V" or even "D" because the channel is noisy and there is little redundancy. However, if you say "Bravo," the recipient is not likely to hear it as "Pravo," "Dravo," or "Vravo." which are not words. That's because of the redundancy you have provided with the sound "ravo," which acts as a kind of backup in case the "B" sound itself is lost.

> **NOTE** Fingerspelling while speaking aloud is also a form of multimodal communication (Hack 48, "Communicate Multimodally").

In Real Life

Rather than illustrate this hack with all the wonderful things you can do if you adopt it, we'll share a true cautionary tale about the kind of world you can expect to live in if you don't. The scene is several years ago, in Marty and Ron's old apartment, before Ron knew the NATO phonetic alphabet.

> **Ron** (*on the phone*): *Hi, this is Ron from apartment P-203. I'd like to order a pizza.*
> **Pizza guy**: *Did you say P-203 or B-203?*
> **Ron**: *P-203.*
> **Pizza guy**: *B-203?*
> **Ron**: *No, P-203.*
> **Pizza guy**: *Is that "B" as in "ball"?*
> **Ron**: *I can't hear you. Did you say, "Is that 'P' as in 'Paul'" or "Is that 'B' as in 'ball'"?*
> **Pizza guy**: *I said, is it "P" as in "Paul"?*
> **Ron**: *I still can't understand you. You're going to have to come up with words other than "ball" or "Paul."*
> **Pizza guy**: *It's very simple. Is it "P" as in "Paul" or "B" as in "ball"?*

Repeat until the desire for ibuprofen exceeds the desire for pizza.

See Also

- ASL University: Fingerspelling (www.lifeprint.com/asl101/fingerspelling) is an in-depth course with proficiency objectives, learning games, and more.

Hack 45: Read Lips

Lip reading isn't a magical way to know exactly what someone is saying from a great distance, as in the movies. Nonetheless, it can be a fun and useful skill to develop, and can even enhance your understanding of conversations you can hear.

For many of us, reading lips is one of those mental skills with a high glamour, something spies do, or the killer robot HAL in *2001: A Space Odyssey*. However, there are a lot of situations in which reading lips is extremely practical. It's obviously useful if you have a hearing impairment, and many deaf people use it in combination with sign language and other communication skills (see Hack 44, "Spell It Out"). Anyone can have limited hearing in some situations — in a crowd, for example, or in a noisy restaurant or club. Furthermore, as you (and your loved ones) age, hearing loss may affect you in the future, even if it hasn't been something you've needed to worry about so far.

Perhaps your ambition is high-minded, or perhaps you just want to eavesdrop on people at other tables in restaurants, learn what people are muttering under their breath, or figure out what the TV censors bleeped. Either way, lip reading is a skill you can develop with a little attention and practice.

In Action

To begin learning to lip read, start paying attention when people are talking. Watch your friends and family closely when they speak. In a mirror, carefully pronounce different words and note the shape of your mouth when you do. Try to find a variety of phonemes to say. (Phonemes are the phonetic building blocks of a language; while they're hard to define distinctly, most experts think there are about 40 phonemes in English.)

If you want to get scientific about it, you can seek text that's designed to test pronunciation, either for linguistic analysis or speech therapy. The following paragraph is used by a project that tracks accents and dialects, and contains most of the basic sounds and clusters of English:

> *Please call Stella. Ask her to bring these things with her from the store: Six spoons of fresh snow peas, five thick slabs of blue cheese, and maybe a snack for her brother Bob. We also need a small plastic snake and a big toy frog for the kids. She can scoop these things into three red bags, and we will go meet her Wednesday at the train station.*[1]

We also strongly recommend the following text passage, usually known as the *Rainbow Passage*; it's very commonly used to assess accents, as well as to test text-to-speech software. The Rainbow Passage was devised by linguists to contain a very wide variety of phonemes and combinations typically found in English:

> *When sunlight strikes raindrops in the air, they act like a prism and form a rainbow. The rainbow is a division of white light into many beautiful colors. These take the shape of a long round arch, with its path high above, and its two ends apparently*

beyond the horizon. There is, according to legend, a boiling pot of gold at one end. People look, but no one ever finds it. When a man looks for something beyond his reach, his friends say he is looking for a pot of gold at the end of the rainbow.

Throughout the centuries men have explained the rainbow in various ways. Some have accepted it as a miracle without physical explanation. To the Hebrews it was a token that there would be no more universal floods. The Greeks used to imagine that it was a sign from the gods to foretell war or heavy rain. The Norse men consider the rainbow as a bridge over which the gods passed from Earth to their home in the sky. Other men have tried to explain the phenomena physically. Aristotle thought that the rainbow was caused by a reflection of the sun's rays by the rain. Since then physicists have found that it is not reflection, but refraction by the raindrops which causes the rainbow. Many complicated ideas about the rainbow have been formed. The difference in the rainbow depends considerably upon the size of the water drops, and the width of the colored band increases as the size of the drops increases. The actual primary rainbow observed is said to be the effect of super position of a number of bows. If the red of the second bow falls upon green of the first, the result is to give a bow with an abnormally wide yellow band, since red and green lights when mixed formed yellow. This is a very common type of bow, one showing mainly red and yellow, with little or no green or blue.[2]

With practice, you'll be able to see small differences between similar sounds. Bear in mind, though, that some phonemes are made by the same lip positions, with changes in voicing, tongue position, or other factors you can't see. For example, you'll have to determine the difference between "pin" and "bin" (different voicing) or even "pen" and "men" by context. Even though they're visually subtly different, you'll probably have similar problems with "bin" and "been" as well. Reading the lips of people with different accents will pose some difficulties, and strangers will be harder to read than people whose speech patterns you know. Nevertheless, study will generally pay off.

You can also seek out courses in lip reading that will provide you with some extra study materials and other resources. Some people also find it useful to take a class with a professional, if one is available in their area. However, you don't really need to buy anything to learn and practice.

There are many ways to practice, once you start to learn what to do. One of the most effective is to use video, either on your TV or computer. Start with a movie you've seen before, so you know something about the context of the speech. Watch the actors' mouths, and turn on the captioning so you can see the words as they're spoken. (You may find some inaccurate captioning, but most of the time captioning should help.) Turn the sound down very low as you get more confident. Use the video controls to pause and study mouth positions, or replay bits of speech. Eventually try turning the sound off completely, and then try it without the captioning.

When you gain a little confidence, start practicing in public places, such as on buses or while waiting in lines. Watch people talking and practice your skill. Watch their expressions and body language; this will help immensely in conveying extra meaning. Try to remember how your mouth felt when you made certain sounds in practice; using that kinesthetic sensory memory will help you remember the sound.

At first, make sure you can see the speaker's whole face; it's much harder to read lips from more than ten feet or if someone is turned away, even partly. Because you're really reading the whole face, lighting is also very important — it's easier to read people who are well-lit, and who don't have strong light behind them that shadows the face. For similar reasons, you'll have a harder time reading people who obscure parts of their faces with their hands or people who have facial hair.

Context is extremely important in lip reading — one of the first things to do when you start reading a conversation is to try to establish some key words, moods, and other information that will help you resolve ambiguous words or dropped information in the course of the speech. Once you know what the speech is generally about, it's also very helpful to actively interpret sentences and try to anticipate where they may be going. This, too, will help if you aren't sure of certain words or you miss parts of the sentence. If you're ready for an extra challenge, put on headphones to make sure you can't hear the talking, even a little, or to provide distracting sounds.

Needless to say, you should be respectful as you practice and use your new skills. If it seems that people are having a very personal conversation, it may be courteous to practice on someone else. However, if they're talking in public, they probably realize they can be overheard anyway. If someone seems clearly uncomfortable about your watching or staring at them, though, it's better to look somewhere else . . . and it might even be dangerous not to.

How It Works

Lip reading, of course, works partly by learning how the mouth moves to make specific phonemes of a language and form words, and interpreting those movements. Even when you become very skilled at lip reading, however, don't expect to be able to transcribe speech verbatim. Only a very small amount of spoken language is conveyed by the actual words people speak. That's why it's very important to learn to read facial expressions, body language, gestures, glances, and other semi-linguistic cues as well. These factors will help a great deal to convey mood, emotional content, and other crucial contextual content.

Be aware that you'll never be perfect at lip reading, but it's a skill you can continue to hone for a long time, as you get better at noticing details and encounter new people with different speech patterns. You may eventually even be able to try lip reading in multiple languages. Generally speaking, though, concentrate on increasing how much you understand, not worrying about how much you miss.

Some final food for thought: Many experts who study communication posit that people who are participating verbally in a conversation often miss a great deal of it, as their attention strays; even with its incompleteness, you may actually be getting more out of a conversation by lip reading because of the intense focus it requires.

In Real Life

Again, lip reading is most commonly associated with deaf people, who undoubtedly find it very useful. People with Asperger's syndrome can also use lip reading to great effect; one symptom is difficulty separating conversation from background noise, and even normal levels of background noise make it extremely difficult for them to parse what someone is saying. In addition, people with Asperger's syndrome often have trouble interpreting facial expressions and other social cues, so learning to focus on noticing and using all the available information in a conversation together can greatly increase their ability to understand it.

Lip reading can also be an excellent tool for people who have a workplace that is consistently noisy. For example, table servers find it easier to take diners' orders, and flight attendants can better hear passenger requests against the steady white-noise drone of airplane engines as well. This can also be a safety issue on an airplane.

Sometimes lip reading can even be a matter of life or death. Industrial workers can save time or even prevent an accident if they can "hear" a warning or other important information even against a backdrop of noise. Moreover, emergency workers like fire fighters and paramedics have saved lives by being able to read the lips of people in distress who can't speak loudly (or at all), and health professionals who aren't in an emergency situation can help ease patients' anxiety and frustration if they can figure out what they need when speaking is difficult.

See Also

Lipread (www.lipread.com.au/Products.html) is a well-regarded line of lip-reading educational products from Australia.

Notes

1. "Speech Accent Archive," Steven Weinberger, George Mason University, accessed May 8, 2011, http://accent.gmu.edu.

2. Grant Fairbanks, *Voice and Articulation Drillbook, Second Edition* (New York: Harper & Row, 1960), 124–39.

Hack 46: Emote Precisely

Brett Douglas Williams

The artificial language Lojban has special words for precisely and concisely expressing emotions inexpressible in English. Stick your toes into this ocean of emotion, and venture out onto the deep sea at your leisure. You might never use this hack in its entirety, but maybe it will help you find just the right words for an emotion you've never been able to express before. As a bonus, learn to communicate on two channels with a few gestures of your fingers.

English has a few emotional words, like "yay" and "ouch" and "argh" and "phew" and "yuck," but have you ever wished for a more accurate or intricate way to express emotions? In this hack, you'll learn a set of emotive words, borrowed from the constructed language Lojban (pronounced LOZH-bahn, with a long O), that can combine systematically to elegantly express complicated feelings. You may want to say, for example, "I am beginning to feel a little social stress," or "I am very tired physically, but attentive," or "I don't believe that mentally, but I do believe it emotionally." Using Lojban attitudinals will help you do that. You'll also learn how to use *fingerspelling* to spell out your emotions as a special hidden channel of communication, secretly letting your friends know how you really feel about what you're saying.

> **NOTE** The logical language Lojban is a descendant of Loglan, a language invented in 1955 by James Cooke Brown in part to test the Sapir-Whorf hypothesis (that a language affects the character of the thoughts of those who speak it) by creating a language specifically intended to expand and clarify the thinking of those who learned it. After more than half a century of maintaining and continuing this vision of a language that enables clear thought and communication, the Lojbanists have amassed a vast toolbox of interesting and useful ways to express themselves with unusual directness and clarity. Even though it's a relatively simple language, however, it usually takes a few years of study for someone to learn all of its systems well enough to converse without a dictionary (such as several perspectives on tense, several ways of rearranging sentences, and several forms of logical connection, for example). This hack is designed to more quickly give you a small taste of Lojban's mind-stretching perspective.

In Action

Now called *cniglic* (*cni* = "emotional" + *glic* = "English," pronounced a little like "Schnigglish"), the practice of intermixing Lojban's *attitudinals*, or emotional words, with English text was first discovered roaming wild in the hills of Lojbanistan. In their IRC chat, for instance (#lojban on Freenode), Lojbanists can often be seen responding to each other's statements with attitudinals in place of words like "hmm" or "yup" or "uh-huh," even when speaking English. Once you know them, it's difficult to resist using these convenient little words that show exactly how you feel about what was just said.

For instance, it's very common to see people responding to something that makes them feel happy by just saying *.ui* (pronounced "whee!" and meaning "happiness"), responding to something they agree with by saying *.ie* (pronounced "yeh!" and meaning "agreement"), or to something that makes them sad with *.uu* (pronounced "woo!" and meaning "pity" or "sympathy" in a positive sense). Sometimes someone will express a more complex attitude, like *.ua ro'i bu'o* ("wah RO-hee BOO-ho," or "understanding (emotional) beginning," colloquially "I'm starting to get it" or "I'm starting to feel it"), and occasionally people will have an entire conversation just in attitudinals, as shown in Table 46-1.

Table 46-1: A Lojban Conversation

	LOJBAN	PRONUNCIATION	MEANING
Person A	*.ui pei*	"wee pay"	How happy are you?
Person B	*sai .ui pei*	"sigh wee pay"	Pretty happy. How about you?
Person A	*nai ru'e*	"nigh ROO-heh"	A little unhappy
Person B	*.uu*	"woo"	Oh, that's too bad!
Person A	*.i'o .oi nai ro'a bu'o*	"EE-ho oy nigh RO-hah BOO-ho"	I appreciate that! Now I'm beginning to feel good socially.
Person B	*.i'i*	"EE-hee"	We are together.

This hack will provide a rough pronunciation wherever there's a Lojban word. For more information about pronouncing Lojban words, see *The Complete Lojban Language*, Chapter 3.[1]

How It Works

To fully specify your emotional state with attitudinals, it's possible to indicate your current position on at least 234 different scales — the 39 basic attitudinal scales, multiplied by six categories (social, mental, emotional, physical, sexual, and spiritual), specifying a precise position in *234-dimensional space* for your emotion (for more on multidimensionality, see Hack 43, "Enter the Fourth Dimension"). Of course, in practice this is only done occasionally as an exercise! You can specify as many or as few scales at once as you want, and it's most common to see just one or two at a time.

To express your emotional intensity in each of the dimensions, you can use the seven-point scale shown in Table 46-2, from the most intense, through neutrality, down to most intensely the opposite.

Table 46-2: The Lojban Seven-Point Scale

LOJBAN	PRONUNCIATION	MEANING
cai	"shy"	A very intense emotion (rarely used in casual conversation)
sai	"sigh"	A fairly intense emotion
ru'e	"ROO-heh"	A less intense emotion
cu'i	"SHOE-hee"	Neutral, the midpoint of the scale
nai ru'e	"nigh ROO-heh"	Less intensely the opposite emotion
nai sai	"nigh sigh"	Fairly intensely the opposite emotion
nai cai	"nigh shy"	Very intensely the opposite emotion (also rarely used)

It's also possible to use just a bare attitudinal, meaning an unspecified degree of the positive form of the emotion, or just the attitudinal plus *nai* ("nigh"), meaning an unspecified degree of the negative form of the emotion. For instance, Table 46-3 shows variants of *.a'u* ("AH-hoo"), basically meaning "interest," or that something seems interesting, attractive, or tasty.

Table 46-3: Variants of .a'u (Interest)

LOJBAN	PRONUNCIATION	MEANING
.a'u cai	"AH-hoo shy"	I'm extremely interested.
.a'u sai	"AH-hoo sigh"	I'm fairly interested.
.a'u ru'e	"AH-hoo ROO-heh"	I'm a little interested.
.a'u	"AH-hoo"	I'm interested.
.a'u cu'i	"AH-hoo SHOE-hee"	I'm disinterested, neither attracted nor repelled.
.a'u nai	"AH-hoo nigh"	I'm repelled/disgusted to an unspecified degree.
.a'u nai ru'e	"AH-hoo nigh ROO-heh"	I'm a little repelled/disgusted.
.a'u nai sai	"AH-hoo nigh sigh"	I'm fairly repelled/disgusted.
.a'u nai cai	"AH-hoo nigh shy"	I'm extremely repelled/disgusted.

Table 46-4 describes the 39 basic emotions of Lojban, and how they combine with the seven-point scale.

Table 46-4: The Basic Emotions of Lojban

LOJBAN	PRONUN-CIATION	POSITIVE MEANING	NEUTRAL MEANING	NEGATIVE MEANING
.ai	"eye"	Intent	Indecision	Rejection/refusal
.au	"ow"	Desire	Indifference	Reluctance
.a'a	"AH-ha"	Attentive	Inattentive	Avoiding
.a'e	"AH-heh"	Alertness		Exhaustion
.a'i	"AH-hee"	Effort	No special effort	Repose
.a'o	"AH-ho"	Hope		Despair
.a'u	"AH-hoo"	Interest	Disinterest	Repulsion
.ei	"ey"	Obligation		Freedom
.e'a	"EH-ha"	Granting permission		Prohibiting
.e'e	"EH-heh"	Competence		Incompetence/inability
.e'i	"EH-hee"	Constraint	Independence	Challenge/resistance against constraint
.e'o	"EH-ho"	Request		Negative request
.e'u	"EH-hoo"	Suggestion		Warning
.ia	"ya"	Belief	Skepticism	Disbelief
.ie	"yeh"	Agreement		Disagreement
.ii	"yee"	Fear		Security
.io	"yo"	Respect		Disrespect
.iu	"yoo"	Love		Hatred
.i'a	"EE-ha"	Acceptance		Blame
.i'e	"EE-heh"	Approval	Neutrality	Disapproval
.i'i	"EE-hee"	Togetherness		Privacy
.i'o	"EE-ho"	Appreciation		Envy
.i'u	"EE-hoo"	Familiarity		Mystery
.oi	"oy"	Complaint		Pleasure

LOJBAN	PRONUN-CIATION	POSITIVE MEANING	NEUTRAL MEANING	NEGATIVE MEANING
.o'a	"OH-ha"	Pride	Modesty/humility	Shame
.o'i	"OH-hee"	Caution		Rashness
.o'e	"OH-heh"	Closeness		Distance
.o'o	"OH-ho"	Patience	Mere tolerance	Anger
.o'u	"OH-hoo"	Relaxation	Composure	Stress
.ua	"wa"	Discovery		Confusion/searching
.ue	"weh"	Surprise	Not really surprised	Expectation
.ui	"wee"	Happiness		Unhappiness
.uo	"wo"	Completion		Incompleteness
.uu	"woo"	Pity/sympathy		Cruelty
.u'a	"OO-ha"	Gain		Loss
.u'e	"OO-heh"	Wonder		Commonplace
.u'i	"OO-hee"	Amusement		Weariness
.u'o	"OO-ho"	Courage	Reticence/caution	Cowardice
.u'u	"OO-hoo"	Repentance	Innocence	Lack of regret

Each of the 39 emotional scales comes in six different "flavors," as shown in Table 46-5.

Table 46-5: The Emotional Flavors of Lojban

LOJBAN	PRONUNCIATION	MEANING
ro'a	"RO-ha"	Social
ro'e	"RO-heh"	Mental
ro'i	"RO-hee"	Emotional
ro'o	"RO-ho"	Physical
ro'u	"RO-hoo"	Sexual
re'e	"REH-heh"	Spiritual

Table 46-6 shows an example of how you can "flavor" a basic emotion, using the attitudinal *.oi* ("oy!"), which expresses the emotion of pain or complaint.

Table 46-6: Flavoring a Basic Emotion

LOJBAN	PRONUNCIATION	MEANING
.oi ro'a	"oy RO-ha"	I feel social pain (embarrassment or loneliness, for example).
.oi ro'e	"oy RO-heh"	I feel mental pain (like struggling to figure out a difficult problem).
.oi ro'i	"oy RO-hee"	I feel emotional pain (grief or misery).
.oi ro'o	"oy RO-ho"	I feel physical pain (you've just actually stubbed your toe or something).
.oi ro'u	"oy RO-hoo"	I feel sexual pain (feeling unsatisfied, that is; if you're enjoying the pain, it would be .oi ro'o .oi nai ro'u!).
.oi re'e	"oy REH-heh"	I feel spiritual pain (the pain of sin, perhaps).

Another important modifier is *bu'o* ("BOO-ho"), which marks where and when you are in the process of feeling an emotion — whether it's just starting (*bu'o*), is ongoing (*bu'o cu'i*), or is just ending (*bu'o nai*). Table 46-7 describes some useful expressions with this modifier.

Table 46-7: Useful Expressions with bu'o

LOJBAN	PRONUNCIATION	MEANING
.ua ro'e bu'o	"wa RO-heh BOO-ho"	I'm beginning to understand mentally. I get it.
.u'i bu'o nai	"OO-hee BOO-ho nigh"	My amusement is coming to an end. This is starting to get boring.
.a'i ru'e bu'o	"AH-hee ROO-heh BOO-ho"	I'm starting to have to make a little bit of an effort. This is getting a little hard.
.oi nai ro'o bu'o cu'i	"oy nigh RO-ho BOO-ho SHOE-hee"	I'm continuing to feel physical pleasure. That still feels good.
.ui nai ru'e ro'i bu'o nai	"wee nai ROO-heh RO-hee BOO-ho nigh"	I was slightly unhappy emotionally, but now it's ending. I'm starting to feel better.
.i'u nai re'e bu'o cu'i	"EE-hoo nigh REH-heh BOO-ho SHOE-hee"	It continues to feel spiritually mysterious.

Now that you know how to combine the attitudinal scales with markers for intensity, category, and contour, you can further combine those phrases to make larger compound emotions. Just say the emotions one after another, each with its own optional markings. Table 46-8 describes some examples.

Table 46-8: Combining Lojban Phrases

LOJBAN	PRONUNCIATION	MEANING
.oi ro'o .ui	"oy RO-ho wee"	I feel physical pain and I'm happy.
.oi ro'e .oi nai ro'a	"oy RO-heh oy nigh RO-hah"	I feel mental pain and social pleasure.
.ui nai ru'e ro'i .ui sai re'e	"wee nigh ROO-heh RO-hee wee sigh REH-heh"	I feel a little unhappy emotionally and very happy spiritually.
.i'u nai ro'e bu'o cu'i .a'u sai ro'e bu'o	"EE-hoo nigh RO-heh BOO-ho SHOE-hee AH-hoo sigh RO-heh BOO-ho"	I continue to feel mysterious mentally and I'm beginning to get very mentally interested.

Note a few last useful words:

- The word *dai* ("dye") marks an *empathetic* use of an attitudinal; you're speaking it for someone other than yourself. For example, *.iu dai* ("YOO dye") means "someone is feeling love."

- The word *pei* ("pay"), which you encountered in the dialogue at the start of this hack, turns an attitudinal from an expression of your emotion into a *question* about how the person you're talking to is feeling. It's answered by specifying a point on the scale you're being asked about: *.o'u pei* ("OH-hoo pay") means "How relaxed or stressed are you?" and you can answer, for instance, *sai* ("sigh," "quite relaxed") or *nai ru'e* ("nigh ROO-heh," "a little stressed").

- Of course, you may not always want to wear your heart on your sleeve, or you might be feeling something but not know for sure what that is. For such circumstances, there's the blandly agreeable word *ge'e* ("GEH-heh"), which just means "I am feeling some unspecified emotion." You can even combine *ge'e* with the scales and modifiers, to say things like *ge'e ru'e ro'i bu'o* ("GEH-heh ROO-heh RO-hee BOO-ho"), or "I am beginning to feel a little something emotional."

In Real Life

You can use these attitudinals just as they are when chatting online with other people who know them, but you and your friends might get strange looks if you started going around all day saying "OO-hee" and "EE-heh." Here's another idea: Use fingerspelling to spell out attitudinals, adding a second, secret channel to your communication. You can use the same fingerspelling that commonly supplements ASL, American Sign Language (Hack 44, "Spell It Out").

The period at the beginning of words that start with vowels (it represents a pause or glottal stop) should be left out, and the apostrophe should be replaced with the letter "h." Then you can discreetly spell out your real attitude about what you're saying. Suppose you're reporting to your friend that someone said he was going to be somewhere, but you know he's a flake and is probably not really going to make it. At the same time that you say out loud "He said he's going to get there on time," you could show you don't actually believe it by spelling out *.ia nai* ("ya nigh," "disbelief"), as shown in Table 46-9.

Table 46-9: Fingerspelling .ia nai

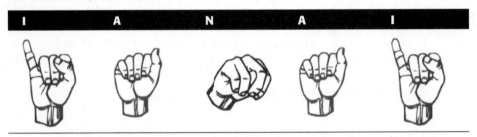

I	A	N	A	I

Or suppose your friend is about to do something sketchy, and you want to warn them without alerting or offending the other people around. You could just quickly sign *.o'i* ("OH-hee," "caution"), as shown in Table 46-10.

Table 46-10: Fingerspelling .o'i

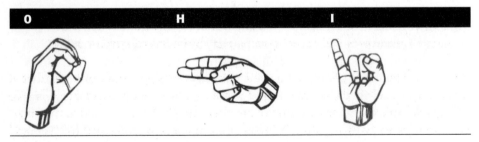

O	H	I

The Lojbanists have found over the years that their attitudinal system has brought them closer together by enabling them to clearly express their feelings, and by being a lot of fun. I hope you'll find it enlightening and useful too.

See Also

- www.lojban.org has much more information about the Lojban language and community.
- http://groups.google.com/group/cniglic is a mailing list where Schnigglish is spoken and discussed.
- http://groups.google.com/group/coi-language is a gentle on-ramp to begin studying Schnigglish or Lojban.

Notes

1. John Woldemar Cowan, *The Complete Lojban Language* (Fairfax: Logical Language Group, Inc, 1997). Chapter 3. Also available online at www .lojban.org/publications/reference_grammar/chapter1.html.

Hack 47: Streamline Your Shorthand

Learn a few prefixes and suffixes to speed up your handwritten notes written in Speedwords, or almost any other shorthand system that uses the Roman alphabet.

Instead of presenting a new technique or skill, this hack builds on an existing skill to improve it. Dutton Speedwords is a kind of shorthand that uses the Roman alphabet, and therefore can be typed on a keyboard as easily as written by hand.

NOTE See the "Notes" section for some sites from which you can learn Dutton Speedwords and other Roman alphabet shorthand systems online.

One problem that people who use Dutton Speedwords have noted is that at times the Speedwords system is maddeningly idiosyncratic and irregular. To cite an example from the designer of another alphabetic shorthand (a reformed version of Speedwords called Briefscript), the Speedwords word for "school" is not *rystu*, or "learning building," but *ryu*, "favorable building." However, a college is a *ryue*, or "very favorable building," which apparently Reginald Dutton thought was the opposite of a shed (bizarrely, *ryat*, or "very unfavorable building").[1]

Ron uses Speedwords frequently, and this kind of idiosyncrasy doesn't bother him much. No one else has to read his notes, so he doesn't write in standard Speedwords but tends to use a more commonsense vocabulary. For example, for "school," he's much more likely to write something like *rystu* than *ryu*, no matter what the dictionary says. However, one Speedwords irregularity that has given him trouble is its *correlatives*, corresponding to words like "how" and "who" and "this" in English. Therefore, he decided to institute a small-scale Dutton Speedwords reform of his own.

The new Speedwords Correlatives provide a way within Speedwords to quickly and elegantly generate many words and phrases such as "that," "what," "how much," "now," "then," "here, there, and everywhere," and so on. Table 47-1 shows an example of the old Speedwords usage, contrasted with the new way of doing things. Notice the haphazard derivation of the old forms.

Table 47-1: Speedwords Old vs. New

ENGLISH	DUTTON SPEEDWORDS	SPEEDWORDS CORRELATIVES
"where?"	*qo*? (from Latin *quo*)	*qp*? (from *qu ep*, "which place?")
"here!"	*ir*! (from English "here")	*cp*! (from *c ep*, "this place")

Although this hack is based on Dutton Speedwords, you should be able to use it with almost any alphabetic shorthand system,[2] of which there are many. You could even use it with ordinary English, to speed up your writing and note-taking in classes and meetings.

How It Works

This hack steals the highly successful mechanism of the *correlative table* from the most successful (in terms of number of speakers) constructed language of all time, Esperanto.[3] In turn, Esperanto's system is simply an extension and regularization of words in existing languages. For example, in English we have "someone," "somewhere," "no one," "nowhere," "anyone," and "anywhere." However, "somewhen," "nowhen," and "anywhen" are considered peculiar at best. The Esperanto equivalents are perfectly acceptable, and the same can now be said of Speedwords Correlatives.

To create the correlatives, we've simply taken each Esperanto correlative root and found a Dutton Speedwords equivalent, then combined the results in a way similar to Esperanto. Readers who already know Speedwords will recognize most of these roots, which should make them easier to remember. For example, *qk*, "what kind?," comes from the Speedwords *qu kla*. The suffix *-d* comes from *od*, or "way," and the suffix *-r* comes from *er*, or "person."

Some of the new words derived from these roots correspond to existing Speedwords (such as the new *cp*, which you've seen corresponds to the old *ir*). Others, such as *jd*, "in every way," are entirely new, as far as we know.

In Action

Table 47-2 shows how to combine the prefixes and suffixes of Speedwords Correlatives. Don't try to memorize the whole table; instead, learn the roots and practice combining them by gradually sprinkling them into your notes.

Here are a few rules to make these correlatives even more powerful and flexible:

- Make plurals with *z*. For example, *cm*, "this thing"; *cmz*, "these things."
- Make possessives with apostrophes. For example, *qr*, "who"; *qr'*, "whose."
- Double or triple the *c-* prefix for useful effects. For example, *cr*, "this person"; *ccr*, "that person"; *cccr*, "yonder person."

In Real Life

As a prolific note taker, Ron uses Dutton Speedwords every day, and because his "notebook" is a stack of index cards, everything that helps him squeeze more useful real estate out of the 15 square inches of surface on one side of a three-by-five card is extremely welcome.

Table 47-2: Speedwords Correlatives

	kind = -k	reason = -y	time = -z	place = -p	way = -d	one = -r	thing = -m	amount = -t
what/which = q-	what kind? = qk	why? for what reason? = qy	when? at what time? = qz	where? at what place? = qp	how? in what way? = qd	who? which? which one? = qr	what? what thing? = qm	how much? what amount? = qt
this = c-	this kind = ck	because, for this reason = cy	then, at this time = cz	here, in this place = cp	in this way = cd	this one = cr	this, this thing = cm	this much, this amount = ct
some = u-	some kind = uk	for some reason = uy	sometime = uz	someplace = up	somehow, in some way = ud	someone = ur	some, something = um	some amount = ut
every = j-	every kind = jk	for every reason = jy	(at) every time = jz	everywhere, in every place = jp	in every way = jd	everyone = jr	everything = jm	all, all of = jt
no = n-	no kind = nk	for no reason = ny	never, at no time = nz	nowhere, at no place = np	in no way = nd	no one = nr	nothing = nm	none, no amount = nt

Since he developed Speedwords Correlatives a couple of years ago, Ron has steadily phased out his use of their irregular equivalents. He hasn't made a longitudinal study of note-taking corpuses in Dutton Speedwords with and without correlatives, but his subjective impression is that they save a little space over regular Speedwords, and a little time writing them — perhaps a lot over time. However, the real and obvious savings are on your memory, as you need only memorize a few roots that combine in regular ways, instead of a few dozen irregular and idiosyncratically formed words.

Notes

1. "Speedwords word-building presents problems," Ray Brown, The Briefscript Project, accessed 14 July 2009, www.carolandray.plus.com/Briefscript/ SWwords.html.

2. "Shorthand Systems," Mentat Wiki, accessed 14 July 2009, www.ludism .org/mentat/ShorthandSystem. Links to a variety of alphabetic shorthands, including much material on Dutton Speedwords.

3. "The Esperanto Correlatives," Don Harlow, accessed 14 July 2009, http:// donh.best.vwh.net/Esperanto/correlatives.html.

Hack 48: Communicate Multimodally

Meredith Hale and Dave Howell

Communicate information more clearly by providing the same information in more than one form — give them a "belt and suspenders" scheme.

Most of us need to share information with other people every day. We don't usually spend a lot of time thinking about how to do it; we'll just jot down some directions, or whip out a quick recipe in e-mail. When we do think about what we're saying or writing, most of us try to be as clear as possible by making it as simple as possible. However, supersimple does not always equal superclear. We make assumptions that others will read or hear information in the same way we do. When they don't, something that seems crystal clear to us can be confusing or even baffling to somebody else.

Mixing in some thoughtful redundancy can make the information easier to understand. By augmenting one mode of information with supporting information in another mode — relative as well as absolute information, for example, or visual as well as verbal information — you can save time in the long run by preventing misunderstandings and resulting mistakes.

In Action

There are many ways to make information multimodal and redundant, such as including different kinds of wording, adding visual elements such as icons or color, or adding kinesthetic or "hands-on" elements. For example, if a group of people are learning a new game, some may find it easier to read the rules for themselves, some might learn how to play more easily if the rules are read to them or summarized for them by another person, and others might just want to jump in and play after getting a very basic overview, and figure out the rest of the rules along the way. Even using a very basic visual aid with a presentation is a way to communicate multimodally — in our game example, some players might learn more easily if they have a player's aid that includes a summary of key rules accompanied by diagrams or symbols on the pieces that help reinforce them.

A classic example of information that can be improved by making it multimodal is driving directions:

- Some people navigate by landmarks, so they want directions like these: "Exit the freeway at the off-ramp by the hill. Turn left at the intersection with the dry cleaning store, turn left at the restaurant, and park on the right side of the street after you pass the school and before the gas station." These people navigate subjectively by association and positioning themselves spatially; they find visual information easy and quick to parse.

- Others want very specific facts, such as you might find on a map: "Get off the freeway at Exit 161, turn north onto 80th Avenue, then turn west onto 10th Street and park on the right side of 10th after you've passed 77th Avenue." These people prefer absolute location indicators and objective information.

- Still other people want relative information: "Exit the freeway at the third off-ramp after the bridge. Turn left at the first stoplight. Turn left again at the next stoplight. Park on the right side of the street about three blocks later." These people think in terms of process, navigate sequentially, and count as they go.

Some people are most comfortable thinking in terms of landmarks. Some people navigate best with a map, and some are most at ease using relative positioning. Really good instructions will combine these different modes to make one set of instructions that work well for different styles of thinking, and provide some redundancy. Consider the following:

"Exit the freeway at the third off-ramp after the bridge, which is Exit 161. Turn left at the first light, by the dry cleaning store, onto 80th Avenue. At the first stoplight on 80th, turn left just before the restaurant onto 10th Street. Park on the right side of the street after passing the school, about three blocks down.

If you get to the gas station on the corner of 10th Street and 75th Avenue, you went too far."

Including several styles of information helps ensure that your various friends all get where you want them to go. Another example: "Please come to our party on Saturday, April 16th." "Saturday" is partially redundant with "April 16th." You can make it even better by saying "Please come to our party on Saturday, April 16th. That's the Saturday after this coming weekend," or possibly "the Saturday before Easter."

You can also mix modes by using graphical elements to supplement words, again leveraging the fact that people absorb information more easily in different formats. For example, if you're preparing a schedule for a musical performance, you might need to have the dancers show up early so they can be dressed, be on stage to warm up, then clear out so the singers can take over and get used to the acoustics, with the instrumentalists arriving a bit later (see Figure 48-1).

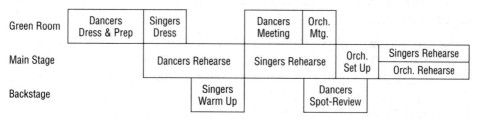

Figure 48-1: The performance schedule, in "monomodal" format

If the schedule shows each group in a different color, or with each group using a unique shape, then you're using the name of each group (one mode) with the colors and shapes (two more modes) to provide redundancy and accommodate different styles of comprehension, thus reducing the likelihood that somebody will make a mistake when reading it (see Figure 48-2).

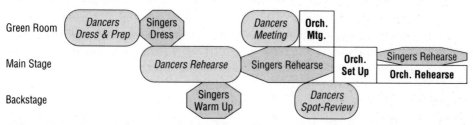

Figure 48-2: The performance schedule, in improved, multimodal format

To return to the game idea, many board and card games communicate multimodally. A card might have a color, an icon, and text; for example, in a game where a card might indicate skipping a player's turn, each "skip" card is blue, has an arrow symbol, and says "skip" on it. A piece that represents a color might also have an individual pattern — for example, all red pieces have a spiral pattern.

This way, people who absorb information more easily in one way than another (or those who can't absorb information in one way at all, such as color-blind people) have an even shot at the game.

Sports teams employ this idea by using a name, a symbol, and a distinctive color scheme. So do other corporations, especially those that need to get your attention quickly, such as fast-food restaurants. When you're driving, you have only a few moments to recognize a restaurant as you go by; a fast-food chain will grab your attention with a big sign that includes the name of the company, sometimes a logo or character, a distinctive color scheme, and even a distinctive building shape and design. These same elements will appear in their commercials, reinforced with verbal slogans and music or sounds, so that when you're looking for somewhere to eat, you can identify their outlets in a split second. You can benefit by adopting this technique yourself.

Taking yet another basic example, many will argue that communicating with someone face-to-face is highly effective because text (instant message, e-mail, etc.) is missing the other modes that accompany talking in person, such as gestures, facial expressions, and vocal inflections. These modes help to get the information across clearly when words alone might not. The evolution of "emoticons" was a way to fill this gap and make text communication multimodal.

How It Works

It's important here to define redundancy in relation to multimodal communication. In this sense, redundant doesn't mean saying the same thing over and over or having more than one of an identical item; it means conveying the same information in different ways. While repetition can be useful in certain situations, that isn't what we're referring to here.

Your body is multisensory and constantly takes in information to help keep you safe and learn things — think about how often this process is multimodal. The burner on the stove is glowing red, the dial says it's on high, and you can feel the heat radiating from it. These are all ways to determine that something is hot and you should avoid touching it. Multimodal communication uses different parts of your brain to make the whole message clearer than any single part.

Multimodal communication can make the conveyance of information more accessible to a wider range of people, and speed up the absorption process. Scanning a page for photographs, charts, or any other graphic is likely to be faster than reading a whole page, it is definitely faster than processing verbal content, and it might provide just the right amount of information to readers. When they have more time, they can go back and get more meaning from the words themselves.

In Real Life

Meredith plays the Celtic harp. Teaching students to play an instrument is often done with multimodal communication. Both when she was first learning to play and now when she learns new music, Meredith's teacher will play the piece through so she can hear how it sounds before she starts to try to play it. Listening to the song is one mode. Then she'll watch where his fingers are on the strings and how he strums them and moves from one string to the next. Finally, she'll take a look at the music in written notation. Combining these three behaviors makes learning the tune fast and easy, and she has references later to help reinforce what she learned with her teacher.

Another example is this hack! You are reading the words and learning about multimodal communication through the writing, but the figures emphasize the idea.

See Also

- Edward Tufte, *The Visual Display of Quantitative Information* (Cheshire, CT, USA: Graphics Press, 2004). Tufte's other publications are also worth checking out.

- Donald A. Norman, *The Design of Everyday Things* (New York: Basic Books, 2002).

- David McCandless, *The Visual Miscellaneum: A Colorful Guide to the World's Most Consequential Trivia* (New York: Collins Design, 2009).

Hack 49: Mediate Your Environment

It's fun and productive to willingly suspend judgment on what people are literally saying long enough to find out what they mean. Build a mediator module, in your brain and in your browser, and watch some of the gibberish around you resolve into perfect sense.

It's all too easy to dismiss someone who's saying something you don't understand. Sometimes we don't even want to understand, because the other person is communicating in a way that annoys us. They might be using jargon we find opaque, a dialect that arouses nationalist, racist, or classist reflexes in us, or an antiquated or obscure mode of speech we never took the time to learn. Yet someone you don't understand may have information you desperately need that you won't find from your usual sources. After all, if you don't understand what that person is saying, it's more likely that their information is novel — truly *news*. Broadening your ability to listen to unfamiliar modes and sources provides you with a much wider pool of information.

In Greg Egan's science fiction novel *Schild's Ladder*,[1] set far in the future (Hack 31, "Mine the Future"), most humans have a brain implant called a *mediator* that performs various communication tasks for them, such as translating languages and prompting them with etiquette expected by other cultures. Egan's mediators are extremely useful; his profoundly egalitarian future society could not function without them. Even if someone comes from the other side of the galaxy, a mediator enables his characters to understand them, or make a good guess about what they're trying to say.

This hack explains how to install a software component into your web browser that will perform some of the functions of an Egan-style mediator while you're surfing the web. Similar software has existed for a long time; text filters, such as the one that used to make Usenet posts look as though they were written by the Muppets' Swedish Chef, the Google option that enables you to display your interface in Klingon, or the Facebook option to display the site using pirate-speak, have been around since the dawn of the Internet. The script we'll be using is more general than such applications, and, of course, is applied in a less frivolous way.

In addition to the software component, this hack also has a "wetware" component. The fundamental idea of the hack is about changing some of your basic attitudes toward communicating with others. Therefore, if you like what the web mediator does for you, you can learn to apply its most important functions with your naked brain.

In Action

The principle that states we should give the benefit of the doubt to people we're talking with is called Miller's Law (www.adrr.com/aa/new.htm). It was stated by psychologist George Miller and popularized by linguist and science fiction author Suzette Hadin Elgin. It is simply this:

> *To understand what another person is saying, you must assume that it is true and try to imagine what it could be true of.*

Elgin expands:

> *In order for other people to understand what you are saying, you must make it possible for them to apply Miller's Law to your speech.*

Also relevant is a proverb called the Robustness Principle (http://tools.ietf.org/html/rfc761), which was originally meant for Internet software but is just as relevant to *human* communication protocols. Formulated in 1980 by computer scientist Jon Postel, it advises the following:

> *Be conservative in what you do; be liberal in what you accept from others.*

Miller's Law tells us to focus on the intent of what someone is saying, and ignore its surface expression, while Elgin's Corollary encourages us to be as clear as we can ourselves. The Robustness Principle elegantly sums them up. You can apply these ideas directly to your own thinking and interpretation (see the "In Real Life" section), and you can use software to apply them to translating online content so that you can absorb it more easily.

How It Works

The following *mediator script* translates common — but potentially irritating — symbols that people use online to show they think something's funny, such as ROTFLMAO ("rolling on the floor, laughing my ass off"), or HAHAHAHAHAHAHAHA into the more innocuous string <laughter>, within the Mozilla Firefox web browser:

```
// ==UserScript==
// @name          Mediator
// @namespace     http://ron.ludism.org/
// @description   Web mediation script from Mindhacker, based on a
                  script from Greasemonkey Hacks by Mark Pilgrim
// @include       *
// ==/UserScript==
var arReplacements =
{
"LOL": "<laughter>",
"ROTFLMAO": "<laughter>",
"ROTFLMFAO": "<laughter>",
":-D": "<laughter>",
"[HAha]{4,}": "<laughter>"
};
    var arRegex = new Array( );
    for (var sKey in arReplacements) {
        arRegex[sKey] = new RegExp(sKey, 'g');
    }
    var snapTextNodes = document.evaluate("//text( )[" +
        "not(ancestor::script) and not(ancestor::style)]",
        document, null, XPathResult.UNORDERED_NODE_SNAPSHOT_TYPE, null);
    for (var i = snapTextNodes.snapshotLength - 1; i >= 0; i--) {
        var elmTextNode = snapTextNodes.snapshotItem(i);
        var sText = elmTextNode.data;
        for (var sKey in arReplacements) {
            sText = sText.replace(arRegex[sKey], arReplacements[sKey]);
        }
        elmTextNode.data = sText;
    }
```

Greasemonkey is an add-on for Mozilla Firefox that enables users to filter text and images on web pages. To install and use this module, take the following steps:

1. Install Greasemonkey from https://addons.mozilla.org/en-US/firefox/addon/748 if you haven't already.

2. Download and extract the mediator script from this book's official website (see Introduction).

3. Open the script `mediator.user.js` within Firefox by clicking File ➤ Open File....

4. Click Install when Firefox asks whether you want to install it.

That's it! Now that you've installed the script, if you're a cranky Internet old-timer like us and the expression "LOL" makes you scoff at someone you should really be learning from, you can neutralize your own kneejerkiness and learn to re-appreciate the anarchic diversity of the Net, however it's expressed.

Of course, if the silly ways people laugh on the Internet don't bother you, there's probably something else that does: split infinitives? Writing out dates as 31/12/2009 instead of 12/31/2009? The word *ginormous*? Even if you're extremely tolerant, there's certainly some form of communication you don't understand or like. If you want to write your own version of the mediator with different conventions in mind, try starting with a script containing no text replacements, and loop over your target as follows:

1. Display the alien text with the help of the mediator.

2. Note any words or phrases you need to clarify.

3. Add them to the mediator with suitable replacements.

4. Keep returning to step 1 until the text makes sense to you.

Be persistent. As with debugging a computer program, making surface fixes will often reveal deeper layers of "errors" underneath.

After you've written a few mediator scripts like this, why not try improving the mediator in other ways? Here are some possible improvements to our serious application of this old "fun" technology, all fairly straightforward.

■ Add a simple graphical user interface.

■ Create pop-up translations as your cursor hovers over phrases, rather than embed them into the page.

■ Enable two-way communication — translation from your jargon to that of whomever you are talking to, as well as vice versa.

■ Provide automatic unit conversion, such as miles to kilometers (Hack 39, "Notate Personally").

Please let us know if you make any of these improvements!

In Real Life

A software mediator is a proof of concept that someone you don't understand, or have never *wanted* to understand, has something interesting to say. Once you know this, you can learn their language and enter their *discourse community*. Then you can learn to think in that language directly, instead of treating it as a code requiring translation. If you have ever learned a foreign language to a high level, you'll be familiar with this phenomenon. Here are a couple of examples of useful, real-life mediations, one dealing with fairly abstract matters, one with matters of life and death.

Software Component

The website Tetraspace (`http://teamikaria.com/hddb/classic/`), a fan site for the fourth dimension (Hack 43, "Enter the Fourth Dimension"), is a great example of why Miller's Law is important. Although Ron is fascinated by the fourth dimension, he used to have a strong aversion to the fannish jargon on Tetraspace, especially the Fourth Dimension Glossary.

For example, the denizens of the site sometimes use the noun *realm* for the third dimension, and the adjectives *realmar* and *realmic* instead of the perfectly good words *three-dimensional*. However, after Ron plugged in the following list of substitutions to help translate their jargon into more standard terms, and read their Glossary through the mediator script, he discovered that the site is crammed with important information, and it's a hub for many interesting people. The mediator served as scaffolding for him to look beyond the overwhelming jargon and discover an entirely new community.

> **NOTE** The following Javascript code must be copied and pasted over the corresponding `arReplacements` array in the mediator script from the "How It Works" section to function. Alternatively, you can just download the script `4d.user.js` from the Mindhacker website.

```
var arReplacements =
{
"apos": "furthest ana",
"bionian": "2D being",
"bulk": "4D hypervolume",
"delta": "kata",
"flune": "4D hyperplane",
"glome": "4D hypersphere",
"gongyl": "4D ball",
"pentaspace": "5D space",
"planespace": "2D space",
"tetrealm": "4D hyperplane",
"tetrealmic": "4D",
"realmar": "3D",
"realmic": "3D",
"realmspace": "3D space",
"realm": "3D hyperplane",
"skring": "4D spring",
"sphone": "4D cone",
"surcell": "4D hypersurface",
"swock": "4D sheet",
```

```
"tesserobject": "4D object",
"tetracube": "tesseract",
"tetral": "4D",
"tetraspace": "4D space",
"tetronian": "4D being",
"trength": "spissitude",
"trionian": "3D being",
"upsilon": "ana",
"wint": "ana",
"zakos": "furthest kata",
"zant": "kata"
};
```

Historian Andrew Ward's book *The Slaves' War: The Civil War in the Words of Former Slaves* is a more substantial use of mediation. To begin with, Ward excises all instances of the "N word" from the slave narratives he quotes, "for the sake of shedding more light than heat, and in consideration of readers who cannot read when they see red."[2]

Moreover, he also performs a far more radical mediation — or rather unmediation. He writes:

> Students of slave narratives will note that I altered the dialect form of many of the original interviews. Some . . . editors were so determined to present this material in what they deemed "authentic Negro dialect" that if they received an interview accurately transcribed in the "proper" English of the interviewee, they sent it back to be reworked with all the stereotypical usages with which black speech was represented at that time . . .

> I am concerned, however, not so much with how they may have sounded but with what they said. I hope that what is represented in these pages as slave speech is at least as authentic as anything the old dialect forms ever accomplished, and far more immediate and accessible. All dialect achieved was to distance the reader from the speaker, to remind the presumably white and educated reader that he or she and most especially the transcriber were above the kind of quaint rhetorical lapses of the poor, uneducated black. It thereby made transcriber and reader accomplices in a caricature that was not only gratuitous and degrading but grossly inaccurate. Cleaning up these transcriptions may have cost them a measure of their theatricality, but I think something more important has been gained: the sensation of listening respectfully and without mediation while an ancestor is speaking.

The result is gripping. No longer is one alienated by the jarring, even incomprehensible, language attributed to the former slaves. Now they come across as intelligent and sensitive, sometimes throwing their former masters into clownish relief.

It would be interesting to learn whether Ward employed any significant software assistance with his task of unmediation. If so, perhaps it could be applied to other texts. What about creating an *Unmediated Huckleberry Finn*, in which Jim, already a sympathetic character, is no longer portrayed as speaking in "authentic dialect"? What happens if you change Huck's dialect, for that matter? The text is in the public domain and widely available, so Ron thinks he might try this someday. If you do, be sure to let him know. (See the "See Also" section for more information.)

Wetware Component

Of course, you can't carry Greasemonkey around with you for face-to-face conversations, but you can give the people you encounter the benefit of the doubt, more or less installing a mediator module within your own head. For example, you can create a behavioral reminder to yourself by writing Miller's Law and the Robustness Principle on a small index card and carrying it with you. Ron has a section of his notebook that he calls his "outlook," where he keeps just such reminders. Alternatively, put a picture of someone you consider to be tolerant and a good communicator on your desk or wall, such as Abraham Lincoln or a brilliant friend.

See Also

- As *Mindhacker* was nearing completion, a controversy broke out about censorship of *Huckleberry Finn* by means of a kind of mediation similar to the one in this hack. There was an immediate satirical response, involving further mediation. We'll let the creators of *The Adventures of Huckleberry Finn: Robotic Edition* tell their story:

    [Huckleberry Finn] has been banned from many schools and libraries ever since its first publication, originally because it portrayed the African American character Jim as being human and now because of the book's use of the word "n-word" over two hundred times.

    Publisher NewSouth Books is attempting to get the book back on library shelves and in classrooms by publishing a new version that removes the controversial word "n-word" and replaces it with the word "slave."

    Critics are calling this "censorship" and "whitewashing of history." We call it "not far enough."... Statistically, people prefer robots to the word "n-word." The word "n-word" is ugly and pejorative. Robots are fun and cool...even when they're trying to take over our world! So we've decided to take the word "n-word" out of Mark Twain's classic and replace it with "robot."... Robots have a long history in literature and popular culture of being used as a metaphor for slavery and oppression.

See www.kickstarter.com/projects/dianidevine/
replacing-the-n-word-with-robot-in-huck-finn for more information.

- George Miller, who stated Miller's Law, has had an illustrious scientific career. For example, he authored one of the seminal papers on human short-term memory, "The Magical Number Seven, Plus or Minus Two: Some Limits on Our Capacity for Processing Information," (http:// cogprints.org/730/1/miller.html) which was the indirect inspiration for the technique in Hack 53, "Train Your Fluid Intelligence."

Notes

1. Greg Egan, *Schild's Ladder* (London: Gollancz, 2002).
2. Andrew Ward, *The Slaves' War: The Civil War in the Words of Former Slaves* (Boston: Houghton Mifflin Harcourt, 2008).

## CHAPTER 8

Mental Fitness

Like increasing your physical fitness, increasing your mental fitness will improve how you deal with everyday problems and emergencies, and how you feel afterwards. If just trying to sit down and focus on a tax form or a writing assignment for school causes you the mental equivalent of panting and wheezing, these hacks will help you boost your mental strength, flexibility, and endurance.

This chapter is about a broad-based conception of mental fitness, from increasing your intelligence using a computer-based method that has shown results in the lab (Hack 53, "Train Your Fluid Intelligence") to increasing your fundamental capability to cope with the world, whether it results in measurable increases in intelligence or not (Hack 55, "Take the One-Question IQ Test"). It will help you broaden your tastes and remain agile by continuing to try new things (Hack 50, "Acquire a Taste," and Hack 51, "Try Something New Daily"), and it will coach you in changing your behavior by using the scientific method (Hack 54, "Think, Try, Learn").

Your brain needs its trips to the gym as much as your body does if you expect it to stay in top condition and ready to serve you for years to come. Give some of these warm-ups and workouts a whirl and see what they can do for you.

Hack 50: Acquire a Taste

Why be a hater? Acquire a taste for things you don't like, from foods to ideas and art, and thereby stretch your mind to gain a few more degrees of personal freedom. Follow Ron as he learns not to loathe cilantro.

Do you passionately hate a certain food, or kind of food? Do you find yourself going out of your way to avoid it, especially when eating out? Hating certain foods, or other kinds of phenomena, is restrictive. It cramps your style. Why not learn to like those things, or at least coexist with them? The more things you like and enjoy, the bigger your world will become, and you will become freer — and perhaps even smarter (Hack 55, "Take the One Question IQ Test") — as a result.

Cultural omnivorousness is currently a trendy way to live. For once, trendiness coincides with wisdom, but do the right thing for the right reasons. Be omnivorous not because it gains you "cultural capital," but because it makes you free.

Liking what you eat, metaphorically speaking, is one of the themes of this book, which also contains hacks about learning to speak the language of people alien to you, expanding your tastes in art, and trying new things on a regular basis. Part of the philosophy we hope you'll gain from this book can be summed up by the Roman saying *Homo sum: humani nil a me alienum puto* (I am a human being, so nothing human is alien to me).[1] This is true freedom, and true intelligence. See Hack 27, "Seek Bad Examples" for expansion of this idea.

Ron has never disliked many foods to start with, but the ones he disliked, he *really* disliked. Nevertheless, he's consciously and deliberately acquired tastes for two of those foods now (tomatoes and cilantro), not to mention the tastes he's developed incidentally, such as for beer. Read on to find out how he went about it.

WARNING   This hack is *not* intended to help you learn to enjoy foods that actually *will* make you sick, such as peanuts if you have peanut allergies.

In Action

Before Ron began trying to hack his disgust for cilantro, he asked the Hive Mind (Hack 16, "Ask the Hive Mind") for advice.[2] It gave him plenty. This section contains an amalgam of techniques he discovered to work, and ones that other people have found to work for them. We'll call the food for which you're trying to acquire a taste the *target food* or *target*.

- Just eat it.

   As in the Weird Al Yankovic song, just eat it. From personal experience, 80% of acquiring a taste seems to be willingly putting the target food into your mouth with an open mind. The other 20% seems to consist largely of doing it repeatedly. We can perhaps call this the Pareto Principle (http://en.wikipedia.org/wiki/Pareto_principle) of Taste Acquisition.

- It's seldom as bad as you think it is.

  If it has been years since you ate the target food, your sensory apparatus may have changed spontaneously in the meantime. Did you gag on carrots and peas as a child? If so, do you still gag on them?

- Acclimate yourself to the food a little at a time if necessary.

  Keep trying it often. As a first step, try bits of the food off your friends' plates when eating out, if you know them well enough to ask for a taste.

- Eat like a native.

  Try the target food as part of various global cuisines. You may like it better in some than in others.

- Eat the food cooked with other ingredients that are culturally appropriate.

  This is not a euphemism for "politically correct." Rather, generations of cooks in a culture where the target food is traditional may know more about how to cook and season it and which other foods taste good with it than the upstart downtown bistro that throws it into everything because it's featured on the Food Network this month.

- Be your own chef.

  Try cooking the target food yourself in different ways. Learn to cook the cuisines that include the target, so you have fine control over your experimentation. Balance the target food with other flavors. The idea is not to smother the hated flavor, but to nicely complement it. Don't overuse the target!

- Reward yourself.

  Eat the target with something else you already find delicious. Eat it in dishes that have plenty of calories so that your body will form a positive association for it. In a sense, you're training your body to recognize that the food is not poison.

- "Come not in that form!"

  Eat the freshest, youngest, purest form of the food you can find. Try the same food as it's grown or raised in another part of the world. Try keeping the food around just to smell for awhile. See if you like it better raw or cooked.

- Try cognitive behavioral therapy.

  Try a kind of cognitive behavioral therapy for your food hatred. Change your feelings about the target food by changing your thoughts. For example, contemplate the fact that many other foods may look, smell, or taste disgusting to you until prepared properly, such as asafetida and raw eggs.

If you associate the target food with something else you find disgusting ("I can't eat that, it looks like . . ."), make yourself realize that it's not the same thing. For example Marty couldn't eat shrimp as a child because she thought they looked like insect larvae; now that she's older and has overcome that association, she's happy to eat them.

- Pretend you're a food critic.

  Don't label the target "disgusting." Pretend it's a totally new taste. How does it taste in expressive, neutral terms? Is its strong flavor "smoky" perhaps, or tart, or earthy? Can you think of the "weird" aftertaste as a "subtle" aftertaste instead? Sometimes just stopping to consider the taste on its own terms, instead of panicking, can help change your mind.

- Don't dwell on negative tastes.

  If you taste something you truly don't like, don't roll it around on your tongue to identify it. Keep chewing, swallow, and move on.

How It Works

One classic example of an acquired taste is beer. Most people seem to dislike their first taste of it, but many people come to enjoy and even love it. The mechanism for acquiring this taste seems to be related to the alcohol lighting up the pleasure center of your brain, rewarding you for drinking the beer.

Indeed, the pleasure buttons that drugs like alcohol and caffeine press in our brains mean that people who drink beer, coffee, and so on often have not only favorite microbrews and blends of coffee beans, but also favorite mugs to drink out of, favorite snacks or creamer to drink them with, and even little rituals to accompany the drinking.

In this hack, among various other techniques, we're trying to harness the same mechanism that enables you to acquire a taste for beer and coffee and their accoutrements, but using different rewards: calories and flavor.

You might also think of this hack as a kind of gustatory semantic pause (Hack 57, "Take a Semantic Pause") that will enable you to reevaluate your subjective impressions of a food. As Gandhi, who experimented with his diet throughout his life, said, "The real seat of taste [is] not the tongue but the mind."[3] In the case of food, familiarity often breeds not contempt, but tolerance and even enjoyment.

In Real Life

Here are two case studies of this hack in practice in Ron's own life: learning to enjoy tomatoes, and learning not to fear cilantro. Because this section is very personal to Ron, he'll be speaking in the first person here.

Tomatoes

When I was 20, during a romantic breakup, my soon-to-be-ex-girlfriend told me she didn't like me anymore, and that she had *never* liked me. I told her — I swear that this is true — "But you could *learn* to like me."

She replied, "You can't make yourself like something," and we parted. However, I was proud and curious, and I wanted to see if I could prove her wrong on that point, at least. I vowed I would learn to like two things that she liked but I had always loathed: tomatoes and the Xanth fantasy novels by Piers Anthony. At the time I saw this as a kind of Nietzschean expression of my will. (Hey, I was 20 and on the rebound.)

Except for ketchup and spaghetti sauce, I had hated tomatoes my whole life, but I started eating them anyway. I forced myself to eat tomato slices on hamburgers, and today I prefer the tang of fresh tomatoes to ketchup on burgers. I thought I would never be able to choke down stewed tomatoes, which literally smelled to me like vomit. Today, while I've never sunk my spoon into a sopping bowlful of them, I'm happy enough to eat stewed tomatoes in mixed vegetables. In fact, about the only form of tomato I seldom eat now is the cherry tomato popular in salads. Even those, however, I consider dispreferred indifferents (as in Stoic philosophy) rather than pure evil.

Cilantro

With the tomato episode as a template, I decided to free myself of my reflexive loathing of cilantro in the spring of 2009, at the wiser (one can hope) age of 43. At this point in my life, hating cilantro was becoming a lifestyle. I frequented `ihatecilantro.com`. Marty wrote a song about my hatred of cilantro to the tune of "Fernando" by ABBA. I was becoming as tiresome about cilantro at dinnertime as I previously had been about such topics as nanotechnology and open-source software, and for much more trivial reasons. It was time to stop.

Apparently I lack the gene to tell me that cilantro "really" has a delightful citrus flavor, so instead it has always tasted to me like filth (to be specific, unsaturated aldehydes).[4] That I would be acquiring the "wrong" taste, that is, a taste for "filth" or unsaturated aldehydes instead of citrus, was immaterial for my purposes. I wanted to be free of the fear I experienced when I entered a Mexican, Indian, or Thai restaurant.

My first steps toward reconciliation with cilantro were tentative, with salsa and corn chips before dinner in a Mexican restaurant. I tried a little salsa, but the cilantro was undetectable; this was my first surprise, as I had long thought I was a kind of cilantro supertaster who could detect the most minute quantities of cilantro in any food, and this restaurant didn't usually stint on it in their salsa.

It was a heady experience to order dinner without begging the server to ask the chef to omit the cilantro, feigning an allergy if necessary. While we waited for the main course to arrive, I had some more corn chips with salsa. After about 20 of them, I tasted a little cilantro in the back of my throat. It wasn't too bad; in fact, it was much milder than I expected.

My entree, a fajita, arrived, and it too had a manageable amount of cilantro. (Before that night, I had considered any nonzero amount to be unmanageable.) I began to feel liberated and a bit giddy, and to dig into my fajita with a relish I had seldom felt before in a Mexican restaurant, even when I asked for dishes without cilantro — because I often found it on my plate uninvited.

A few nights later, Marty made a tomato soup for a party, and I spontaneously thought it could use some cilantro. Then, over the next several months, I encountered somewhat stronger cilantro several times in Mexican and Indian food; none of those instances distressed me.

One day, a burrito I bought at lunch contained some strong cilantro that actually did seem fairly unpleasant to me. It was so strong that I suspect even someone who had never disliked cilantro might have thought it heavy-handed. It was at this point that I thought of applying a kind of cognitive behavioral therapy (see above), and finished my lunch with equanimity.

Despite sometimes wishing a spicy dish had a little cilantro to make it even spicier, I still don't seek out cilantro the way I've come to seek out tomatoes. However, I've only had a couple of years to recalibrate my taste buds; in the case of tomatoes, I've had more than 20 years. Of course, I never really supposed I would begin to eat cilantro by the handful like chocolate candies anyway.

What I have received from this hack is comfort in the knowledge that I can walk into a restaurant or the cafeteria at work and never worry about whether one of the dishes contains the herb I used to hate so much. Since cilantro doesn't bother most people, all this hack has really done is freed some mental energy and brought me up to the human baseline, but it feels as though I'm invulnerable to bullets.

I never did learn to like Xanth novels, though.

See Also

- Roger-Pol Droit, *Astonish Yourself: 101 Experiments in the Philosophy of Everyday Life* (New York: Penguin, 2003). This book also contains a kind of hack about acquiring a taste, but more for the sake of amusement and philosophical wonder than for practical reasons. The whole book is full of interesting things to try that will change your viewpoint and open your mind, well worth perusing.

- Matthew Amster-Burton, *Hungry Monkey: A Food-Loving Father's Quest to Raise an Adventurous Eater* (Boston: Houghton Mifflin Harcourt, 2009). A book about teaching kids to like all kinds of food.

Notes

1. "Citation of Terentius," trans. by Jos van Geffen, accessed July 2009, www
   .xs4all.nl/~josvg/cits/terence/index.html. (An interesting page. It
   contains the original Latin version of "nothing human is alien to me," and
   its translation into 51 other languages.)

2. "How to Acquire a Taste for Cilantro," Ask Metafilter, accessed 18 Jul 2009, http://
   ask.metafilter.com/115309/How-to-acquire-a-taste-for-cilantro.

3. Mohandas K. Gandhi, *Autobiography*: *the story of my experiments with truth*
   (Dover: Courier Publications, 1983).

4. "Getting to the Root of the Great Cilantro Divide," Josh Kurz, National
   Public Radio, December 26, 2008, www.npr.org/templates/story/story.
   php?storyId=98695984.

Hack 51: Try Something New Daily

Mark Schnitzius

Do days, weeks, months, years seem to fly by for you, unremarked and even unnoticed? This may be due to a lack of variety in your life. The New Game is a game you can play that will ensure that every day holds at least a bit of uniqueness.

As human beings, we each have a sort of internal thermostat that defines how much variation we crave, versus the safety and comfort of routine. Many people seek out a high level of routine, and are uncomfortable with any novelty — witness Elvis Presley, who at one point in his life is rumored to have eaten meatloaf every night for a month.

Chances are good that if you're reading this book, you have an inquisitive mind and are open to trying new things, just for the novelty of it, but even the freest spirits occasionally find themselves falling into a rut. Work, school, or family commitments can often soak up your spare energy, so that the remainder of your time is spent zoning out. When this happens, it seems that days, weeks, months, even years fly by, because there is nothing to distinguish today from yesterday or tomorrow.

You only get so many days before you die, and letting any slip past you is a minor tragedy. In poetry, literature, and film you can find countless admonitions to "seize the day," or take "The Road Not Taken," as Robert Frost described it, so that you don't regret not having done so later. But beyond the philosophical reasons, there are cognitive benefits to adding novelty to your life. Exposure to new experiences positively affects your ability to remember and learn.

Therefore, here is a simple way to ensure that every day contains at least some small bit of uniqueness for you.

In Action

The New Game is a game you can play by yourself, and it consists of just a single rule: *Do something new every day.* The trick, of course, is how you define "new" — by design, it's entirely up to you! Your definitions should include things that:

- Make you feel brave or proud for having had the courage to try.
- Might lead to a discovery of something that could become a new favorite for you.
- Improve your knowledge or skill in at least some small way.
- Give something back to the arts, the community, or to humanity as a whole.

It's best to start with a simple set of rules, and then add new rules as you go, if you need them. Adding new rules may seem like cheating at first, but you'll know when a rule is right for you, because it will involve doing things that give you the same feeling of satisfaction, or rush of adrenaline, as the things that fit your existing rules.

Here are the basic rules I use. I consider my "new" for the day to be satisfied when I do any of the following:

- Eat at a new restaurant. This is easy enough if, like me, you work in a large city and eat lunch out every day.
- Eat a dish that I've never eaten before. Have you tried everything on the menu at your favorite restaurant, or do you always order the same thing?
- Prepare a meal from a recipe I've never tried before.
- See a movie I've never seen before, especially a classic.
- See a television show for the first time. Yes, there's a lot of garbage on the tube, but with all the new channels these days there are some gems to be found.
- Finish a new book. You might want to only count *starting* a new book, but if you're like me, you start a lot more than you finish.
- Explore a new neighborhood in town.
- Take a new, untried route to or from work.
- Learn and use a new word.
- Listen to a new song, a new radio station, or a whole new musical genre.
- Use a new technique or new tool at your job, such as a new function or algorithm, if you're a computer programmer.

- Create *anything*. This can include writing, painting, songwriting, etc. If I'm bringing something new into the world, that definitely counts.

- Learn anything new. This includes any kind of study, or working on a new skill, such as playing an instrument, juggling, public speaking, or computer programming. The "new" here is the new and improved you!

The list could go on and on. If you are so inclined, keep a log of your daily new activities, either on paper or in an online calendar or private blog. Consider color-coding your entries by category (food, media, physical exploration, etc.) to ensure that you don't consistently choose the same kind of new experience and fall — ironically — into a rut in your novelty! Also, you might want to consider playing the game with a friend or acquaintance. This may make it more fun, and will provide motivation, support, accountability, and even protection (if you're thinking of wandering into strange neighborhoods).

How It Works

How does the game work to improve your cognition? Studies conducted at University College London have shown that the midbrain region, which regulates our motivation, responds better to completely new experiences than to familiar ones. This is the same part of the brain that controls the dopamine levels in the frontal and temporal regions of the brain, which regulate our ability to predict reward. Novel information is often highly rewarding, and further studies have shown that slightly familiar information is consistently remembered better — almost 20% better in some cases — by test subjects when mixed with completely new information during the learning process (www.medicalnewstoday.com/releases/48722.php). Thus, it's probable that playing the New Game will also improve your memory of your day-to-day activities.

In Real Life

When I first started playing the New Game, it was quite an eye-opener to discover how many of my days were just vanishing down the memory hole, never to be recovered. I often found myself scrambling late in the day to find my "new" for the day. As I got into it, though, it was amazing how often it would force me to try something I was skeptical about, and end up leading to the discovery of a new favorite that came to be part of my regular rotation. Strange, isn't it, that enforced novelty can lead to improved routine?

I've also found that it's not always the major things that are the most satisfying to check off; often, it's the things that I'd heard about for a long time but for whatever reason never managed to get around to trying. For instance, I had my first taste of Turkish Delight while playing the New Game. Seeing an old classic movie that's new to me is another favorite — even if I end up not liking it, at least afterwards I can say I have seen it.

If you decide to give the New Game a try, unless you partner up, there will be no one to enforce its single rule for you. Nevertheless, commit yourself to keeping it going for at least a month to start with, and don't quit, even if you happen to miss a day. Eventually newness will become part of your mindset, and even if you decide to quit playing strictly, you will still find yourself choosing the unfamiliar option more often, when faced with a choice.

If you're reading this book and trying to improve your mental agility, then by my rules your "new" for the day has been satisfied, so start with the New Game in earnest tomorrow!

Hack 52: Metabehave Yourself

Work directly on your behavior, rather than your thoughts or feelings, to further your plans, break bad habits, and establish good ones, using the principles pioneered by behaviorism.

Although this book is called *Mindhacker*, sometimes what we want to affect is our behavior, not our thinking process — we want to change how we act, and what we think or feel is somewhat irrelevant. One way to affect an undesired behavior is to make small changes to related habits, shaping the undesired behavior indirectly. This may be easier than directly changing it, for a number of reasons.

The school of psychology that concerns itself most with shaping behavior is known as *behaviorism*. We'd like to propose a neutral term for the aspect of behaviorism that has been called *behavior analysis therapy* until now. At least within the context of this book, we'll be calling it *metabehavior*, which simply means "behavior applied to behavior" or "behavior acting on behavior." Metabehavior is analogous to the much-studied phenomenon of *metacognition* or "thinking about thinking" (Hack 38, "Think Clearly about Simple Errors").

This hack contains nine mini-hacks, gleaned from various works on behaviorism, behavior analysis, and even behavioral economics. This may sound like a fringe field, but President Obama has at least one prominent behavioral economist, Cass Sunstein, in his administration.

Many of these techniques are common, although not everyone has heard of all of them. Maybe you learned some of them from your mom as a kid and have let them languish since you grew up, but dust them off and take another look — your mom passed them along because they work. Moms and dads are experts at low-tech behavior modification!

We have used all of these techniques, and they seem to work for us. Note that the self-referential quality of this hack means that we'll be taking many of our real-life examples from our own work situations and writing process.

In Action

The following "external" hacks enable you to manage yourself by managing your external environment.

Tracking

Tracking simply means *monitoring*, or keeping track of, your behavior. This is one of the most basic metabehavioral techniques, so it's the first on the list.

You can't modify your behavior if you don't know how often you're performing the action in question, or even whether you're doing it. Tracking can help uncover triggers or patterns of a behavior, useful in formulating a strategy for changing it. Therefore, one of the first steps in getting control of your finances, for example, is tracking what you spend your income on as closely as you can.

When you're working, it's often useful to track how many work items you've completed in a work session. It not only helps you to pace yourself, it is encouraging to see your "to-do" items drop in number and your "done" items rise. You can track items with anything from hash marks in a notebook to sophisticated digital tracking systems. Even looking at the item count at the bottom of a folder on your computer screen can be helpful.

Metabehavioral tracking can work on a national or planetary level too. Consider proposed regulations that would require corporations to reveal their levels of greenhouse gas emissions. Again, you can't modify your behavior if you don't monitor it.

Reminders

Reminders are another core metabehavioral technique. The basic principle behind reminders is that you can't act on what you're not aware of, and we're not always aware of everything we should be. Even more important, we're usually not aware of what we're not aware of. Thus, we should remind ourselves of important but hidden or non-obvious factors when deciding how to act.

A reminder might be as simple as putting a sign or picture on the wall in your office to remind you to change your behavior in a desired way, or it might be a more elaborate system (Hack 1, "Remember to Remember").

It's relatively simple to construct a system to automatically remind you of to-do items with a stack of index cards and a repeating timer called a Motivaider. (For more information about how to do this, see www.ludism .org/mentat/MindPerformanceHacks_2fBuildAnExoself.) The Motivaider (http://habitchange.com) is itself a simple yet powerful device that can act as a reminder of anything with which you choose to associate it, from standing up straight, to being kind to people, to checking your to-do list. You set the timer for an interval — let's say 23 minutes — and stick it in your pocket. It will then vibrate every 23 minutes, reminding you intermittently to do what you were trying to remember to do.

Smartphone apps have begun to appear that can duplicate the Motivaider's functionality, such as Annoyster for the iPhone (www.annoyster.com). There are other alternatives as well.

Organizing Your Environment

Rearrange your environment so it supports your goals, rather than opposes them. Sometimes this can entail changing things that may not seem directly related to what you're trying to do, but are distracting you nonetheless. Robert Epstein has described an example of this that happened to the behaviorist B. F. Skinner:

> Sometimes the results were grand, and sometimes they were silly. [Skinner] used to write in his study in the early mornings, and at one point I remember him being concerned about his fidgeting. He would write for a few minutes and then fidget in his chair and get up. What, he wondered, was causing him to stop writing? Could it be the seat of the chair? He slit open the sides of the cushion, pulled out some foam, and stuffed new foam in, shaping the cushion to conform to his posterior. Sure enough, the bottom line improved: He was able to write for far longer periods with the modified (but very shabby!) cushion. He had changed his environment in a very simple fashion in order to change his own behavior.[1]

Another example: Ron had trouble getting up in the morning, so he bought a Chumby (www.chumby.com), a programmable, Internet-capable alarm clock. He can set it to wake him in a variety of ways; he's found over time that the best way, with occasional small variations, is to set an alarm with *Morning Edition* on the local NPR station half an hour before he has to get up, then to switch to a recording of a bugle playing "Reveille." The NPR doesn't wake him all the way up — it just prepares him for the day — but "Reveille" does. In addition, the snooze time for Reveille is set as low as it will go — one minute — so his cunning morning self has to be craftier than usual to sleep in, because hitting the snooze button doesn't buy much time. This may sound like a ludicrously contrived way to get up in the morning, but Ron will assure you that he's never gotten up so reliably before in his life. If you sleep in a lot but don't have a Chumby, you can try something similar with your laptop and a capable timer program such as KAlarm (www.astrojar.org.uk/kalarm). At minimum, try two different alarm clocks; this works best if you place the second clock across the room so you have to get up to turn it off. As a last resort, you can try Clocky (www.nandahome.com), "the alarm clock that runs away" — it literally rolls off your bedside table and across the room all on its own, so that you have to chase it down to turn it off.

The point is to organize your environment in a way that enables you to get things done. If you have to carve up a perfectly functional seat cushion so you can sit still long enough to write, do it. If you're a heavy sleeper and you have to buy a fancy Internet alarm clock or write a bunch of cascading shell scripts on your laptop to get up in the morning, do that. Fold, spindle, mutilate, and organize your environment. Don't kill anyone or break their stuff, obviously, but otherwise, do whatever it takes.

Truncation

Truncation means nipping something in the bud, stopping it before it can even start, let alone become a problem.

Truncation works by setting obstacles for yourself that act as force multipliers for your good intentions. In general, it's easier to say no to temptation before it happens than while you're hip-deep in it. For example, we've found that if we check e-mail and social networking sites first thing in the morning, it's easy to get caught up in them. Therefore, it's usually better never to get online before work in the first place.

Ron has sometimes gone so far as packing up his netbook and its accessories the night before he has to be at an important meeting or when he is expecting some especially interesting e-mail. That way, in order to get online in the morning, it's necessary to unpack the netbook instead of just turning it on — another obstacle. If this ever fails to be enough, he can pack his whole bag for the morning, netbook and all, and put it downstairs by the front door, or even in the car. Then he would have to get dressed, walk downstairs, bring the bag into the house, power the netbook up, and so on. It's easier to defer checking e-mail until later, at least until he gets to work on time. He has a similar rule about web surfing before bedtime.

Experiment with how big the obstacles you set yourself must be, and be sure to track your experiments. There will come a time when it's easier to stop your bad behavior than to "walk around" the obstacle. This technique works especially well if you're essentially lazy by nature; Ron uses it often.

Commitments

Making public commitments is a great way to follow through on your intentions. Classic examples of this include giving a trusted friend a $100 bill to burn, or a sealed letter revealing embarrassing secrets to mail, if you fail to meet a deadline.

There are new twists available on these old tricks, such as www.stickK.com (Hack 28, "Turn a Job into a Game") or Scrumble (Hack 29, "Scrumble for Glory"). We have used both Scrumble and stickK to help write this book. Ron also considered posting public drafts of chapters as soon as he finished them. It's hard to make a more public commitment than that, at least for this kind of project.

The following "internal" hacks work more directly on your behavior than the external hacks do.

Homework First

We call this technique Homework First because of the common parental injunction to kids to do their homework before watching TV or playing video games. The key here is if you do the important but difficult, unpleasant things first, you'll probably have an uninterrupted stretch of time to do fun things with a clear conscience, whereas if you do the fun things first, you might get caught up in them and never get to the important things. (See "Momentum" below.)

For example, when Ron arrives at his day job in the morning, he starts up his computer, logs in, and reads work e-mail before he even gets coffee. Then he gets coffee and does any work he can that arrived overnight before he reads his personal e-mail. He gets his work done on time, and as a side effect, this routine has often led to his discovering and reporting build and network problems before any of his co-workers do. He doesn't know how much this fact has helped his work reputation, but it doesn't hurt.

Inspiration

Ron has sometimes felt inspired by a Muse, especially when designing board games; while he doesn't believe in the literal truth of this, there are neurological correlates for this kind of inspiration that suggest it's not merely imagination.[2]

This means that inspiration is a real phenomenon in your brain. However, it doesn't mean that if you want to do something creative, you should loll about on your divan awaiting a bolt of lightning. Certainly, if you want to be a creative professional, you need to work every day, whether inspired or not.

However, you shouldn't resist inspiration when it strikes either. If you feel inspired to write a poem, stop what you're doing if you can, and scribble it down. If you feel inspired to buy a gift for your spouse, do it. For that matter, if Phosphatia the Dish Muse visits and you feel inspired to wash several loads of dishes, your spouse or roommate might be grateful for that too. You can get a lot of work done this way! Use the energy in the moment it comes to you.

Speaking metaphorically, the Muse often comes to visit at inconvenient times. Ron's likes to drop in around 3:00 in the morning. For that reason, he keeps a notebook by the bed, and carries it with him throughout the day.

As a concrete example of inspiration, we scheduled the writing of this book by week, with a certain number of hacks per week depending on how busy we were, and then scheduled particular hacks for particular weeks. Ron usually took notes during the work week and wrote hacks on the weekend. However, sometimes ideas for a different hack — even a completely new one — came to him during the week. In that case, he simply abandoned himself to the new hack. It was much easier than fighting it, he got plenty of work done with less effort, and usually he felt inspired to write the hack he was skipping sometime later (Hack 24, "Knock Off Work").

Momentum

When you don't have inspiration, momentum can carry you through. The trick is to get the ball rolling in the first place, and then go with it.

If you need to write a term paper, and you're not inspired to, or you're experiencing writer's block, or you simply don't want to, do this: Open a new document in your word processor, and sit in front of it for five minutes. That's all you have to do. You don't need to write anything, but if you do, so much the better. Don't start doing anything else; just sit there.

If you can't write anything, come back in an hour and sit in front of your computer for another five minutes. Do it again and again. Eventually you'll be annoyed, and the suction of the blank page in front of you combined with the pressure of your annoyance will push some words onto it.

Once you do start writing, relax and let the words and ideas flow. When you have to get up from your computer, stop writing in mid-thought instead of getting to a "stopping point." Your mental momentum may carry over when you sit down again.

This is good or "positive" mental momentum. It's important to stop negative mental momentum before it can accumulate — use truncation (above) to do that.

Extremes

Going to extremes may sometimes be helpful. For example, if you're trying to quit drinking coffee, you can commit (publicly or not) to drink three cups of coffee whenever you backslide and drink one. That is, whenever you allow yourself a single cup of coffee to kill the cravings, you must quickly chug two more of the same size.

You will probably find the resulting caffeine jitters fairly punishing; you might even be sick. Thus, if you're foolish enough to try a cup of coffee even once under this regime, you'll probably think twice — or thrice — before doing it again.

How It Works

This hack uses many ideas from the school of psychology known as behaviorism, as we mentioned above. Some behaviorists have historically believed (they would say "behaved as if") mind and consciousness do not exist, or at least have no place in science. More recent incarnations of behaviorism, such as behavior analysis, have downplayed this claim somewhat.

Metabehavior can be thought of as a kind of low-tech psychological technique. When J. B. Watson founded the behaviorist school of psychology in the early twentieth century, he was able to draw some fairly sophisticated conclusions about animal behavior, simply by directly studying the behavior as such, without twenty-first-century equipment like MRI scanners that can provide supplemental information about accompanying phenomena like brain states.

Today the metabehavioral approach has spawned some surprising descendants, such as behavioral economics and even the "low-tech" *behavioral robotics* of Rodney Brooks and colleagues (Hack 30, "Salvage a Vintage Hack"). With this hack, you'll be able to apply metabehavioral techniques to change your own behavior.

Metabehavior works because you're motivating yourself with the things you know motivate you best. It doesn't matter whether the things that motivate you seem boring, silly, or childish to anyone else. No one needs to know but you, except perhaps for a friend you can trust to follow through on smashing that no-longer-mint, but still beloved, Boba Fett action figure you handed her in case you didn't follow through on your commitment.

What motivates and shapes your behavior is by definition extremely personal. You already have a long history of it influencing your behavior. You don't need to tell anyone about it — but at the same time, don't be afraid to exploit it for all it's worth.

If you would like to create a portable mental toolbox of these behavioral techniques, Ron suggests making a mnemonic acrostic of them. THOTCRIME works well, as it ironically alludes to the Orwellian quality of some early behaviorist writing that denied the existence of consciousness or thought.

Tracking

Homework First

Organizing Your Environment

Truncation

Commitments

Reminders

Inspiration

Momentum

Extremes

See Also

■ Robert Epstein, *Self-Help Without the Hype* (Tucker, GA, USA: Performance Management Publications, 1997).

- Steve Levenson and Pete C. Greider, M.Ed., *Following Through*, Second edition (Bloomington, IN, USA: Unlimited Publishing, 2007).

- Richard H. Thaler and Cass R. Sunstein, *Nudge: Improving Decisions About Health, Wealth, and Happiness* (New Haven, CT, USA: Yale University Press, 2008).

Notes

1. Robert Epstein. "Skinner as Self-Manager," *Journal of Applied Behavior Analysis*, 30 (1997), 545–568.

2. Alice Weaver Flaherty, *The Midnight Disease: The Drive to Write, Writer's Block, and the Creative Brain* (Boston: Mariner Books, 2005).

Hack 53: Train Your Fluid Intelligence

M. W. Fogleman

Learn about a task you can perform online that can increase your intelligence by exercising your working memory. It may not be exciting, but it's highly effective.

Psychologists who study intelligence make a distinction between fluid and crystallized intelligence. *Fluid intelligence* is based on your ability to handle new problems in new situations, whereas *crystallized intelligence* is based on more specific knowledge (such as your multiplication tables) acquired over a period of time. Psychologists knew that crystallized intelligence could be taught and learned, but they weren't sure whether fluid intelligence could be improved.

The Nintendo DS video game Brain Age had a subtitle of "Train Your Brain in Minutes a Day!"; in other words, it implied that it could improve your fluid intelligence. Although Nintendo worked with a Japanese neuroscientist while developing the game, they cautiously labeled the game as entertainment, not as a training exercise scientifically proven to improve mental performance.

While some studies with Brain Age and other kinds of "brain fitness" training exercises have been done, it is not always clear that practicing a specific task or tasks causes general improvement, and Brain Age is no exception (www.telegraph.co.uk/health/healthnews/7610884/ Popular-brain-training-games-do-not-make-users-any-smarter.html). But in 2008, a study released by Susanne Jaeggi and others offered evidence that something called an *n-back task*, or what is commonly referred to as *dual n-back*, could possibly improve fluid intelligence and working memory.[1] (Working memory is the ability to hold information in your mind that you need to perform complex tasks.)

Essentially, you are presented with a sequence of stimuli (generally two or more kinds simultaneously, such as audio and visual), and you attempt to compare the present stimuli with past stimuli a certain number (n) of turns ago. For this reason, what is commonly referred to as *dual n-back* would more accurately be called *x n-back*, *x* being the number of kinds of simultaneous stimulus and *n* being the number of each kind of stimulus that you are trying to keep in your head at one time. For example, if you were playing mono 2-back with alphabet letters (x=1, n=2), and I gave you the sequence of letters A-B-A-C, when the second A comes up you should acknowledge that it matches the letter A two turns ago. However, when C appears, you should realize that it does not match the letter two turns before that, B.

While this seems quite simple, increasing the number of stimuli and the number of turns that you need to remember makes it much more difficult. The n-back game works to increase those variables over time, which usually increases how many items you can keep in your working memory, which may lead to improvements in your fluid intelligence.

In Action

There are several implementations of the n-back game, for different platforms and with different variations. I use Brain Workshop, which is open source and available for Windows, Mac, and Linux, but you may want to look into a different solution if you want to practice on a smartphone or tablet. The n-back FAQ lists several mobile solutions.[2] To get started, download and install Brain Workshop from `http://brainworkshop.sourceforge.net`.

Once you have installed and launched Brain Workshop, you'll find a menu with various options (see Figure 53-1).

Brain Workshop adds many variations to the n-back task. Its default settings should work for now, so press the space bar to go to the game screen, which looks like a tic-tac-toe board (see Figure 53-2).

The game places rectangles in different positions on the tic-tac-toe board, while saying different letters through your speakers or headphones. These are the two basic stimuli: locations of rectangles on the board *and* letters that you hear. Brain Workshop defaults to dual 2-back, so that you have to remember these two stimuli for two positions. Press the space bar again to try a game and see your baseline. When the third letter/space combination comes up, you have to compare each stimulus to its respective stimulus from two turns ago. If the rectangle's position matches, press A; if the letter you hear matches, press L (see Figure 53-3).

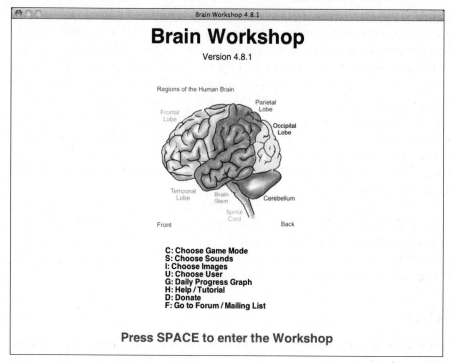

Figure 53-1: Brain Workshop menu

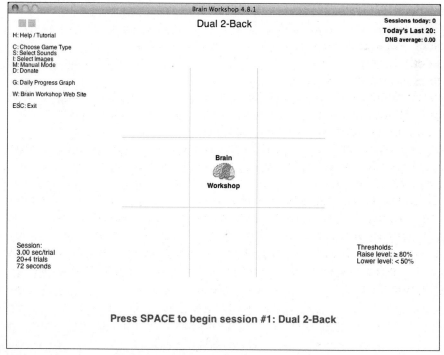

Figure 53-2: Brain Workshop game screen

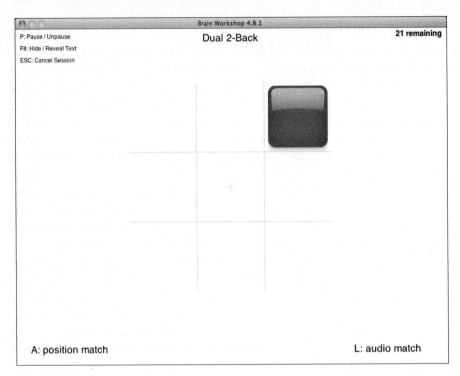

Figure 53-3: Brain Workshop in action

You'll find the first few times you practice the n-back task with Brain Workshop to be very difficult — don't get discouraged! If you are having trouble understanding exactly what it is that you are trying to do (I had trouble at first), I recommend watching the Brain Workshop screencast or reading the tutorial.[3] Keep playing — you will improve very rapidly with regular n-back practice.

As you get better, Brain Workshop will increase the n variable, or how many positions you have to remember for each stimulus, from the default setting of 2 to 3, 4, and onwards. If you get really good, you might try playing with some of the alternative modes. To the letter and audio stimuli, you can add colors and shapes, as well as a second audio channel and arithmetic.

It's important to establish a routine for training with n-back. The Brain Workshop website recommends spending 25 minutes per day, four or five times each week. As with most skills, the more you practice, the better you'll become; unlike most so-called brain training games, practicing the n-back task improves your working memory and fluid intelligence, so it will benefit more areas of your life than just the task itself. N-back improves your fluid intelligence quantifiably; it's emphatically not true that practicing the test improves your score on the test but has no real world implications.

How It Works

The 2008 study conducted by Jaeggi et al. tested the hypothesis that there is "a strong relationship between *working* memory and *Gf* [fluid intelligence]" by means of the working memory training method of the n-back task. When they found that the n-back task worked as expected, they then hypothesized that the relationship "between working memory and *Gf* primarily results from the involvement of attentional control," which is requisite for both working memory and fluid intelligence. Additionally, they state that the n-back task itself was optimal for training fluid intelligence by means of working memory because of its "adaptive character," which requires the "continual engagement of executive processes [cognitive functions that control and manage other cognitive functions] while only minimally allowing the development of automatic processes [akin to habits] and task-specific strategies [ways to solve a problem that don't transfer to other problems]."

Psychologists have known for some time that if you repeatedly test something, a subject can improve at the test but not necessarily improve at what the test is supposed to measure. Similar problems have occurred with other purported intelligence-training tasks. However, because the n-back task changes as you improve, developing specific strategies to improve at the task itself is difficult. This is even truer if you increase or change the number or kind of stimulus, or what we've been calling x.

The study notes that executive processes, which the n-back task requires, are also quite useful for most tasks that require fluid intelligence. The n-back task requires you to:

- "inhibit irrelevant items."
- "monitor ongoing performance."
- "manage two tasks simultaneously."
- "update representations in memory."

It also "engages binding processes between the items (i.e., squares in spatial positions and consonants) and their temporal context." All these factors combine to make n-back a very promising development for psychology (even if the task itself may not be very exciting to practice). The study concludes,

The finding that cognitive training can improve Gf is a landmark result because this form of intelligence has been claimed to be largely immutable. Instead of regarding Gf as an immutable trait, our data provide evidence that, with appropriate training, there is potential to improve Gf. Moreover, we provide evidence that the amount of Gf-gain critically depends on the amount of training time. Considering the fundamental importance of Gf in everyday life and its predictive power for a large variety of intellectual tasks and professional success, we believe that our findings may be highly relevant to applications in education.

That said, there have been some criticisms of the Jaeggi study. The n-back FAQ lists several studies that found no improvement, but some of these studies have themselves been criticized, and the findings of the Jaeggi 2008 study have also been replicated by several other studies (www.sciencedirect.com/science/article/pii/S0160289610001091 and http://ieeexplore.ieee.org/xpl/freeabs_all.jsp?arnumber=5454984). While it's worth considering the findings of these different experiments, it may be more effective to simply try the n-back task for yourself.

In Real Life

In my own use of Brain Workshop, I noticed two effects: I remembered my dreams more often, and my meditation practice improved. The n-back FAQ keeps a list of people who have reported how regular n-back practice has affected them, in terms of both IQ tests and other, more subjective changes. Some report drastic, noticeable changes; some notice minor changes; and some notice no benefit at all. Some particular benefits that are listed include improved dream recall, productivity, concentration, general understanding, learning speed, curiosity, creativity, and even calmness and happiness.

See Also

- You may find training on your smartphone or tablet more convenient than training on your desktop or laptop. After examining multiple dual n-back apps for mobile platforms, it seems to me that the best of them are IQ Boost and Brain N-Back (the version by Phuc Nguyen) for iOS and Android respectively. Both are currently free and available from the appropriate app store.

- Wired wrote an article about the n-back game: www.wired.com/science/discoveries/news/2008/04/smart_software.

- Wikipedia also maintains an article on the n-back task: http://en.wikipedia.org/wiki/N-back.

Notes

1. S. M. Jaeggi, et al., "Improving Fluid Intelligence with Training on Working Memory," *Proceedings of the National Academy of Sciences*, vol. 105 no. 19 (2008): www.iapsych.com/articles/jaeggi2008.pdf.

2. "N-back FAQ," accessed April 2011, `www.gwern.net/N-back%20FAQ.html`. Maintains a list of software for different platforms, as well as online websites where you can practice the dual n-back task.

3. "Brain Workshop: A Dual N-Back Game," Paul Hoskinson and Jonathan Toomim, accessed April 2011, `http://brainworkshop.sourceforge.net/tutorial.html`.

Hack 54: Think, Try, Learn

Matthew Cornell, M.S.

Live life as a series of scientific experiments.

This hack outlines an approach to living that's based on the set of practices that has impelled humanity through tremendous progress for the last 400 years: science. Treating life as an experiment enables you to look at problems as opportunities to explore, and to have a sense of rational, yet ultimately rich, control over what you choose to do. Living experimentally empowers you with control of your thinking and behaviors, and this helps you to cope with life's inherent unpredictability and limitation of control. Additionally, it can lead to your being more fully engaged and mindful of the frankly amazing world around us.

In Action

There are two facets of putting this approach into action: how to experience your world with a life-as-experiment mindset, and how to use concrete practices to try new things experimentally.

The Experimental Mindset

First, how do you *choose* where to apply experimental methods? Here are five main characteristics that define an experiment. The more of these that apply to the problem, question, or opportunity under consideration, the more likely it is a candidate for the experimental approach.

- **Novel:** *Something that is new to you, unfamiliar and untested*
- **Speculative:** *Something about which you have questions, or that arouses your curiosity*
- **Unpredictable:** *Something you can't make good predictions about with your current level of knowledge*

- **Improvisational:** *Something that lends itself to changing actions during the process, or to a certain flexibility in how you approach it*

- **Provisional:** *Something that can be changed in response to what you learn, or that will be done repeatedly, possibly differently each time*

Following are a few examples of experiments that people have done to improve themselves and their lives, and some ways you could consider them experimental, based on the preceding characteristics.

Trying a New Hobby

Learning to cook, for example, is most fun when you're experimenting. It is unpredictable (a burnt casserole is an occupational hazard), improvisational (pictures and instructions are one thing, but actually putting together a meal is another), and provisional (you might not stick with it if you didn't enjoy cooking or eating it, or you might cook something else next time).

Taking a New Medication

Finding the best treatment for a medical condition is often complicated and time-consuming. Treating it as a formal experiment can make the process shorter and more effective.

How can taking a prescribed drug be an experiment? If you think about it, recommended dosages are ones that work acceptably well, based on average results for large groups of people; what matters most, however, is determining what amount works best for a specific person — you — and that's something you cannot know without experimenting (under professional supervision, of course). It is certainly unpredictable (who hasn't looked at a prescription's "scare sheet" of side-effects without suspecting they have half of them?), improvisational (while you have a specific dosage plan to follow, you need to pay attention to your reaction, and act accordingly), and provisional (it's an excellent idea to keep in mind that there is usually more than one medication or combination you can try for a medical condition, and this can be a source of hope if one doesn't work out).

WARNING Keep it safe! Like anything you do, it is important to ensure that your experiments are benign and ethical. We can take a cue from the Belmont Report, which outlines three principles (`http://ohsr.od.nih.gov/guidelines/belmont.html#gob`) that address experimental ethics: Experiments should respect the people involved, be beneficial, and be just. For experiments with relationships, you should consider carefully letting others know what you're doing. For medical experiments, check with your medical professional for help setting them up safely, monitoring while you're trying them, and analyzing your results.

Getting Started

To begin trying this method in your life, start with something small, such as an experiment that you could complete in less than a week. Pick an area of your life that needs changing, a problem you want to work on, or something you've been thinking of trying for a while but haven't had the gumption yet. Figure out just one change you'll make, and one or two things at most that you'll measure during the experiment. Many people start with a health or lifestyle focus, such as eating smaller portions, starting to exercise, or improving sleep.

Another starting point might be a hack from this book. After all, they are all about making changes to improve your life, and experimenting is a principled way to incorporate and evaluate how much they end up helping. Just find one that jumps out at you and then set it up using the Think, Try, Learn process.

Experimental Practices

To actually implement the mindset, you'll apply the basic practices of identifying experiments, designing them, carrying them out, and analyzing and learning from the results. Overall, it helps to think of the process as having three interconnected components: *think* (design and direction), *try* (experimentation and observation), and *learn* (analysis, reflection, and integration), as shown in Figure 54-1.

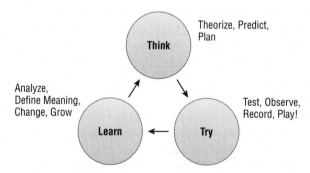

Cycles: Iterations, Recursions, Interleavings, and Orderings

Figure 54-1: The Think, Try, Learn process

These three elements form the framework for the specific practices and tools that you can use to live an experiment-driven life.

Think

In this stage, you decide what you want to experiment on, how you'll go about it, and possibly capture your expectations with predictions of what might happen.

It's a reasonable starting point for many experiments, although any entry point is valid, such as by accidental discovery during the Try phase.

After you've used an experimental mindset to find appropriate subject matter for an experiment, you need to thoughtfully decide how to approach how you'll test a solution in the Try phase. It's helpful to ask the following four questions, which I've taken from my Edison site, a tool that helps people track, share, and learn from their experiments.[1]

- What will you do?
- How will you test your idea and measure success?
- How will you know you are done?
- How will you enjoy the journey?

Regarding the actual structure and sequence of the experiment you come up with (the first three questions), several approaches are possible. The most common is the *Reversal*, or *ABA design*. The steps of the design are as follows:

1. Define the question you're trying to answer.
   "Is grinding during the day causing my tooth pain?"

2. Decide on one thing that you're going to change.
   Wear a night guard during the day.

3. Decide on at least one corresponding measurement you'll make.
   Rate pain on a scale of zero to two.

4. Start taking measurements for a while.
   You're in the first "A."

5. Implement the change and keep measuring.
   Now you're in "B."

6. Cut out the change and continue measuring until you're done.
   This is the final "A."

Try

How exactly do you run an experiment once you've designed it? Think of it as being composed of four interrelated activities:

- Carry out the changes you decided on in the Think phase.
- Make observations about what you're experiencing during the process.
- Record your measured data.
- Regularly analyze where you are in the experiment.

It's helpful to capture your personal observations throughout the experimentation process by recording any stories, ideas, insights, and relevant thoughts that occur.

An essential practice of self-experimenting is to keep an experimenter's log, or journal, where you record the expectations, observations, data, and experiences and results before, during, and after your experiment. The tool you choose must be readily accessible so that you can easily record observations when they're fresh. Keeping a log has multiple benefits:

- It provides the data you need to identify exploitable patterns.
- It's a source of information for possible troubleshooting.
- It provides motivation for your experiment and keeps you engaged.
- It develops your observation skills.
- It helps you be more optimistic and grateful — reflecting on your day reminds you that good things have happened.
- If shared with others, it helps them learn from your work and may motivate them to try it too.

You may want to consider the new technology options available for monitoring your results, which are in vogue due to the rise of mobile technology and embeddable sensors for self-monitoring. The ability to take measurements that are ubiquitous, wireless, and consolidated opens the door to major changes in how we think about taking control of our health, and it can give us useful data for developing insight into how we operate as habitual creatures — what Jim Collins calls "a bug called you."[2] Some examples include Fitbit for walking, calories, and sleep (www.fitbit.com/); Nike+ iPod Sport Kit for running (www.apple.com/ipod/nike/); Zeo Personal Sleep Coach (www.myzeo.com/); the Withings scale and blood pressure home devices (www.withings.com/); and GlowCaps for prescription compliance (http://rxvitality.com/). Nearly all of them offer web-based tools for data collection, analysis, and sharing. For an excellent introduction to these options, see Gary Wolf's article in the *New York Times*.[3]

Finally, you evaluate how your experiment is proceeding, and whether you need to make any changes to it. Are you facing obstacles? Are you not getting adequate results? Are you still learning anything? You may decide to continue the experiment, make an adjustment to what you're doing, or call it completed and move on.

As with the overall Think, Try, Learn process, there is no strict ordering of these activities. You are guided instead by your results and intuition, plus any advice you can get from others, professional or otherwise.

Learn

In the Learn stage, you make sense of your experiment's results. You analyze any data you've collected, reflect on what you've learned about the subject, and assimilate the outcome into your life. Reviewing your experimenter's journal is an excellent starting point. Ideally, you've discovered something that improves whatever area you were targeting, and which you can permanently incorporate into your life via a new perspective or behavior.

If you've collected quantitative data in addition to your observations, this is when you analyze it. Your goal is to see the connections, and to look for cause and effect, between the thing you changed (known as the *independent variable*) and the resulting effect on the other thing you tracked (the *dependent variable*).[4] If you're doing an ABA type of experiment, the transition points will be of interest: A-to-B and B-to-A. Try using simple visualization tools, such as an X-Y plot, to help you find patterns.

For example, if you were doing an ABA experiment to test whether recent fatigue you are feeling relates to how much sugar you eat, you might record two things each day: total sugar consumed (mg) and overall vitality during the day (using three levels such as low, OK, and high, for example). The A portion would be continuing your current intake of sugar (for a week), and B might be halving it, also for a week. Then you would go back to your original consumption. Afterward, you would plot sugar consumption and vitality against time to determine whether the latter changes along with the former.

Note that it can be difficult to identify definitive cause-and-effect relationships between our actions and results because of the complex interrelationships between things in our lives. You might decide that your mood varies with how much sugar you eat, yet there may be confounding factors[5] such as major life stressors going on at the time, the timing of your sugar intake over the course of a day, and so on.

When you've collected your information and analyzed it to glean any new insights or correlations from what you've learned, you're ready to move back to the Think stage, to see if applying your new knowledge leads to developing a better solution to try next.

In Real Life

Here are two examples of larger experiments I've done over the last few years.

Experiment: Improving Sleep

Like many people, I sometimes suffer from insomnia; in my case, I typically have trouble falling asleep. Not too long ago it was especially bad and started to affect my ability to work, so I decided to experiment; over the course of a year I ended up trying a bunch of possible solutions, though not at the same time.

Following are the solutions I've tried:

- Counting breaths and doing relaxation visualizations.
  Result: No improvement.

- Taking melatonin.
  Result: No improvement.

- Adopting the "no computer" rule in the evening.
  Result: No improvement, though worth further experimentation.

- Not eating right before bed.
  Result: No improvement. Ditto for not exercising right before bed.

- Avoiding bright lights at night, primarily from playing on my phone in bed.
  Result: I decided that although the light probably has an impact, the relaxing nature of the play is worth any trade-off.

- Not napping during the day.
  Result: Left me more tired than ever. The opposite experiment, napping when I felt tired (30 minutes max) worked very well (I felt better during the day) and didn't seem to harm falling asleep at night.

- Finally, going to bed when I first felt tired.
  Result: This one ended up being extremely effective, and I try to do it each night.

Note that I ran each of these as its own experiment, working the Think, Try, Learn cycle before moving on to the next one. For each, I (1) came up with details for what I would do and measure; (2) tried it for some time, recording observations and data; and then (3) assessed the experiment and repeated the cycle, sometimes making small variations on the current experiment, and for others trying something very different.

If you also suffer from insomnia, here is a detailed description of another sleep experiment I ran. Because it is common knowledge that caffeine is a stimulant that can affect falling asleep, I wondered if there were a relationship between sleep and the two cups of chocolate I drank each day, which contain a little caffeine. I came up with an ABA test in which I would consume my current two cups per day for three days (the first A), then do a B phase of stopping completely for three days (be brave, experimenter!), then go back to my normal dose (the final A). I recorded sleep quality each morning using a simple three-value scale of restedness: groggy, slightly drowsy but awake, or alert.

At the end of the ninth day, I did some analysis in the Learn phase, and in my case the results were conclusive: The chocolate did not hurt my sleep. This was frankly a relief, as I love the stuff! Don't ask me what I would have done otherwise.

Experiment: Becoming More Productive

Staying on top of work can be a struggle. Fortunately, you can easily apply the Think, Try, Learn methods explained earlier to get more productive. Combining it with the productivity system Jetpack (Hack 21, "Get Control of Yourself") makes both techniques stronger. Briefly, that system organizes your work so that you work from a calendar and three consolidated lists (tasks, waiting, and projects). Those lists can provide a concrete starting point for running a number of helpful experiments. Here are a few examples.

Daily Planning

Creating a daily "to do" list is a classic time-management idea. The idea is to create a temporary list of tasks to do each day that will accomplish a strategic mix of work, and that will give you a sense of satisfaction at the end of your day. A straightforward test is to try daily planning for a week, and then switch back for a few days and evaluate any difference in productivity. You might measure your overall feeling of accomplishment at the end of the day, or your ability to prioritize and focus on critical tasks. Or simply tally how many tasks you completed each day.

"Just 10 Minutes"

This is an experiment in procrastination-busting whereby you limit the duration of all tasks to no longer than 10 minutes. This addresses the common problem of feeling too overwhelmed to even get started.

Interruption Log

Because interruptions are a common productivity drain, try the experiment of simply tracking them. Record who interrupted you, when it happened, how long it lasted, and the reason. Do it for one week, and then study the results to find preventable interruptions. You might encourage the people who interrupt you to use alternative forms of communication such as e-mail, or think about how you can delegate better. If it's bad enough, you might even try a separate experiment, such as closing your door with a sign on it: "Do not disturb. Will be free at 1:30 p.m."

In my case, I've tried all of these at one time or another, and found the daily planning technique to be extremely helpful. I now use it every day because it gives me a "focus anchor" when phone calls, e-mail, and other distractions pull me off course. It also gives me a concrete sense of accomplishment at the end of the day, which lets me enjoy my down time in the evening. Finally, it's a great way to become more accurate at estimating how long it takes to finish particular tasks, which makes planning smoother and more effective.

How It Works

As humans, we are wired to be curious, and we have an innate drive to explore the world. Living experimentally is a natural application of these traits. To be reminded of this, just watch children playing for a few minutes, and notice their boundless enthusiasm to question and investigate. Unfortunately, we often lose sight of this as we get older.

Change and Control

There is an evolutionary basis for assuming that change represents a threat — we might lose something dear to us, or we might encounter new situations for which we don't feel prepared. Ancestors who mastered their surroundings were more successful, so we are happier when we have influence. However, nothing is static, and outside factors often limit the practical power we can wield.

Treating goals as experiments gives us a feeling of more control over how we view or approach our options, and turns our fear of change into excitement about the potential of the unknown to surprise and delight us.

Desire

It's natural to want things, but unwavering attachment to a particular outcome can make us unhappy because it means we are open to only one outcome, the particular one we desire. But life rarely cooperates by giving us exactly what we want. Attachment to the end product closes us to the rich opportunities that can actually unfold, ones that are different from our initial desire (Hack 33, "Make Happy Mistakes"). Also, it sets up a lose-lose success metric that disappoints us, regardless of whether things are looking positive (in which case we worry about losing something good), or when they're not going our way, which also disappoints.

To feel more equanimity, we can apply a healthy sense of detachment via objective observation. This way of treating the process and results as data allows us to stay flexible and enjoy what's actually unfolding, rather than clinging to our expectations going in, which may conflict with reality.

Mindfulness

In our busy, complex lives, it's easy to become distracted by rehashing the past or worrying about the future. But each moment we live is where the action is; it's where we experience the world through our senses, are able to exert our influence, create memories and stories, and discover the unpredictable fruits of our efforts. The vigilant observation that's integral to experimenting is a sustainable way of experiencing each irrecoverably precious moment.

Finally, I'd be remiss if I didn't encourage you to think of this hack itself as an experiment. If you try it, ask yourself if it helps *some* aspect of the way you see the world or interact with it. Don't take my word for it; prove it to yourself.

See Also

- Stewart Friedman, *Total Leadership: Be a Better Leader, Have a Richer Life* (Boston: Harvard Business School Press, 2008). This impressive book thoroughly applies the Think, Try, Learn idea to business, and shows leaders how they can use it to be healthier and more well-rounded people.

- A great starting point for getting to know the self-experimentation community is the *Quantified Self* blog ("Self Knowledge Through Numbers"): http://quantifiedself.com/. You can also visit my blog, *The Experiment-Driven Life*, where I cover Think, Try, Learn, along with Edison stories and experiment ideas.

- A helpful clearinghouse for sites and tools of all types is *The Complete QS Guide to Self Tracking* (http://quantifiedself.com/guide/).

Notes

1. The self-experimentation movement is on fire, and you can choose from many creative tracking tools. They run the gamut from the simple to the sophisticated, though most of them are specific to a domain, such as mood, exercise, sleep, or sex. Edison, the Think, Try, Learn Experimenter's Journal (http://edison.thinktrylearn.com/) is an integrated data- and observation-recording tool, along with a helpful community of motivated self-experimenters. It enables you to create and track your individual experiments, set up group experiments that you can invite fellow experimenters to participate in, and give and receive encouragement and advice using social collaboration features.

2. From Stanford's Entrepreneurship Corner with Tom Kelley of the IDEO design firm: "Young at Heart: How to Be an Innovator for Life": http://ecorner.stanford.edu/authorMaterialInfo.html?mid=2054.

3. Quantified Self founder and *Wired* writer Gary Wolf's seminal *New York Times* article:"The Data-Driven Life," Gary Wolf, www.nytimes.com/2010/05/02/magazine/02self-measurement-t.html?_r=1&pagewanted=all.

4. While I've mostly avoided scientific experimental terminology in this hack, some of it is helpful for self-experimentation. This is a complex topic that is essential for sophisticated scientific studies, but you can find some general characteristics of good experiments at http://answers.yahoo.com/question/index?qid=20090124093953AAPO4zf.

5. Confounding factors are variables that you haven't accounted for but which affect the results of your experiment. For example, in working on improving sleep, you might not realize the impact of recent stressful events. Read more at www.experiment-resources.com/confounding-variables.html.

Hack 55: Take the One-Question IQ Test

Determine how smart you are at a given moment with a test that's not much longer than this sentence.

Although psychologists used to think that the intelligence of a person tends to remain constant and static, it is now widely accepted that intelligence can wax and wane throughout your life.[1]

It can even change in the course of a day. For example, the amount of sleep you get can cause enormous variation in mental performance; just take a long look at yourself on the morning after a long night of partying or studying, when you trip over the cat.

What if there was a quick mental thermometer with which you could take your intellectual temperature, a way that you could tell in a few seconds whether you're shining like a crazy diamond or acting and thinking as dull as a doornail? What if this thermometer could tell whether you were continuing to get duller or more brilliant? You could use this feedback, not to feel smug, or to punish yourself for being dumb, but to maximize your intelligence, so as not to make stupid mistakes.

If you're reading this book, you probably want to be smarter, but even if you don't, you almost certainly don't want to be stupider. Yet, you might be storming around in a momentary rage, breaking crockery and scaring pets and children, temporarily too stupid to notice.

In Action

Philosopher and humorist Robert Anton Wilson gives the following two criteria as a quick perceptual test of intelligence that also indicates in which direction your intelligence level is headed:

- If the world seems to be getting bigger and funnier all the time, your *intelligence* is steadily increasing.
- If the world seems to be getting smaller and nastier all the time, your *stupidity* is steadily increasing.[2]

Simply use the preceding criteria to take your perceptual measure; then, if you're doing something that's making you stupid, such as screaming at fellow drivers cutting you off in traffic, *do something else*. On the other hand, if you're doing something that's making you smarter, *do it more*.

Let us be more specific. What we're about to tell you may seem to be the plainest common sense, but surprisingly few people really seem to believe it: You can change how you *feel* by what you *think* and *do*. We often react to our feelings, letting them influence what we do and believe, but it also works the other way — your feelings react to your thoughts and actions as well.

Thus, if you feel as if the walls are closing in on you (your world is getting smaller and nastier), you can take a semantic pause (Hack 57, "Take a Semantic Pause") and first assess your situation for "basic need emergencies" with the mnemonic HALT: Have you let yourself become too Hungry, Angry, Lonely, or Tired?

- If you're hungry, raise your blood sugar with a sandwich.
- If you're angry, meditate or punch a pillow.
- If you're lonely, phone a good friend.
- If you're tired, take a nap.

If you've addressed your immediate needs and the walls are still closing in, try some cognitive behavioral therapy. If that doesn't work, try whatever seems as though it might plausibly help. Try doing the things that you'd rather be doing if you felt better; just doing them may help you feel better and push back those walls a little. Do something kind or helpful for someone. Be scientific about it; if a tactic you supposed might work doesn't, abandon it and try something else, until you find something that does help (Hack 54, "Think, Try, Learn"). If all else fails and you really don't know what to do, just do or change *something*. Often, any change will jolt you out of a bad state, or at least give you an idea of what might work better by comparison.

NOTE You can learn about meditation and cognitive behavioral therapy from online sources in the "See Also" section below.

If, on the other hand, your world is getting bigger and funnier, you probably don't need much advice. Just be sure to note what you're doing so you can do it again. By noting what you're doing and continuing to check your mental temperature, you can create a feedback loop that will teach you what you need to do to stay happier and smarter more of the time.

How It Works

Although *bigger* is the opposite of *smaller*, *funnier* is not necessarily the opposite of *nastier*, so a feeling that the world is getting bigger and funnier is not clearly the absence or opposite of the feeling that it's getting smaller and nastier. Therefore, let's look at both sides of Wilson's heuristic.

First, the smaller and nastier side. A sensation that "the world seems to be getting smaller and nastier all the time" can be seen as a kind of *anomia*, a social-psychological term meaning a condition "characterized by a breakdown in values," that is, the feeling that nothing really matters, "and a feeling of isolation" as well as "social malintegration" and "interpersonal alienation."[3] In short, anomia is a feeling that life sucks and other people are to blame for it, so you're better off without them (www.sociologyindex.com/anomia.htm).

Research seems to support the idea that anomia and intelligence are negatively correlated — that is, the more intelligent you are, the less anomic you tend to be, and vice versa. In a study titled "Is Ignorance Bliss? A Reconsideration of the Folk Wisdom," political scientist Lee Sigelman found that "intelligence has no independent impact on either happiness or life satisfaction, but that it is a good predictor of anomia . . . even when the effects of all the other variables in the analysis are controlled, more intelligent people tend to be less anomic." In fact, Sigelman found that intelligence was more highly correlated with low anomia than any other variable in his study, including education, health, race, church attendance, political participation, and income.[4] In other words, if we define the feeling of a continually smaller and nastier world that Wilson describes as anomia, then the smaller and nastier that people feel their world to be, the less intelligent they probably are.

The fact that anomia and intelligence are negatively correlated means that you can predict the absence of one by the presence of the other to a significant degree, whatever way causation runs — whether being smart makes you less anomic, or being less anomic makes you smart — and this is enough for our quick-and-dirty "intellectual thermometer." The same is true for the other correlations described in this hack. You're not necessarily changing one variable by changing the other. You're experimentally changing some aspect of your thought or behavior, and then measuring the effect with the thermometer.

Turning to the bigger and funnier side of the question, researchers have been able to show significant correlations between the ability to appreciate humor and other abilities, including visual search, handling abstractions, mental flexibility, and working memory. All of these are important components of intelligence, so it seems that the ability to appreciate the humor in the world around you is also an indicator of intelligence. Further, these abilities seem to be mediated by the right frontal lobe of the brain, which also enables us to "integrate 'extrapersonal space' with the 'internal milieu'"[5] — in other words, make sense of the world, thereby combating anomia. Perhaps a similar mechanism is at work *both* when the world ceases to seem small and nasty and when it starts to seem big and funny, wondrous, and delightful.

In short, who is more likely to intelligently learn from what they encounter: someone who anomically treats every new experience as the "same old same old," or someone who mentally exclaims, with Robert Louis Stevenson, "The world is so full of a number of things, / I'm sure we should all be as happy as kings"? The answer is the basis for our one-question "IQ test."

In Real Life

If you want to try to make your world bigger and funnier very quickly, spend some time perusing Wikipedia's Unusual Articles page: (http://en.wikipedia.org/wiki/Wikipedia:Unusual_articles). The assortment of widely varying subject matter that you've likely never heard about before, combined with Wikipedia's relentless "neutral point of view" policy (http://en.wikipedia.org/wiki/Wikipedia:Neutral_point_of_view), which can transcend the resistance you may have to important new information, will quickly make your head (if not your world) explode in bright colors.

In this case, even the slightly creepy information that might, in a more sensational source, incline you to see the world as bigger and nastier rather than bigger and funnier, such as the articles on the Bloop (http://en.wikipedia.org/wiki/Bloop) and the Hum (http://en.wikipedia.org/wiki/The_Hum), are refreshingly devoid of scare tactics, so you may well find something funny in them too.

See Also

- *Happy to Burn* is an excellent free ebook that can teach you the basics of meditation: www.sankhara.com.au/.

- A free PDF from our previous book, containing the full text of a hack explaining the basics of cognitive behavioral therapy, "Learn Your Emotional ABCs," is available online: http://oreilly.com/catalog/mindperfhks/chapter/hack57.pdf.

Notes

1. M. Howe, "Can IQ Change?," *The Psychologist*, 11 (1998): 69–71.
2. Robert Anton Wilson, "Stupidynamics (John Dillinger Cabal, Position Paper 23)," *The Illuminati Papers* (Berkeley, CA, USA: And/Or Press, 1980).
3. Leo Srole, quoted in Mathieu Deflem, "From Anomie to Anomia and Anomic Depression: A Sociological Critique on the Use of Anomie in Psychiatric Research." *Social Science and Medicine*, 29 (1989): 627-634.
4. Lee Sigelman, "Is Ignorance Bliss? A Reconsideration of the Folk Wisdom." *Human Relations*, 34 (1981): 965-974.
5. P. Shammi and D.T. Stuss. "Humour appreciation: a role of the right frontal lobe." *Brain* 122 (1999): 657–66.

Clarity

Once you've made your mind strong and flexible, added skills and speed, and shaped it into a superb tool, clarity enables you to focus all that power in the right direction. Clarity helps you apply your abilities directly to your chosen task, without dissipating energy in unproductive attitudes.

People whose minds are clouded and distorted by strong emotions such as fear and anger often make mistakes that are dangerous to themselves and others. That's why this chapter focuses on several methods for clearing your head, such as Hack 57, "Take a Semantic Pause."

Sometimes it's not strong emotions that distort our ability to think clearly, but weak ones that persist over a long time, such as coming to think of ourselves as "losers" (Hack 59, "Get Used to Losing"). The hacks in this chapter offer solutions to those problems too. Sometimes the best way to get a clear view is to throw everything you think you know away and start over (Hack 56, "Cultivate Beginner's Mind").

The human race has devised many mind hacks in the quest for a clear and sharply focused brain, from coffee to meditation. We're only offering you a sample; if you discover new ones, we hope you'll write and tell us about them. After all, strengthening the mind is a terrific pursuit, but learning to control and focus it — while extremely rewarding — never ends, and we'll always be looking for new directions.

Hack 56: Cultivate Beginner's Mind

You can learn nothing new about something you think you already understand completely. Learn why you must unlearn everything you know, at least once in a while.

Shoshin is a concept from Zen Buddhism that translates to "beginner's mind." It refers to creating and maintaining the state of mind that a novice to a subject has — open, eager, without preconceptions — even when you approach a subject you know well. Zen teacher Shunryu Suzuki used the phrase in the title of his seminal book *Zen Mind, Beginner's Mind*, which reflects a saying of his regarding the way to approach Zen practice: "In the beginner's mind there are many possibilities; in the expert's mind there are few." Another way the Zen tradition expresses the benefits of beginner's mind is to say that you can't fill a cup that's already full. When your mind is filled with the experiences, opinions, knowledge, and ideas that you already have, there's no room for new ideas to come in.

With beginner's mind, you can approach the fountain of the world with an empty and clean cup, ready to be filled. You can see new possibilities every time you look at something, and old ideas don't affect your views toward different aspects of a situation, or prevent you from seeing new solutions to a problem. The excitement and wonder of staying in the moment and being alert to the new keeps your energy high, your boredom low, and your creativity at its peak.

In Action

Reverting to beginner's mind sounds simple, and essentially it is. It's learning to forget (temporarily, perhaps) whatever you know about an object or situation. In practice, this can be difficult, and it takes a lot of persistence and self-monitoring until you get the hang of it.

Before you take steps, it helps to create a generally positive state of mind. Yvonne Rand, a longtime Zen practitioner, recommends intentionally placing your mouth in a half-smile position, and holding it for the space of three breaths (www.scientificamerican.com/article.cfm?id=smile-it-could-make-you-happier). Frequently, this automatically generates a happier and more positive emotional state; Rand refers to it as "mouth yoga," and it seems to work like hatha yoga and other systems that change mental state by changing body position, but on a smaller scale. Recent scientific research bears this out; several studies have found that the expressions you adopt change your emotions, even when you adopt them consciously and without accompanying emotional stimulus. Your initial reaction may be against "faking a smile," but start practicing beginner's mind right now and try to see it as a neutral step toward your goal! (http://web.psych.ualberta.ca/~varn/bc/Kleinke.htm)

An important part of beginner's mind is "don't-know mind," in which you accept the state of not knowing: not knowing what something is or what it will do, or what you expect of it, which allows you to stay open and responsive. This state can be excruciating for adults, especially Americans. We all want to know what's going on, and exactly what to do — we all want to be the expert in any situation, and we're culturally conditioned to value taking initiative, pushing ahead, being proactive rather than passively waiting to see what happens. However, being the expert has its drawbacks. It can begin to define and restrict you, giving you a position to defend, an opinion that people expect to hear, validation that your experience is important, and so on.

All of these can blind you to new possibilities. If you can let go of the need to be an expert and, instead, rest inside a state of don't-know mind, you're ready to do what needs to be done in the moment, and you're starting from scratch to analyze what's really in front of you, objectively and without the blinders of expectation. You don't waste effort reacting before you know what you're dealing with, and the effort you make is used effectively. Because you don't know what's going to happen next, your situation becomes exciting and suspenseful, suffusing you with enthusiasm and energy.

Letting go of being an expert also means letting go of the fear of failure and appearing absurd. This, too, is crucial to beginner's mind; beginners expect to fail, and don't take it personally when they do. It's all part of the learning process, and they don't let it stop them from striving toward success. Babies don't care how much they amuse us when they're learning to walk. If they acted like adults — worried about looking silly, worried they'll never learn because it's too hard, worried about doing it incorrectly or about hurting their bottoms — nobody would ever learn at all. As a Japanese proverb says, "Fall down seven times, and get up eight times."

Beginner's mind isn't meant to negate the benefits of experience or knowledge. Adopting it doesn't mean that you must continually "reinvent the wheel" in a practical sense. It's simply a way of learning to use what you know in fresh ways and applying it to situations as they really are, rather than as you assume they are. You can go back later and solve the practical problems, but beginner's mind teaches you not to let pre-emptive problem-solving block you from finding good ideas and new angles. Not only can your beliefs obscure real understanding and potential solutions, but you can waste a lot of energy solving problems that you don't have yet. After you find the new ideas, you can tackle the detailed solutions all the better, because you know exactly what needs to be done.

Here are some concrete games and techniques for stimulating the beginner's mind viewpoint:

- Be aware of the language you use. Ask more questions, make fewer statements.

- Pretend you're an alien or an archaeologist: How would you report on your situation? Describe it in the present tense and in the moment. Teach somebody else about it (Hack 9, "Learn By Teaching").

- Note specifically what you know about your situation or object, then ask yourself "what else" repeatedly until you can't add anything to your list. This seems to be dwelling on what you already know, but when you exhaust those things and push yourself to keep looking, you find new things you hadn't noticed before.

- Try to solve a problem incorrectly, or come up with the worst possible solution (Hack 27, "Seek Bad Examples").

- If you're trying to get to know an object, try to approach it in a novel way. Try drawing it. Explore it as a small child would: Put your face on it, or your foot. See if it makes a noise or has a smell. Call it by a different name. Make it into a character and have a conversation with it.

- Find a real child or someone else who doesn't know anything about your problem, and ask them what they would do. Be serious and listen carefully and respectfully to the answer you get.

How It Works

The brain is wired to respond to what's new in its surroundings. This is a survival trait with a lot of evolutionary value, because it constantly makes you aware of, for example, items that could be food, or creatures that could pose a danger. To make way for a constant flow of information about new items and situations, the mind forms mental models, attaching a few attributes to an item or situation — tasty, not mine, frightening, sexy, familiar, stinky, get more, avoid this, and so on — and then files them away. When a model is retrieved from its pigeonhole, you tend to take the mental shorthand as the reality of the object; because it takes effort to add information and re-analyze, we tend to avoid changing what we think we know.

When the "attribute pegs" are filled for a mental model, your attitude becomes like the full cup mentioned earlier in the hack — there's no room left for new ideas. More and more, you forget that your mental image of something isn't the same as the item or situation itself. You forget that it is actually more than you've included in your model, and you probably forget what it really is, what it can do, or how you could potentially use it.

Beginner's mind "resets" the mental models, enabling you to redefine things and see new possibilities for them, from the perspective of your current mental state and the rest of your situation, which may be very different from the state in which you initially formed the model. Also, because the mind is naturally excited by what's new, you can generate and maintain energy and enthusiasm by constantly seeking new information. Because everything has many more aspects than you can initially understand, and even more as its context changes over time, there's always new information to gather.

In Real Life

Marty tries to use beginner's mind as much as she can. It takes vigilance, but she finds it worthwhile. Ron has a little more trouble with it sometimes. One example that's become a favorite family story involves cultivating beginner's eyes. Because Ron enjoys eating cups of yogurt, Marty had bought a batch and stored them in the door of the refrigerator. Within a couple of days, most of them were gobbled up, but a couple languished uneaten. She wondered if the reason was because these particular cups had been stored upside-down. She flipped them over, and sure enough, they disappeared posthaste. Marty realized that Ron had a mental image of the yogurt containers that included a red lid, and he had been looking for that in the refrigerator shelves. In his mind, the red lid was a crucial attribute of the yogurt, so when he didn't see the red lid, the yogurt became "invisible" to him. A moment of beginner's mind to help him see the refrigerator contents without preconceptions about their appearance might have helped him find the treat sooner.

A more substantial way that Ron leverages beginner's mind, however, is that he frequently asks Marty to consult when he's writing a tricky Perl script or a code sample for his technical writing and runs into something that just won't work. Marty is generally technically competent and has had a few classes in computer programming, but she doesn't know Perl and is not an accomplished coder. Nonetheless, the act of showing her the code and the naive questions she asks about it have frequently led Ron to see where he took a wrong turn. Sometimes Marty can see where he's made an incorrect assumption or forgotten a step, and from there he's able to springboard into the right solution.

See Also

- Shunryu Suzuki, *Zen Mind, Beginner's Mind* (New York: Walker/Weatherhill, 1970).
- "Cultivating Beginner's Mind," Yvonne Rand, www.goatintheroad.org/ cultivating.html.
- Alan Watts, *The Way of Zen* (New York: Pantheon, 1957).

Hack 57: Take a Semantic Pause

Jonathan Davis

Some thinkers, such as Malcolm Gladwell, advocate the cultivation of first impressions. This hack advocates the opposite: taking a deep breath, counting to ten, and doing whatever else is needed to make a second or even third evaluation of a situation, so that you can avoid prejudice and hasty decisions.

The semantic (or cognitive) pause is a powerful tool that can enhance critical thinking, mental health, and effective communication. In essence, it is simple: You pause what you are doing so that you can objectively assess your situation and, if needed, reformulate your strategy, attitude, words, impulses, or ideas. The semantic pause is a key defense against coercive persuasion,[1, 2] and a useful skill in activities as diverse as principled negotiation and psychotherapy.[3] Semantic pauses range from taking a deep breath during an argument (to give you time to think and calm down) through to full-life retreats, where individuals pause their daily lives, retreat from their responsibilities, and reflect on their lives.

A variant of the semantic pause — the weekly review — is the central component of David Allen's "Getting Things Done" methodology,[4] whereby gaining control and perspective is achieved by taking a weekly break from life and work to purposefully review and organize one's systems, lists, and horizons of focus (i.e., your goals, areas of responsibility, and active projects).

You can even find the idea in military doctrines on grand strategy, where disrupting the enemy's ability to stop, plan, and think (their "OODA Loop"),[5] while maintaining your own situational awareness and orientation, is considered the key to winning wars.

This hack offers some ways in which you can activate and use this critical tool when you need it most, such as when you need to wake up to reality; when you are in a rut; or when you are angry, aroused, confused, or disoriented. I will show you how you can program cognitive interrupts into your mind, systems, and environment to ensure that when critical thresholds are breached, you are able to signal yourself to snap to attention, take a semantic pause, and summon your rational side to take charge.

How It Works

There are two types of semantic pause: the higher-level *contemplative pause* or review and the lower-level, in-the-moment *tactical pause*.

The contemplative pause, or structured review, is part mnemonic aid and part alarm that wakes us from the slumber of habit and complacency. It helps us to remember important things we may have forgotten, reminds us about standards we are committed to maintaining, and challenges us to truthfully confront the real state of our world. A contemplative pause can give us perspective we may have lost, ground us in values and principles we have allowed to atrophy, and reconnect us to people who give us strength and guidance. Sometimes it merely serves to shock or sting us into action.

The tactical semantic pause, conversely, interrupts negative cycles of behavior by seizing back control of our mind after it has been hijacked by the primitive brain functions of the autonomic system.

The key to how this hack works is the structure of the brain, which is divided into three parts that have progressively evolved over time. The oldest part of the brain is the *reptilian brain*, which controls autonomic functions like breathing and heart rate. We share this brain part with reptiles, hence the name. The second oldest part, the *mammalian brain* or limbic system, controls our emotions. We share this part of the brain with all mammals; in some ways, you and your dog or cat have the same emotions, although you may define and understand them differently. The most recently evolved part of the brain, the *neocortex*, is unique to humans and controls higher functions like consciousness, free will, decision making, and self-control.

These structures result in two cognitive systems and ways of thinking. The autonomic system, or System 1, is powered from the reptilian and mammalian parts of the brain, is primarily unconscious, automatic, and affective, and relies on heuristics or mental "shortcuts." It processes information very quickly and uses pattern-matching rules (heuristics) to make speedy judgments that help us to survive. Reflexive reactions like ducking or jumping out of the way of a car are examples of System 1 in action.

The reflective system, or System 2, is based in the neocortex, primarily the prefrontal cortex. It manages our controlled processes. It is slower, conscious, and rule-based. It is also responsible for inhibition of drives and impulse control.

System 1, then, is connected with your gut reaction, while System 2 is connected with your conscious thought. System 1 is useful, especially in emergencies, but somewhat error-prone. Its heuristics are, after all, just rules of thumb. System 2 monitors System 1 and corrects or overrides its bias-laced automatic judgments and decisions. You can flinch at what you think is a spider (System 1's immediate reaction), but seconds later realize with embarrassment that it's just a bottle top (System 2 correcting the bias-based judgment).

The problem is that System 1 can inhibit and even paralyze System 2 under certain circumstances, such as when we are under stress. Its heuristics are not corrected, biases become embedded, and we can lose control of our drives and impulses, leading to poor choices with deleterious consequences. Much of the magic of the semantic pause is that is restores primary control of your mind to System 2 (the reflective system) when System 1 (the autonomic system) has seized control. The semantic pause is designed to short-circuit System 1 so that System 2 can take over again. This applies both to when we have lost control in the moment and to when we are operating from faulty heuristics, coasting along mindlessly, accepting our status or environment, unaware of our biases and bigotries.

In Action

This principle of interrupting yourself to force awareness into a situation and calmly assess options serves us in two ways:

- It can *wake us up* when routine, complacency, and our tendency to overuse heuristics leads us to operate in a mindless or forgetful state — when we are sleepwalking through life, blind to opportunities and threats, or when we are taking too much for granted and have become complacent.

- It can *calm and clarify* us when we are under stress, being deliberately manipulated, or victims of our inherent human biases and cognitive blind spots.

In other words, you need to be able to *recognize the need for semantic pause, force a semantic pause*, and *use a semantic pause effectively*.

The keys to this hack are being able to focus attention on yourself when needed (trigger self-awareness); being able to recognize what's happening to you (observe and orient); and having the mental tools at hand to get out of the negative state and regain control of yourself (act on rational choices).

How to Recognize the Need for a Semantic Pause

How do you "snap out of it"? How do you remember to "count to ten" when System 1 is ordering your body to fight to the death? Where do you find a reservoir of calmness and wisdom when you are utterly confused? How do you force yourself to remember what (and who) is important in your life when you have lost perspective or are "too busy" to care?

The answer lies in three linked practices: *prevention, preparation,* and *planned pauses.*

Prevention

The best scenario is not to need a semantic pause at all, but to avoid letting matters get so out of control that you need one. The trick is to escape tempting situations or break behavior cycles while you still have full control.

After passions or appetites are aroused, it becomes much more difficult to control yourself and act in your own best interests. If you know from experience that certain situations inevitably lead to undesirable outcomes, try to prevent the outcomes by breaking or disrupting the predictable negative cycles of interaction *before* they arise again.

Do you argue with your parents after too much wine at dinner? Decide before you have dinner with your parents to break the cycle by not drinking or avoiding contentious topics. Do you impulse-buy at certain stores? Separate the process of choosing from actually buying by leaving your wallet at home when you go to that store, and return the following day to make your purchase. In short, learn *metabehavior* — changing your behavior with your behavior (Hack 52, "Metabehave Yourself").

Take the time to discover your own emotional triggers or "hot buttons." Avoid people, subjects, or situations that activate them. A good example is the old rule found in pubs in Ireland: Never discuss religion or politics.

Wherever possible, structure cooling-off periods during which you can reverse your decisions easily and without penalty. For example, instead of trying to force yourself to hold off on sending an angry e-mail, set your mail client to only send messages after a 30-minute delay, so you have a chance to cancel it after you have calmed down.[6] Instead of trying desperately to *not* drunkenly call your ex-girlfriend to tell her you still love her, simply delete her number from your phone before you go out drinking, or use a service that temporarily bars you from calling certain numbers.[7]

Preparation

If you cannot avoid certain situations completely — for example, if you have an abusive boss or your job involves periodic high-pressure situations — you can prepare for them by practicing and training yourself to automatically trigger semantic pauses when you need them.

The emergency services have something to teach us in this area. They have perfected the art of handling the sudden high-stress situations that they expect to encounter in their jobs. Bitter experience has taught them that the best defense against dysfunction under stress is relentless practice to develop automatic lifesaving responses. Training drills, practice runs, and live fire simulations are all designed to ingrain these responses by training the autonomic system to respond rationally and save lives.

The Department of Justice, responsible for the welfare of America's police men and women, consider preparation in the form of realistic training to be a vital factor to officer survival in violent confrontations with criminals.

> *"Training often determines which persons survive and which ones suffer injury or death. Training that is realistic, repetitive, understandable, and believable potentially reduces the nonadaptive effects of evolution.* In preparing for a highly-charged emotional event, effective and realistic training can reduce its intensity (levels of arousal), allowing higher cognitive functioning to prevail."[8] *[Emphasis mine]*

If you are able to anticipate a situation in which you could benefit from a semantic pause, then you can prepare for that situation by training yourself to react in an optimal manner.

Here is a simple but effective way to train yourself to handle anticipated situations with thought experiments and visualization:

1. Identify your trigger. Your trigger is something tangible that you can recognize as signaling the need for a semantic pause. It could be someone else's behaviors, like shouting or sarcasm, or it could be a physiological sensation such as excessive blinking, rapid heartbeat, or a dry mouth. Your trigger will serve to alert you to the fact that you are in a bad situation, possibly in a psychologically suboptimal state, and that you should trigger a semantic pause immediately.

2. Decide *beforehand* exactly what your response will be if you are triggered. Write down your response as a *policy* — for example, "If anyone shouts at me on the phone (trigger), I will end the call immediately (semantic pause) and report the incident to my human resources representative (rational response)."

3. Keep your policy highly visible. You could stick it on your computer monitor, so that you can refer to it quickly if necessary.

4. Repeatedly imagine yourself responding to your trigger in the best possible way. In the preceding example, you might visualize yourself calmly putting down the phone, taking a deep breath, and calling human resources. Try not to fantasize about stinging put-downs or violence against your tormentor. Focus on what concrete actions you will take in the situation. Run a movie in your head of the situation. Try to be as detailed as possible, and include how you would like to feel — perhaps calm, confident, even slightly amused.

5. When someone triggers you in reality, it should activate your pre-decided response: If someone shouts at you on the phone, you should hang up calmly and call human resources. You may find it helpful, at first, to refer to the policy, but eventually it will become ingrained as an automatic response, an unconscious habit triggered automatically by unacceptable behavior.

You can program dozens of these policies into yourself. They are, after all, innate. We all have boundaries, principles, and standards — mental territory we defend as fiercely as our physical territory. Triggering a semantic pause is just a way to do so rationally and with maximum effect.

Planned Pauses (or Structured Review)

The best way to recognize the need for a semantic pause, and to set in motion the process for triggering one, is to deliberately plan for routine structured reviews of your day, week, projects, goals, responsibilities, relationships, or even your whole life. In this context, "structured" means that you conduct your review using checklists and key questions to ensure that you bring your full attention to all the areas of your life requiring it.

Additionally, when going into meetings, negotiations, or stressful situations, you can use pattern-interrupt alarms on yourself and schedule deliberate pauses.

To do this, you could add an agenda item like "Take a pause," or write a note to yourself on your meeting agenda, asking "Are you comfortable and in control?"

These checkpoints and planned contemplative pauses help you keep an eye out for "warning signs." At a tactical level, they can alert you that a meeting or discussion has gone off-track or that a situation is beginning to unravel. At a higher level, they can help you to ensure that key relationships and areas of responsibility are not being neglected.

How to Force a Semantic Pause

While these contemplative pauses and weekly reviews are vital for maintaining control and perspective in your life, sometimes merely becoming aware of a problem is not enough. The key benefit of semantic pauses is to be found at a tactical level: in a high-stakes crucial conversation with a colleague or partner; during a fraught negotiation or heated argument; when pressured to make a decision; or when in the grip of panic, rage, or confusion.

Many people do indeed become self-aware ("Wow, I'm sweating!") and recognize that they need a pause, but they cannot break out of the arousal state or think clearly enough to respond in a reasonable way. This is because when we experience stress (such as through frustration or conflict), our cognitive abilities are severely impaired — System 1 has taken over, often to our detriment.

To release your brain from its grip, you need to short-circuit System 1. The objective is to regain enough self-control and presence of mind to use a semantic pause properly and quickly return to a state of equilibrium, clarity, and positive focus. One of the most effective ways to regain control from System 1 is to trick it into believing all is well. One way to do that is to deliberately slow your breathing and, oddly enough, your blinking. Controlling your breathing and blinking has an immediate calming effect, which allows you to get a thin "wedge of consciousness" into your brain and spark the semantic pause.

The original article on the wedge is "The Wedge of Consciousness: A Self-Monitoring Device" by Milton Dawes (`http://miltondawes.com/formal-essays-handouts/the-wedge-of-consciousness-a-self-monitoring-device/`).

How to Use a Semantic Pause

Now that you have established a beachhead of sanity and clear thinking in your brain, you need use your semantic pause to reassert complete self-control over yourself and your situation. One of the best ways to do this is to guide your thinking and behavior with prepared material in the form of checklists (Hack 1, "Remember to Remember"), plans, scripts, key questions, and mantras that you can bring to mind to ground and calm yourself.

When astronauts encounter technical difficulties, it usually comes in the form of blinking lights — red lights come on, orange lights flash, or green lights fail to come on. After the astronauts have eliminated the possibility of false alarm, they do not bicker amongst themselves or debate with Mission Control; they crack out the procedure manual and run through the procedure or checklist for that activating event. In the same way, you can create a "procedure manual" for yourself, with situations you might find yourself in and prepared procedures or checklists to guide your thoughts and actions during your semantic pause.

If you don't have such a checklist or procedure to follow, you can still ground yourself with positive rules of thumb, usually expressed as a short mantra or power phrase. The word "mantra" means "mind tool" or "that which protects our mind." They can be extremely useful for reminding us of wise beliefs or principles at times when we are tested.

In *Time Management for System Administrators*, Thomas A. Limoncelli writes:

> *Rules of thumb are like habits that don't happen regularly. They are ways to mentally record responses that are generally good for particular situations. When I activate a rule of thumb, I have a mantra that goes along with it. For small tasks I am likely to procrastinate on, my mantra is:* Sooner is better than later.[9]

Your mantras can be truisms, aphorisms, technical proverbs, or a simple reminder not to take it all too seriously. Use whatever it takes to recapture perspective and act. (See Hack 31, "Mine the Future" for the similar concept of the *outlook*.)

In Real Life

Perhaps the most salient use of the semantic pause hack for me is my weekly review, part of the Getting Things Done methodology. Once a week, usually on a Sunday evening, I spend an hour or two reviewing my complete inventory of projects, activities, and areas of responsibility.

First, I *get clear* by processing notes, clearing inboxes, and using checklists to remind me of areas that may need my attention or things I might need to do. The key is to get items out of my head and into a trusted system.

Next, I *get current* by reviewing all of my projects, roles, calendars, and other lists (such as key people or areas of responsibility). Here I am taking stock, clearing out the obsolete information, and forcing myself to think in a structured way about each element. The focus is on resisting inertia, on keeping things moving, the key question usually being "What is the next action?"

Finally, when I have captured all my commitments and tasks on my lists, clarified them using structured thinking, and organized them into concrete next-actions, I can *get creative*. With the peace of mind that results from getting on top of my commitments, I can then think about all the hare-brained ideas I have, daydream, and generally let creative juices flow. This is not something that I do, exactly; rather, it's the state I get to when I have captured, clarified, organized, and reflected upon everything that has my attention and for which I'm responsible.

At work, we use semantic pauses of both types all the time. I have one-on-one meetings with my direct reports once a week to ensure they are OK, clear, and engaged. My team and I also meet regularly and voluntarily, usually not during work time, just to take stock and reset our counters. Since we operate in a high-pressure technical operations environment, it's vital for us to maintain perspective on our full portfolio of responsibilities, and not fall into the trap of responding only to the latest and loudest problems. Our Operations diary (group tickler file) contains randomly timed instructions and questions that challenge us to pause and review our commitments, principles, and goals.

We have also learned the value of preparation, especially in the domains of change control and business continuity. My team and I have frequently been saved by our foresight in creating prepared plans and detailed procedures to guide our thinking if we find ourselves in pressure situations. When klaxons are sounding, phones are beeping, managers are shouting, and customers are screaming, the last thing you want to do is try to work out a troubleshooting process, or make a decision about how long you should keep trying to fix something before rolling the system back. It's best to do your crisis thinking before the crisis, but if you didn't, take a semantic pause immediately. Let the phones and e-mail hold their messages, silence the alarms, calm yourself (and everyone else), and then focus on the problem at hand, develop a strategy, and act on it.

In my personal life, I have several "circuit breakers" that can be used by myself or others to help me get a grip when necessary. For example, my wife and I have an agreed-on safety phrase — in Danish — that we use when we are in public or traveling, so that we can tactfully veto each other's decisions without argument or embarrassment, especially when we are under pressure or in situations of danger or recklessness. We've agreed that we can discuss the matter at home later, but we need to be able to signal that a situation is deadly serious and have the other partner comply immediately. This relies on both parties having complete trust in each other and never abusing their powers of veto, but it can save time and trouble, and possibly life and limb, if one of us is out of control.

To help me execute semantic pauses, I sometimes use keyboard shortcuts to load text files with my mantras, checklists, and self-admonitions. When I'm in pressure situations — arguing, negotiating, or dealing with angry customers, for example — I can type "row" (which is British English for "an angry dispute or fight") into Mozilla Firefox to load a simple text file with reminders to myself about how to handle these situations. You could as easily do this with any program launcher, like Quicksilver (Mac), Launchy (Windows), or GNOME Do (Linux), as well.

Usually my text file contains key questions or mantras, like "Why would a kind, reasonable, intelligent, and well-meaning person say, think, or do this?" (See Hack 49, "Mediate Your Environment.") It lists the Harvard Negotiation Project's five core concerns: Affiliation, Appreciation, Status, Autonomy, Role (the ultimate checklist for dealing with emotional negotiation).[10] It also lists the STATE process from *Crucial Conversations*:

- Share your facts.
- Tell your story.
- Ask for others' paths (What).
- Talk tentatively.
- Encourage testing (How).[11]

I also have similar files and shortcuts for my staff, co-workers, boss, and important clients. Those files include their DISC types (http://en.wikipedia.org/wiki/ DISC_assessment), personal information, salient events, current activities and projects, and any other information that is relevant to dealing with that person. A former boss of mine, for example, can come across as rude and domineering even though he is a thoughtful and kind person. He cannot stand extraneous small talk before business matters are handled. He wants BLUF (Bottom Line Up Front). Whenever I had a meeting or call with him, or when I felt an argument brewing with him, I would pause to bring up my file to remind myself how to get the best out of our encounters. People could not understand why I was the only person who was "spared" his wrath. The truth is that because I had done some basic preparation and used a semantic pause, I seldom triggered his wrath, and on the rare occasions I did, I managed the conflict professionally.

The key to this hack, for me, lies in the Latin proverb *Festina lente* ("Hurry slowly"). It means that, regardless of the circumstances, it's beneficial to do things the proper way instead of hurriedly and heedlessly: See urgent things through, but in a thorough manner. It is a beautifully succinct call to temper hotheadedness and the tendency to be sloppy and error-prone when hurried or stressed. I find it extremely useful to call this to mind when I am being rushed or allowing circumstances to get the better of me. So when I feel out of control or find myself in a funk, being buffeted by overpowering emotions and situations, I merely say "Festina lente" to myself to automatically trigger a semantic pause: I stop, reset, and proceed mindfully. This injects equilibrium, clarity, focus, perspective, and engagement back into any situation and works for me every time I use it, even in circumstances of extreme pressure.

So try taking a semantic pause when you think things may be heading out of control. Your semantic pause skills will evolve naturally with regular practice, but it's easy to get started: just stop and breathe.

See Also

- "Fight, Flight or Freeze — Understanding and training within the sympathetic nervous system," Kevin Davis, www.officer.com/web/online/Operations-and-Tactics/Fight−Flight-or-Freeze/3$34515.

- " 'Fight, Flight, or Freeze' Reactions, Ongoing Stress and Health," Darling G. Villena-Mata, Ph.D., C.H.T., www.brooksidecenter.com/fight_flight_or_freeze.htm.

- "Does 'Fight or Flight' Need Updating?" H. Stefan Bracha, M.D. et al., http://psy.psychiatryonline.org/cgi/content/full/45/5/448.

- "Blinking — Control It or Show Your Worst," H. Bernard Wechsler, http://ezinearticles.com/?Blinking---Control-It-Or-Show-Your-Worst&id=204865.

- Richard H. Thaler and Cass R. Sunstein, *Nudge*: *Improving Decisions About Health, Wealth, and Happiness* (New Haven: Yale University Press, 2008).

- Nance Guilmartin, *The Power of Pause*: *How to be More Effective in a Demanding, 24/7 World* (San Francisco, CA, USA: Jossey-Bass, 2010).

Notes

1. Kathleen E. Taylor, *Brainwashing*: *The Science of Thought Control* (Oxford: Oxford University Press, 2004). See particularly her "Stop and Think" advice.

2. Robert B. Cialdini, *Influence*: *The Psychology of Persuasion* (New York: Collins, 2007). See particularly the "Click, whirr" response.

3. See Rational Emotive Behaviour Therapy, specifically the APET Model modification, http://www.wiltshirehumangivens.org/human_givens/apet.html.

4. David Allen, *Getting Things Done* (New York: Penguin, 2003).

5. The OODA Loop (for Observe, Orient, Decide and Act) is a concept applied to the combat operations process, often at the strategic level in both the military and commercial operations. It was created by military strategist and U.S. Air Force Colonel John Boyd.

6. Gmail has introduced a feature called "Undo Send" that gives you a short time — five or ten seconds — to undo sending e-mail. You can enable it via the Google Labs icon.

7. There is a wonderful service in Australia that allows you to bar yourself from using certain numbers during a specified period. It is designed to prevent you from "drunk dialing." See `http://www.virginmobile.com.`
`au/why-choose-us/fun-stuff/dialling-under-the-influence/`.

8. Anthony J. Pinizzotto, Ph.D. et al., *Violent Encounters: A Study of Felonious Assaults on Our Nation's Law Enforcement Officers* (report, U.S. Dept. of Justice, 2006).

9. Thomas A. Limoncelli, *Time Management for System Administrators* (Sebastopol, CA, USA: O'Reilly Media, 2006).

10. The mission of the Harvard Negotiation Project (HNP) is to improve the theory and practice of conflict resolution and negotiation by working on real world conflict intervention, theory building, education and training, and writing and disseminating new ideas. See `www.pon.harvard.edu/`
`category/research_projects/harvard-negotiation-project/`.

11. Kerry Paterson et al, *Crucial Conversations: Tools for Talking When Stakes Are High* (New York: McGraw-Hill, 2002).

Hack 58: Retreat and Reboot

Every once in a while, during a creative project, a relationship, or a lifetime, it's helpful to withdraw from the world and collect yourself, or start your project anew.

Both retreating and rebooting can be powerful tools for successful work. *Retreating* means withdrawing strategically from distraction to focus on creative work, such as writing a novel, composing a song, or solving a math problem. *Rebooting* means starting over, clearing your mind and stopping all the "programs" that have stuck or crashed and are slowing it down.

In many ways, rebooting is the opposite of retreating, because most creative retreats are about focusing on your work rather than clearing your mind. On the other hand, you can often use a more traditional retreat from the world to reboot and return to your work refreshed. The two generally work together in some combination, regardless of the direction from which you approach them.

In Action

There are many ways to creatively retreat, reboot, or both. The following sections describe a few.

Working Retreat

A working retreat is one in which you retire from ordinary activities to concentrate on your work. It can be useful to physically remove yourself from your usual environment, but you can retreat without doing so, if that's not convenient or comfortable. The important thing is to remove your distractions so that the work is all that's left.

Optimally, you should bring nothing else to your retreat to occupy your mind; your work should be your only focus. For example, if you have to write a paper, writing it longhand can help remove a lot of distraction associated with working on a computer (Hack 30, "Salvage a Vintage Hack"). If you must work on a computer, turn off Internet access so that you can only use local word processors and text editors. If you must access the web for research, either do the research ahead of time and bring your notes, or save the web pages you need either on paper or as files. (Ubuntu and Mac OS already have the ability to print to PDF, and it can be added to Windows easily enough.) You may also be able to use something like parental controls or a piece of JavaScript to limit the websites you can access.

If there's a TV or radio where you're working, turn it off, unplug it, and stick it in the closet. Turn off your phone and put a Do Not Disturb sign on your door. Try to approximate the cell of a medieval monk: just you, four walls, something to sit on, and your work. Four bare walls are boring, and soon you'll find that even the work you've dreaded and postponed is more entertaining than they are, so you'll probably get to work. The moment that that happens, this hack is in action.

Sleep on It

Studies have shown that when you're stumped by a difficult problem, rebooting by sleeping on the problem often produces better and more creative results than continuing to bash at it mindlessly (www.newscientist.com/article/dn8732). The function of sleep is still not fully understood, but some researchers believe that during sleep, especially REM or dream sleep, the brain processes "loose ends" left over from the waking day. Psychologists call this *memory consolidation*. A productivity expert might call it "closing open loops"; a computer scientist might call it "garbage collection."

Of course, if you're exhausted, you probably can't think clearly whether you need to reboot or not, so you might as well try getting some sleep to help remove that obstacle. However, it's sometimes possible to reboot by simply napping; although the "reboot effect" is most pronounced after REM sleep, it's best to nap for at least 90 minutes to get one or more REM periods in.

Sleeping on a problem may give you a more direct result than you expect. Studies at Harvard Medical School have shown that it's possible to "incubate" solutions to problems by concentrating on the problems before going to sleep. In one Harvard study, a third of the participants had dreams that actually solved their problems in a novel way, according to both the participants and outside observers (www.asdreams.org/journal/articles/barrett3-2.htm). Dream incubation, or something like it, has been practiced in cultures as diverse as ancient Greece and modern Islam, where it is known as *istikhara*.

Meditation

Meditation is a technique that is deliberately used to clear one's mind, refresh oneself, and renew one's focus. Research has shown that meditation may even decrease your need for sleep (www.biomedcentral.com/content/pdf/ 1744-9081-6-47.pdf). It's like a micro-retreat. Ron is particularly devoted to using meditation as a tool to increase his clarity; when his mind is full of worrisome garbage, he has often found that 20 minutes of following his breath can give him the detachment he needs to reboot.

There are many sources of instruction about meditation. You can learn from teachers, books, or many freely available sources online, such as the Mentat Wiki (www.ludism.org/mentat/MediTation).

Recreation

Recreation comes from the roots *create*, "to make" and *re*, "again or anew" — that is, to repair or make like new. You might think that playing games is a waste of time when you have something to get done, and sometimes it is. However, if you're trying to reboot, a little fun can provide some relaxation while keeping your mind engaged and active, and can give you some shifts in perspective and a different train of thought than the one you had been working on. These can all contribute to increased creativity and productivity when you return to your work. The combination of changing activities and "keeping the motor running" in your mind with the shot of relaxation can be more powerful than either simply switching tasks or taking a complete rest break. Thus, the next time you're creatively blocked, you might try a game of Risk or going to a movie.

Switch and Combine Modes

You may find you can solve problems better if you mix your modalities a little so that you use different parts of your brain together or alternately. For example, combine modes by talking to yourself or teaching someone else while you're trying to repair something (Hack 9, "Learn by Teaching"). Draw pictures and diagrams when you're stumped about writing. This engages both the verbal and nonverbal parts of your brain, so that you're effectively multi-tasking inside your own head.

You can also switch modes, so that you can do more in a particular stretch of time. Do some physical work at the end of a day at school or office as a "palate cleanser," so that the analytical part of your mind can take a rest while the kinetic part takes over and gets its chores done in turn. There's truth in the proverb "A change is as good as a rest"; in fact, athletes often cross-train rather than take time off because "detraining" can cause them to lose muscle tone. Thus, a change may be *better than* a rest in certain situations (www.pponline.co.uk/encyc/detraining-1113). You can use a similar strategy to good effect with your brain.

Exercise

Aside from helping you mentally cross-train, exercise has its own specific merits. It can help make you a better thinker by tuning your physical brain chemistry, such as elevating your mood and your oxygen intake. It often involves taking yourself out of your normal environment to a special place such as a park or gym, and giving your mind little to focus on except your ideas, so it can be an excellent mini-retreat. If you work more with your head than your hands, exercise can be a valuable way to reboot by switching hemispheres, and it can also be a way to reboot through recreation if you enjoy exercise or sports. Of course, if you work more with your hands than your head, "exercise" might mean mental exertion, such as a game of chess, Sudoku, or a session with a challenging book.

Reboot by Retreating

You can also reboot by going on retreat — but not a working retreat, the kind described earlier. Instead, go on a more traditional retreat, such as a meditation retreat. Many monasteries will even rent you a room for your own personal retreat, which need not intersect with the other inhabitants of the monastery except at mealtimes.

Alternatively, take a room at a resort motel during the off season, or even the dead of winter. It will be cheap, you'll be waited on assiduously, and most important, it will be quiet. You'll be able to sleep, meditate, play board games, and go running all you like, thereby achieving many ways to reboot simultaneously. Essentially, this is a retreat where the project you're focusing on is rebooting; use the same intense concentration on the problem of resting and repairing your mind that you'd use on any other project.

How It Works

Total sensory deprivation, as in a flotation tank, eventually causes the human brain to hallucinate. Mild, partial sensory deprivation during a retreat seems to lead to a similar but less overwhelming flow of thoughts about the material you've brought into your isolation, often in the form of creativity and productivity.

You're always putting out energy, work, and attention, but usually it's dissipated in details and switching among different tasks, so when you retreat to focus everything on one task, you have a lot of resources to use. It's the difference between a sprinkler and a water jet.

Knowing that you're on a purely voluntary retreat can also have the effect of renewing your commitment to your project. After all, if you can leave at any time but you don't, you may conclude you actually like, or even love, what you're doing, and return to your usual work environment with renewed purpose. By committing your time and money to your project in the form of retreat, you prove its worth to yourself, too. Retreating to focus on a project in its purest form may also reconnect you with what you like about it, helping you to dissolve any frustration attached to your work.

Thus, if you're stuck on a problem and metaphorically beating your head against the wall in frustration and rage, it should help to get out of the frustrated, angry state by sleeping on the problem, by meditation, by distraction, or by some other means listed earlier. You're likely to forget most of the stale, broken approaches you were taking, and a fresh approach will have room to emerge. Even in less intense situations, relaxing removes emotional static that interferes with thinking, and permits solutions to bubble up from non-conscious parts of the brain that may be working on the problem. In a way, you'll have renewed your beginner's mind (Hack 56, "Cultivate Beginner's Mind").

Similarly, Kay Redfield Jamison, a psychiatrist who has written on bipolar disorder, and is herself bipolar, said "I write when I'm manic and edit when I'm depressed."[1] If you write when you're in a good mood, you'll be at your most creative, but you may produce some purple prose. If you revise your writing when you're in a bad mood, you'll be inclined to cut the worst of your excesses.

In Real Life

Early in the process of writing this book, Ron took 10 days off from his day job to write as much as he could, and, along with some contributors, wrote first drafts of 20 hacks, or about a third of the book. Marty was on a trip, so for most of the time, all Ron had to do was take care of our two dogs, eat, sleep, and write. We live in a quiet suburb, so the atmosphere was calm and conducive to writing.

This was a productive period for Ron, and when he returned to his day job, he learned to turn lunch hours into micro-retreats by bringing nothing with him to the cafeteria but some notes and a few sheets of blank paper. Not eating lunch with his coworkers didn't make Ron popular, but writing is a solitary activity. One of his coworkers, however, was a moderately well-known writer. When asked how he managed to stay productive with a demanding day job, he told Ron (ironically, as Ron would have liked to know him better) that one of his main methods was to cut off all social contact during a project.

Douglas Adams said, "I love deadlines. I love the whooshing noise they make as they go by." Perhaps as a consequence, he was locked in a hotel room by his publishers to finish writing novels on no less than two occasions.[2] Even Adams admitted that the books he produced this way (*So Long, and Thanks for All the Fish* and *Mostly Harmless*) are not among his best work, but they are still in print today, more than 25 years later.

The important thing to remember about this hack is that it works on a variety of scales. From turning off your phone and closing the door for a few minutes, to donning a robe and spending the rest of your life getting cozy with the scripture of your choice, the basic principle of eliminating distractions can help you focus on what is important to you like a scanning tunneling microscope.

Notes

1. Peter D. Kramer, *Against Depression* (New York: Viking, 2005).
2. M.J. Simpson, *Hitchhiker: A Biography of Douglas Adams* (Boston: Justin, Charles & Co., 2003).

Hack 59: Get Used to Losing

Most of us lose most of the time, but that doesn't make us "losers." Adjust your thinking about competition to gain more, even when you don't win.

Many of us are taught from childhood to adopt a life strategy that focuses on "winning" at all costs. This is especially true of Americans, although it extends to many cultures. However, focusing on winning can often be costly in the long run. In reality, you may gain more if you focus on understanding what winning really means in a larger sense.

How It Works

Despite folk wisdom, winning is not simply a matter of "wanting it enough." Factually, you *will* lose most of the time. In almost any situation for which the idea of winning is meaningful, there will only be one "winner." Everyone else involved will lose, even if their skills are evenly matched. Those who lose will always outnumber those who win in any situation with more than two players. This is so obvious that it almost doesn't bear discussing, yet we continue to repeat to each other and ourselves that if we don't win, it's a matter of personal failure and we are "losers."

However, not being the winner is not the same as being a loser. If you think of situations only in absolute terms, only in terms of whether you win or lose, you can potentially lose many benefits you would have had otherwise:

- You may commit more to the effort of winning than you should.
- You may devalue the benefits you would gain in the course of the effort.
- You may lose the benefits, such as cooperation and learning, that you could have gained from the other people whom you have cast as your competitors, rivals, and enemies.
- Defining yourself as a "loser" may affect your self-confidence and reduce your ability to achieve your goals.

In Action

Expect to lose. Suppose you go to a job interview. You find out there are four other interviewees. You have to assume everybody else is approximately as smart, skilled, and qualified as you are, because you were all chosen by the same person to interview for the same position. That means that on the face of it, you have only one chance in five, or 20%, of getting the job. Only one person can get the job this time; everyone else will lose.

Understanding that you will always lose more than you win, and that this is completely normal and OK, is one step toward breaking down the limits that result from focusing too much on a win/lose dichotomy. Winning feels great, but it's not the only thing that matters.

In almost every situation — even situations overtly defined as competitions — there are benefits you can gain if you don't win. You can recognize them, and change your actions so that you increase them, by determining what's really important and what's broadly available to gain.

One way to do this is to perform a cost-benefit analysis. Every victory has its cost. Is winning at whatever you're doing going to cost you more than you're likely to get out of it? If getting that startup job you want means behaving unethically toward the other candidates, and you learn the "prize" consists of vicious superiors, 60-hour workweeks, and hypertension, maybe you should take a fall in this match, champ.

When you know what the competition costs — that is, what you stand to gain or lose by winning or not — you can "change the victory condition," a gaming term that means determining for yourself what "winning" represents for *you*. You can then let go of winning in the technical sense, and win in your own way.

For example, consider a sales competition at your job, where you sell an average of 10 solid-unaffordium macguffins a week. During the week of the competition, you sell 35 macguffins, but your colleague sells 38. You have lost the competition by a frustratingly small margin and you won't get the prize. However, you've also increased your sales for that week by 250% and gained a large bonus in commissions, and you've probably made some new contacts and developed some new macguffin sales strategies. You may even have surprised yourself, never having thought you could sell so much. The confidence, the commission bonus, the contacts, and the sales skills are all "prizes" you won in the competition, even though you technically lost. They will probably keep benefiting you long afterward, too. If you were only focusing on being the technical victor, though, you might not have realized or used what you actually "won".

Concentrating on winning competitions separates you from the other people involved, because it makes you define them as opponents. This can prevent you from interacting with them positively, or at all. However, they often have much in common with you, or they wouldn't be involved in the same competition. Learning to see such people as like-minded opens you to learning from them and cooperating with them in similar, less-competitive situations. Maybe the winner of the sales competition didn't know you before, but was impressed with your performance. If you don't see each other as enemies, you can potentially share strategies, work together on difficult sales, goad and encourage each other to higher achievements, and generally use each other as resources and allies, or at least the esteemed opposition. This is the essence of good sportsmanship, a value that has grown a bit neglected in modern times, but one that is well worth dusting the sticky cobwebs off and polishing up.

The attitude we're promoting here goes further back than "sportsmanship," however; it goes at least as far back as the ancient Stoics. William Irvine, in his introduction to Stoic ethics, *A Guide to the Good Life*, puts it admirably:

> [A Stoic] will be careful to set internal *rather than* external goals. Thus, his goal in playing tennis will not be to win a match (something external, over which he has only partial control) but to play to the best of his ability in the match (something internal, over which he has complete control). By choosing this goal, he will spare himself frustration or disappointment should he lose the match: Since it was not his goal to win the match, he will not have failed to attain his goal, as long as he played his best. His tranquility will not be disrupted.
>
> . . . playing to the best of your ability in a tennis match and winning that match are causally connected. In particular, what better way is there to win a tennis match than by playing to the best of your ability? . . . If we consciously set winning a

tennis match as our goal, we arguably don't increase our chances of winning that match. In fact, we might even hurt our chances: If it starts looking, early on, as though we are going to lose the match, we might become flustered, and this might negatively affect our playing in the remainder of the game. . .[1]

Irvine goes on to discuss how this Stoic model can be applied to other areas of life. For example, he suggests that rather than try to make your beloved love you, just be as lovable as you can. It's telling that people unlucky in love are often cruelly called "losers"; the "winner take all" ethic is everywhere in our culture.

If you don't win anything else by adopting these goals and attitudes, however, you can gain self-respect from approaching competition this way. You can be glad you exercised rationality over emotional reaction to a battle. You can push yourself to always give your best effort and improve on your previous performance. You can learn all you can about how to handle the situation better next time. These are all skills you can use throughout your life, long after you have quit the job, forgotten the score of the game, or broken up with your love interest anyway.

In Real Life

As we've mentioned elsewhere, we belong to a long-standing board game group. Over the years, this experience has changed Marty's approach to gaming and competition profoundly. When the group started, she was a *very* competitive gamer, and because she's a smart, skilled player of many games, she expected to win a lot of the time. However, several other members of the group are as good as she is, or better — at least at certain types of game. She quickly realized that she had two options: Give up gaming with these friends every week or learn how to lose. Instead of giving up the group, she decided to reevaluate the win condition and keep her eyes on the redefined prize.

We have both learned that in many games (San Marco comes to mind, if you're a Eurogame fan), an overall win comes from many small second-places. In life, an impressive heap of your best work may be worth more than someone else's one big "win," which might be a fluke anyway (Hack 35, "Ratchet").

Furthermore, you don't get better at games by repeatedly playing opponents who are weaker than you so you can improve your chance of "winning." That's just bullying. If you want to scale the skill ladder of a game and get really good, play people who are better than you. If you're 12, don't play checkers with your three-year-old sister; play with Grandpa. You will lose, and lose, and lose again, but one day you will win. Beating your three-year-old sister is nothing, but beating Grandpa? *There's* glory for you.

While Marty still enjoys winning, she's become much more appreciative of what she gains by playing, whether she wins or not: better skills, the satisfaction of playing the best game she can, the respect of her fellow players for doing well even without the win, and (not least) a lot of fun with people she enjoys spending time with. She has even gained some true friends. While she may go for weeks at a time without a technical victory, she considers her time with the group to be a huge win, and the ability to extend the skill of evaluating win conditions and keep her focus on what's really important in any competition is priceless.

This principle also came into play recently when Marty and her sister entered a cupcake-baking competition. The two of them entered the competition in hopes of winning a large cash prize, which would help them launch their cake business. While they didn't win the cash — nor did they expect to, in keeping with this hack — they worked hard on developing new recipes, learned a lot about product development, and got a lot of practice producing large numbers of cupcakes quickly. It would have been fun to win, and the cash would have helped the business, but the skills, experience, and original recipes will help launch it as well.

Notes

1. William B. Irvine, *A Guide to the Good Life: The Ancient Art of Stoic Joy* (New York: Oxford University Press, 2009).

Hack 60: Trust Your Intelligence (and Everyone Else's)

You may not be the smartest person in the world, but you don't need to be. Greg Egan's concept of "general intelligence" and the mathematical model called the Universal Turing Machine suggest that, given time and resources, you can think and create along with the finest human minds.

If you bought this book, there's a fair chance you did so with the notion of becoming smarter, but just how smart can you expect to become, both now and in the future, when strap-on second and third heads become *de rigueur* fashion accessories? Just how smart is "smart," what does "smart" even mean, and should you care?

In Action

In this section, we'll look at a couple of ways of estimating human intelligence on a cosmic scale, and argue that once you're as smart as a human, becoming much smarter is no big deal.

The Sentience Quotient

In 1984, nanotechnologist Robert Freitas, Jr. postulated a measurement called the Sentience Quotient, which he says is "a sliding scale of cosmic sentience universally applicable to any intelligent entity in the cosmos. . . Generally, the more information a brain can process in a shorter length of time, the more intelligent it can be." (www.rfreitas.com/Astro/Xenopsychology.htm)

The Sentience Quotient is calculated with the equation

$$S = \log_{10} (I / M)$$

where

- I – the rate at which the brain can process information in bits/second.
- M = the mass of the brain.
- The $\log_{10}$ operation takes the order of magnitude of I/M — that is, its power of 10.

NOTE If you haven't used exponents since high school, remember that 10^1 is 10, 10^2 is 10 x 10, or 100, and so on. 10^3 is 10 times bigger than 10^2, and 10^4 is 10 times bigger than that. Also, 10^0 is 1, 10^{-1} is 1/10, 10^{-2} is 1/100, and so on.

To translate completely, 10^3 is 10 x 10 x 10 is 1,000 (1 with the decimal moved three places to the right). 10^{-3} is 1/1000 is .001 (1 with the decimal moved three places to the left). We'll keep the exponents to a minimum in this hack, but we can't lose all of them, so buckle up — the numbers are going to get very big (and very small) very fast.

Individual human neurons mass about 10^{-10} kilograms and can process between 1,000 and 3,000 bits per second, so the human I/M is $10^3/10^{-10}$ or 10^{13} bits/second/kilogram. Thus, human beings have an estimated SQ of 13. You can also multiply both I and M by the number of neurons in the brain, and get 10^{13} bits/second processed by about 1 kilogram of gray matter, thereby deriving the same figure, 13.

Freitas calculates that the stupidest possible brain, which would consist of one neuron with the mass of the known universe, and would take the entire age of the universe to process one bit of information, would have an SQ of -70. Near the middle of the scale, most plants have an estimated SQ of -2. At the other end, the smartest possible brain would have superfast neurons that existed at the Planck scale (Hack 40, "Notate Wisely"), and therefore an SQ of 50.

Because Freitas's paper was written in 1984, these numbers could probably use some updating; the important thing to take away from these estimates is their sheer size. On this enormous scale, the smartest human who ever lived is almost certainly not an order of magnitude smarter than you are. Indeed, no human has a significantly different SQ from a dog or a cat.

NOTE Freitas's paper was about xenopsychology, the study of alien intelligence. Of course, in 2011, we don't even know if alien life exists, let alone how smart it is. Freitas was trying to set upper and lower theoretical bounds on the kinds of intelligence the human race might encounter. These limits might just as well apply to our own descendants. After all, if the human brain is a computer — a big if, we admit, but the theoretical basis for this hack — it ought to be possible to improve its raw performance considerably, as we've done with all our other computers. Thus, even if humans are alone in the universe, the hypothetical upper ranges of SQ may yet have some relevance.

Kurzweil's Estimate

The Sentience Quotient is good as a first pass at thinking about intelligence on a universal scale, but most researchers since Freitas have preferred to estimate brain power using some form of operations per second, whether FLOPS (floating-point operations per second), MIPS (millions of instructions per second), or the more general cps (calculations per second). Let's invent a new measurement like the Sentience Quotient that's the $\log_{10}$ of the number of calculations per second a brain can do and call it the New Sentience Quotient, or NSQ. A device that can perform 100 cps has an NSQ of 2, which, please remember, is 10 times more powerful than an NSQ of 1.

By emulating human visual and auditory processing capabilities on computers, measuring how much human neural tissue is devoted to those functions (for example, in the optic nerve), and comparing it to the total mass of the brain, artificial intelligence researchers Hans Moravec, Ray Kurzweil, and colleagues have been able to estimate how much processing the average human brain can do. Their estimates range from NSQ 14 to 15. Kurzweil, an AI advocate, surveys these efforts in his book *The Singularity Is Near*,[1] and decides on a more conservative estimate of NSQ 16 (10^{16} cps) — more conservative in the sense that he'd like to build a human-equivalent computer soon, and doesn't want to underestimate the power of the human brain.

General Intelligence

When Marvin the Paranoid Android complains in *The Hitchhiker's Guide to the Galaxy* that he still has to do menial jobs even though he has a "brain the size of a planet," exactly how smart does he mean? According to computational neuroscientist Anders Sandberg, a well-engineered AI with about the mass of the Earth might have an NSQ of 61.[2] That means Marvin is approximately 10^{45} times more powerful than today's human brain. However, according to the estimate by Freitas, the upper end of intelligent performance is SQ 50, which is only 10^{37} or 10 trillion quadrillion quadrillion times smarter than the human norm — quite a bit less optimistic than Sandberg's estimate, but still vastly more intelligent than a human.

If you could increase your intelligence by a similar factor, what would be in it for you? Would you believe us if we said that — in some sense — not so much?

Consider that the first generation of IBM PCs built in 1981, with Intel 8088 microprocessors, can theoretically perform any calculation that the fastest PCs or even the fastest supercomputers of today can perform. It would make those calculations more slowly, but with sufficient peripherals (such as a big hard drive, a better video card, and so on), an 8088 can do everything the latest processors can do, only slower. Such a PC is "Turing-equivalent" or "Turing-complete" in a practical sense, meaning that it's equivalent to a Universal Turing Machine (see "How It Works") and therefore a fully general-purpose computer. In other words, you could theoretically render *Avatar* with the original IBM PC, but you'd better be prepared to swap a lot of floppies.

Let's mine the future once again (Hack 31, "Mine the Future") and examine science fiction writer Greg Egan's idea that something like Turing completeness applies to human beings as well. He calls it *general intelligence*.

> *It was a rigorous result in information theory [in the future] that once you could learn in a sufficiently flexible manner — something humanity had achieved in the Bronze Age — the only limits you faced were speed and storage; any other structural changes were just a matter of style.*[3]

If Egan's science fictional hypothesis holds, it's both good news and bad news. The bad news is that there is no magical procedure, such as becoming a cyborg or uploading your personality, that will let you vault the human condition into an unimaginable candyland of unlimited superintelligence and power. The good news is that you don't need one. With enough time and sustained effort, you can already think any thinkable thought and solve any soluble problem.

How It Works

Do we have reason to believe that Egan's idea of general intelligence applies to humans, in the same way that Turing equivalence applies to computers? The answer is yes, of course, if humans are computers.

A Universal Turing Machine (UTM) is a mathematical model of an ideal computer developed by mathematician Alan Turing in the 1930s; it served as a conceptual prototype for building real computers later in the century.

A UTM both reads from and writes to an abstract tape, changing internal state with each read or write operation. The UTM can compute any computable program, because the UTM's tape (which serves as both its RAM and its long-term storage) is infinite, so the UTM has an infinite memory and infinite storage. This is an advantage over real-world computers, which can have only finite memory and storage. Also, of course, as a mathematical abstraction, the

UTM will never wear out. Combining these specifications means that UTMs can perform some calculations that real-world computers cannot.

That said, for most practical purposes, a real-world computer is very close to a Universal Turing Machine, although it might need more memory or storage than it has for difficult calculations. Excepting issues of speed and storage, however, any computer that's equivalent to a Universal Turing Machine is equivalent to any other Turing-equivalent computer. The same goes for languages and programming environments such as LISP, Perl, and Python (Hack 40, "Notate Wisely").

Artificial intelligence experimenters and advocates such as Ray Kurzweil and Hans Moravec tend to think that the brain is just another computer, albeit one that runs at a speed of around 10^{16} calculations per second. Such a computer currently cannot be built by humans, except in the traditional way that *Homo sapiens* has been doing it for 200,000 years. But if the brain is just another computer, any brain that's Turing-equivalent can do anything any other such brain can do: It can think any thought that any other Turing-equivalent brain can think, feel anything an equivalent brain can feel, and so on.

We don't quite know what it takes for a human brain to reach Turing equivalence, but it's probably not much in human terms. If the brain is a sophisticated computer, then most likely, any mentally competent adult has what Egan calls general intelligence.

In Real Life

What does the principle of general intelligence mean for you? The "real life" we'll be discussing in this final "In Real Life" section of the hack is your own.

Have you ever complained that someone was "too stupid to live"? You may be what psychologist Albert Ellis called an *intellectual fascist*: "Intellectual fascism . . . is the arbitrary belief that individuals possessing certain traits (such as those who are intelligent, cultured, artistic, creative, or achieving) are intrinsically superior to individuals possessing certain other traits (such as those who are uneducated, uncultured, unartistic, uncreative, or unachieving)." According to Ellis, intellectual fascism can cause needless friction with your neighbors, prevent you from learning unconventional information, and finally cause you to trip up or freeze at a critical moment when you apply your overly harsh standards to yourself. (http://classic-web.archive.org/web/19990128234207/rebt.org/essays/aug98essay.html)

People on the autistic spectrum — people with autism, Asperger's syndrome, and related developmental disorders — have pioneered *neurodiversity*, the concept that human brains come in diverse forms and that people with autism, for example, ought to be appreciated for their unique gifts and societal contributions, instead of being shunned because they seem a little strange to "neurotypical" people. We welcome the concept of neurodiversity and would like to see its definition extended, not only to encompass a broader range of disorders outside the autistic spectrum, but also to encourage people on the broad human spectrum of IQ to respect and appreciate one another more than they do.

Embracing the idea of general intelligence can help fight intellectual fascism. Everyone is about as smart as everyone else if general intelligence holds; if it doesn't hold, the differences among individual humans are still tiny on the cosmic scales we've been discussing, whether you're counting in calculations per second, or bits per kilogram per second.

General intelligence means that your IQ is not as important as how well you use it, and optimizing that is exactly what this book is about. Intelligence is fluid and relative, state-dependent, and situational. If, as the proverb has it, "Genius is an infinite capacity for taking pains," then perhaps patience is a gift more suitable to wish for than notionally higher intelligence.

Classic IQ tests and definitions of "smart" tend to favor those skilled at formal, intellectual ways of approaching information, whereas many new definitions of intelligence and even kinds of intelligence are being studied. One example is *social intelligence*, the idea that the driving force behind the evolution of our large brains was the necessary processing power to negotiate complicated interpersonal situations such as extended family life, complex social life, politics, altruism, collaboration, and so on.

All this points to the idea that there's no sensible reason to overly value intellectualism, and that our similarities far outweigh our differences when it comes to using our brains. It makes sense to respect and be kind to other people, even when they don't live up to some intellectual ideal.

It also makes sense to be kind to yourself when you fall short of your own ideals. If the principle of general intelligence holds, after you reach a certain stage in your mental development, you're basically not going to get any smarter. In fact, that's probably already happened, and the best you can do is improve your skills and learn to be more efficient and flexible in using your intelligence.

So why wait any longer? Learn something you've been putting off because it seems too hard. Create a work of art. Write a symphony; write a book. Get better at using the brain you have, with this book and others like it. Along with patience, perhaps you had better hope for a longevity pill so you can complete all your projects.

See Also

- Thomas Armstrong, Ph.D., *Neurodiversity: Discovering the Extraordinary Gifts of Autism, ADHD, Dyslexia, and Other Brain Differences* (Cambridge, MA, USA: Da Capo Lifelong, 2010). This is a broad and deep look at the rights of people whose brains are "different" and potential coping strategies for them, including people who probably don't have what we have been calling general intelligence.

Notes

1. Ray Kurzweil, *The Singularity Is Near* (New York: Viking, 2005).
2. Kurzweil, Chapter 6
3. Greg Egan, *Schild's Ladder* (New York: EOS, 2002).

The Unboxed Games Manifesto

Board gamers of the world, unite! You have nothing to lose but your boxes.

We, the founders of the Unboxed Games movement, revolt against boxes — boxes of all sorts and sizes — except the soapbox.

Unboxed games are designer games for the people, toppling the tyranny of the boxed commercial game. With the proliferation of game systems such as the piecepack in the twentieth and twenty-first centuries, there is no longer any other excuse for the existence of boxed commercial games than greed. How many hit commercial card games can be played with only a couple of standard decks and a sharpie? We condemn you, Uno. We denounce you, Phase 10. We rebuke you, Lost Cities. We belittle you, "Great" Dalmuti.

Unboxed games are green, ecological — scorning boxes of components. We repudiate the bourgeois "parakeet" gamer who is only interested in a game if it has "nice," shiny bits. Hundreds of bits in a box times hundreds of boxes on a shelf times tens of thousands of devoted gamers equals *hundreds of millions* of redundant pieces of four-color parakeet droppings. Boxed games look nice on the shelf but provide little more than bragging rights, consuming unspeakably more natural resources than a simple rule sheet. We say enough. Unboxed games are the Hercules that shall cleanse gaming's Augean Stables.

Unboxed games are free, merrily robbing the cash boxes of corporate sharks like Hasbro and their pusillanimous remoras. As gamers, we want to play, not pay. As game authors, we want to be played, not paid. Johan Huizinga said in

Homo Ludens that games exist in a magic circle. It's time to cast the moneychangers out of the magic circle. Games must be free — not only free as in free beer, but also free as in free speech: free to travel the world via the Internet and cell phones, free to be scratched in the sand, as free as the ancient air.

Unboxed games are elegant and spontaneous, obsoleting the ten-pound box of rulebooks. You can carry the rules to an unboxed game in your head and play pickup games *anywhere* with *anything*, so they're low tech, but also high tech — the natural home for unboxed rules is the Net as much as the neighborhood pub.

Unboxed games are portable and universal, shredding the boxes that separate Chess sets from Poker sets from Monopoly and the Settlers of Catan. Let your pieces run free. Let the Chess King woo and marry the Queen of Hearts — or the King of Hearts, for that matter. One day you will play Poker with a Chess set, Chess with a Poker set, everything with a computer, and emulate any computer program with a pen and paper.

Unboxed games are tested by the aeons, recalling the relics of our mighty-thewed progenitors from the box in the attic to which they had been relegated. We bow reverently before Saint Sid Sackson and *A Gamut of Games*, Robert Abbott and *Abbott's Original Card Games*, David Parlett and his *Original Card Games*. Game design has advanced far since these great works were published (and largely because of them). As authors, we can apply what we've learned to today's unboxed games.

Unboxed games are magical, revealing as illusion the boxes of limitation around ordinary things. We have witnessed wonders born of egg cartons and string. We have seen the Multiverse born of pen and paper; we have seen unboxed metagames swallow themselves and evert like the World Snake Ouroboros. Henceforth, the newest games shall be played with the oldest materials.

Unboxed games are good for your imagination, mocking the boxes that lock in the minds of gamers who can't believe that a poker chip is a pirate ship, or dice are ice floes. Any mentally competent adult can pretend one thing is another. Let A = B. Let this Ace be Beowulf. Let this Queen be Grendel. We call these *playlike games*: "Play like this penny is a race car." "OK, now play like it can fly."

Free our games. Free our culture. *Play outside the box.*

3D Visualization

John Braley and Ron Hale-Evans

The following figures are meant to accompany the "In Real Life" section of Hack 42, "Enter the Third Dimension."

Figure B-1: A 3D checkerboard of gray and white cubes

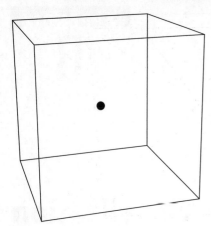

Figure B-2: A black point in the center of a white cube

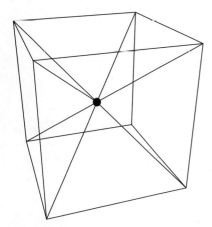

Figure B-3: Eight lines extending from the center point to the vertices subdivide the cube into six pyramids.

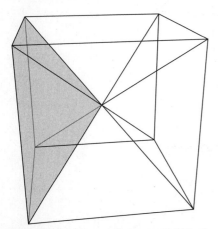

Figure B-4: One of the pyramids in the white cube becomes gray.

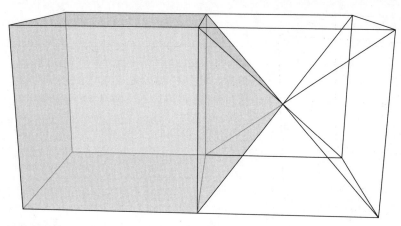

Figure B-5: The gray pyramid in the white cube joins up with a neighboring gray cube.

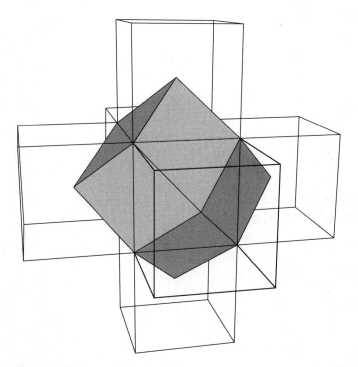

Figure B-6: A central gray cube joined with six neighboring gray pyramids becomes a rhombic dodecahedron.

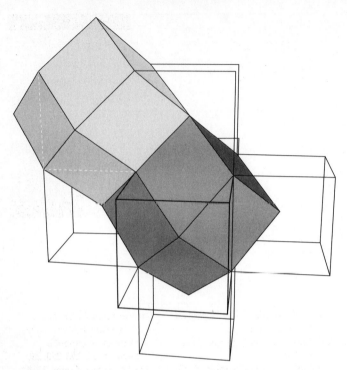

Figure B-7: Two adjoining rhombic dodecahedra

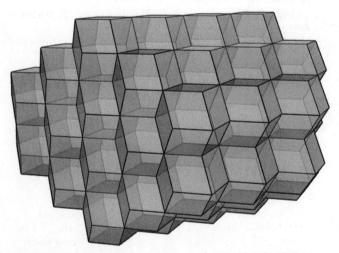

Figure B-8: All cubes are now transformed into rhombic dodecahedra, filling space as the cubes did.

Index